Kelly Hoffman

Public Administration for the Twenty-First Century

Public Administration for the Twenty-First Century

Phillip J. Cooper | *University of Vermont*

Linda P. Brady | *Georgia Institute of Technology*

Olivia Hidalgo-Hardeman | *University of Pittsburgh*

Albert Hyde | *The Brookings Institution*

Katherine C. Naff | *San Francisco State University*

J. Steven Ott | *University of Utah*

Harvey White | *University of Pittsburgh*

HARCOURT BRACE COLLEGE PUBLISHERS
Fort Worth   Philadelphia   San Diego   New York   Orlando   Austin   San Antonio
Toronto   Montreal   London   Sydney   Tokyo

Publisher	Earl McPeek
Acquisitions Editor	David C. Tatom
Product Manager	Steve Drummond
Developmental Editor	steve Norder
Project Editor	Charles J. Dierker
Art Director	Brian Salisbury
Production Manager	Serena Barnett Manning

ISBN: 0-15-500481-6

Library of Congress Catalog Card Number: 97-72037

Address for Editorial Correspondence:
Harcourt Brace College Publishers, 301 Commerce Street, Suite 3700, Fort Worth, TX 76102

Address for Orders:
Harcourt Brace & Company, 6277 Sea Harbor Drive, Orlando, FL 32887-6777. 1-800-782-4479

Web site address: http://www.hbcollege.com

Harcourt Brace College Publishers may provide complimentary instructional aids and supplements or supplement packages to those adopters qualified under our adoption policy. Please contact your sales representative for more information. If as an adopter or potential user you receive supplements you do not need, please return them to your sales representative or send them to:

Attention: Returns Department, Troy Warehouse, 465 South Lincoln Drive, Troy, MO 63379

Printed in the United States of America

7 8 9 0 1 2 3 4 5 6   039   10 9 8 7 6 5 4 3 2 1

The authors respectfully dedicate this volume to the memory of the many public administrators who have died in the performance of their public duties, and to their families. These victims of bombings, assassinations, kidnappings, and other moments of madness have honored their nations and their people at least as much as those who have sacrificed their lives on the battlefields of the world.

Preface

Public Administration for the Twenty-First Century is about the future. With the coming of the new century, public administrators need to focus on how to do a better job of serving the people—all the people—in creative, new ways. We must contemplate better ways to work across levels of government. We need to develop partnerships with not-for-profit institutions and other nongovernmental organizations. We must begin the new millennium fully aware of the many responsibilities and obligations presented to us as administrators of the people's government.

These tasks, now and in the future, do not occur in a vacuum. They take place in an environment where legal statements of authority and constraint are not only more lengthy and complex, but also of growing importance. At the very time that new modes of governing are being tested, the challenge of integrating these approaches into the body of law, which underlies all legitimate use of political power, becomes more significant than ever before. We must better understand the global dimensions of public administration so that professional managers can become more effective, regardless of where they might work. This requires not only forthright efforts to integrate a comparative perspective in our profession, but also a need to understand the nature and role of international institutions.

These challenges are the focus of *Public Administration for the Twenty-First Century*. The thematic threads that run throughout this textbook are the globalization of public administration, the importance of diversity in its many manifestations, the crucial role of law and legal processes, the significance of intergovernmental and interorganizational relationships, and a need to engage the challenges of the future rather than looking backward too much to reform movements of the past. Taken together, these threads weave a set of perspectives, practices, issues, and obligations that seem very likely to be the basis for public administration in the twenty-first century.

This textbook begins with an introduction that develops these themes. We explore the importance of appreciating the past (and not merely an ethnocentric one) and an even more crucial need to contemplate the future—one where managers are always facing forward. These themes, along with concerns about diversity, intergovernmental and interorganizational relationships, global forces in public management, and public law, flow through all the chapters that follow.

Chapters 2 and 3 focus specifically on the public law foundations of public administration and ethics, two areas that are often ignored in introductory texts but ones that are central to the lives of professional managers. Chapters 4 and 5 address intergovernmental relations in a way that moves beyond the usual total focus on fiscal federalism to consider a full range of issues, with considerable attention paid to the responsibilities of local government in addition to the standard focus on state and national capitals. These chapters also emphasize the contemporary forces of change in intergovernmental relations. Chapters 6 and 7 provide a crisp but thorough discussion of public policy. Rather than attempting to compress all of the crucial elements of policy into one chapter, we have added a second one that focuses on what happens after policies are adopted. It covers the implementation, evaluation, and termination phases of the process.

Chapters 8 and 9 address organization theory and behavior as well as crucial management techniques. These two chapters carefully weave together our historical knowledge about organizations and the most recent trends in organizational thinking. Chapter 10 is devoted to contemporary trends and issues. It stresses the importance of understanding the growing diversity of the workforce, not only in terms of race and ethnicity, but with particular regard for gender. Chapter 11 explores contemporary budget issues not merely as technical matters but as an arena in which the most fundamental political debates occur. Chapter 12 provides a basic understanding of international institutions and governance, a dimension that is often ignored in other public administration texts. Chapter 13 then goes on to take a comparative view across governments, countries, and cultures, with a particular emphasis on contemporary trends.

In all of this, *Public Administration for the Twenty-First Century* presents the central themes and the broad spectrum of basic public administration knowledge in a fashion intended to interest new students but also to respect the experience of those public service professionals who are returning for advanced education.

It may seem surprising, but there has never been a better time to be a public administration professional. Of course, it is also probably the most difficult time to be a member of our profession as well. Clearly, bashing bureaucrats has become not just an American pastime, but also an international fad. Griping about bureaucrats—the term being pronounced almost as a four-letter word—probably ranks only slightly below enthusiasm for soccer in worldwide popularity. However, politicians' complaints about excessive regulations, project delays, and inflated costs became boring two decades ago, and their criticisms have not become any more helpful with age and repetition. Their continuous and sometimes disingenuous rhetoric is ironically hypocritical, because it has most often been those same elected legislators and executives who wrote the policies that have mandated the very regulations about which they complain. These same leaders, too, are quite often responsible for increased project or program delays because of their actions in heaping piles of procedural obligations on ministries and administrative agencies while at the same time cutting related operating budgets and staffing levels.

The very fact that the profession faces so many challenges makes public administration a worthy calling for the very best of our men and women. It is time to recall that commentators first coined the phrase, "the best and the brightest," not during the John F. Kennedy administration but during the New Deal of Franklin D. Roosevelt. Then, the best and the brightest were encouraged to join government service. They were sought to fight the ravages of the Great Depression, and, later, to face the perils of World War II and its aftermath. Today the challenges are different, but the need for talent, commitment, and effort remains. Despite the excesses of political rhetoric concerning problems in the public sector, it is always our task to strive toward providing the public with better, more responsive and effective service.

The contemporary world of public administration has truly become a global commons in which it is no longer enough to focus on one's own capital city as the center of power and the place in which to pursue the public interest. We have a global marketplace where the cost of building a city hall is determined in part by traders on financial exchanges half the world away. Public managers today must effectively deal with the pace and level of change that accompanies this kind of dynamism.

The profession also is affected by a growing realization that old notions about the existence of a few superpowers and many small, supposedly unimportant developing nations were wrong when they were first articulated, are absolutely counterproductive today, and will be positively destructive in the twenty-first century. Some years ago, an internationally known economist, speaking at the annual conference of the International City/County Management Association, said that if the podium were covered with buttons, each of which represented the ability to eliminate a country, he could push many of them without causing a major impact on the world's economic well-being. Modern public administrators around the globe know that he was absolutely wrong. He was wrong in economic terms, because the centers of growth in the dramatically expanding world population are in the developing nations of Africa, Latin America, and Asia. Markets there are growing, with large portions of the global workforce busily producing goods and creating competitive forces that are driving major changes in the worldwide economy.

This economist also had it wrong in more important human terms. The economic dimension is but one facet of the public management task. Indeed, economic effectiveness is not an end in itself but a means to an end. The end is professional effectiveness in pursuit of the public interest. The public interest is an inclusive concept that does not write off large numbers of people because they are poor or because they face major social challenges. The concept recognizes a need to address problems of equity and inequality not only in one's own country, but elsewhere in the world as well. With that recognition comes an awareness that people live and work in widely varying cultural traditions that affect not only how they live, but also how they are governed. It recognizes as well the need to address environmental issues and other challenges that are important to the quality of life for all the world's citizens.

This is also a time when public administrators must face the future. Change is coming too rapidly to stand in the present and face toward the past. Some of us have been guilty of doing just that. It is important to understand the reform tradition of public administration and to celebrate the foundations of the field, but that is not enough in the contemporary world. There must be a forward outlook, a perspective provided in the pages that follow.

The authors of this book comprise a diverse group with varied perspectives who have come together to face that future and meet its challenges. We may start from very different interests and experiences, but we agree that these themes are important and that they have too often been ignored or under-appreciated in introductory textbooks for public administrators. We believe that *Public Administration for the Twenty-First Century* represents a step toward remedying those omissions.

The authors also recognize, however, that although diverse perspectives are useful in a textbook, they must also be fashioned into a coherent whole with consistent themes and a continuity of ideas. Therefore, after all of the chapters were individually prepared, reviewed, and revised, the lead author performed a final, overall revision to ensure the readability and continuity of the text. Thus, although the book has many authors, it is a single work with a clearly articulated set of guiding themes, stronger for its diversity but, we believe, also effective as a unified volume.

Each of us benefited from the assistance of many colleagues at various stages along the way. Because there are so many of us and so many of them, we hope that a general and collective statement of our gratitude will suffice. We do wish, however, to specifically acknowledge the help of our reviewers. Although they took the time to offer specific comments on the ideas and presentations found within this textbook, the authors bear the sole responsibility for the end result. The reviewers were: Carl Bellone, California State University-Hayward; Irving Dawson, University of Texas-Arlington; Andrew Glassberg, University of Missouri-St. Louis; Arie Halachmi, Tennessee State University; Ronald Hy, University of Central Arkansas; Richard C. Kearney, University of Connecticut; Raymond Pomerleau, San Francisco State University; Mary Ann E. Steger, Northern Arizona University; S. Yan Tang, University of Southern California-Los Angeles; William L. Waugh Jr., Georgia State University; and John A. Yoegel, formerly of Pace University-New York. We must also acknowledge the efforts of David Tatom and the staff at Harcourt Brace, who endured throughout the lengthy development of this textbook. We appreciate your patience and support.

Above all, we want to express our appreciation to the many public administration professionals who have answered the call to public service. They are often unrecognized and inadequately rewarded for doing the most important work in the world—feeding the hungry, bringing medical care to the sick, tending the environment, educating our young people, and maintaining the forces that ensure our security.

The Authors
August 1997

About the Authors

Phillip J. Cooper is the Gund Professor of Liberal Arts and director of the Master of Public Administration program at the University of Vermont. He has served as a consultant to the United Nations and to governments both foreign and domestic at the national, state, and local levels. He was the first recipient of the Charles Levine Award for excellence in public administration scholarship, teaching, and service. His scholarship has emphasized the role of public law in public administration, public policy, sustainable development administration, and comparative and development administration.

Linda P. Brady is a professor of International Affairs and chair of the Sam Nunn School of International Affairs at the Georgia Institute of Technology. She formerly served in the U.S. departments of State and Defense and was an advisor on arms control for the Jimmy Carter and Ronald Reagan administrations. Dr. Brady has been honored for her work with students and for her work in diplomacy and foreign policy, and has written extensively on international negotiations. She was formerly the John M. Olin Distinguished Professor of National Security Studies at the United States Military Academy.

Olivia Hidalgo-Hardeman is an assistant professor of Public Policy at the Graduate School of Public and International Affairs at the University of Pittsburgh. She received her Ph.D. from Purdue University and has taught at a number of universities, including the University of California-Riverside, Pan American University, and Kentucky State University. Dr. Hidalgo-Hardeman maintains an interest in methodology, public policy, and in comparative and development administration.

Albert Hyde is a senior staff member at The Brookings Institution's Center for Public Policy Education. He was formerly a faculty member at American University, the University of Pittsburgh, and San Francisco State University. At the latter two universities, Dr. Hyde served as chair of the public administration departments. He has published widely in the field of public administration, and has authored other textbooks for Harcourt Brace College Publishers.

Katherine C. Naff is an assistant professor of Public Administration at San Francisco State University. She was formerly a senior research analyst with the U.S. Merit System Protection Board, and holds a Ph.D. in Government is from Georgetown University. Her research focuses particularly on women and minorities in government employment and on the impact of organizational change on the federal civil service.

J. Steven Ott is a professor of Political Science and director of the Master of Public Administration Program at the University of Utah. He is widely published in the field of public administration and has authored other textbooks for Harcourt Brace College Publishers. Dr. Ott's research focuses in particular on organizational theory and behavior, with special interest in innovative management theories and techniques.

Harvey White is an associate professor of Management and Policy at the Graduate School of Public and International Affairs at the University of Pittsburgh. He is a former city manager who combines municipal experience with his academic credentials in coordinating the Municipal Manager Program at GSPIA. Dr. White is currently president of the Conference of Minority Public Administrators and was formerly a faculty member at Southern University. He has published in the areas of public finance, environmental policy, and diversity issues.

Contents in Brief

Contents in Detail

Chapter 3   Law against Ethics: Legal Accountability and Ethical
Responsibility   75

Chapter 4   The Intergovernmental Policy Structure
and Action   94

Chapter 7   Policy Implementation, Evaluation, and Termination   185

Chapter 8   Managing Public Organizations   201

Chapter 9   Organization Development, Participation,
and Culture   235

Chapter 1

Public Administration for the Twenty-First Century: Beyond Reform

Reinventing government is old news.[1] Despite all of the hype and headlines, there is nothing new or revolutionary about the quest to "make government work better."[2] Indeed, public administration as a field has always been an enterprise aimed at reform. Woodrow Wilson, in an article usually taken to mark the start of the field, declared, "It is getting harder to run a constitution than to write one."[3] Since the late nineteenth century, the time when the field was founded as a profession and an academic study, public administration has been about elimination of corruption, improvement of efficiency, and enhancement of service delivery in pursuit of the public interest.[4]

The Heart of the Job

What has changed is the nature of the world in which we live and work and the range of problems, constraints, and opportunities confronting public administrators within it. Public service professionals can no longer afford to be ethnocentric, inward looking, focused on the past, and defensive. We must be forward looking, globally oriented, innovative, adaptable, and ready to take advantage of opportunities to serve the community more effectively. It may seem odd to say it in an era of downsizing, deregulation, decentralization, and decrementalism, but public administration, if it is to be done well, is and must be an aggressive, not a passive, enterprise. We must be aggressive in pursuit of the public interest.

Nearly half a century ago, Stephen K. Bailey wrote that one of the most important characteristics for public service is optimism.[5] That does not mean silly simple-minded boosterism or an unwillingness to recognize problems and challenges. That kind of attitude is useless at best and reckless and disingenuous at worst. Rather, the optimism stems from a well-justified understanding

1

that the enterprise of public administration is a worthy endeavor. It is essential to the maintenance of a quality of life in the modern community: for any community and at every level of society.

At the same time, public service professionals must be aware that it is a worthy endeavor because the stakes are high and the global situation, from the smallest town to the largest international institution, is complex and dynamic. Where the quality of life and the future of our communities are at stake, there will be competition and confrontation as well as negotiation and accommodation. There will be increasing intergovernmental interdependency even as contests for control of markets and resources are waged. There will be an increased need to recognize global realities even as calls grow louder for decentralization and an emphasis on local communities. Governing in this complex and exciting world is the subject of this volume.

Back to the Future

Public administration is in several important respects a matter of education. Whether one is working with a city council, subordinates in county government, superiors in a state agency, peers in another cabinet department, ministry at the national level, or negotiating partners from other nations, it is essential that the public administrator be able to convey a sense of what is, what can be, and what will work. However, the "what works" question is not simply a matter of expertise. What works in one setting may not work in another. Most people have seen a newly minted professional, fresh from college or graduate school, who has all the technical answers and can make a computer sing, but cannot get things done. The critical mix is a blend of expertise and experience applied in a manner that is sensitive to cultural and other factors that shape administrative reality. Experience is knowing about what has been tried and what can work; it is not merely the ability to design a technical fix for a problem. The effective public manager is aware that experience can be acquired in more than one way. It can, to be sure, simply be lived, but uneducated, unchallenged life experience can be nothing more than habit. It can be defensive, egocentric, rigid, and unresponsive, all the characteristics of bureaucracy that people all over the world love to hate. Besides, one lifetime is too short to experience more than a fraction of what the profession has learned over the generations.

Consider an inelegant but effective way to understand the task before us. As public administrators in the business of educating those we serve and those with whom we work, we can see the challenge in the following homespun homily:

You can't no more teach
What you ain't learned
Than you can go back
To where you ain't been

Anonymous

Put differently, public administration is an eminently practical profession, though based in an important body of theory, and we can only understand what it can be tomorrow by understanding what it is today and how it came to be over the years.

This Is an Old, Old Enterprise

There is a tendency to think that what is termed "the bureaucracy" in contemporary parlance is new, or at least that it came about because of the expansion of health, social service, and poverty programs of the 1960s or the New Deal era. Nothing could be further from the truth. Public administration is a global enterprise that traces its roots far back into antiquity and has undergone centuries of change and development.

It is clear that both ancient Asia and Egypt developed relatively complex administrative structures.[6] In Egypt the pharaohs' governments used priests and military officers for a wide range of administrative and civil engineering tasks both at home and in conquered provinces. Given the complexity of the annual flooding of the Nile and its impact on agriculture and gathering, the development of relatively sophisticated astronomical and mathematical techniques was critical. The task of governing a growing population and an expanding empire meant there were many needs for organization, analysis, and development.

By the time of the Roman Empire, the concept of public administration was acquiring a significant level of scope and complexity. The Romans learned from the Egyptians and the Greeks and applied what they had learned as they first conquered and then governed a huge empire. The Romans were sophisticated enough to operate a variety of governing systems. First, there was the system needed to govern Romans, not only those living in Rome and its environs but also those engaged in various activities around the empire. Beyond that, the Romans developed systems in individual areas of the empire that blended Roman principles with the traditions and customs of that kingdom or province. To manage that complexity, the Romans developed effective legal systems for both domestic and provincial applications. The size of their military operations required relatively sophisticated organizational skills. It also became necessary for the Roman leadership to be concerned about financing a far-flung operation, though the methods they used to acquire resources would not meet with much approval in our time.

The end of the Roman era was followed by a number of changes in the part of the world formerly included in the empire. These changes took a very long time but ultimately had dramatic consequences. In particular there followed the creation of empires based in Byzantium (later known as Constantinople) and the beginning of what came to be known as the Holy Roman Empire under Charlemagne.[7] Over time, wars of consolidation and succession among the princes of Europe ultimately led to what we refer to now as the nation-state.

The other major development was the rise of the Roman Catholic Church. The popes developed a complex system of hierarchy and control. The church also evolved its own governing structure, which grew as the church sent its priests out with European missions of conquest. As the church developed a widespread ecclesiastical empire with significant secular political involvements, its own governing operations grew increasingly complex. Like other rulers, popes acquired a court, called the *curia* (which is Latin for court), that remains the central governing operation of the church to this day.

The growth and increased complexity of life in Europe and in the colonies required development of new systems of law and trade. In a time when cash machines and credit cards are common, it is difficult to visualize just how much complexity was involved in creating enough infrastructure to permit a trader in Genoa to ship goods to Marseilles with some certainty that the goods would get there and that payments would be made to the proper parties along the way in the correct amount and in an acceptable form. The development of currency, banking, commercial paper, transportation systems, and mechanisms for resolving disputes arising in the process required creation of a host of what we would now call soft technologies. The building of this infrastructure, the organization and operation of government, the maintenance of military arms, and the control over international interests meant a need for increasingly effective systems of tax collection, record keeping, and administration.[8]

It Was Not All in Europe

In part at least because the United States inherited so much from its European forebears, because the United States has contributed a great deal to the literature of public administration since then, and because of no small amount of ethnocentrism by Americans and Europeans, there is a tendency to forget that not all development of the means of operating societies took place in Europe or the United States.

The cultures of Asia, Africa, and Latin America were many and varied. The great religions and philosophies of Islam, Hinduism, and Confucianism had profound impacts on the shape of societies and, consequently, on the form and character of their governing bodies. Certainly the Mandarins (people we would today refer to as members of the Senior Executive Service) played a central role in the governance of the Chinese Empire. In Africa and Southeast Asia, traders as well as military conquerors spread and shared religion and culture, creating new governing institutions and processes as the need for social and economic infrastructure expanded. Europeans were not the only countries to develop colonies.

In the western hemisphere, Aztec, Mayan, and Incan cultures were complex and, in a number of important respects, very sophisticated. The Mayans' development of city planning, architecture, and mathematics created communities that bring admiration even today.

A variety of causes, including conquest, had devastating impacts on a number of these historically significant societies and the governing systems they had developed. Although many of the indigenous systems were displaced by colonial governments, important elements of their cultures and social systems remained for generations. Indeed, one of the important difficulties for colonial powers was to build administrative systems that could operate in those communities. In places like Africa, where European conflicts led to partitions of colonial possessions, historically important social systems were altered or displaced. The education of talented colonial citizens in Britain, France, and Spain were part of efforts to inculcate the languages and social systems of Europe in what is now known as the developing world. Following independence, a number of former colonies have gone through turbulent periods as they have attempted to fashion administrative institutions and processes that take advantage of useful practices from the colonial period while recovering historically important local traditions and cultures.

Max Weber, a German sociologist who developed much of what is today called the theory of bureaucracy, considered this history and the contemporary situation and came to several conclusions:[9] (1) Complex societies require complex economies, legal systems, and mechanisms to ensure security. (2) The governing structure is essential to ensure a workable infrastructure not only to allow those in positions of authority to rule but also to allow private individuals to undertake the many business and personal tasks they seek to achieve. 3) Given those historical realities, bureaucracies are needed to support governmental and social efforts. As Joseph Shumpeter put it, "bureaucracy is not an obstacle to democracy but an inevitable complement to it."[10]

A bureaucracy is not some kind of evil monster, but merely a form of organization with certain general characteristics that have developed over time. They include hierarchy, formal authority, division of labor by specialization, employment by merit, merit judged by education and other formal preparation, compensation based on performance of official functions, complex systems of record keeping, and standard operating procedures to enhance efficiency. At the same time, Weber recognized that a source of great tension was the fact that while bureaucratic organizations were necessary for many of the things modern societies need to have done, they also have dehumanizing tendencies that can alienate even those who serve within them. Since Weber's time, of course, the effort has been both to create the complex organizations that are essential to modern governance and simultaneously to attack the characteristics of bureaucracies that are disliked in many societies around the world. Later chapters will discuss just how that task has been addressed.

Reformers and a New Era of Professional Public Administration

In the United States, concern with development of public administration extends back before the crafting of the Constitution. Even after independence, however, the United States, like many former colonies since, had difficulty building the kind of administrative infrastructure needed to construct a new nation.

   Much of the discussion concerning creation of the Constitution was about solving problems that stemmed from that lack of infrastructure. Although the Constitution did not speak directly to what we would today call public administration, it is not true that the framers ignored the subject. The Constitution speaks of the president's power to appoint "Officers of the United States." It gives the president "the executive power." The president has the power to "require the Opinion, in writing, of the principal Officer in each of the Executive Departments, upon any Subject relating to the Duties of their respective Offices." It allows the Congress to "vest the Appointment of such inferior Officers, as they think proper, in the President alone, in the Courts of Law, or in the Heads of Departments." Thus, heads of executive departments may appoint other officers. The Congress is also given power "To make all laws which shall be necessary and proper for carrying into Execution the foregoing Powers, and all other Powers vested by this Constitution in the Government of the United States, or in any Department or Officer thereof." The "foregoing powers" include a host of matters from the "laying and collecting of taxes" to the military to the regulation of commerce, all of which require active administration. During the ratification debate, Alexander Hamilton even went so far as to argue that the president should respect professional public officials because they are essential to a successful government and should not be able to fire them simply on political grounds.[11] Even with all of the fears of the newly formed central government, the framers had learned the lessons of the years before the Constitution and concluded that there had to be a national government powerful and complex enough to be effective in meeting the needs of a growing and geographically expanding nation.

By the late nineteenth century there had been many changes in American society. Two were of particular importance. First, industrialization had created powerful business concerns with major facilities around the nation. Second, there was burgeoning growth as the large industries located in cities where a labor market could be found. Their presence, in turn, attracted others in search of work. The lure of jobs also attracted large numbers of immigrants. However, the marketplace that attracted residents and built industry did not take care of the human difficulties that came with burgeoning urban growth. The need to address those problems allowed political machines to grow, trading services and privileges for votes and other political support.

Reformers reacted against abuses in the city, state, and national governments in the 1880s. One of these voices of reform was Woodrow Wilson, a lawyer trained at the University of Virginia who went on to study what was then called political economy at Johns Hopkins University. When he became interested in the problem of running a constitution rather than simply designing governments and policies, he found himself switching from a focus on Great Britain to the lessons that could be learned from the German (then Prussian) tradition, one of the world's leading centers of administrative development.

In 1887 Wilson authored a paper designed to spark interest in the study of public administration. It was really a combination of three papers. In the first, originally entitled "The Courtesy of the Senate," Wilson attacked partisan political patronage, the meting out of favors and jobs for political support. To that Wilson added his work on the importance of learning how to govern and not merely how to frame a government, which is what dominated the writings of political scientists of the day. Finally, he spoke of how lessons on how to administer government better could be learned from a wide variety of sources, including governments with whom we did not share values, like the Prussian bureaucracy. He gave his paper as a speech, and, when the editor of a journal contacted him about publishing the piece, Wilson demurred, warning that it was only a first approach to the subject of public administration, too thin and superficial to be worthy of publication. Even so, the editor pressed him and the article was published as "The Study of Administration,"[12] and it is regarded as the founding essay for the field.

Wilson argued that administrators could concentrate on operating the government rather than on substituting their judgment for that of elected officials, an idea that has come to be called the politics/administration dichotomy.

Those administrators could study mechanisms of administration not only in use by other governments but also by those employed in private industry.

When the reform movements found ways to attack corruption, focus on meeting the needs of growing cities, and adapt techniques of scientific management from the much admired private sector, the field of modern public administration was under way. It was led by a group of reformers emphasizing a professional perspective on operating government in the public interest. Authors of early books in public administration were lawyers who were not experts in management. Newer texts, like those authored by Leonard White and W. F. Willoughby emphasized "management, not law."[13] The scientific management movement of the 1920s and 1930s quickly came to dominate the field, advocating the idea that there were generic, scientific principles of management applicable to any kind of organization, whether public or private.

It was no surprise that when President Franklin Roosevelt sought advice on how to manage the executive branch, which was growing in an effort to fashion solutions to the devastations brought on by the Great Depression, the result was a document entitled "The Papers on the Science of Administration." Nor was it surprising that "The Papers" asserted: "Efficiency is axiom number one in the hierarchy of administration."[14] There were, however, numerous social, economic, and political demands facing government, and it became increasingly clear, particularly after World War II, that efficiency was only one of the values that Americans wanted administrators to emphasize.

After the war, thousands of servicemen and -women returned home to build families and careers, focusing much of the effort of administration on local governments and states where housing, schools, jobs, and manifold public services were needed. At the same time, there were demands for the national government to build an infrastructure adequate to support the changing national economic and social life. There were also calls for the United States to address long-festering wounds caused by a history of racial discrimination and to play a responsible role in the international community as well. Then there was the demand that the nation do something about the problem of poverty, and the Great Society was born. All of these forces fostered new and different types of public administration organizations and responsibilities.

Many of these forces were echoed in countries around the world recovering from the ravages of war and the demands of the modern age. Countries like Germany and Japan were rebuilt. In the case of Japan, a new constitution was virtually imposed by occupation forces, though it was by most assessments an amazingly progressive document. It was the beginning of the end of colonial rule in Asia, Africa, and Latin America, though not everyone was able to gain independence. Caribbean, Pacific, and Asian states remained under foreign control. The most recent changes came in the transfer of Hong Kong from the British Commonwealth to the People's Republic of China and the process of transition to independence in Micronesia. The number of "new" countries that emerged from the end of World War II through the 1980s has had mapmakers reeling, most recently with the breakup of the former Soviet Union into what came to be known as the Newly Independent States of Central and Eastern Europe. In some nations, although the boundaries remained, the transformation of society was as great as if an entire new country had been created. Certainly South Africa provides a leading example. All of these new or transformed nations had to be governed and their people served.

However, there were also increasing frustrations with the size, complexity, and cost of government by the same people who continued to demand more and better services at all levels of government. A number of political figures of both major political parties began to achieve success by running against government. In the midst of this period came the Watergate episode that led many critics to feel justified in their attacks on government in general and the bureaucracy in particular. It did not matter that those at the heart of Watergate were political appointees (and mostly lawyers as it happens) rather than career civil servants. Ironically, during the same period, there were calls for increased safety, health, and environmental protections from government and a simultaneous revolt against regulation supported again by both Democrats and Republicans.

The 1980s were a period in which the conflicting demands continued along with growing attacks on government and bureaucracy. Efforts were undertaken to cut back the size and complexity of national government and to trim expenses, at least with respect to domestic programs. The Margaret Thatcher government in Great Britain was one of the first of the developed countries to signal a dramatic transformation in attitude and approach to the public sector before the shift became evident in the United States. In the developing world, countries like Bangladesh launched privatization efforts well before that trend was popularized in Washington, D.C.

With the 1990s came the end of the Cold War; as the former Soviet Union collapsed, numerous formerly authoritarian governments fell, and even the few remaining Marxist regimes, like the People's Republic of China, were radically transformed. To the calls for domestic cuts was added a demand that the nation take a "peace dividend" by cutting defense expenditures just as it was seeking to continue cuts in domestic spending. Still, the number of countries known or thought to possess nuclear weapons increased significantly, and others, like China, moved to update their weapons systems by purchasing equipment and expertise from debt-ridden and poverty-stricken former Soviet republics, now independent nations.

There are enough ironies in many of these developments to make anyone's head swim. At the very time that the attacks on public service have
been the loudest, demands for more and better public services have been the
most intense. At a time when there has been a desire to downsize (or as the
term is presently used, right-size), there have been more large-scale and increasingly complex problems that government has been called on to address,
not merely in the writing of policy but in its implementation and day-to-day
administration.

Over the Horizon: Watch Where You're Going!

So much for nostalgia. History is valuable, but only prologue. The hard part
is keeping those lessons of the past in mind while focusing on the future.
There are some keys to meeting that challenge.

Grounded in Fundamental Values, Not Mired in the Past

There is a real irony in the contemporary demand for change and the simultaneous longing for a restoration of basic values. That is a theme in many
communities and cultures around the world. Developing countries appreciate some of the benefits of modernization but regret the loss of tradition and
homogenization of culture that accompanies it. Developed nations know
they must adapt to changing global environmental limits, economic pressures, and social diversity concerns, but fear that they are losing touch with
the values that have united their people in the past. Even small towns feel the
strain as they become exurbs or even suburbs. Although they have a host of
new services and conveniences, citizens fear the loss of characteristics that
made the towns attractive places to live in the first place.[15]

Similarly, contemporary public administrators often look forward to the
opportunity to expand their horizons, to deal with other people and cultures,
to surf the Internet and other telecommunications and information technology global highways, to eliminate unnecessary constraints on creativity, and
to explore new organizational and interjurisdictional structures. At the same
time, many fear that so much attention to that which is new means a loss of
concern for the enduring values that ought to define the profession, that set
it apart and make it a noble enterprise.

To be sure, there are valid concerns in all these areas. James Q. Wilson has
pointed out an interesting irony: Because the concept of fundamental values
has been so used and abused, "Virtue has acquired a bad name. To young
people it is the opposite of having fun, to older ones it is a symbol of lost
virtue that politicians now exploit for partisan purposes, and to young and

old alike it is a set of rules that well-meaning but intolerant bluenoses impose on other people."[16] However, the values of public service have meaning and are important.

The commitment to use professional expertise in the public interest has been an avowed purpose of public service since at least the Progressive era, when the field—in its modern sense—was born. It is why Wallace Sayre said that public administration and business administration are "alike only in all unimportant respects."[17] It is why Paul Appleby wrote that "government is different."[18] This is also why successful private sector managers do not, as a group, have a very strong record when they step into government to make government run more like a business. Woodrow Wilson wrote, "Business-like the administration of government may and should be—but it is not business. It is organic social life."[19] Public service entails many obligations that will be discussed throughout this volume, but it can be summarized in a comment made by Benjamin Franklin. As he emerged from the Constitutional Convention, Franklin was approached by a lady who inquired what kind of a government the framers had given them. He replied, "A republic, if you can keep it." It is the task of public administrators to help the people keep it.

In sum, there is no need to focus only on the future or predominantly toward the past (in terms of preservation of fundamental values.) That is a commonly implied but dangerous false dichotomy. The task of public administrators is to maintain values while meeting the need for change.[20]

The Danger of Reform

The term *reform,* notwithstanding its critical place in the history of public administration, has become a problem. It is a problem because it has been so badly abused that it has lost much of its value. It is also troublesome because, ironically enough, it keeps us focused on the past and on the negative instead of on the possibilities of the future.

In its nature, *reform* means to change for the better. It does not mean simply to change. The term is normative and *was,* at least, focused on improvement. Sadly, the term has been devalued because every change is called a reform. Instead of improvement, in the sense of better quality or more efficient service or other criteria on which most professionals would agree, the measuring rod has come to be overnight opinion polls or the ideology of the dominant political players at any particular moment. For example, regulatory reform in contemporary parlance usually does not mean doing a better job of operating regulatory programs, but deregulation (and deregulation is often a matter for elected officials rather than for administrators).

The other reason that reform is so problematic is that the nature of reform is to correct a problem or to improve over past performance. In either case, the emphasis is on the past and how we have been doing our job.

To put the matter in slightly more concrete terms, consider the "Smith and Jones rules." Every organization has them, though they do not necessarily have names, and the exact details of how they came into being may be lost in the mists of time. In essence, a problem once emerged with employee Sam Jones or manager Susan Smith. In responding to the problem, several managers spent days of meetings and countless hours of staff time, all to produce rules and procedures to make certain the same problem would never happen again. From that point forward one or more aspects of life in that agency would never be the same. The moral of the story is that it is always important, whenever the phrase "we'll fix it so it never happens again" is used, to ask whether we are managing by facing backward, toward the past, or forward, into the future.

Long Horizons and Short-Term Futures

The question is, of course, What do we mean by the future? That is not as strange a question as it may at first appear, and the answer can matter a great deal. The simplest response is that it is not the past or the present. The implication is that we think forward and not toward the past. It also means that we try hard not to get so bogged down in surviving current problems that we fail to keep a longer run perspective. That much having been said, How far is the future? It varies depending on the position one occupies in an organization and the type of activity in which one is engaged.

Futurists and many strategic planners say the future is more than twenty years out. The reason is that using a long time horizon frees organization members from being locked into current ways of thinking. It allows a "what if" mentality. This kind of time horizon is most often a luxury enjoyed by the most senior managers. On the other hand, as organizations are flattened (meaning that hierarchy is reduced), middle management is trimmed, and line administrators are asked to play a greater role, this kind of strategic thinking is less the preserve of the elite leadership and more something that is everyone's business.

The medium-term future is often three to ten years out. The medium term matters because most significant reorganizations, new programs, or human resource development strategies are usually contemplated in that range. It is close enough to allow specific action but far enough in the future to avoid causing serious anxiety.

Political appointees often see the time frames in political cycles of two and four years rather than in the policy cycles or managerial cycles noted above.

Executive branch officials tend to think in terms of presidential or gubernatorial terms. Legislators often see the world in the language of legislative terms. The situation is somewhat different in parliamentary governments where elections may occur at regularly scheduled times but may also come about if there is a political crisis such as a vote of no confidence. Since members of the cabinet in this instance are also members of the legislative body, they do not have quite the difference in time perception that one finds in a system based on separation of powers.

The short-term future is usually thought of in terms of one to two years. This parallels budget and administrative planning cycles and allows contemplation of the next one or two benchmark evaluation periods. This is not the time frame for long-term plans or program development. It is usually concerned with the implementation and operation of previously established priorities. Much of the line manager's time is spent in this time frame, but hopefully not too much.

Of course, it is always important to remember that there are cultural differences in the perception of time. Some indigenous peoples have difficulty with concepts of contracting because they think it presumptuous to assume that one can bind the diety to a particular future. Other cultures do not assume a linear concept of time, but tend to operate in cyclical frameworks. That may sound unusual to a generation that did not learn to tell time from hands on a clock face but from digital readouts, but it was not so long ago that rural families in the United States operated in a similar fashion, focused on the seasons of the year.

Similarly, there are sometimes differences in the way timeliness is to be understood. Many Europeans and Americans assume that time is valuable, that appointments are to be kept on time, and that a failure to arrive in a timely manner is an insult to others involved in a planned meeting or social event. In other cultures, time is a more relative concept, and tardiness is expected or at least not condemned. This difference has manifested itself occasionally when tightly scheduled professionals resent clients who arrive late for meetings, such that the session begins with a tension that may result more from differing concepts of time than from intentional snubs or lack of concern.

Fear of the Future: Realities, Goals, and Mega-Change

In addition to differences in temporal assumptions, there is one other thing that is important to remember about the future: It is always changing. That may sound trite, but it is a truth managers too often forget. It has to do with the differences between goals and realities. Realities are empirical; they are situations in the world. A key player may leave the organization unexpectedly, budgets may be cut, and crises—either natural or man-made—may occur.

Goals, by contrast, are always in the future, always pushing the envelope. Indeed, that is the very purpose of a goal.

If it is relatively easy to break the big concept *the future* down into chunks that public administrators can handle without choking, why does the term engender so much anxiety? First, of course, there is fear of the new (or of the unknown, which is often the same thing). While there will always be unknowns that create some degree of anxiety, others will regard those surprises as excitement and opportunity. The dangers of the unknown can be reduced considerably through the processes of contemplating the future and planning to meet it. Second, there is fear of losing a good situation that one, or one's organization, enjoys presently. As for that anxiety, all the effort in the world to behave defensively and build a redoubt around the status quo will not stop the future from arriving. The usual consequence of such a defensive attitude is to render one's self more vulnerable and less prepared when the future arrives.

Another cause of failure to contemplate the future is that futurists, both professional and popular, have made the future seem too shocking to contemplate. They warn of mega-change that will sweep away all we have known and that can only be faced by those willing to radically transform their lives. Consider the work of Alvin and Heidi Toffler, whose books are entitled *Future Shock* and *The Third Wave*. The Tofflers give us a framework for the politics of the third wave, but if they are correct that the pace of change continues to accelerate, then surely the third wave will be followed by a fourth, fifth, and so on, each of shorter duration. There is no reason to believe that those waves will be less important than the third. However, social, political, economic, and even technological change rarely occurs at a moment in time but as a process and in stages, more like a confluence of changing currents than a tidal wave. The same is true of response to change. It tends to develop over time. It is true that environmental issues are terribly important, and there is now a remarkable level of consensus on the need to take significant steps to address those issues. On the other hand, it has now been a quarter century since the Stockholm world environmental conference of 1972 that led to the concept of "sustainable development" as a critical force in global and even local affairs. Much remains to be done, even though it has now been more than five years since the Rio Earth Summit. It is true, if very nearly trite, to recognize that we are in an age that is being dramatically influenced by information technology, but most people, at least in developed countries (and many in developing countries) have adapted to computers over a substantial period of time.

The point is not that the pace of change is less than dramatic, nor is it that the consequences of change will be less than very serious. It is that change, the movement into the future, is normal and inevitable. Moreover, if we contemplate it, plan for it, and move toward it with a spirit of opportunity and adaptability, we may not need to be "Future Shock[ed]."

What Is in the Public Administration Future?

The rest of this book will explore what appears to be coming in the future for public service professionals in each of the major functional areas of the field. More broadly, however, we will emphasize themes which seem to us to be extremely important human changes. They include the globalization of public administration; the increasing complexity of intergovernmental and intersectoral relations; the growing importance of diversity; the significance of limits, environmental, economic, or social; and the continuing importance of public law and legal processes, whether formal or informal, to resolve tensions and provide tools for meeting new challenges.

Globalization of Public Administration

Contrary to popular opinion, there are many things that public administrators do very well. Most people can expect that the basic services they need every day will be available regardless of economic fluctuations, political turbulence, or even the weather. Police, fire, water, sewage disposal, roads, transportation infrastructure, and emergency communications, operate for most people most of the time the way they are expected to, and many citizens when asked about their direct experiences with government reply positively.[21] There are many places in America where creative things are being done and hard choices made by a wide variety of public managers despite daunting economic and political pressures.[22] Also, contrary to the rhetoric used by some politicians, there is no systematic evidence that private sector organizations are on the whole more efficient than public ones or that there is more fraud, abuse, or waste in public service than in private business.[23] There is much argument that public administrators should be concerned with customer service, like the public sector. However, most people who have clashed with a credit card company, a bank, an insurance company, an automobile dealership, a cable television company, or a major airline may want to consider whether the issue is one of superiority of the private sector over the public.

There is always room for a great deal of improvement, and there are always the occasional horror stories. There are also many stories of excellence and commitment.[24] Public administrators have long sought to learn lessons from the private sector, academic disciplines, or wherever better ideas might be found. In the past two decades, efforts have been underway to get the best advantages of private sector and not-for-profit organizations while maintaining the accountability demanded in the public sphere. But the most important sets of lessons cannot be learned using the traditional focus of American public administration, or for that matter public management in other nations, on purely domestic concerns.

The most ominous criticisms of American public administration for the long term are not about efficiency or integrity, but about its ethnocentric and geocentric focus. Indeed, in most countries, the focus is inward, on the local tradition and contemporary issues, without looking out to understand what is common and what is unique. Which problems have already been addressed in other countries, with what solutions, and with what degree of success?

Public administration must globalize as a profession and as a field of study, for it is surely doing so as a matter of fact. From the global coverage of CNN, to the communications channels of the information superhighway (like the Internet), to the impact on local governmentals from international trade agreements like the North American Free Trade Agreement (NAFTA) and the General Agreement on Tariffs and Trade (GATT) that created the World Trade Organization, the borders of political jurisdictions, of economies, and of societies are increasingly porous. There are three absolutely crucial lessons that everyone in our field needs to learn about the global future. They concern growth of diversity, the importance of culture, and the significance of limits. Consider these dimensions from the perspective of public administration in the United States, but similar arguments could be made for the other governments of the world as well.

Diversity

The population of the United States is a distinct minority. The U.S. population is roughly 270 million, or about 4.5 percent of the world population that now is nearing six billion. It is only about one-tenth the population of Asia, which represents over half of the global census. There are three times more Africans than U.S. citizens. There are more Latin Americans, Europeans, and residents of the former Soviet Union. Less than two billion of the world's nearly six billion citizens are Christian, and more than half of those are Catholic. Many Americans think of Hispanics as minorities, but, if we compare percentage of population, the number of U.S. citizens in the world is slightly more than half the proportion of Hispanics to the whole U.S. population. That is, Americans represent a smaller percentage of the global population than do Hispanics in the U.S. population. We are a distinct minority. In short, White, Anglo-Saxon, Protestant American men and women are distinctly atypical of the world's population.

Mosques, such as this one located in Dhaka, Bangladesh, represent the religious center of a community and serve as a crucial cultural influence for the more than one billion Islamic people of the world.
(Photo courtesy of Phillip Cooper.)

Moreover, population projections suggest that in the years ahead, the United States will represent an even smaller proportion of the world's residents. "The future growth will be concentrated in Asia, Africa, and Latin America. About 97 percent of the growth in world population between 1990 and 2050 will take place in what we now call the developing countries, 34 percent of that in Africa and 18 percent in Southeast Asia."[25] At that medium-level projection by the United Nations, the annual growth will reach ninety-seven million in the next five years, or the equivalent of the entire population of the United States every three years.[26] Not only that, but the population of the United States is aging while the global population, largely the population of developing countries, is growing younger.[27]

Economically, with the addition of Austria, Finland, and Sweden, the European Union now has a GNP of 7.3 trillion dollars, which is "an economy 10 percent larger than the United States' and 64 percent larger than Japan's."[28] By 1991, the United States ranked only sixth in per capita Gross Domestic Product (GDP) at $23,100 per person per year (with more than one billion people in the world at under $370 per year).[29] With the rise of trading blocs like the European Union and NAFTA, individual national economies become less dominant. The World Trade Organization promises to reduce the level of controls on international trade by individual countries, making nation-states even more porous in financial terms than they have come to be already.

In sum, residents of the United States are also members of a global community in which their nation is only one part. The borders are increasingly porous, and the impact of change in one part of the world can be quickly felt in another. The collapse of the Mexican peso in 1994 caused immediate alarm among U.S. leaders as President Clinton issued a call for forty billion dollars in loan guarantees to shore up the Mexican economy: There was fear not only that other Latin economies would be rapidly affected, but that there would be significant losses for American investments under NAFTA. The Kobe earthquake in Japan instantly put the world's sixth largest seaport out of operation. Political and ethnic strife in Africa and the former Yugoslavia caused an influx of refugees into Scandinavian countries, economies (particularly Finland and Sweden) that were already under stress. The end of South African apartheid had a rapid impact on global investment. Those global markets operate by computer twenty-four hours a day around the globe, responding to changes everywhere that might have an impact on the global economy, in specific regions and nations, or in particular financial sectors. The status of national economies, currency exchange rates, inflation levels, and interest rates all affect who makes investments and in what, including in the purchase of government securities, whether they are federal bonds to cover national debt or state or local bonds. Changing investment expectations, the rise of new financial instruments, and pressure for performance caused a locally elected treasurer in Orange County, California to drive the county into bankruptcy by putting large sums of public funds into high-yield (but also high-risk) investments that went bad.

The issue is not that it is a small world. It is large and complex, but it is increasingly one global community in which nation-states are no longer quite the islands they once were, just as local communities are no long as insulated from national trends and problems as they used to be. Public administrators in all countries and at all levels of government need to be aware of that reality. It affects everything from the cost of bonds to build a new school, to the presence of a major employer in the county and how much property tax they will pay, to the way a state government administers social policies paid for by various forms of taxation, and ultimately to the quality of life we all enjoy.

The Importance of Culture

On the other hand, while it is increasingly a global community, it is a diverse world with dramatically different cultures. Those differences are important, and they influence how problems are perceived and addressed.

On a global scale, language and culture affect everything from communications to social values. In its most isolationist periods, Americans travelling abroad expected everyone to speak English. Europeans warned Americans that it was important to learn French and German, the languages of international diplomacy. Of course, those were the languages of diplomacy because they were the languages of the dominant countries during the years of colonial rule. Increasingly, government and business officials from Latin America and Asia are insisting that there are far more people who speak Spanish and Chinese than there are residents of the United States, Britain, France, or Germany. Indeed, Latin Americans have been trying to convince residents of the United States that the term American is not restricted to citizens of the fifty states.

Culture counts. Cultural distinctions are critical not merely in the world of those who jet around the globe, but locally as well. Chicago is one of the largest centers of Polish culture in the world. Los Angeles has one of the largest Portuguese-speaking communities. New York has a sizable Russian community complete with Russian-language newspapers and radio stations. More and more communities who want to serve all of their residents are finding it necessary to convey community information in Spanish as well as in English. In the United States, as in other parts of the world, indigenous cultures have come to play a more recognized and important role after years of neglect. Increasingly, representatives of this plethora of cultures are demanding a voice at city hall, the state capitol, and in Washington, D.C., as well as in international organizations like the United Nations.

At a more specific level, the presence of multiple languages and cultures directly affects the operation of programs and delivery of services. Schools quickly feel the impact of cultural change. Local social service agencies encounter it. Health care programs are affected by significantly different ways of viewing health and medicine. Different cultures have different perceptions of time. They differ as to styles of negotiation or dominant patterns of authority. The level of formality that members of one culture accept may be difficult for those of another. The issue is not that every public administrator will understand all of the nuances of cultural differences, but that he or she will be alert to the fact that differences do exist and be willing to understand the needs of the people he or she serves.

The Significance of Limits: Environmental, Economic, and Social

If it is important to understand the rich diversity of people and cultures and to see that the interrelationships among them are crucial, both internationally and domestically, then the other fact of contemporary public administration life is that we live in a world of limits.

During the nineteenth and for much of the twentieth centuries, the presumption was, particularly in developed Western countries like the United States, that growth was essentially boundless and that technology and the marketplace would supply what was needed. As we enter the twenty-first century, however, there is a very different reality. There are limits of several types that affect the day-to-day work of public administrators, from demands by local residents not to locate a waste-treatment facility in their neighborhood (the so-called NIMBY problem for "Not in my back yard!"), to expectations for more water resources to support construction of new homes, to demands for state governments to fashion strategies to meet clean air standards, to efforts by regional leaders to address the need to change their economies because of the loss of resources, to the loss of agricultural land, to the need to rethink local and regional planning to accommodate new residential patterns, to the loss of small town social patterns brought on by growth.

Two of the most important sets of limits go to fundamental realities of the modern age. Humankind is now in a position to do what we have never before able to accomplish: We could destroy the environment we need to survive, or we could destroy ourselves in war. The decisions about those possibilities are not in the hands of one or a few nations. A nuclear exchange between India and Pakistan, or Israel and one of its Arab neighbors would have dramatic global impact without regard to anything done by the United States, NATO, or the United Nations. Environmental disasters do not respect national boundaries. Deforestation and desertification (the process by which once fertile land deteriorates into desert) can drive large numbers of environmental refugees out of their homeland in search of a reasonable quality of life elsewhere.

Many of the important issues of limits do not arise because of specific crises: great cataclysms like in civil strife in Rwanda, wars in the former Yugoslavia, earthquakes like the disaster in Kobe, or floods like those in Italy. They develop slowly over time as boundaries are reached and pressures mount. Consider the following facts.

"If the medium prognosis is fulfilled, there will be double the present number of people on earth in 2050."[30] Before that, "the total number of rural poor in the Third World may reach 1.25 billion—more people than now live in the entire industrial world—by 2015."[31] The global consumption of water has increased from about ninety-five cubic miles of water in 1900 to an expected 1,240 cubic miles within the next five years; that is out of a total available estimated 2,150 cubic miles.[32] Of course, that water is unevenly distributed, as are rates of consumption. Even in the United States, which has large amounts of fresh water, there are tensions over available water supplies. The floor of California's central valley has dropped more than twenty-five feet because of the amount of water drained from underground

The world's poor are very poor. When a natural disaster occurs, as in this flooding of hovels in downtown Dhaka, Bangladesh, the poor have no recourse but to endure. (Photo courtesy of Phillip Cooper.)

aquifers. Much of four western states is dependent on the water in the large Ogalala aquifer that is being rapidly used.

While it is true that there is a hydrological cycle that permits substantial amounts of the used water to be used again, the situation is more constrained than it may appear. Present rates of industrial use mean that substantial amounts of the water are not adequately treated to eliminate toxins and other hazardous wastes. Industrial and even household wastes that were improperly disposed of in past decades seep into underground aquifers, contaminating water sources on which many communities depend. As those aquifers that are sources of pure water are drained at rates too rapid to allow for normal recharging, they can crush under the man-made and geological pressures such that they will not be available in the future or will at least not be as productive as in the past. There are locations in the United States, such as portions of Florida, where the water table is less than two feet below ground level. Defor-estation eliminates watersheds, which reduces the capacity of an ecosystem to store water that can later be released to support plants and animals as well as to maintain stream flow, to support irrigation, and to recharge community water reservoirs. The loss of watershed can have catastrophic effects if it is too severe or too rapid. Thus, Honduras has experienced a dramatic loss of electrical power in recent years and can provide only about seven hours per day of electricity because deforestation has destroyed watershed, which in turn crippled the nation's ability to produce hydroelectric power.

The "green revolution" of the 1960s has continued, with many nations achieving extremely high levels of agricultural productivity. Even so, more than a billion people lack adequate nutrition. Ironically, some of the green revolution crops develop so fast that they have inadequate amounts of key minerals. Of course, with the levels of population increase even the most dramatic levels of production have upper limits. In a number of Third-World countries, agriculture has been a major element of the economy and has shifted to crops that can earn the maximum return in the international market. This is essential for those countries to pay the interest on huge levels of international debt. That has meant that some traditionally productive agricultural countries have had to import staple foods because so much of their capacity is given over to commodities. That has also meant a decline in the diversity of crops in some places as more and more land has been put into export-oriented production.

Another major problem all over the world has been the loss of farmland. Studies have found serious damage to 300 million hectares (a hectare is the equivalent of 2.47 acres of farmland). "Agricultural activities accounted for 28 percent of this degradation, overgrazing about 34 percent, and deforestation another 29 percent."[33] The other major cause of loss of productive land is that it has been developed to meet the housing and other construction needs of burgeoning populations. In order to meet dramatically increasing demands for food and fiber with less available land, most countries have employed substantially increased quantities of chemical fertilizers and pesticides that, in turn, produce increased water pollution. See Figure 1-1.

Even with the most efficient farming techniques, there are limits, and pushing those limits raises the danger of spillover problems like water pollution and the excessive use of toxic chemicals.

Think of it this way. Consider Table 1-1, which shows consumption patterns from 1970 to 1990.

The other major problem with consumption patterns is that they are extremely uneven. "[T]he average American baby represents twice the environmental damage of a Swedish child, three times that of an Italian, thirteen times that of a Brazilian, thirty-five times that of an Indian, and 280(!) times that of a Chadian or Haitian because its level of consumption throughout its life will be so much greater."[34] That is one reason that the developing countries

Figure 1-1
World Population Growth Patterns

*Despite an optimistic decline in the number of new people added to the world's
population each year after the turn of the century, there will continue to be a need to
increase food production. That need will put added strain on the world's environment.*

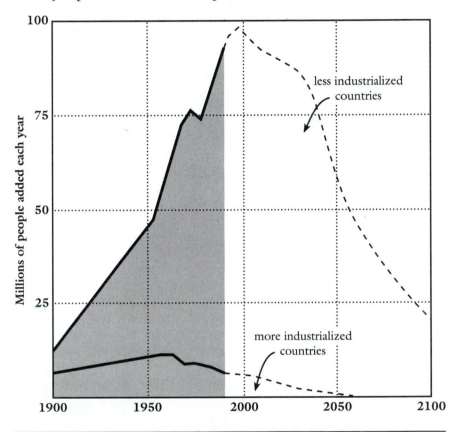

Source: Reprinted from *Beyond the Limits,* copyright © 1992 by Meadows, Meadows and
Randers, p. 15. With permission from Chelsea Green Publishing Co., White River Junction,
Vermont.

responded so harshly to the developed nations at the Rio Earth Summit
when the Third-World countries were told that they had to institute conservation programs to protect their natural resources, like rainforests, against
exploitation. Their answer was that the developed countries had done
tremendous damage to the environment over generations so that they could

Table 1-1
Worldwide Growth in Selected Human Activities

	1970	1990
Human population	3.6 billion	5.3 billion
Registered automobiles	250 million	560 million
Kilometers driven/year*		
by passenger cars	2584 billion	4489 billion
by trucks	666 billion	1536 billion
Oil consumption/year	17 billion barrels	24 billion barrels
Natural gas consumption/year	31 trillion cubic feet	70 trillion cubic feet
Coal consumption/year	2.3 billion tons	5.2 billion tons
Electric generating capacity	1.1 billion kilowatts	2.6 billion kilowatts
Electricity generation/year		
by nuclear power plants	79 terawatt-hours	1884 terawatt-hours
Soft drink consumption/year	150 million barrels	364 million barrels
(U.S. only)		
Beer consumption/year	125 million barrels	187 million barrels
(U.S. only)		
Aluminum used/year for		
beer and soft drink containers	72,700 tons	1,251,900 tons
(U.S. only)		
Municipal waste generated/year*	302 million tons	420 million tons

*Organization for Economic Cooperation and Development (OECD) member nations only.

Source: Reprinted from *Beyond the Limits,* copyright © 1992 by Meadows, Meadows and Randers, p. 7. With permission from Chelsea Green Publishing Co., White River Junction, Vermont.

enjoy a high standard of living and now that they have created a global mess they want Third-World countries to give up the opportunity to meet their own quest for a better life to make up for years of abuse and degradation by others. The answer was a resounding *No!*

Environmental and population constraints are by no means the only kinds of limits that public administrators confront. Others include the limits of space, time, and money. Communities are often part of a metropolitan area with a hundred or more cities, counties, authorities, and special districts, each with its own boundaries, legal powers, and financial resources. It is no longer possible in many communities simply to expand by annexing new land and re-zoning it to help meet community needs for new facilities or as new tax base.[35] The same is true of states, or in other countries, regional governments. Alone, they cannot control behavior that produces difficulties in other states, like the burning of inexpensive fossil fuels to produce electricity

*As more countries drive headlong in their development efforts, they must also confront
such accompanying perils as the alarming increase in air pollution found in Bangkok,
Thailand. However, people in developing countries resent those from already developed
nations who demand restraints on progress so as to ease the world's pollution problem.*
(Photo courtesy of Yvan Cohen and ASIAWEEK.)

in one part of the country when the resulting pollution falls as acid rain in another. The use and abuse of water supplies in one place affects states down-
stream who use that same water as a drinking-water source. Economically, it
occurs when one state gives away large tax breaks or exemptions from state
regulations to businesses to locate there, forcing neighboring states to
change their policies and requirements in order to compete for jobs. Some
states have large portions of their land owned and operated by the federal
government. This land is enjoyed by the citizens of other states but may not
be taxed or used by the host state for its own needs.

There are also limits to financial resources. While there are increasing demands for services by government, there is little willingness to pay additional
taxes to support those expectations. Indeed there have been strong demands
to reduce taxes and other costs for services. That trend has been one of the
reasons why the call to "reinvent" government has focused on the effort to
do more with less. There have been those who have argued that modern societies can grow their way out of the constraints of financial limits, but even

some economists are coming to believe that unconstrained economic growth is not sustainable over the long term without significant impacts on the environment and other crucial dimensions of modern life.[36]

All of these are limits. Many nations have lived with limits for generations, but finding new ways of living with limits while maintaining the quality of life everyone seeks is one of the most interesting challenges facing those who govern.

The Increasing Complexity of Intergovernmental and Intersectoral Relations

One of the important consequences of confronting limits has been a growing recognition of the interdependencies among public sector organizations and between those organizations and private firms and not-for-profit institutions. Our concept of intergovernmental relations has changed from fairly simple notions of federalism to complex federalism to intergovernmental fiscal relations to multijurisdictional and cross-sectoral cooperation and competition with a mix of local, state, regional, national, and even supranational participants.

For a long time, when Americans thought of intergovernmental relations they thought of federalism, the relationships between the national government and the states. As cities and their surrounding suburbs grew, it became clear that the interests of the metropolitan areas and of the rest of the state in which they were located often seemed to be in competition with one another. That was a difficult competition where state legislatures were structured such that rural interests could exercise a veto over state policy making. Besides, local governments are creatures of the state and are constrained by the authority of the state. As communities expanded and new areas of the country experienced dramatic growth—particularly in the west, southwest, and southeast—the complexity of metropolitan government increased. There were new special districts, school districts, and city governments, as well as dramatically expanded expectations of county governments.

Responding to these dynamics, the federal government began to construct a complex set of grants and transfer payment programs that not only involved the states but also sent resources directly to the local governments. During the 1970s and 1980s there emerged increased demands for what the Richard Nixon administration and later the Ronald Reagan administration called "the new federalism."[37] The driving force was the argument that authority and discretion over policy decisions and expenditures should be sent back to the states and localities to make programs more responsive and more accountable.

The problems of the new federalism were two. The first was that local majorities have not historically tended to attend very much to the needs of minorities, which is why many of the federal programs came with so many strings attached when they were originally designed. Therefore, there was pressure to maintain controls on programs as they were decentralized to the state and local governments. The second problem was that one of the driving forces of the 1980s and 1990s was budgetary, such that when the programs came to the state and local governments, they often came without dollars attached. The states have often done to the localities precisely what the national government did to them, sending down program responsibility but not resources. These dynamics gave rise to the revolt by states and localities against what are termed "unfunded mandates."

The job still needed to be done. One result of these dynamics has been increased efforts by communities and states to find new ways of meeting their obligations. Often they have elected to contract with not-for-profit organizations or private profit-making corporations to provide services. They have also entered into interjurisdictional agreements for the exchange or purchase of services, such as ambulance operations. States have developed similar relationships and have also created interstate compacts which, when approved by the Congress, can be used to meet regional needs. The same is being done in other nations around the world.

In addition, supranational agreements, whether regional like NAFTA, or global, such as the GATT or international environmental accords, are important parts of the intergovernmental mix. The United States Environmental Protection Agency must carry out U.S. obligations under more than a hundred international accords. But since many of the national environmental policies are actually administered by the states, and in some cases the local governments, that means a relatively direct impact of global action on local administrators. The European Union has already had dramatic impacts on domestic policies in Britain, France, and Germany, even down to such matters as land use and business regulation. There are also direct negotiations between states and even localities and other similar units abroad on issues of commercial cooperation and technical assistance.

The Importance of Public Law and Legal Processes

The forces of globalization as well as the increasing complexity of intergovernmental and intersectoral interdependencies and competition have, perhaps ironically, made public law and legal processes more important than ever before. Although there has been an international reaction against excessive regulation and frustration with what have seemed to be legal constraints on management flexibility, increased attention to public law issues is required to help structure the new infrastructure needed to deal with increasingly complex fiscal, social, and economic relationships; to provide tools for meeting new

*When the rule of law is removed, people lose their protection from unreasonable
governmental action and sudden harm. Often they must flee for their lives, as happened
in Rwanda when Rwandan Hutus streamed into Zaire to escape feared Tutsi
retaliation. Thousands of such refugees—in Africa, the Balkans, and
elsewhere—further strain efforts to reestablish governmental organization.*
(Photo courtesy of AP/Wide World Photos.)

challenges, including enhancing our ability to resolve tensions; and to meet growing demands for accountability that come even as so many voices are heard calling for empowerment and enhanced flexibility. Indeed, what has taken place in Bosnia, Rwanda, and Somalia clearly demonstrates what can happen when the rule of law breaks down and there is no meaningful regulation of behavior.

Infrastructure. As the republics emerging from the former Soviet Union have discovered, there is nothing natural about a complex market-based economy or a sophisticated modern democracy. They require a great deal of infrastructure. One of the important elements of that infrastructure is a body of law that facilitates the new types of relationships. Even an advanced nation like Germany has faced a huge task in attempting to supply infrastructure and address problems arising in connection with the unification of the former East Germany into the West.

Developing nations, moving from authoritarian regimes, have had to see law in a new way and to construct the kinds of legal systems, from constitutions to the most detailed laws governing local business activities, that are needed when very powerful centralized governments fall. They must do that even as they are in the process of developing a new political culture, a set of understandings about who should govern and with what range of power.

In the United States, the same problem existed in the early years of the republic. Article I, section 8 of the U.S. Constitution is in significant part a set of powers given to Congress to be able to construct an infrastructure, including the ability to build an economic foundation, to develop roads and other services, to regulate commerce, and so on. In its more recent manifestations, the problem of building a set of legal relationships that allow order and predictability while permitting the freedom to pursue personal and public goals goes on. The task of building and changing the infrastructure to meet new demands and circumstances is never ending. For example, while many love the freedom of the open road, the conduct of some users on the "information superhighway" has led to collisions that require controls. The problem of punishing abusers of the Internet has triggered a large discussion of what kinds of laws and processes are needed to support the new information infrastructure. Again, there is nothing natural about such a system of law. It is a human creation, and the body of laws needed to make it work must all be created as well.

New Tools and New Tensions. As various units of government move to meet these demands for legal support, it becomes necessary to fashion new tools and processes. The use of contracting to provide services is a very popular device. Indeed, many state and local governments contract for large amounts of their social service and maintenance operations. However, contracting with governments is different and far more complicated than simple agreements between private organizations. There are special constraints on governments and special accountability requirements that private sector firms need not consider. If contracts between government and the private sector are complex, working agreements among governmental units may be even more so.

At the national level, the complexities are even greater. When a government agrees to take action under a treaty, it must still do things at home in conformance with a variety of existing domestic laws. That means reconciling international procedures and authority with domestic. When, for example, the federal government agrees to an environmental program for which states and localities do the actual work on the ground, there are several sets of relationships that must work in harmony if anything is to happen at the end of the day.

Then there is the problem that increased complexity in an era of limits can lead to frustrations and tensions that must be resolved in some reasonable way to avoid a breakdown of the system. We have seen too often around the world in recent years what happens when there is no adequate legal system or when the mechanisms of conflict resolution fail. Thus, there has been an effort to construct better processes, both formal legal decision-making and alternative dispute resolution techniques to meet these challenges.

The Accountability Problem. Despite the reaction against law and lawyers that is common in many societies, public law plays an increasingly important role in public administration. One of the most important forces behind public law development is the ever increasing demand for more and better accountability. While there are many forms of accountability and many means for assuring it,[38] the legal tools remain extremely important. Even governments that have traditionally relied on concepts of ministerial responsibility in which the approach is to hold the government in power politically rather than legally responsible for its behavior are facing more demands for legal mechanisms of accountability.[39]

As new kinds of organizations and new interorganizational relationships are created to meet new problems, though, old devices for ensuring accountability must be refined and new types of tools must be fashioned. This problem is cast in high relief in countries that have emerged from authoritarian or traditionally centralized hierarchical forms of democracy. Several governments have fallen in developing countries in recent years, for example Brazil and Venezuela, and others have experienced significant shifts in policy, as in the case of Mexico during 1993 and 1994, in ways that would have been unheard of in an earlier time. Demands for accountability in Africa and in the republics of the former Soviet Union call for new approaches, including legal institutions and processes.

Conclusion

In short, welcome to the fascinating and obviously challenging world of public administration for the twenty-first century. For those new to the field, it is far more dynamic than most would have expected. To those who come to the field of public administration as "a second profession," it is a good time to place experiences in context and look toward the future. Despite the fact that the challenges are formidable, so are the opportunities for impact and growth. The chapters that follow will move through the more specialized elements of management, policy, and politics that make up the field, with particular attentions to the dynamic forces described above.

Notes

[1]The concept originated with and has been popularized in recent years as a result of publication of David Osborne and Ted Gaebler, *Reinventing Government* (New York: Penguin, 1993).

[2]The phrase comes from the Report of the National Performance Review, *From Red Tape to Results: Creating a Government That Works Better and Costs Less* (Washington, DC: Government Printing Office, 1993). For evidence that it is not new, see John Rohr, *To Run A Constitution* (Lawrence, KS: University of Kansas Press, 1986).

[3]Woodrow Wilson, "The Study of Administration," *Political Science Quarterly* 2 (1887): 209–213.

[4]Luther Gulick and Lyndal Urwick, *The Papers on the Science of Administration* (Farifield, NJ: Augustus M. Kelley, 1977), originally published by the Institute of Public Administration, New York, 1937.

[5]Stephen K. Bailey, "Ethics and the Public Service," in Roscoe Martin, ed., *Public Administration and Democracy* (Syracuse, NY: Syracuse University Press, 1965).

[6]E. G. Gladden, *History of Public Administration* (London: Frank Cass, 1972).

[7]Dwight Waldo, *The Enterprise of Public Administration* (Novato, CA: Chandler & Sharp, 1980), 7.

[8]Henry Jacoby, *The Bureaucratization of the World* (Berkeley, CA: University of California Press, 1973).

[9]H. H. Gerth and C. Wright Mills, eds., *From Max Weber: Essays in Sociology* (New York: Oxford, 1946).

[10]*Capitalism, Socialism, and Democracy,* 3rd ed. (New York: Harper & Row, 1950), 206.

[11]Alexander Hamilton, James Madison, and John Jay, *The Federalist Papers* (New York: Mentor, 1961).

[12]Woodrow Wilson, *op. cit.,* 197–222.

[13]Leonard D. White, *Introduction to the Study of Public Administration*, 4th ed. (New York: Macmillan, 1955), xvi.

[14]Lee Luther Gulick, "Science, Values and Public Administration," in Gulick and Urwick, eds., *op. cit.*

[15]Robert Wood, *Suburbia* (Boston: Houghton Mifflin, 1958).

[16]James Q. Wilson, *The Moral Sense* (New York: Free Press, 1993).

[17]Wallace Sayre, "The Unhappy Bureaucrats: Views Ironic, Helpful, Indignant," *Public Administration Review* 18 (Summer 1958), 245.

[18]Paul H. Appleby, *Big Democracy* (New York: Alfred A. Knopf, 1945), 1.

[19]Arthur S. Link, ed., *The Papers of Woodrow Wilson*, Vol. 5 (Princeton, NJ: Princeton University Press, 1968–69), 689–690.

[20]See John Nalbandian, *Professionalism in Local Government: Transformations in the Roles, Responsibilities, and Values of City Managers* (San Francisco: Jossey-Bass, 1991).

[21]Charles Goodsell, *The Case for Bureaucracy*, 3rd ed. (Chatham, NJ: Chatham House, 1994).

[22]Indeed, for all of its critical content, *Reinventing Government, op. cit.*, was in truth a catalog of public administration innovations.

[23]George W. Downs and Patrick D. Larkey, *The Search for Government Efficiency* (New York: Random House, 1986).

[24]Terry L. Cooper and N. Dale Wright, eds., *Exemplary Public Administrators* (San Francisco: Jossey-Bass, 1992); James W. Doig and Erwin C. Hargrove, *Leadership and Innovation* (Baltimore: Johns Hopkins University Press, 1990).

[25]Ingomar Hauchler and Paul M. Kennedy, *Global Trends* (New York: Continuum Publishing, 1993).

[26]*Ibid.*

[27]"In 1990, the U.S. Census Bureau estimated that 31.6 million people (12.6 percent of the total population) were sixty-five years of age and older. And Rece and Wick have predicted that "by the year 2030, sixty-four million people (20 percent of the population) will be age sixty-five or older." Robert Parson, *et al.* "Assessing the Needs of Our Elders," *Public Management*, February 1995, 14.

[28]*The Week in Germany*, January 6, 1995, 1.

[29]Paul Kennedy, *Preparing for the Twenty-First Century* (New York: Random House, 1993), 49.

[30]Hauchler and Kennedy, *Global Trends, op. cit.*, 111.

[31]Roger D. Stone, *The Nature of Development* (New York: Alfred A. Knopf, 1992).

[32]*Ibid.*, 298.

[33]World Resources Institute, *World Resources, 1992–93* (New York: Oxford University Press, 1992), 97.

[34]Kennedy, *Preparing for the Twenty-First Century, op. cit.*, 32–33.

[35]David Rusk, *Cities Without Suburbs* (Washington: Woodrow Wilson Center Press, 1993).

[36]Herman E. Daly, *Beyond Growth: The Economics of Sustainable Development* (Boston: Beacon Press, 1996).

[37]Michael Reagan, *The New Federalism* (New York: Oxford University Press, 1972).

[38]See e.g., Barbara Romzek and Melvin J. Dubnick, "Issues of Accountability in Flexible Personnel Systems," in Patricia W. Ingraham and Barbara S. Romzek, eds., *New Paradigms for Government* (San Francisco: Jossey-Bass, 1994).

[39]C. Neal Tate and Torbjorn Vallinder, eds. *The Global Expansion of Judicial Power* (New York: New York University Press, 1995).

Chapter 2

Legal Basis and Framework of Public Administration

In the summer of 1992 a variety of dramatic, profound, and even tragic events around the world posed the same questions in several different ways: Who has the power to govern, and what are the limits of that power? In the United States, there were the Los Angeles riots that flared in the wake of the acquittal of police officers accused in the beating of Rodney King. In the days following the outbreak of violence, several dozen people were killed and many more injured. Countless homes and businesses were destroyed. In Lima, Peru, President Fujimori, citing corruption in government and threats from the Shining Path revolutionaries, claimed dramatic emergency powers, swept aside normal constitutional processes, shut down the legislature, and assumed dictatorial authority over the nation. In Sarajevo, in what used to be Yugoslavia, news reporters flashed video footage of the destruction of a community and its people. In Russia, the republic that was once the seat of government of one of the greatest powers on earth, the people struggled to deal with massive unemployment and economic collapse as a new government tried to transform the society and the economic structure that supported it. In Western Europe, political leaders worried that the French people would vote *no* in a referendum, thereby rejecting the Maastricht Treaty implementing the planned European Union, as Denmark had already. (The EU places major central authority outside traditional national sovereignty in a wide range of fields, from regulatory controls to monetary exchange rates.) In Rio, leaders from around the world met at the Earth Summit, one of several world summits on critical issues during the 1990s. (These summits ended with Habitat II, the so-called City Summit in Istanbul in 1996.) The challenge for the leaders in Rio was to address the need to protect the environment while simultaneously ensuring the opportunities for all nations to pursue the economic development necessary to lift the Third-World countries out of poverty and dependence in order to ensure self-determination and dignity for all peoples. It was the challenge of sustainable development.

Behind all of these events were the ever-present questions of who has the power to govern, and what separates proper authority to act from naked political, economic, or military might. The situation in each case was different, as were the power relationships, the lines of authority. In the case of Los Angeles, there were questions about abuse of power and the breakdown of authority at the local level within a state and nation with a strong constitutional tradition. In Peru, the debates were over the very survival of the constitution itself and the form of government it created. In Sarajevo, the battle raged between various ethnic and religious groups and among the republics that emerged from what was Yugoslavia, resulting in a campaign of "ethnic cleansing" reminiscent of the behavior of the Nazis during the Third Reich. In Russia, the problem was to remake a republic into a sovereign nation and transform its entire system of authority, to re-create the legal and economic relationships both among its citizens and between them and the people of other republics of the former Soviet Union. In Rio, sweeping declarations were issued as to the importance of sustainable development, but, even in a setting with so much apparent agreement, there were dramatic disagreements as to what authority should exist to compel environmentally responsible behavior, ensure economic accountability for environmental restoration, and establish protection against unfair trade practices that would undermine environmental goals. The questions of how much authority should exist, where it should be placed, and how it should be limited against abuse remained unresolved as the heads of state returned home to claim victory for their environmental policies. Such questions of authority are presented in particularly graphic terms in times when economic stresses are strong or when periodic episodes of ethnic, religious, or national prejudices are particularly intense.

The issues raised in the several situations mentioned above were not questions only about some lofty debate over philosophy or the structure of constitutional republics. Most of these problems arose when the effort was made to use authority, not merely to define it. As Woodrow Wilson put it; "It is getting harder to run a constitution than to write one."[1] The challenge is not simply about how authority is to be defined, but how it is to be used on a daily basis by the people who must operate the ongoing functions of government and implement new policies, the public administrators.

The Problem of Authority

As the terms of the discussion to this point suggest, there are differences between power and authority. The robber in an alley with a gun has power over his or her victim, but certainly no authority to use it. If, as some scholars define it, power is "the capacity or ability to cause others to act in a predictable manner," or "the ability of A to cause B to act in a manner that he would not act otherwise,"[2] then the robber has power. However, the mere possession of physical, military, economic, or political power, in and of itself, is no reason for anyone to regard its use as proper.

Of course, power may come from a formal claim or it may be simply a matter of influence, informal power that arises from the ability to persuade. It may come from the ability to build consensus or form effective coalitions but, if that is all there is to it, it remains power rather than authority.

When we say, for example, that a health department has the authority to deny a license to operate a restaurant or to shut down a paint factory, we mean that it has power properly conveyed to it by an acceptable source in an appropriate manner. Administrators, who are not elected and may not look to the ballot box for support, must be content with the authority given to them by law. Because constitutions rarely mention administrative agencies, and even less often specify any of their powers, administrators must rely on authority vested in their agencies by legislatures in the form of statutes. While agencies may have the raw power to act beyond the matters delegated to them by law, they do not have the authority to do so. When we speak of abuse of authority, we mean either that an administrator exercises a power for which he or she has no authority (sometimes called an arrogation of power) or that he or she uses authority in a way that violates some legal limit on that power.

Max Weber, one of the leading scholars of bureaucracy, recognized legal delegations as one type of authority, what he termed rational/legal authority.[3] He also spoke of traditional authority, which comes from the recognition that a particular office has historically been permitted to exercise a specific kind of power. The third type of authority he referred to as charismatic in nature. It comes from the ability of a leader to move his or her followers by force of character, personality, or special skills such as talent as an orator.

In most modern democracies, however, charismatic and traditional authority are forms of power or influence. Rational/legal authority is the formal requirement for authority. Whatever label is used to describe it, the way we think about authority often has something to do with the perspective from which we view it. (This idea that "where someone stands on something depends on where he or she sits" is referred to as Miles' Law, named after Rufus Miles, although the credit for this particular line has been claimed by a number of people.) As administrators, we are producers of administrative action and, as such, we view various kinds of authority delegated to our organizations as tools with which to manage others involved in the operation and do the job assigned to the agency. As public servants and citizens, we are consumers of administrative decisions rendered by our superiors in government or by other agencies that have jurisdiction over our activities. From that perspective, we see authority as a constraint on our behavior that we may be inclined to accept, challenge or circumvent. In nations such as the United States that purport to operate under the rule of law, all officials "from the highest to the lowest, are creatures of the law and are bound to obey it."[4] Wherever we sit, to use Miles' phrase, it is extremely useful to think in terms of the perspectives of both the consumer and the producer of administrative action.

Of course, the type of rational/legal authority that we encounter depends in part on the kind and location of the activity in which we are engaged. Thus, local government administrators must operate within local authority, state restrictions, and national laws. Moreover, since the obligations of domestic governments are increasingly defined by regional organizations involving a number of countries or global agreements including many or most nations, the numbers of authorities that affect a given administrative action are increasing. However, before plunging into the details of discussions about the more specific contemporary issues of authority and its limits, it is useful to consider what rational/legal authority means in terms of the kinds of laws that most often empower and constrain administrators.

Legal authorities include constitutions, statutes, executive orders, treaties, regulations, and judicial decisions. Constitutions are, of course, fundamental law and are superior to other legal authorities. Although there may be debates about who has the authority to interpret constitutions and how it should best be done, the plain fact is that Article 6 of the United States Constitution provides that "this Constitution, and the Laws of the United States which shall be made in Pursuance thereof; and all Treaties made, or which shall be made, . . . shall be the supreme Law of the Land; and the Judges in every State shall be bound thereby, any Thing in the Constitution and Laws of any State to the Contrary notwithstanding." This is the so-called supremacy clause. The constitutions of other nations, or of the states within the United States, sometimes contain similarly bold declarations of authority, but even if they do not, they are supreme within their sphere. Of course, there are nations like Great Britain, in which there is no single document called the constitution but a collection of guiding state papers which, taken together, are considered to be the equivalent of a constitution. In any case, constitutional law is primary.

Statutes are, of course, the bills passed by the legislature and signed by the chief executive. As they move through the legislature, proposed legislation carries a bill number. When it is adopted by both houses of the U.S. Congress, it acquires a public law number that is a combination of the number of the Congress and a chronological numbering beyond that. Thus, P.L. 104-121 would be the 121st statute passed by the 104th Congress. In the states, the newly passed bills are given a session law number, which is essentially the same idea as the congressional numbering system except that it corresponds to the state legislative sessions, which are different from those of Congress. The legislation collected by subject and updated to include all current amendments is called a code. So, we most commonly look for statutes in the U.S. Code Annotated (USCA) or, if looking for state statutes, something like the Kansas Statutes Annotated (KSA). The term "annotated" refers to the fact that these versions of the codes contain some other reference and historical information in addition to the language of the statutes themselves. Similar codes are constructed for local ordinances.

Treaties are also legal authorities, and increasingly important ones. Such international accords as the General Agreement on Tariffs and Trades (GATT), the North American Free Trade Agreement, and numerous international environmental agreements to which we are signatories have important consequences not only for the activities of federal agencies but also for state and local agencies. They affect regulatory programs, commercial activities, and the design and compatibility of various communications and transportation systems.

Treaties in the United States are normally ratified by the Senate, a process quite different from most countries, in which no independent ratification is required. The call for ratification of the European Community integration plan mentioned earlier has produced enormous complexities, with Denmark, the first nation to undertake a ratification process, rejecting the accord. Some European nations are now coming to have a greater appreciation for the problems they see with ratification in the United States. However, the U.S. Supreme Court has ruled that presidential agreements that have not been ratified by the Senate still have the same effect as treaties, assuming of course that they do not violate the U.S. Constitution or statutes and have not been opposed by Congress. An example is the Iran hostage agreement supported by both Presidents Carter and Reagan.[5]

There is another form of executive action not necessarily involving Congress that carries the force of law: Executive orders are edicts issued by the president (or in the states by governors) to one or more agencies or officers of the executive branch commanding or prohibiting some practice. Some thirteen thousand such orders have been issued by the president since the numbering system was created to track them, and the truth is that no one seems to know precisely how many there are. They are legally binding, as are similar orders issued by state governors to executive branch officials under their control. Different countries have different constitutional authority for the issuance of decrees. The matter tends not to be as significant in parliamentary governments since the prime minister controls a majority or a coalition that can act relatively quickly on serious matters, unlike the model in the United States based on separation of powers.

Regulations issued by agencies under the powers granted to them by statute represent another form of legal authority. Like statutes, administrative rules are published chronologically in the Federal Register as they emerge from the agencies, or in the state registers at that level of government. Each year all related regulations are collected, reorganized, and updated into a Code of Federal Regulations (CFR). Similar codes exist at the state level. At the local level, policy is promulgated in the form of ordinances.

Finally, there are what are often termed precedents, rulings by the courts interpreting the law in the various forms in which it exists. More will be said about these rulings shortly, but, for the moment, it is useful to note that they are produced by federal and state courts. The rulings issued by the courts of one state carry interpretive authority only in that state. Similarly, rulings issued by trial level courts in the federal system are binding only within their districts. However, rulings by the U.S. Supreme Court plainly affect the entire nation. Of course, most countries do not share American style federalism and many do not have common law legal structures. Local governments may be responsible for carrying out many important policies, but they often lack the authority to issue ordinances. In code law countries, the use of precedent is more limited than in the Anglo-American system, though there has been a growing tendency even in European-style code-based legal systems to use judicial precedents.

The discussion of authority under international agreements becomes considerably more complex since different treaties set forth differing procedures to be used to resolve disputes arising under the terms of the particular accord in question. There is a World Court, located in the Hague, the Netherlands; however, nations make decisions as to whether to subject themselves to the jurisdiction of that court. The World Court's real authority is somewhat limited, though it does issue rulings that are generally understood to carry the weight of precedent.

Merely describing the various legal authorities, though, tells us relatively little about the dynamics of the law and its importance in the daily life of administrators. Bearing in mind the fact that law is not only an enabling force (a source of authority) and a set of constraints, let us consider each of the major areas of law as it affects public administration.

Constitutional Premises of Public Administration

John Rohr has argued vigorously and effectively that public administrators are, at least in the United States, constitutional officers whose power ultimately stems from the Constitution and who in turn owe a duty to ensure its faithful execution.[6] Rohr is right, of course, but in order to understand the meaning of the role of public administrator as constitutional officer, it is important to investigate the constitutional premises of the enterprise.

It is surprising how frequently people, particularly Americans, speak of the Constitution, often in reverential tones, and yet seem to know relatively little about its meaning and significance. Such behavior raises the distinction between the idea of a constitution and the concept "constitutionalism."[7] It is no great feat to claim that a nation has a constitution. After all, to most people who have read it, the Constitution of the former Soviet Union seemed to be an extremely progressive document, with manifold provisions purporting to protect the liberty and equality of its citizens as well as the responsibility of the government.[8] However, as one delegate to a recent international meeting put it, some countries, including his (which was, by the way, not the Soviet Union), are extremely "accomplished at the fine art of writing political poetry," constitutions and laws that sound wonderful but do little.

On the other hand, those who live under a regime that supports a concept of constitutionalism expect that the Constitution is a living document, an institution of government that binds both the rulers and the ruled. It conveys powers to government that citizens are bound to acknowledge and obey on pain of punishments up to and including the loss of their lives. However, it also constrains those who hold office in the government. If they exceed or abuse their powers, they no longer act in the name of the people and cannot claim authority for their actions. In this sense, we sometimes borrow a concept from corporate law that holds that if the officers of the corporation violate the authority delegated to them by the stockholders, they are acting *ultra vires* (meaning "beyond the power"). At that point they are acting for themselves, and the stockholders should not be held responsible for their behavior. Similarly, when an officer of government violates the Constitution or other laws, he or she is acting *ultra vires* and cannot purport to act in the name of the people whose government it is. Increasingly, people around the world are declaring that their country should not merely have a constitution but should practice constitutionalism.

Efficacious Government and Limited Government

The language used to describe constitutionalism seems to suggest that the main purpose of a constitution is to constrain government behavior. That is only partly true. It is also the document that creates and defines government and thereby gives to the institutions and officers of government the powers they are to exercise. It is an enabling and empowering document.

The primary purpose of the U.S. Constitution was not to create limited government but to build efficacious government. If the framers had wanted only to ensure limited government, they needed to do nothing more than maintain the Articles of Confederation that existed prior to the drafting of the new charter. It had no independent and coequal executive or judicial branch, could act on individual citizens only through the state governments, and could exercise only those powers "expressly delegated" to the central government. It is true that the framers, according to James Madison (often regarded as the leading influence in the creation of the Constitution), wanted a situation in which they could "oblige [the government] to control itself" and not become a tyrannical force over its citizens. However, Madison preceded those words about control of government by noting that "you must first enable the government to control the governed."[9]

The framers did indeed construct a constitution that chartered what should be an effective government and not merely a limited one. They began in the preamble itself by rejecting the idea of the Constitution as something that emanated from the states by positing that this government was established and ordained by "We the people" and declaring that its purposes were indeed "to form a more perfect union, to establish justice, ensure domestic tranquility, and to promote the general welfare." The document itself is fairly simple in design, a fact of considerable importance to the framers, who wanted a document that would last and did not want to attempt to bind future generations too closely to the lifestyle of the late eighteenth century. Still, the relatively brief charter made important changes in addition to setting its base in the people rather than the states.

The U.S. Constitution created a strong executive branch and gave it authority to carry out the executive functions of government, to make critical appointments to office, to operate as commander in chief in times of war, and to make treaties "by and with the advice and consent of the Senate."[10] It allowed the executive to obtain the opinions in writing of the heads of departments, which of course clearly implied that there were to be executive departments. That expectation was sustained as many of the framers who served in the first Congress busily set about the task of creating various executive departments. The Constitution spoke of the president's power to appoint "Officers of the United States" and to vest in them power to appoint subordinate officers, which clearly implies that there were to be not only executive officers other than the president but subordinate executive officers below them—so much for the idea that the framers did not contemplate a public administration.

The Constitution also created a strong and independent judiciary, vesting the judges with what amounts to life tenure and protecting them from attempts by others to punish them by reducing their pay while in office. It gave to the Supreme Court and such inferior courts as the Congress would establish the judicial power which consists of the authority to decide "all cases in law and equity arising under this Constitution, and the laws made in pursuance thereof, and treaties made or which shall be made," including those cases "in which the United States shall be a party." The judicial power then included the authority to decide constitutional cases as well as statutory issues even if the government itself, and by implication its officers, were parties in the case.[11]

The Congress was given a list of powers allowing it to lay and collect taxes, to appropriate funds, to establish credit, to coin money, to establish and equip military forces, to build a national infrastructure consisting of roads and postal services, and to encourage the development of business and commerce by protecting patents and copyrights. It authorized the legislature to regulate "commerce with foreign nations, and among the several states, and with the Indian tribes." Many of these powers had been precisely the kinds of authority previously denied to the central government under the Articles of Confederation.

It was no accident that the framers eliminated the language that had existed in the Articles of Confederation confining the national government to those powers "expressly delegated" by the Constitution. They instead concluded the legislative article by conferring on the Congress "all powers which shall be necessary for carrying into Execution the foregoing Powers."[12] That this change from the expressly delegated language to the so-called "elastic clause" was no accident is demonstrated by the fact that a similar resolution was reached when the Tenth Amendment was drafted. Again the proposal to state that all powers not "expressly delegated" to the "United States by the Constitution nor prohibited by it to the States, were reserved to the States respectively, or to the people" was rejected. That is, the "expressly delegated" requirement was deliberately rejected, but the rest remained.

This was a Constitution under which the national government could act directly on the people it was to govern as well as on the states. It had more tools with which to do the job and more authority to employ those tools. The measure of its success and the goal of its creation is the efficaciousness of the government it created. As Hamilton clearly explained in *The Federalist,* a strong executive is the very definition of good government. However, even Hamilton recognized that a strong executive did not mean only a strong president but also an effective civil service. Though he obviously did not use that term, Hamilton warned that the president should not be able to use simple political preferences as the basis for hiring and firing all the key people in government.[13]

Indeed, one of the clear efforts of the framers was to protect the process of governance from the day-to-day pull and haul of public opinion and short term political pressures by establishing a representative, rather than a direct, democracy. The ongoing effort to develop and use legal authority does not depend on frequent plebiscites. Even with all the changes in access to the ballot, in the much modified processes for direct election of senators, and in the mechanisms of presidential election, there remain filters between legal authority and day-to-day public opinion.

Of course those in state or local government, and administrators who must consider international issues, must be aware that there is considerable differentiation in the purpose and character of the many other constitutions apart from the national charter. Many states trace the lineage of their constitutions back to the early days of independence, predating the U.S. Constitution. Some states had ambivalent views on the powers of their chief executive, though they did ensure independent and potent judicial powers. The tensions between local governments and state officials remain very important even now, and there are differences among states as to the nature and extent of local autonomy. That is a critical issue because, from the view of the national Constitution, states have independent constitutional stature while local governments do not.[14] Local governments exist by virtue of state constitutions and laws and not otherwise. Their powers are dependent on state governments.

Constitutional Powers and Limits

With those premises in mind, let us sketch, and only sketch, some of the critical elements of constitutional authority for public administration. It is possible to understand constitutional authority in terms of the powers of the three branches, the constitutional foundations of political economy, and the evolving concept of federalism.

Separation of Powers. There are few administrators or would-be administrators who have not been confronted on more occasions than they care to remember with the traditional formula that the legislature makes the laws, the executive enforces them, and the judiciary interprets them. Like most things in government, however, that apparently simple construct turns out to be considerably more complex in operation. What many people may have once understood to be the rules of separation of powers have changed considerably. For the moment, there are a number of themes that are important to understand as one comprehends the relationships among the branches and the significance of separation of powers in the contemporary administrative environment.

The first reality is that much, if not most, of the world does not utilize what Americans understand to be separation of powers. Parliamentary governments draw their executive leaders from members of the governing party in the legislature and may also provide, as in Britain, for some kind of judicial function by one or both houses of the legislature through appeals from the courts to the "law lords" or their equivalent. A continuous support of at least a majority of legislators for the executive performance of the government is essential or the current government will fall and face a new election. In a number of countries, that maintenance of support is even more complex than it sounds because the governing majority in the parliament is not a single party but a governing coalition built by agreement among a number of parties. In the end, though, the parliamentary regimes have neither the same concept of separation of powers nor the same idea of relationships between executive and legislative functions. These differences are important when American administrators attempt to work with their counterparts abroad. They are also important because the lack of familiarity with our concept of separation of powers makes it difficult for our international colleagues to understand the behavior of our government.

The second reality is that our concept of separation of powers is not entirely accurate either, at least if it is understood in the fairly simplistic terms in which it is often described. We do not have three airtight branches of government in which all powers are neatly categorized and separated. Indeed, the Constitution nowhere states that there shall be a separation of powers. Instead, it says in Article 1 that "all legislative powers" shall be vested in a Congress, consisting of a House of Representative and a Senate, that "the executive powers" shall be exercised, according to Article 2, by a president of the United States, and that, according to Article 3, "the Judicial Powers" shall be exercised by "one supreme Court, and in such inferior Courts as the Congress may from time to time ordain and establish." Just what those powers mean and where their boundaries are to be drawn and by whom has been the stuff of separation of powers debate ever since.

The fact that the separation of powers is complex and not nearly so absolute as many Americans believe does not mean that it is an unimportant concept or that it has no real constitutional meaning. It does. Battles are still waged among the branches, with some programs falling by the wayside as casualties because one branch or another hits the outer boundaries of the separation of powers.[15] The separation of powers remains an important factor in administrative life.[16]

In addition to providing the government a variety of powers to respond to the particular problems that had plagued the fledgling nation since independence, the framers very intentionally divided up many of the powers that had been particularly troublesome when exercised by the British crown during the colonial period. These included the war powers, the ability to tax and spend (so often associated with foreign adventurism by the king), and the ability to create and fill offices that had been used by the crown to maintain support among potential adversaries or rivals. The president was to be commander-in-chief of the armed forces in time of war, but Congress was to retain the power to declare the state of war. The president was to administer the government, but could not lay taxes and could only spend subject to the so-called audits and accounts clause of the Constitution. The creation of taxes was vested in the legislature, as was the power to authorize expenditures. The president was given the power to appoint officers of the United States, but just what offices would exist and how many officers there would be remained within the province of Congress to determine.

This separation of powers was bolstered by checks and balances. Thus, the president has the power of appointment, but it is exercised "by and with the advice and consent of the Senate" for most important offices. Congress has the power to legislate, but it is required by the presentation clause to face a presidential check in the form of a veto, although it may override a veto with an extraordinary majority of two-thirds of both houses. Presidents may have the authority to appoint judges to the federal bench but, once there, the president has no ability to remove them from office, nor does Congress have the ability to punish them by reducing their pay during their period of service.

Although they are frequently lumped together, the fact is that the separation of powers and checks and balances are two separate ideas, the latter intended to protect the former. The provision that a particular power vested in one branch has a check in another branch does not mean, at least not in constitutional terms, that it is shared. The check merely ensures that the power is exercised within its proper limits.

The fact that the separation is not airtight does not support the view that there is no separation at all. Even by today's worldly wise and sometimes cynical perspective, the separation of powers still defines the principal character and function of the branches and, at particularly critical points in our history, defines the limits of individual branches as well as the power of opposing branches to draw a line. Thus, when President Nixon suggested that he might not obey a ruling by the Supreme Court in the Watergate case to turn over disputed tape recordings, it became immediately clear that whatever else he may or may not have done to that point, he would be removed from office for refusing to obey the constitutional judgment of the Supreme Court. When opposing parties in the White House and on Capitol Hill decided to raise the stakes in their interbranch disputes during the 1970s and 1980s, it produced a dramatic list of complex and controversial Supreme Court rulings seeking to address the separation of powers.

Most of the time, however, we operate under what Louis Fisher has called a "constitutional dialogue."[17] It is defined by a set of interactions among the branches that continues over time. The Supreme Court may have given in-

*The U.S. Supreme Court is the home of an active participant in the ongoing
"constitutional dialogue" between the three branches of the nation's government.*
(Photo courtesy of Howard Ball.)

terpretations to a variety of civil rights statutes in 1988 that many in and out
of Congress found incorrect, but that was not the end of the story. Within
two years the legislature had written a new law changing those statutes, in effect overturning the Supreme Court. Indeed, on some occasions, the courts

will respond to a statute by indicating that the law presents serious difficulties but that those problems must be fixed by the legislature, in effect inviting a legislative response.[18] When the White House moved to interfere in the issuance of agency rules through a regulatory review process, Congress countered by threatening to eliminate the appropriations needed to keep that White House office in operation.

Fisher teaches three critical lessons. First, the fact that a court rules on a dispute between branches is not the end of the matter, but may indeed trigger a host of additional actions and reactions among the other players. Second, many battles that could present constitutional separation of powers contests in the Supreme Court never get to a court at all but are resolved by political exchanges among the other branches. And even if they should generate a legal challenge, they tend to be resolved without ever reaching the Supreme Court or engendering what would be considered a constitutional crisis. Finally, most interbranch interactions are managed through a system of informal understandings and exchanges. Agencies work with Congress most often through communications between agency and congressional committee staffs who negotiate important issues before they ever develop to a stage of formal contest, whether political or legal. The same arguments apply by extension to state-level interbranch exchanges as well.

The courts have often worked to facilitate this flexible understanding of separation of powers by permitting innovative legislative designs such as the many decisions, beginning early in the nation's history, to permit delegations of authority to administrative agencies to issue rules having the force of law. They have permitted agencies to adjudicate disputes arising under their statutory mandates with proper guarantees of due process of law and the availability of judicial review to serve as a check. They have even upheld the creation of independent regulatory commissions and protected the members of those commissions from political control by the president. They have, as we have already observed, recognized the power of the president to issue executive orders and proclamations having the force of law. Similarly, they have recognized the power of the president to enter into executive agreements with foreign powers that have binding legal consequences in this country. They have implied powers and protections for the president, like executive privilege and absolute immunity from civil liability, on grounds that these were essential to the proper performance of the executive function.[19] In sum, the judiciary has usually been willing to cooperate in the dialogue and interpret the separation of powers with a generous and cooperative spirit.

There have, however, been periods in history when the dialogue has gone badly, when one or another of the institutional players has refused to resolve matters informally and has precipitated formal legal, as well as complex political, confrontations. Some of these engagements arose because one branch thought that what some regarded as an innovative solution to a problem was too much of a stretch into its separation of powers protected turf.

Examples include the creation of a Federal Election Commission to control campaign financing, with members to be appointed by the leaders of the legislature as well as by the president;[20] development of an independent counsel (usually called special prosecutor) statute to take investigation and prosecution of some cases involving political officials outside of the normal Justice Department control;[21] and expanded use of legislative vetoes in statutes designed to permit congressional intervention into the rulemaking processes of administrative agencies.[22] Other cases developed from adoption of the Gramm-Rudman-Hollings budget deficit reduction program that would have had the comptroller general of the United States issue a mandate to the president to sequester funds from previously enacted appropriations legislation[23] and from the enactment of new federal criminal sentencing guidelines calling for creation of a sentencing commission staffed by judges who would adopt the mandatory sentencing ranges to be used by all judges.[24] Still other disputes arose regarding the outer boundary of the Article 3 judicial functions when revised bankruptcy legislation created bankruptcy judges who fit neither the Article 1 court model nor the requirements of Article 3 judges.[25] Some disputes also centered on administrative agencies that seemed to be moving well beyond the normal adjudicative functions of regulatory bodies and into the realm of Article 3 courts.[26]

The lessons of these disputes seem to be that the courts are willing to maintain a great deal of flexibility for the legislature and the executive to work out solutions to policy problems. During an oral argument in one of these cases, attorneys told the justices of the Supreme Court that their adversaries were merely trying to scare the Court by suggesting that the wrong decision in that case would undermine the legitimacy of all independent regulatory commissions and many other administrative agencies. To this, Justice Sandra Day O Connor replied, "Well, they scared me with it!"[27]

Still, when the ability to resolve disputes through the dialogue breaks down, the courts will respond and interpret the separation of powers and checks and balances in ways that seek to maintain their essential integrity without accepting simplistic and overly rigid formulations. The basic approach is functional. What are the essential attributes of the executive function? At what point does a decision process become, in truth, more like an Article 3 judicial proceeding and less like a limited administrative adjudication? At what stage can it be said that the legislature has tried to move beyond ensuring oversight and is actually interfering in the implementation of programs?

Because agencies operate on the basis of powers delegated to them by the legislature, in most instances under the direction of the chief executive and

The members of the U.S. Supreme Court are often called on to mediate disputes or check imbalances arising between the executive and legislative branches. In one such case, Justice Sandra Day O'Connor saw danger in some separation-of-powers arguments. (Photo courtesy of the U.S. Supreme Court.)

with the check of judicial review before them, these ongoing discussions of the living separation of powers matter mightily. Since agencies have only the power accorded them by statute, administrators must always be prepared to provide a reference to the legal authority for their actions and to defend their definitions in court if the need arises.

Constitution and Political Economy. For federal agencies, most of the statutes that create them (called enabling acts) and provide them with authority (authorization acts and appropriations acts) are based on some combination of three provisions of the Constitution: the commerce power, the taxing and spending clause, and the so-called necessary and proper clause. There are a variety of other provisions in Article 1, section 8 which, taken together with these three, allow and even seem to require Congress to construct a national infrastructure consisting of an economy, a transportation system, a national security and defense establishment, communications (which in those days involved a postal system), a means of ensuring control over access to citizenship and the assurance of the rights of citizens, and adequate regulatory mechanisms to protect the operation of all of these. After all, it was in large part the effort to remedy the problems caused by the lack of these powers that led to the writing of the Constitution in the first place. Still, for many of the laws Congress adopts, it is the commerce, taxing and spending, and necessary and proper clauses that are most important.

The Supreme Court played a major role in supporting an expansive reading of those powers of the legislature so as to permit the national government to establish an economy and protect its operation from abuses by states or localities as well as to carry out the tasks most often identified by the general public as governmental. The Court supported the government's claim to be able to establish a national bank and prohibit state efforts to interfere in the operation of the national economic infrastructure.[28] It sustained the authority of Congress to regulate not merely the movement of goods across state lines, but also to include persons as well as products in the definition of interstate commerce and to reach not merely what was carried but the means of conveyance as well.[29] It permitted Congress to reach beyond borders and into states to deal with intrastate activities that have important effects on interstate commerce.[30]

Still, there are a variety of activities that do not fit within the authority of the congressional commerce power, even with such an expansive definition. The states, under the Tenth Amendment reserve powers clause, have what is commonly known as "police-power," the authority to regulate health, safety, and public welfare. Thus, Congress is limited in its authority to get at problems of true national importance, such as health care and education, directly. Instead, it has been able to develop policy in these areas largely by the use of taxing and spending powers, promising states grants of federal funds if they will comply with national standards, and, not incidentally, threatening them with the loss of federal dollars they currently receive if they refuse to comply. Thus, the federal government was able to force states to raise their drinking age to tweny-one or face the loss of federal highway dollars.[31] Similarly, most educational and health care standards have been enforced through threat of loss of federal education grants.

The taxing and spending powers are not used only to move the states and local governments but also to govern individuals and businesses as well. Targeted tax increases, tax cuts, and tax credits are all devices regularly employed as policy tools by the national government.

These powers are not merely regulatory in a narrow sense. They also build the infrastructure on the basis of which the economy and the community function. Consider the modern metropolis. Whatever their historical roots, most modern cities are active transportation, communications, commercial, and service centers. They depend on the federal programs that establish the financial system and maintain its operation, ranging from the Federal Reserve to the bank regulators and the Securities and Exchange Commission. They can be efficient parts of a national transportation and communication system because of the uniform laws administered by the Federal Aviation Administration and the Federal Communications Commission. Their highways, airports, and mass transit systems are funded with large amounts of federal dollars. The tax advantages available to purchasers of municipal bonds help them finance some of the remaining costs. Urban development programs and various tax programs provide incentives to economic development.

Many of the people who work in the cities actually live in the suburbs or, increasingly, even in the surrounding rural counties. They are able to get to work because of the existence of superhighways built as part of the interstate highway system funded primarily by the national government.

One reason for the suburban growth was the availability of inexpensive land and therefore lower-cost housing. Of course, the purchase of even these homes has been possible largely because the federal government helped to construct and maintain a mortgage market with sufficient financial guarantees to assure a flow of funds to these projects. The mortgage infrastructure permitted developers to make available more property at a lower interest rate with lower down payments than would otherwise have been available. That meant that would-be home owners could get into the market and, if they were willing to incur enough debt, qualify for and purchase a nicer and more expensive home than they would otherwise have been able to contemplate. One major reason that buyers can make such choices is that they pay a substantial amount of their monthly payments as interest that the federal government permits them to write off on their federal taxes. It also makes most home owners eligible to itemize other deductions that might relieve them of a considerable tax burden they could otherwise face.

Of course, these new communities require services that are provided by counties, cities, and, in many cases, special districts. These, in turn, are supported in large part by property taxes. Like the mortgage interest taxes, the federal government subsidizes these services by permitting taxpayers to write off the property taxes on their federal returns. Since states base their returns on the income figures generated from the federal returns, the deductions help the taxpayer at both levels.

To the degree that direct federal assistance is available in local economic development, the property owner benefits as he or she watches the value of the property appreciate. As that taxpayer approaches later life, she or he may sell the property without paying capital gains taxes on that increased property value. The taxpayer can also anticipate Social Security and Medicare assistance during retirement.

Finally, the federal regulatory authority, whether exercised through the commerce power or taxing and spending powers, can aid states that wish to innovate, protecting them from destructive competition from other states. Thus, during the Great Depression, several states that had been considering enactment of unemployment compensation programs based on taxes on employers hesitated, fearing that neighboring states that did not charge the taxes would lure businesses away. The federal government stepped in and enacted a program in which all states faced taxes on employers, but those with minimally adequate programs would get the money back from the federal government.[32] In this way, the disincentives were removed from those states that wanted to create programs, and the perverse incentives were removed from those states that might have wanted to take advantage of their more progressive neighbors by avoiding business taxes and thereby capturing firms seeking to escape states with unemployment programs.

Twenty-First Century Federalism. As these examples indicate, the simplistic ideas of federalism so often learned by schoolchildren, which picture federalism like a layer cake where there is a clear line between those powers exercised by the states and those controlled by the federal government, bear little relation to reality. There are some traditional elements of federal/state relations that remain important, but there are critically important new aspects as well.

All of the federal government activity notwithstanding, it is still true that many of the most important features of government in the lives of citizens are the responsibility of states and local governments. Most criminal law is state law, as is domestic relations law. It is a local government office that handles the recording of a birth certificate and that files the death certificate at the other end of life's journey. The laws governing property transactions as well as regulating property use are also state and local. Decisions about most crucial issues of health, safety, and education remain state or local matters. Thus, the reserve powers exercised by the states (under the Tenth Amendment) and localities (by delegation from the states) remain critically important constitutional matters and essential factors in the lives of Americans.

It is important to note that the idea of decentralization, in one form or another, is increasingly important around the world as well as in the United

States. Even in nations with unitary national governments, as compared to our federal system, leaders are increasingly sending the service, and even some of the regulatory, functions to regional or local units. While decentralization has the danger of a lack of uniformity and consistency, it is responsive to the call for greater participation by the citizens and more sensitive to local or regional issues. It meets the practical needs of many developing countries where there simply is no national capacity to carry out essential responsibilities.

Among the more important features of contemporary American federalism are preemption, the new regulatory framework, and the role of the state and local governments as market participants as well as market regulators in a changing economic environment.

The supremacy clause of the Constitution makes it quite clear that where the national government has the power to act, its decisions are binding on the state and local governments regardless of anything in state constitutions or laws to the contrary. On the other hand, there are a variety of areas, like taxation for example, in which both the national government and the states have authority, what is referred to as concurrent power. Moreover, the Supreme Court has ruled in a host of cases that peculiar local circumstances may exist that permit state governments (or local governments if authorized by the states) to legislate in ways that affect interstate commerce.[33] So the question often arises as to where the outer boundaries of state decision making are to be found. To the degree that states are in economic competition with one another or are seeking to block or force national policy making, these questions become particularly important.

There are four basic situations in which this judgment about state authority must be drawn. They include cases: (1) in which Congress approves state action; (2) where it has said nothing about state moves; (3) where the authority at issue is shared between Congress and the states; and (4) where Congress opposes or controls state activities. The first category is where Congress has clearly agreed with the state claim to authority. Thus, Congress has recognized that states have the power to regulate insurance companies even though there is no serious question that the national government could take over that task if it chose to do so.[34]

The second situation arises where Congress has said nothing about state authority but where states or localities find action necessary. Common examples of this kind of situation involve regulation of trucks on state highways or the attempt to block shipment of possibly diseased animals or plants into or through the state. In such situations the states or localities must demonstrate the important local interest they are seeking to protect, ensure that there is no more burden on interstate commerce than is essential to meet those legitimate local interests, and avoid policies that discriminate against interstate commerce. Where, for example, the state of Illinois had a policy that forced trucks entering the state to stop and install a certain type of mudguard unlike that required by most other states, the Supreme Court found an excessive burden on interstate commerce.

The discrimination problem can arise in two different ways. One set of difficulties exists where a state practices "protectionism," such as shielding its businesses from competition from other states. Thus, when the state of North Carolina tried to force Washington state apple producers to stop using their well-respected system for grading and advertising their apples, the Supreme Court found this a clear discrimination and struck down the policy.[35] Similarly, where states try to regulate businesses operating in neighboring states so as to protect themselves, the courts have had no difficulty drawing the lines. This problem arose when some states tried to dictate liquor prices that could be charged in their state based on the wholesale prices charged by distributors in other states.[36]

Another set of discrimination conflicts involves situations in which states or localities have attempted to insulate themselves from national problems or those of neighboring states. As long ago as the 1930s the Supreme Court made it clear that "[t]he Constitution was framed . . . upon the theory that the peoples of the several states must sink or swim together and that in the long run prosperity and salvation are in union and not division."[37] It was on this theory of discrimination against commerce that the Supreme Court struck down efforts by the state of Alabama to restrict shipments of hazardous waste to the nation's largest licensed toxic waste facility located in Emelle, Alabama. The state might be able to limit transportation and disposal of any hazardous waste, but it could not develop controls aimed at waste moving in interstate commerce as distinguished from similar toxic wastes developed within the state.[38]

All of this does not mean that the states and localities have been closed out of an opportunity to obtain recognition for local needs in complex regulatory programs—quite the contrary. During the 1960s, many social service programs were developed that provided funds for federally developed programs to state and localities that actually delivered the services. Since the 1970s, the same thing has been done with regulatory programs. Under the contemporary design, states are permitted to develop their own standards in, say, environmental matters, so long as they are at least as rigorous as the federal standards. Once the standards are approved by the relevant federal agency, the states are allowed to enforce those standards. The idea is simply to adjust standards to local needs but not permit them to be diluted, while also allowing local administration in order to ensure that enforcement officials are sensitive to local problems and needs. Where states will not or, as is often true, cannot develop their own standards, they may nevertheless be permitted to enforce federal standards themselves. In many cases, states simply do not have the expertise or facilities to do the scientific work needed to develop acceptable standards, but they can enforce standards with a degree of sensitivity to local problems. Finally, if the states will not or cannot develop or enforce existing standards, the federal government may step in and carry out the entire regulatory function itself.

This kind of policy framework is a partial preemption, a decision by the federal government to exercise some, but not all, of its power in a given arena, leaving a degree of discretion for the states and localities.[39] The problem is that Congress often does not specify in clear terms what, if any, authority it intends to leave to the states. In these settings, the courts must investigate the degree of what is termed *implied preemption* that exists. In such situations the courts either will try to determine whether the federal scheme is so pervasive that it preempts the field, leaving no room for state action, or will try to assess the degree to which there is a conflict between what Congress has mandated and what the states propose.[40]

Preemption can be done by federal administrative agencies as well as by Congress. If an agency adopts rules under a valid delegation of authority from Congress that conflict with state policy, the federal rules prevail. Thus, when some states contested the Federal Communications Commission's rules governing portions of cable-television regulation, the Supreme Court upheld the FCC.[41]

Sometimes state and local governments are themselves the targets of federal regulation. The Supreme Court has held that if an activity is within the regulatory power of Congress under the commerce clause, the controls may be applied to state and local governments as well as to those in the private sector. Thus, local government employees are covered by the provisions of the Fair Labor Standards Act just like other employers.[42]

In the contemporary world, state and local governments, not just in this country but in many other nations around the world, are active participants in the marketplace, as well as regulators of it. There is great pressure for governments to contract out for, or contract to deliver, services and even to become entrepreneurs in their own right. Moreover, the subnational governments are very much affected by the shifts and changes that emerge in the regional, national, and even the international economies.

As businesses have changed so that the local plants that manufactured goods distributed in local retail stores have given way to national or international suppliers who vend their wares through mail-order catalogs using toll-free telephone numbers, cable-television marketing systems, or computer-based purchasing or sales, the old ways of contemplating business regulation and taxation have been significantly modified. The fact that states other than those in which a firm maintains its headquarters or major facilities have been prohibited from taxing mail-order firm business in their state has a major impact in the way states can consider their relationships to business. (That is especially true given that at the time of the most recent major case on the matter, mail-order business amounted to over $180 billion in sales.)[43] Similarly, when the national economy undergoes major shifts, such as the deregulation movements that swept the late 1970s and 1980s, there are important consequences as well. Consider states like Kansas, in which natural gas is an important economic resource but also an industry regulated by the state. When natural gas was deregulated, it left the state with a set of public utility regulations that seemed to interfere with the obligations of existing natural gas contracts, an apparent violation of the impairment of contracts clause of the Constitution. The courts have had to work with the states, providing feedback on the outer boundaries of state power in such situations.[44] Similarly, as states and localities have felt economic pressure to actively support economic development, there have been important issues in such areas as the zoning of property and the obligations of firms seeking to move businesses out of the area.[45]

Of course, one of the problems that has come with the desire for governments to be entrepreneurs is that we have had to confront the constitutional problems that arise in comparing government as market regulator with government as market participant. For many years now, it has been clear that when state or local governments engage in activities that are not noticeably different from those of private firms, they may be regulated by the federal government or taxed like any other business.[46] But what limits exist under the Constitution apart from those imposed by the Congress? If a governor flies to Moscow and enters into business arrangements with the Russian Republic, what are the implications? Without addressing the additional complications that may arise if state or local governments run afoul of foreign policy powers, there are some problems even closer to home.

Consider the following example. Boston imposed a restriction on those competing for city construction contracts which required that a fixed percentage of the employees to be used on the work be city residents. Was that a violation of the commerce clause? No, said the Supreme Court, because in that situation the city was not behaving as a government but as a market participant. Under those circumstances the restrictions of the interstate commerce clause do not apply.[47] For similar reasons, the state of South Dakota was permitted to operate a cement plant that sold its products only to in-state businesses.[48] It was allowed to do as a market player what would clearly be prohibited if the state had imposed a similar restriction as a regulator of private businesses. However, when the state of Alaska tried to place a restriction on contracts for timber sales that would have mandated some processing of state-owned lumber within the state before it was shipped elsewhere, the Court concluded that the state was attempting to be both a market participant and a market regulator. In that situation, the commerce clause applied and prohibited the Alaskan policy.[49]

Apart from the commerce power, there is another provision that restricts states and localities called the privileges and immunities clause. The clause is understood to prohibit states and localities from interfering in normal freedoms associated with national citizenship. Thus, when the city of Camden, New Jersey, tried to do something similar in its contracting processes to what Boston had already successfully sustained, it lost because it was challenged under a different provision of the Constitution.[50] The reason was that although the commerce clause may not apply to government as entrepreneur, the privileges and immunities clause does. That clause protects, among other things, the right to travel across state boundaries to pursue a lawful occupation. It may be acceptable for states to place substantial license fees on out-of-state hunters seeking to take big game in a state, but it is not permissible for a state to attempt to force employers to give priority in hiring to a state's citizens before permitting others to have a chance at the jobs.

In sum, the changes in the economy, whether specific policy steps taken by the national government or simply the dynamic changes in the marketplace, constantly test and force redefinition of what the late Justice Hugo Black used to refer to as "Our federalism."[51] Although the courts are willing, in the absence of contrary national legislation, to permit some flexibility to state and local governments to be entrepreneurial, there are limits. Those limits are, at this point, far from clear and anything but fixed.

Constitutional Rights and Liberties

Of course, none of the powers discussed thus far may be exercised in a way that violates constitutionally protected rights or liberties, most of which are set forth in the Bill of Rights or the so-called Civil War Amendments. While the details of constitutional rights and liberties are beyond the scope of this discussion, there are a few simple ideas that any administrator should bear in mind, whatever the kind of agency or level of government in which she or he operates.

Nationalization of the Bill of Rights. The first ten amendments to the Constitution, referred to as the Bill of Rights, were added shortly after ratification to fulfill promises to those in the ratifying conventions who insisted that a written bill of rights was essential to limit the powers of the newly created national government. Thus, the First Amendment states that "Congress shall make no law. . . ." It says nothing about the states.

When the attempt was made to use the Bill of Rights to protect citizens against abuses by state and local governments, the Supreme Court declined

the invitation. It held that the Bill of Rights applied to the national governments and not the states.[52]

However, after the Civil War, the Thirteenth, Fourteenth, and Fifteenth
Amendments were adopted. They ended slavery, attempted to ensure protections against state abuses, and assured the right to vote without regard to
race. Of these, the Fourteenth Amendment has proved the most complex
and intricate to interpret. Unlike the Fifteenth, the Fourteenth Amendment
says nothing about race. It states:

> All persons born or naturalized in the United States, and subject to the juris-
> diction thereof, are citizens of the United States and of the State wherein they
> reside. No State shall make or enforce any law which shall abridge the privileges
> or immunities of citizens of the United States; nor shall any State deprive any
> person of life, liberty, or property without due process of law; nor deny to any
> person within its jurisdiction the equal protection of the laws.

At least as it is written, then, this provision of the Constitution plainly
does apply to the states, and, by extension, to local governments, without regard to questions of race or gender. It applies to "all persons. . . ." The
question that has been argued at length, however, was what the word *liberty*
meant in the due process clause.

Some, like Justice Black, argued that the word *liberty* should be understood to mean those liberties protected by the Bill of Rights, and that therefore all of those specific protections should be applied to actions by state and
local government as well as the national government. Others rejected that
proposition.[53] Although the Court refused to accept Black's complete incorporation argument, as a practical matter, his view has carried the day. In a
long series of opinions, the Supreme Court has engaged in a process known
as selective incorporation in which it has applied most of the protections of
the Bill of Rights to the states.

The Core of the Bill of Rights. The provisions of the Bill of Rights most often
encountered by administrators are the First, Fourth, Fifth, and Ninth
Amendments.

The First Amendment protects the freedoms of speech, association, press,
peaceable assembly, and religion in both the free exercise dimension and in
the prohibition against the establishment of religion. Even these rights, often
called the first freedoms, are not absolute. In particular, administrators are
often called on to address these liberties in situations where the government
has not attempted to prohibit their exercise but rather has implemented
time, place, and manner regulations which condition the exercise of the liberties, such as in the issuance of permits for political demonstrations. Public

administrators are citizens as well as regulators, and it is not uncommon to confront problems of free speech or free exercise of religion on the job as a supervisor or an employee.

The same is true of Fourth and Fifth Amendment rights, protecting against unreasonable search and seizure or self-incrimination. As the cases in which the Supreme Court upheld mandatory drug testing of some public employees demonstrated, the rules for administrative searches and seizures are not the same for criminal investigations as in administrative contexts, even though the Fourth Amendment applies to both.[54] In less dramatic, and less troublesome circumstances, administrative inspections are done all the time for health, safety, sanitation, and the like. Obviously, if the same level of controls that are applied in criminal investigations were used every time an inspector visited a plant or restaurant, the administrator's situation would be untenable. So the Constitution applies, but in a way that accommodates administrative reality.

Fifth Amendment safeguards against self-incrimination do apply when there is a danger of a criminal proceeding, but not in normal administrative operations. Thus, a civil servant can be made to testify about his or her performance on the job on pain of losing a job, but that same employee cannot be made to testify if that testimony might implicate him or her in a criminal matter unless an appropriate level of immunity from prosecution is granted.[55]

By the way, the Fifth Amendment is the basis for a claim of a deprivation of due process of law when the federal government is involved. When the term due process is used, it normally refers to the procedural guarantees that are usually understood to be required to ensure fundamental fairness. These include notice of what is to be done and the legal authority on which the action is based, the opportunity for some kind of a hearing at which one can give evidence and test the evidence used by the other side, a fair decision maker who will provide a reasoned written judgment on the record developed in the proceedings, and some kind of opportunity for an appeal. The government may take one's life, liberty, or property if it does so properly.

The Fifth Amendment has also been interpreted by the Supreme Court to prohibit discrimination by the federal government, as if it included an "equal protection" clause like the one in the Fourteenth Amendment. The reasoning is that the concept of due process prohibits arbitrary decision making when important judgments are made about individuals. A government action that is discriminatory is by definition arbitrary. Therefore, discrimination violates due process.

The Ninth Amendment has been the subject of considerable debate, at least since the ruling by the Supreme Court in 1965 that first recognized a constitutional right to privacy. In that case, Justice Douglas, writing for the majority, relied on several provisions of the Constitution to protect privacy, but several members of the Court thought that the proper clause for the right was the Ninth Amendment.[56] That amendment provides that "[t]he enumeration in the Constitution, of certain rights, shall not be construed to deny or disparage others retained by the people." This particular provision was added because of fears raised during the ratification debates that some would argue that only those rights specifically listed in the Bill of Rights would be protected from government interference when, in fact, the Bill of Rights had been meant to preserve rights and not limit them. Today, the Ninth Amendment arises most often in connection with situations where birth control, abortion, or other medical programs are involved.

The equal protection clause of the Fourteenth Amendment has produced lengthy discussion and debate in situations from school desegregation cases to contemporary arguments about gender discrimination. It prohibits intentional discrimination. However, in an era when statutes rarely contain discriminatory language and when those who wish to practice bigotry have learned enough to speak in code words or to keep their mouths shut, it is extremely difficult to prove an intent to discriminate. Therefore, the number of legal cases brought under the Constitution is small as compared to the number launched under one or more of the pieces of civil rights legislation adopted by Congress. The concept remains important, but the practice has shifted to statutes and administrative guidelines issued by bodies like the Equal Employment Opportunity Commission.

There is a certain danger that American administrators have in contemplating these rights and liberties. We have a tendency to assume that all other governments operate according to the same restrictions. That is not necessarily true. There are constitutions that confer more protections than our own and many that provide far less protection. There are even major concepts like equal protection under the law that we regard as essential and that are generally acknowledged by the international community, but which may not be applied by individual countries that plainly discriminate on the basis of race, gender, or religion in ways that are lawful in their systems. This divergence can be a serious source of tension between American public servants and their counterparts in other lands.

Statutes: From Democracy through the Constitution to Policy in the Street

Although the constitutional foundations of public administration are critically important, most of what administrators encounter most of the time comes directly or indirectly from statutes. Put differently, statutes are the way we get the judgments of democracy through the constitutional processes and limits to policy in the street. While there is much talk of government by judiciary and many debates over the power of the executive, whether president or governor, the importance of the legislative process and the products it provides is often undervalued.

Since all administrators can be challenged to show the source of their power (the so-called *quo warranto* writ demands the official to show what warrants his or her action), and since the overwhelming majority of agencies are created and empowered by legislation, an awareness of statutes is critically important. In part, that requires an effort to overcome the fear most administrators have initially about their ability to read a statute.

Statutory Forms

It is useful to recall that there are basically three kinds of statutes that administrators encounter most often, enabling acts, authorization statutes, and appropriations legislation.

Enabling Acts. Enabling acts create agencies, define their powers, and set the jurisdiction within which those powers may be exercised. Enabling acts are often quite old and, although they may be amended over the years, they are rarely completely rewritten.

Authorization Statutes. Authorization statutes are usually employed to launch a new program or delegate to the agency a new area of responsibility. An agency may have many such statutes, delegating to it a variety of programs. Thus, the Environmental Protection Agency has been given statutes authorizing action on clean air, clean water, insecticides, fungicides, and rodenticides, the regulation of handling and disposal of toxic wastes, responsibility for cleanup of abandoned hazardous waste sites, and more. State agencies often find themselves handling state statutes and federal delegations, such as the so-called "Right to Know" law that requires not only disclosure of the discharge of pollutants by area firms but also development of evacuation plans to be used in the event of a chemical disaster.

A variety of legislation is adopted in order to comply with international agreements, such as the Ocean Dumping Convention and many other environmental or health accords. In these situations, the legislation may be of a peculiar form, requiring unusual action or a different process from what is often employed in standard domestic legislation. Thus, the Coast Guard found itself facing a difficult squeeze in attempting to develop regulations to comply with the international ocean dumping restrictions. The problem was that the Coast Guard, a unit of the U.S. Department of Transportation, had to meet the deadlines of the international agreement and related legislation but also comply with U.S. domestic administrative procedure requirements. Another recent example is the set of complexities associated with the Great Lakes compact, which involves a number of states and Canada.[57]

Appropriations Legislation. Presumably, appropriations statutes merely provide the funds needed by an agency to carry out its assignments. However, appropriations committees often conclude that protection against spending abuses requires substantive controls on an agency. Thus, appropriations legislation may contain clauses prohibiting the use of funds for particular activities or conditioning expenditures on compliance with one or another restriction. A true statutory picture of an agency can only be painted with all of these taken together. For day-to-day purposes, though, administrators often focus on only one statute, and indeed, often on only one part of one statute.

Statutory Interpretation

The answer to statute anxiety is practice and some basic knowledge. In general, courts will read statutes literally. That is, courts assume that statutory language is drawn precisely and that the legislature is perfectly capable of fixing any problems that may arise in the event of misinterpretation. Unlike constitutional amendments, the passage of amended legislation is common.

The courts begin with a deference to what is called *contemporaneous administrative construction,* meaning the initial interpretation given to a statute by the agency charged with its implementation. The basis for this deference is the fact that the agency has both expertise in the field at issue and experience working with statutes in that area. The courts may ultimately disagree with the agency interpretation, but they start with a heavy presumption that the agency was correct.[58]

Courts will also take into account what is called the *judicial gloss* on a statute, meaning the previous interpretations given by courts to the statute. Many of those judicial interpretations are based on a reading of legislative histories, the story of the passage of legislation from introduction to final enactment. At the national level, the documents are readily available to support such an analysis, though discerning what legislative intent truly was can be a very difficult process. At the state level, legislative history research can be nearly impossible because few states provide the kind of fully developed record of the legislative process needed.[59]

Finally, courts consider changing circumstances in their assessments of statutes and their contemporary application. Where an agency has as part of its authority a very old statute, it often becomes necessary to evaluate the meaning of that legislation in the contemporary setting. Many of the regulatory statutes adopted much earlier in the century often force that kind of guessing game.

Statutes for Everyone: Cross-Government Obligations

While each agency functions under a set of enabling, authorization, and appropriations legislation, it also operates under statutes applicable to all public organizations. These fall into three general categories. First, there is the legislation that governs administrative procedure. Second, there are statutes mandating civil rights protection. Third, there are what might be termed general administrative support and management statutes.

The Administrative Procedure Framework. There is nothing like a constitution of administrative law that sets the standards for the general operation of all administration agencies. Instead legislation has developed historically into what is now known as the Administrative Procedure Act (APA). States have comparable legislation, also often referred to as APAs, though they vary considerably from state to state.

The APA concept has grown as a response to a number of important questions. The overall problem is how to structure and define the way agencies under the control of unelected administrators who exercise considerable authority and make decisions having the force of law are to operate such that they can be said to comport with basic constitutional norms and the rule of law. In particular, there have been continuing discussions about the fact that agencies make rules having the force of law, like legislatures, and produce decisions in particular cases, like judges. There is also a question of how citizens and others in government are to know and respond to agency decisions. Finally, there has been a discussion of how to integrate the "quasi-legislative" and "quasi-judicial" decisions from agencies into the larger legal framework of constitution and statutes.

The result of these concerns and discussions has been an APA (and its state equivalents) made up of several elements. First, there are introductions sections that define the terms and also the coverage of the procedure statutes. They generally divide up administrative actions covered into two categories. Quasi-legislative procedures, most often rulemaking, produce general statements of policy issued to implement statutes which prescribe behavior for everyone or groups of people in the future. For example, there are rules governing those trucking firms that haul toxic substances. Quasi-judicial processes are those that produce decisions in individual cases that grant or deny a claim, like a Social Security Disability benefit case, or render a finding, as in a regulatory proceeding that finds a firm in violation of safety rules. The introductions also specify which agencies are covered and which are not, a very important issue at both the national and state levels.

The APA provisions governing the process by which agencies issue rules essentially call on administrators to make certain that rulemaking is open, orderly, and participative. That is, agencies are required to give published notice of their intent to make rules. They must permit participation in the rulemaking process through submission of written comments on proposed regulations (so-called notice and comment procedures) or testimony at hearings, where they are required by statute. The rules eventually adopted must be published along with critical elements of the record developed to support the rule. Finally, there must be sufficient time to implement the new rule before enforcement begins. More recently, Congress adopted the Negotiated Rulemaking Act, which added a preliminary step to this process that permits agencies to assemble representatives of groups likely to be interested in and affected by the planned policy to try to reach preliminary agreement on its terms. The idea is to reduce later conflict and eliminate wasted effort by incorporating critical views at the earliest possible stage of the process. Whatever emerges from that preliminary process is then fed into the normal rulemaking process, permitting expanded notice and participation before the final rule is eventually issued. After they are issued, rules may be amended, replaced, or eliminated, but only if the proper rulemaking processes are employed.[60]

The primary concern when agencies act like courts and adjudicate claims or disputes is that they provide the basic elements of due process of law and that their actions are fundamentally fair. Of course, neither the general concept of fairness nor the more legalistic notion of due process requires that someone win a dispute. Instead, it means that a person must receive the kind of notice and hearing described earlier in this chapter. The most complex problem in administrative adjudications is the fact that agency personnel make the rules, implement them, and adjudicate cases arising under them. The idea is that agencies have the expertise and experience to perform those tasks well, but the problem is obvious. The way that the APA resolves this apparent situation of the agency being the judge and jury in its own case is by providing special status and protections against interference for the administrative law judges who make decisions so that they cannot be punished by agencies for making rulings against the government.

The questions of checks is somewhat larger, though. For that reason, the APA provides for judicial review of agency decisions, both rulemaking and adjudication. This process begins with a large dose of deference to expert and experienced administrators, along with a respect for the need for administrative discretion and flexibility. Still, the courts are available to check actions that are arbitrary or illegal. Judicial review also performs the function of integrating the decisions of agencies into the larger body of law. Court precedents bring the administrative process that began with the passage of statutes full circle, such that one can now read the legislation creating and defining the powers of the agencies, the rules and administrative opinions issued by the agencies that implemented those statutes, and the judicial opinions linking the two and evaluating both in terms of the constitution.

The other major element of APA is a set of fair information practices laws intended to: (1) ensure that information about planned and past agency actions is available; (2) protect against inappropriate acquisition of information about individuals; and (3) ensure the open and participative character of administrative proceedings. With that in mind, the national (and most state) APA contains a Freedom of Information Act, Right to Privacy Act, Government in the Sunshine Act, and Federal Advisory Committee Act.

The Civil Rights Framework. While the APA addresses a wide range of concerns about the rights and interests of those in agencies or with disputes pending before them, the last three decades have witnessed demands for attention to the need to open government to people who were previously excluded. While the equal protection clause demands that "no person" be denied the "equal protection of the laws," it is not always clear precisely what those terms mean. Plainly, it outlaws race and gender discrimination, but what of age discrimination or unequal treatment based on physical disabilities? Could a state force a state trooper to retire from normal street duties in his fifties, even though a physician certified that he was extremely fit and healthy? The Supreme Court upheld the state.[61] Moreover, it can be extremely difficult to meet the legal requirements for proof of discrimination under the Constitution, such as proving the intentions of the person or group who allegedly disadvantaged someone because of gender.[62]

For these reasons, Congress has adopted a set of civil rights statutes relevant to most public administrators. The most pervasive statute in this field is the Civil Rights Act of 1964, and its numerous amendments, which prohibits discrimination in employment, programs funded by the federal government, and places of public accommodation on the basis of race, gender, religion, and national origin. To those strictures have been added the Age Discrimination in Employment Act (ADEA), Pregnancy Disability Amendments, Education for All Handicapped Children Act, and Americans with Disabilities Act (ADA). The Civil Service Reform Act of 1978 attempted to integrate a number of these statutes into a coherent framework covering federal civil servants against discrimination.

The other commonly employed statute in this field is the post–Civil War Civil Rights Act codified as 42 U.S.C. Section 1983, which permits a citizen whose rights under the Constitution or laws of the United States are violated to sue state or local employees and units of government.[63]

The Management Framework. There is another set of statutes that provides tools for managing and controlling agencies. Civil service statutes, whether state or federal, define public employment, prescribe rights for employees, and set procedures for supervision and discipline. Although union contracts are different from statutes, civil service statutes are modified in operation by collective bargaining agreements entered into by government units and employee bargaining units.

Other statutes define relationships between the government and the private sector. Among the most important here is the Federal Property and Administrative Services Act and the many government contract statutes passed since the 1940s that control federal government contracting. States have equivalent legislation. The more government uses contracting to obtain both goods and services, the more important are these contracting statutes. Important to both of these kinds of activity is the growing body of ethics legislation, such as the federal Ethics in Government Act and similar state legislation, that prohibits conflicts of interest and sets other protections against abuse of office. There is also a set of statutes, perhaps well symbolized by the Inspector General Act, providing investigative and auditing authority to ensure that these other statutes are honored. Agency inspectors general are special in-house investigative officers.

In sum, the statutory framework defines the authority of an agency, the jurisdiction within which it may apply that authority, the appropriations available to support that activity, the procedures by which legally significant actions can be taken by the organization in the form of adjudications and rulemaking, the management authority available to operate and monitor administrative practices, the information access and control strictures applicable, and the protections against discriminatory behavior by administrators.

Courts and Administrators

Most often, judicial rulings, called precedents, are incorporated into new or revised statutes and administrative rules. In terms of the need to understand the structure and core design of the law governing administration, it is important to understand the concept of precedent. It is also critical to understand that judges are regular participants in ongoing administrative life.

Precedent: Court Rulings as Judicial Authority

There are several questions about precedent that are useful for administrators to contemplate. What is precedent? How does it develop? What does it mean?

Precedent refers to a legal concept known as *stare decisis,* which means that once a court has answered a legal question, that interpretation should be uniformly applied by others called on to address the same kind of problem.

Although the debates rage over the right precedent to use in a given situation and how it should be applied, the basic idea is relatively simple. Precedent stems from the notion of equal justice under law, according to which people in similar situations should, as a matter of justice, be treated similarly. It is one way of defining fairness.

The reason that precedent becomes important has to do with the relationship between statute and common law. No legislature can possibly write statutes that would be specific enough to cover every situation that might arise. For one thing, it is impossible to know in advance what might come to pass as the economy, technology, society, and politics change. For these reasons, judges continually find themselves faced with the need to interpret statutes and administrative rules in new and unanticipated circumstances.

Sometimes the questions before the courts are completely new and do not fit easily within any existing statutory framework. One of the more famous of such cases concerns government regulations of surrogate parenting.[64] Another concerns a Tennessee case in which a local judge was asked to decide whether frozen human embryos had to be protected and whether to award them to one party or another in a divorce case.[65]

The former cases involve creating precedents that interpret existing authorities. The latter call into play what is termed the common law process, also know as judge-made law, where there is seemingly no clearly applicable alternative authority.

The question of how precedent is made, then, varies somewhat, depending on the kind of authority involved in a given case and the type of interpretation a judge is asked to provide. The basic elements of constitutional and statutory interpretation were discussed briefly earlier. The greatest problem for judges in constitutional interpretation is that they must interpret a document that was admittedly and intentionally written in broad terms so that it would stand the test of time and be usable in a variety of anticipated situations. The other problem, however, is that mistakes made by judges in the interpretation of the Constitution are somewhat more difficult to correct than mistakes made in statutory interpretation. In the latter case, the legislature can simply revise legislation. Constitutional interpretation begins from the language of the Constitution, adds the intent of the framers (to the degree that it is clear, and it rarely is), focuses on the meaning given to the words of the Constitution by previous court rulings, and considers the need for change to fit new circumstances. As a practical matter, when a case arises, the argument is about the current judicial interpretation of the language of the Constitution and whether it ought to be changed to apply to the situation before the court.

Recall that statutory interpretation rules hold that legislation should be interpreted strictly, since mistakes can be corrected with relative ease by the legislature. The initial interpretation given to a statute by the agency charged with its administration is presumed to be valid, although that presumption is the starting point for analysis and is not absolute.[66] The courts will then consider prior judicial interpretations of the statute and, once again, include a judgment as to the need for change in the existing interpretation to fit the case before the court.

In cases of common law development, courts begin from the proposition of *stare decisis.* The parties will attempt to convince the court that there is a precedent, if not exactly like the situation before the court, then close enough so that the principle on which the earlier case was decided should be applied in the current case. Each side will then analyze the precedent it offers to determine what the central principle was in that earlier decision. It will advise the judge as to how that principle should be applied, either directly or in a modified form, to the current case.

The judge may accept one of the authorities presented by the parties as a proper precedent. He or she may then either accept or reject the arguments about the principle on which that earlier case was decided. The judge may do an independent assessment of the precedent to find a principle. Finally, the judge may either apply the principle derived from the precedent directly to the current case, modify it for a better fit, or perhaps even create a new principle on grounds that the existing rules just will not fit the new problem. This is the common law process of decision.

In any case, the opinion that emerges, one explaining the ruling of the court, the disposition of the case (what is to happen next), and the basis for the conclusions reached, represents a new precedent. Arguments about that opinion will arise in the future as others attempt to employ that precedent to support their positions in new cases.

To state that a precedent exists does not indicate exactly what the significance of a precedent is. Judicial opinions are treated as legal authorities, but they are binding only within the jurisdiction of the court that issued the ruling. Since the U.S. Supreme Court issues comparatively few of the rulings handed down every year, most of the precedents issued around the nation have limitations. Moreover, since no two cases are ever exactly alike, it is often possible to have what appear to be conflicting decisions in closely related cases.

In practice, though, the situation is not quite as chaotic as it may appear. When a new statute or rule appears, or when a problem arises like those mentioned above for which there is no applicable legislation or regulations, there is often a flurry of litigation. Initially, these cases may produce a variety of conflicting interpretations. As judges in various jurisdictions read opinions issued by their colleagues elsewhere, they often produce a trend that legislatures may notice and write into legislation. Where conflicts remain, appellate courts begin to sift out the differing opinions and eventually narrow the range with respect to particular questions. This process of resolving conflicts among courts may even lead to a Supreme Court ruling intended to settle the matter.[67] In truth, though, judicial decisions of that sort rarely settle everything. In fact new rulings may spark new cases.

It is important to realize that administrators in different jurisdictions face different court systems, legal authorities, and procedural rules. There are common patterns, but there are also differences. The more intergovernmentally complex the administrative environment, the more important these differences can be.

It is also true that these modes of interpretation and judicial action vary from nation to nation. Countries that operate from a French code law system, rather than an Anglo-American system of common law jurisprudence, view the role of the judge differently and do not accept the same rules of interpretation. On the other hand, there is a tendency in many countries around the world toward some covergence among systems. The French, for example, now have a Constitutional Court that is relatively new and different from their historical judicial tradition. Moreover, some code law courts may use more of the concepts of interpretation familiar to American courts than the classical models might suggest. The point, however, is that a wide variety of judicial structures, processes, and rules of interpretation remain.

The Judge as Participant in Administrative Life

The truth is that judges remain regular participants in the administrative process. There are at least two ways to view this situation.

From the judges' point of view, they do not create the task. People bring cases to court that must be resolved. While it is true that judges can sometimes use procedural devices to duck cases, trial-level and appellate-level courts below the Supreme Court level often must take difficult and contentious cases. Even though the Supreme Court has virtually complete discretion over its own docket (in practice if not in theory), even that high court eventually gets cornered into deciding cases like abortion, affirmative action, or death penalty disputes.

While judges have considerable power and discretion, they also face a variety of serious constraints. They usually have very crowded dockets and a limited amount of time to consider what are often very complex cases that are years in the making before they ever reach a court. Judges are usually generalist lawyers who may be called on, particularly in many administrative law cases, to face scientifically and technically complex problems where a new question is far ahead of current law. They have few staff members, barely enough to push the necessary paper out the door.

In the end, they usually rule in favor of agencies. Contrary to popular opinion, they are most often acutely aware of their own limitations and would rather settle cases than decide them in litigation.

Taken as a group, the justices who make up the U.S. Supreme Court in any given period of time can often be noted for their style and for the role that they play in society and government. The Warren Court of the 1960s, not always a serious group, was noted for its involvement in many issues. In an informal portrait are (left to right, front) Tom C. Clark, Hugo Black, Earl Warren (Chief Justice), William O. Douglas; (left to right, back) Byron White, William J. Brennan Jr., Potter Stewart, Arthur J. Goldberg. (Not shown is John M. Harlan II.)
(Photo courtesy of the U.S. Supreme Court.)

However, judges do have an important role to play in the administrative process, and they do play it. Sometimes, they simply issue rulings in favor of one side or another, but often they issue an interpretation and send the case back to agencies for further action. The next chapter will consider in greater detail some of the types of actions they may take.

What is important here is that because their decisions frequently and necessarily have important policy consequences, judges are legitimately part of the larger law and policy dialogue. Ironically, administrators often act as though judges are interlopers into their arena when, in truth, many of the charges levelled against judges have also been used to criticize administrators.

They are unelected, often seem difficult to control, and make critically important decisions.

Conclusion

Put differently, it is often useful to think of the role of law and courts in public administration in the way we often picture budgets. Budgets are often troublesome. There is never enough money available and there are always strings attached to its use that constrain the ability of administrators to do our jobs. On the other hand, without budgets, agencies would be unable to do anything. Certainly it cannot be expected that the public should sanction the appropriation of large amounts of funds without protections to ensure that unelected officials employ the funds in a responsible way to accomplish the purposes expressed by citizens through the political process.

Similarly, administrators exist by virtue of the legal authority creating our agencies and our offices. Administrators are accorded substantial authority to make sweeping rules having the force of law and to adjudicate important matters affecting the lives and property of the organizations and individuals within their jurisdiction. The required legal processes, along with the judges who review administrative actions, may seem to be intrusive constraints on administrative action but, like the appropriations process, they are the mechanisms to ensure accountability to the body politic. The question of the meaning and use of the tools of accountability is the subject of the next chapter.

Notes

[1]Woodrow Wilson, "The Study of Administration," *Political Science Quarterly* 2 (1887): 209–213.

[2]See David Easton, *The Political System* (New York: Knopf, 1971).

[3]H. H. Gerth and C. Wright Mills, eds., *From Max Weber: Essays In Sociology* (New York: Oxford, 1946).

[4]*United States v. Lee,* 106 U.S. 196, 220 (1882).

[5]*Dames & Moore v. Regan,* 453 U.S. 654 (1981).

[6]John Rohr, *To Run a Constitution* (Lawrence, KS: University of Kansas, 1986).

[7]See Charles Howard McIlwain, *Constitutionalism: Ancient & Modern* (Ithaca, NY: Cornell, 1947).

[8]S. E. Finer, ed., *Five Constitutions* (New York: Penguin, 1979).

[9]Alexander Hamilton, James Madison, and John Jay, *The Federalist* (New York: Mentor, 1961), No. 51.

[10]U.S. Constitution, Article 2.

[11]*Marbury v. Madison,* 1 Cranch 137 (1803).

[12]U.S. Constitution, Article 1, Section 8, Clause 13.

[13]See *Federalist* No. 77.

[14]*Reynolds v. Sims,* 377 U.S. 533 (1964).

[15]See *Buckley v. Valeo,* 424 U.S. 1 (1976); *Northern Pipeline Construction Co. v. Marathon Pipe Line,* 458 U.S. 50 (1982); *INS v. Chadha,* 462 U.S. 919 (1983).

[16]See Rohr, *op. cit.*

[17]Louis Fisher, *Constitutional Dialogues* (Princeton, NJ: Princeton University Press, 1988). See also Louis Fisher, *Constitutional Conflicts Between Congress and the President,* 4th ed. (Lawrence, KS: University of Kansas Press, 1997).

[18]See *TVA v. Hill,* 437 U.S. 153 (1978).

[19]*United States v. Nixon,* 418 U.S. 683 (1974); *Nixon v. Fitzgerald,* 457 U.S. 731 (1982).

[20]*Buckley v. Valeo, op. cit.*

[21]*Morrison v. Olson,* 487 U.S. 654 (1988).

[22]*INS v. Chadha, op. cit.*

[23]*Bowsher v. Synar,* 478 U.S. 714 (1986).

[24]*Mistretta v. United States,* 488 U.S. 361 (1989).

[25]*Northern Pipeline Construction Co. v. Marathon Pipe Line, op. cit.*

[26]*Commodity Futures Trading Commission v. Schor,* 478 U.S. 833 (1986).

[27]54 *United States Law Week* 3710 (1986).

[28]*McColluch v. Maryland,* 17 U.S. 316 (1819).

[29]*Gibbons v. Odgen,* 22 U.S. (9 Wheat) 1 (1824); *The Daniel Ball,* 77 U.S. (10 Wall.) 557 (1871).

[30]*Southern Pacific v. Arizona,* 325 U.S. 761 (1945).

[31]*South Dakota v. Dole,* 483 U.S. 203 (1987).

[32]*Steward Machine Co. v. Davis,* 301 U.S. 548 (1937).

[33]*Cooley v. Board of Wardens,* 53 U.S. (12 How.) 299 (1851); *Kotch v. Board of River Pilots,* 330 U.S. 552 (1947).

[34]*Prudential Insurance Company v. Benjamin,* 328 U.S. 408 (1946).

[35]*Hunt v. Washington State Apple Advertising Commission,* 432 U.S. 333 (1977).

[36]*Healy v. Beer Institute,* 491 U.S. 324 (1989).

[37]*Baldwin v. G.A.F. Seelig,* 294 U.S. 511 (1935).

[38]*Chemical Waste Management v. Hunt,* 504 U.S. 334 (1992). See also *Fort Gratiot Landfill v. Michigan Department of Natural Resources,* 504 U.S. 353 (1992).

[39]See generally, *Hodel v. Virginia Surface Mining,* 452 U.S. 264 (1981), *Hodel v. Indiana,* 452 U.S. 314 (1981).

[40]*Gade v. National Solid Wastes Management Association,* 505 U.S. 88 (1992).

[41]*Capital Cities Cable v. Crisp,* 467 U.S. 691 (1984). See also *Morales v. TWA,* 504 U.S. 374 (1992).

[42]*San Antonio Metropolitan Transit Authority v. Garcia,* 469 U.S. 528 (1985).

[43]*Quill Corp. v. North Dakota,* 119 L.Ed.2d 91, 100 (1992).

[44]See *Energy Reserves Group v. Kansas Power & Light,* 459 U.S. 400 (1983).

[45]*Allied Structural Steel v. Spannaus,* 438 U.S. 234 (1978).

[46]*United States v. California,* 297 U.S. 175 (1936); *New York v. United States,* 326 U.S. 572 (1946).

[47]*White v. Massachusetts Council of Construction Workers,* 460 U.S. 204 (1983).

[48]*Reeves v. Stake,* 447 U.S. 429 (1980).

[49]*South Central Timber Development v. Wunnicke,* 467 U.S. 82 (1984).

[50]*United Building Trades Council v. Cambden,* 465 U.S. 208 (1984).

[51]*Younger v. Harris,* 401 U.S. 37 (1971).

[52]*Barron v. Baltimore,* 32 U.S. (7 Pet.) 243 (1833).

[53]See the opinion of Justice Cardozo in *Palko v. Connecticut,* 302 U.S. 319 (1937).

[54]See *National Treasury Employees v. Von Raab,* 489 U.S. 656 (1989).

[55]*Lefkowitz v. Cunningham,* 431 U.S. 801 (1977); *Lefkowitz v. Turley,* 414 U.S. 70 (1973).

[56]*Griswold v. Connecticut,* 381 U.S. 479 (1965).

[57]See U.S. House, Hearing before the Subcommittee on Oceanography, Great Lakes and the Outer Continental Shelf of the Committee on Merchant Marine and Fisheries, *Great Lakes Water Quality Program,* 102nd Cong., 1st Sess. (1991).

[58]*Rust v. Sullivan,* 500 U.S. 173 (1991); *Chevron v. Natural Resources Defense Council,* 467 U.S. 837 (1984).

[59]See Gwendolyn B. Folsom, *Legislative History* (Charlottesville, VA: University Press of Virginia, 1972).

[60]This applies to substantive or legislative rules, those intended to have the force of law and implement statutory authority, as compared to what are termed procedural or interpretive rules. See *Motor Vehicle Manufacturers v. State Farm Mutual,* 463 U.S. 29 (1988).

[61]*Massachusetts Bd. of Retirement v. Murgia,* 427 U.S. 307 (1976).

[62]See *Personnel Administrator v. Feeney,* 442 U.S. 256 (1979).

[63]See *Maine v. Thiboutot,* 448 U.S. 1 (1980); *Owen v. City of Independence,* 445 U.S. 622 (1980).

[64] *In the Matter of Baby "M,"* 525 A.2d 1128 (Sup. Ct. NJ 1987), rev'd 537 A.2d 1227 (NJ 1988). See also *Anna J. v. Mark C.,* 286 Cal. Rptr. 369 (Ct. of Appeal, 4th Dist. 1991).

[65] *Davis v. Davis,* 15 *Family Law Reporter* 2097 (1989).

[66] See note 58 supra.

[67] A classic example is in the area of the right to die cases. See *Cruzan v. Director, Missouri Department of Health,* 497 U.S 261 (1990).

Chapter 3

Law against Ethics: Legal Accountability and Ethical Responsibility

While law ought to be seen in a more constructive and positive light in public administration than has often been the case, it is nevertheless true that one of the important functions of law and courts is to constrain power, to maintain accountability. On the other hand, accountability is a concept far larger and more complex than any discussion of law can address. Put differently, many of the debates in public life concern what one should or should not do rather than how one must or must not behave. These normative debates are usually collected under the title of public sector ethics. Viewed in a certain light, it is not surprising that efforts have been made over the years to compel public employees to behave ethically through the adoption of various ethics-in-government legislation, civil service rules, conflict-of-interest statutes, and financial-disclosure requirements.[1]

In the post-Watergate era, several presidents have successfully run for office by attacking public servants, even as they undermined the ability of those professional administrators to do their jobs. At such a time, the use of a blend of law and ethics in search of accountability has been an attractive and apparently obvious response to public distrust of government. There was the creation of the Office of Independent Counsel (often called the special prosecutor) to investigate alleged criminal violations. There were reports by agency Inspectors General (IG) of abuses in the State Department with respect to then-nominee Bill Clinton's family travel history. The press reported an Air Force IG disclosure of alleged wrongdoing in contracting procedures done to support a aircraft manufacturer in economic distress. Then there was the eleventh-hour pardon of a former secretary of defense for lying to Congress in connection with the Iran-Contra affair. All of these events reinforce the image that there are serious problems of unethical behavior where tough law enforcement is seemingly needed to ensure accountability.[2] The impeachment of the Brazilian president on corruption charges, the various corruption scandals in Italy, and similar cases in other countries suggest that the problem is not limited to the United States.

The difficulty is that such stories often blur a host of critical distinctions that make a great deal of difference in how we address problems of law, ethics, and accountability. For example, most of the cases cited above involved political appointees rather than career civil servants. Indeed, most of those convicted in the Nixon-era Watergate scandal were not only political appointees rather than career civil servants, but were also lawyers. Some of the behaviors previously discussed alleged violations of particular provisions of law, while others concerned patterns of behavior that appeared to be unethical but were not necessarily criminal. One of the best examples is the Special Counsel report on former Attorney General Edwin Meese. Meese immediately declared that the fact that the special prosecutor did not find a basis for an indictment meant a complete exoneration, a finding of innocence. Asked about that, the special counsel replied in a televised interview that he could not understand how anyone who read the report could find that it cleared Meese of wrongdoing.

In an effort to explore these complexities, this chapter considers the dangers of confusing law and ethics, contemplates ethics on its own terms, and discusses the legal tools of accountability.

The Tempting Trap: The Danger of Confusing Law and Ethics

Word-association quiz: cue "ethics," response "law"; cue "corruption," response "illegality"; cue "ethics statutes," response "confusion."

If there is a positive side to some of the abuses by government officials and those seeking favors or power by corrupt means in the past two decades, it is that their behavior has reintroduced discussions of law and ethics into public administration theory, practice, and education. One of the problems with that discussion, however, is the tendency to combine legal and ethical concepts and policies. The difficulty with that perspective is that law and ethics are not synonymous, and the tendency to meld the two in public administration scholarship and practice can be detrimental to our understanding and use of both. Let us consider the basis of the confusion, the critical distinctions that should be maintained, the fruits of the confusion, the importance of law in its own right, and the fundamental value of ethical discussion in its own dialogue.

Law against Ethics

The tendency to abandon the distinctions between law and ethics and to blur the concepts past the point of usefulness is easy to understand. After all, the implicit connection between law and ethics seems obvious. Law is an expression of the values the society considers important. To speak with relative consistency over time about a set of critical values suggests an ethical framework. Hence, ethics and law are firmly linked. However, the fact that some laws are consistent with some ethical principles, or that ethicists mine the law as a useful ground to discover social and political values, does not make those two concepts synonymous, nor does it erase important differences that may create fundamental conflicts.

There are a number of important distinctions between law and ethics. The simplest difference is the fact that there are many behaviors that are immoral but not illegal and vice versa. Dishonesty is morally wrong, but it is illegal only in particular circumstances, such as fraud or perjury. There are many technical regulations that define the law, but violations of them are rarely considered immoral. Driving five miles per hour over the posted limit is illegal, but most people would be in great moral trouble if driving at that speed were considered unethical. Despite the fact that it was a clear violation of regulations for Veterans Administration officials to treat claims related to Agent Orange as service-connected disabilities, many clinicians at VA facilities found ways around the rules and provided treatment anyway. Few who have studied the matter have considered that behavior immoral.

The differences are often blurred because there are similarities and sometimes connections between law and ethics. Based on a belief that stealing is immoral, most societies have adopted laws against theft. However, precisely what will be punished as robbery, burglary, or embezzlement is defined in law, not ethics. In sum, ethics may be related to law and may even be the basis for law, but it is not law. Law may reflect ethics—and the arguments in law may illuminate ethical issues[3]—but law is not ethics.

Second, law is an external and comparatively objective check that can be enforced without regard to the feelings or beliefs of the persons affected. Ethics, by contrast, is principally a force, often highly subjective in nature, directed by the individual involved. It is an internal, and largely voluntary, check. In fact, when efforts to compel the individual to behave in an ethical fashion reach the point at which the person is no longer effectively able to choose ethical or unethical behavior, ethics begin to lose force and law begins to take over.

Law is often, at least in the context of public administration, an authority-granting, empowering instrument. It is also a management tool. While ethics may, in a philosophical sense, be a foundation for positive and constructive behavior, it is most often regarded as a set of constraints on behavior.

The failure to keep these distinctions in mind has produced a variety of consequences. The first is the myth that we can solve ethical problems with ethics statutes. While society may be able to punish or deter some forms of corruption, that is not the same as compelling ethical behavior. The second consequence has been a deflation of ethics by law. The process of ethical development and education is far more difficult and delicate than passage and enforcement of laws. The idea that passage of appropriate ethics rules will address the issue undermines the effort to achieve a higher level of moral discussion and development. Third, it confuses the central task of administration, the implementation and enforcement of law, with the maintenance of sets of values. These tasks may in some senses be related, as in the administration of civil rights laws, but that is not always true.

Put differently, the confusion of law and ethics often also involves a blurring of the important distinction between authority and legitimacy. An official may have the legal authority to act, but that is no guarantee that the decision made will be correct in the view of those affected by it. Administrators are often called upon to use their authority to carry out tasks they would just as soon not perform. They are also constrained from providing services, say health care, they think it would be right to give. Presumably, if enough citizens regard government action in a particular field as illegitimate, though legally authorized, the law will be changed. However, many administrators frequently find themselves caught between their sense of what is right and what the law compels.It is indeed when these clashes between legal authority and morality catch the public servant that tensions between law and ethics become most apparent. We say that the official is obliged to honor the rule of law as a fundamental principle of public morality. However, while obedience to law may itself be a value, it is mandated whether it is celebrated as a moral precept or not.

Finally, the tendency to combine law and ethics tends to produce circular logic and an avoidance of hard questions. Conversations often drift back into discussions about law. When that occurs there is a tendency for those involved to reason from assumptions about ethics to the requirements of law and from there back to the values and ethics on the basis of which the whole discussion began. It is an understandable circularity but not a helpful dynamic.

The Confusion of Ethics Statutes

The post-Watergate tendency to enforce ethics by law has been the impetus for much of the debate over ethics standards and enforcement for two decades.[4] In fact, the first official act President Clinton completed after taking the oath of office was to sign a new ethics executive order. There has been considerable talk about ethics czars and disclosure statutes at both the federal and state levels, including sharp debates about the unwillingness of otherwise qualified candidates to serve in appointed positions because of some of the rules. The Office of Independent Counsel, created in the wake of the Watergate episode, has been as controversial as many of the people it has investigated. Thus, the very public battle between President Bush and Independent Counsel Lawrence Walsh has been a subject of continuing discussion as calls surfaced for appointment of an Independent Counsel to investigate President Clinton's involvement in Democratic fund raising during the 1996 election.

At the state level, ethics laws have been passed with wide-ranging disclosure statutes, covering not only employees themselves but also their families, even if the employees occupied purely professional positions with no decision authority over financial or personnel matters. The states involved often lacked the administrative capacity to implement the statutes, leaving state civil servants in technical noncompliance with the law while state officials tried to determine how to patch together some kind of coherent process to address the problems.

Ethics in Its Own Dialogue

Once the burden of the law-ethics confusion is lifted, it is possible to focus more clearly on ethics. Debates over the virtuous life, the obligations of public servants, and the responsibilities of participation in the body politic reach back to antiquity, and particularly to the writings of the Greeks. The contemporary discussion of ethics in public service is aimed at reconciling the broad historical discussions of ethics with the obvious, immediate, and very practical problems confronted by administrators.[5] These efforts to address the many conflicts administrators see in their professional lives start from a discussion about the relationship of internal checks to external mechanisms of accountability and contemplate the several quite different perspectives from which ethical judgments are made.

The Internal/External Debate

Carl Friedrich and Herman Finer conducted a dialogue on the subject of administrative responsibility that has come to be the classic debate over the utility of internal constraints versus external controls.[6] This argument took place against the backdrop of rising fears about the growing power of administrative agencies staffed by unelected civil servants exercising a great deal of authority over businesses and private citizens. While Finer insisted that the only real protection was the establishment of a set of external checks in the form of laws and administrative processes to discipline violators, Friedrich insisted on a more subtle approach. His argument was not a soft-hearted position, but a mixture of practical concern and a determination to structure a more positive approach than was suggested by the police-the-bureaucrats perspective.

On the pragmatic side, Friedrich simply stated that it was impossible to create a structure that would catch and curb all abuses. The only way actually to obtain responsible behavior was to recruit the right kinds of people and then socialize them carefully into a set of public service values. Since then, many have tried to formulate that set of values and to find ways to inculcate them into professionals entering public service.

In other countries, the process of professionalization and inculcation of values is done differently. In part because of their long history of colonial administration, the British and French systems of administration have been particularly influential. Historically, the British relied on the generalist tradition, the recruitment of graduates of Oxford and Cambridge whose social backgrounds and education emphasized the kind of broad intellectual tradition and sense of public responsibility that support what came to be known as the British administrative class. These generalists were sent around the world and into a wide range of colonial offices on the theory that a person thus prepared in the OxBridge tradition could handle any challenge.[7] The French developed a quite different approach over the years, emphasizing career development within a particular type of agency or policy area. The most prestigious of these came to be known as the "Les Grands Corps de l'Etat."[8] That system stresses focused and continued career development within a particular functional field rather than the movement of generalists across types of organizations and positions. When developing countries emerged from colonial rule, they often adopted the administrative model of their former colonial rulers.

The American tradition has added an additional dimension since, in this country, public administration is often a second profession.[9] Engineers, health providers, and communications experts go to work in the public sector and soon find themselves promoted into managerial positions. It is often at this point that public administrators return to universities for formal training in the field of public administration. They bring with them the values of their primary profession and must then integrate those principles with the public service values they develop along the way. Sometimes those sets of values are compatible, but not always. Thus, physicians may be upset by fiscal considerations when their primary values focus on treatment modalities that are medically appropriate to their patients. Engineers may become impatient with demands for public participation in decision making when their professional education tells them that there is a logical and technically sound solution to the problem at hand. This second-profession tradition offers administrators who often have a great deal of expertise as compared to generalists, but the French system, in which career development seeks to mesh professional and public service values, often has more consistency and coherence.

Of course, all of this assumes that there is a coherent and consistent set of public service ethics to guide public administrators. Actually, there are at least three different perspectives that establish ethical standards for public service: regime values, situational ethics, and personal ethics. Each concerns a set of duties owed to a different person or group.

Regime Values and Public Ethics

When the concept of public service ethics is used, the immediate response is that the fact that one serves the public implicates a different set of values—often a higher set of expectations—for government officials than for private individuals. Still, it can be very difficult to specify what is meant by higher or special obligations. John Rohr has argued that one can frame that discussion by understanding the Constitution as a repository of national values to which public administrators should look as they seek to understand their place and their responsibilities.[10] He adds that the debates in the Supreme Court over many of these constitutional premises provide a useful source of information for understanding these values and reflecting upon them. Richardson and Nigro add that the materials available from the founding period provide not only an understanding of the premises of the Constitution but also of the frailties of human nature understood by the framers and the "correctives" incorporated into the constitutional framework to address those weaknesses.[11]

The effort to guide one's conduct by reference to these regime values tends to reinforce the legitimacy of official action by supporting the central premises on which the government is based. The idea is not that constitutional law is ethics but that ethical understanding may use features of national constitutional foundations as repositories of values. Put in slightly different terms, it is an attempt to assist public officials in developing their ethical frameworks by concentrating on the role of the public administrator and his or her place in the larger governmental scheme.[12]

It is a crucial but often neglected fact that when administrators deal with their counterparts in other nations, the regime values from which they proceed may be entirely different and even clearly in conflict.[13] To the degree that the perceptions of ethical premises and the ability to communicate values is blocked by an unwillingness to understand and incorporate those differences into decision making, action that will be effective and regarded as legitimate will be limited.

Situational Ethics

While there are processes with which to approach ethical problems and foundations from which to draw ethical premises, few writers are ready quickly to list specific ethical principles to govern individual decisions. The clear reason is that the situations in which ethical problems arise are so varied and

AMERICAN SOCIETY FOR PUBLIC ADMINISTRATION
Code of Ethics

The American Society for Public Administration (ASPA) exists to advance the science, processes, and art of public administration. The Society affirms its responsibility to develop the spirit of professionalism within its membership, and to increase public awareness of ethical principles in public service by its example. To this end, we, the members of the Society, commit ourselves to the following principles:

I. Serve the Public Interest
Serve the public, beyond serving oneself.
ASPA members are committed to:
1. Exercise discretionary authority to promote the public interest.
2. Oppose all forms of discrimination and harassment, and promote affirmative action.
3. Recognize and support the public's right to know the public's business.
4. Involve citizens in policy decision-making.
5. Exercise compassion, benevolence, fairness and optimism.
6. Respond to the public in ways that are complete, clear, and easy to understand.
7. Assist citizens in their dealings with government.
8. Be prepared to make decisions that may not be popular.

II. Respect the Constitution and the Law
Respect, support, and study government constitutions and laws that define responsibilities of public agencies, employees, and all citizens.
ASPA members are committed to:
1. Understand and apply legislation and regulations relevant to their professional role.
2. Work to improve and change laws and policies that are counter-productive or obsolete.
3. Eliminate unlawful discrimination.
4. Prevent all forms of mismanagement of public funds by establishing and maintaining strong fiscal and management controls, and by supporting audits and investigative activities.
5. Respect and protect privileged information.
6. Encourage and facilitate legitimate dissent activities in government and protect the whistleblowing rights of public employees.
7. Promote constitutional principles of equality, fairness, representativeness, responsiveness and due process in protecting citizens' rights.

III. Demonstrate Personal Integrity
Demonstrate the highest standards in all activities to inspire public confidence and trust in public service.
ASPA members are committed to:
1. Maintain truthfulness and honesty and to not compromise them for advancement, honor, or personal gain.
2. Ensure that others receive credit for their work and contributions.
3. Zealously guard against conflict of interest or its appearance: e.g., nepotism, improper outside employment, misuse of public resources or the acceptance of gifts.
4. Respect superiors, subordinates, colleagues and the public.

5. Take responsibility for their own errors.
6. Conduct official acts without partisanship.

IV. Promote Ethical Organizations
Strengthen organizational capabilities to apply ethics, efficiency and effectiveness in serving the public.
ASPA members are committed to:
1. Enhance organizational capacity for open communication, creativity, and dedication.
2. Subordinate institutional loyalties to the public good.
3. Establish procedures that promote ethical behavior and hold individuals and organizations accountable for their conduct.
4. Provide organization members with an administrative means for dissent, assurance of due process and safeguards against reprisal.
5. Promote merit principles that protect against arbitrary and capricious actions.
6. Promote organizational accountability through appropriate controls and procedures.
7. Encourage organizations to adopt, distribute, and periodically review a code of ethics as a living document.

V. Strive for Professional Excellence
Strengthen individual capabilities and encourage the professional development of others.
ASPA members are committed to:
1. Provide support and encouragement to upgrade competence.
2. Accept as a personal duty the responsibility to keep up to date on emerging issues and potential problems.
3. Encourage others, throughout their careers, to participate in professional activities and associations.
4. Allocate time to meet with students and provide a bridge between classroom studies and the realities of public service.

Enforcement of the Code of Ethics shall be conducted in accordance with Article I, Section 4 of ASPA's Bylaws. In 1981 the American Society for Public Administration's National Council adopted a set of moral principles. Three years later in 1984, the Council approved a Code of Ethics for ASPA members. In 1994 the Code was revised.

American Society for Public Administration
1120 G Street NW, Suite 700
Washington, DC 20005-3885
(202) 393-7878
(202) 638-4952 fax

complex that it is nearly impossible to outline specific rules for problems other than the most extreme examples of unethical behavior. The recognition of the situation does not make all things relative. It does mean that there are and must be considerations other than broad ethical principles that matter in individual ethical judgments.

Because the focus of administrative activity is generally in an agency, situational judgments often have to do with the assessment of behavior in terms of its impact on and appropriateness for the organization to which one belongs. Presumably, a positive ethical judgment in such a context means, in part at least, an action that is not destructive of the operating integrity and performance of the organization and that is consonant with the organizational culture according to which members of the organization relate to one another on a daily basis. That approach assumes, of course, that the organizational culture is itself legitimate and consistent with the essential regime values of the society within which it functions.

That kind of assertion includes three important facets. First, situational ethics may dictate very different decisions in a range of organizations. The appropriate set of expectations as to rights and obligations in a strictly hierarchical organization like the military, for example, is quite different from one that is more collegial, like a university. Similarly, organizations that operate on a wage-oriented, fee-for-service system are quite different from organizations consisting largely of professionals socialized into the same or similar sets of rules of professional behavior. Another example can be seen in comparing organizations that produce a technical service or physical product with those that provide care, counseling, or educational services to clients. In any of these cases, an individual may find that an imposition of a personal ethical code has a seriously disruptive and negative impact on coworkers and the organization as a whole.

Second, it is entirely possible to find oneself in an organization that has elements to its organizational culture that are inconsistent with the regime values of the society within which the agency operates. One of the major examples of this kind of problem is to be found in battles over police/community relations.

Reports that large for-profit corporations like Lockheed-Martin and Anderson Consulting had entered bids to assume responsibility for the administration of welfare programs in Texas raised eyebrows for a variety of reasons. One of the sets of concerns involved the question of the possible clash of values between those principles that generally drive profit-making firms and public interest goals embodied in the social policy legislation, as well as those of professional social workers. Of course, some of the bidding firms immediately began hiring experienced professional administrators from the public sector. While that may have had some bearing on the individual value sets possessed by some of those employed by the firms, the question of how well those premises will serve employees in organizations that have traditionally had very different values remains. How well will the ethics of the helping professions fare when they are pitted against opportunities to maximize profits?

Third, given that both regime values and organizational cultures vary dramatically around the world and that American administrators will find it increasingly necessary and desirable to work with their counterparts in other countries and regions of the world, this situational perspective is likely to become somewhat more, rather than less, complex. It can be extremely disconcerting for an American administrator to find herself in a working meeting with colleagues of similar interests and responsibilities when that colleague is from a country whose government is at odds with our own regime values. Administrators must be able to work with each other, but it is possible to do so only if it is understood that each person starts from different premises and operates within different organizational cultures. One of the classic examples is the problem Americans have had in working with people from Arab, principally Islamic, countries. Another example is found in some of the difficulties Westerners sometimes have in working with Eastern Europeans. A third case in point is the continuing awkwardness that many Westerners have in dealings with representatives of Asian governments. These administrators may do very well together on a personal level, but find themselves in quite different positions when decisions must be made.

Personal Values: Noblesse Oblige

Whatever the ethical framework that emanates from regime values or moral guidance derived from a given organizational context, much of the discussion and debate over public administration ethics comes down to the individual. That is one reason why several of the leading authors on the subject urge public service professionals to invest time in a conscious effort to build their own ethical framework, using their own understanding of their backgrounds and beliefs in concert with what they can find in ethics literature and education to prepare themselves for decision making.[14] Virtually all of these analysts agree that there is no time to lay the kind of foundation needed for ethically sound decisions when a problem develops. One either has the foundation or not.

At root, the concept of personal ethics suggests, in the Western tradition, that the individual should not disappear into the work group or the larger society but ought to be moving toward the attainment of the virtuous life or, put in slightly different terms, towards his noblest self. In some cultures, the sense of losing one's own identity to the family, tribe, or the larger society is considered more important than the individuality measure.

This concern is one of the important reasons why some ethicists consider the process of education as a critical "corrective," a way to improve public service professionals even though there is a recognition that they start with the common human tendencies to like and sometimes to abuse the authority they possess.[15] To the degree that the framers of the U.S. Constitution saw themselves seeking to build a government that recognized human weaknesses but sought a system of both internal and external correctives, this approach brings the discussion full circle. Individual ethical frameworks must be carefully developed so that they recognize the legitimate claims of the society as expressed in its regime values yet still acknowledge the importance of situational constraints drawn from organizational culture.

Conflicts among the Perspectives

It is of course true that there are conflicts among these three legs supporting ethical constructs. Regime values may not be consonant with what seem to be the dictates of situational ethics, as in the case of the Rodney King beating by Los Angeles police officers. Clearly, in that instance, the organizational culture of the Los Angeles Police Department violated American regime values. Personal values may reach the point of impasse when driven against contradictory situational norms, as in the problem of the whistleblower who feels the need to go outside the organization to call attention to an organizational culture gone awry.[16] Also, there may be extreme conflicts between personal ethics and regime values, either American regime values or those guiding the actions of representatives from other cultures. Thus, when an American refuses to subordinate his or her individuality to the group enterprise, it may engender serious negative reactions in international work groups.

The issue is of both ends and means. How do we develop premises and modes of thought and behavior that simultaneously recognize the critical interaction between duty to regime values, pursuit of a moral community, mutual obligation to situational problems, maintenance of civil and effective working relations within organizations, and the individual's concern with noblesse oblige, the search for a virtuous public and private life?

Law in Its Own Right:
Legal Tools of Accountability

However diligently we work toward ethical development, few citizens are willing to abandon what the framers of the Constitution termed "auxiliary precautions" when it comes to checking the power of public officers.[17]

Hence, there remains a significant variety of legal limitations. In fact, as the earlier portion of the chapter indicated, there continues to be a desire to combine ethical concepts with legal restraints. The legal restraints may be either judicial or nonjudicial in nature.

Nonjudicial Responses

Administrative law imposes a set of procedural requirements on agencies that act as legal restraints on administrative discretion. Presumably, the fact that administrators are constrained to provide due process in agency adjudicative procedures, including personnel actions, ensures fundamental fairness as well as compliance with the basic constitutional guarantees. Rulemaking requirements, on the other hand, which require documentation for later review, are intended to structure the process and encourage reasoned decision making. Requirements regarding fair information practices seek to keep the process open and accessible while simultaneously protecting the privacy of individuals whose lives are affected by administrative decisions. Above all, the administrative law requirements are intended to discourage administrative behavior that is "arbitrary, capricious, an abuse of discretion, or not otherwise in accordance with law."[18] Of course, the requirements imposed by statutes are backed by the possibility, indeed often the likelihood, of a later judicial review. They are meant to be more than mere encouragement.

Alternative dispute resolution techniques, by contrast, are intended to encourage agencies and those parties facing conflicts with them to resolve their differences out of court. On the rulemaking side, the Negotiated Rulemaking Act encourages the use of preliminary negotiations between the agency and groups likely to be affected by a proposed regulation with the hope that later challenges can be avoided. The Alternative Dispute Resolution Act focuses more on what are often considered adjudicative problems, situations in which an agency takes action against an individual or business firm. This statute calls on agencies to attempt to resolve problems short of formal litigation through the use of a variety of alternative dispute resolution (ADR) techniques. (At the time of this writing, neither of these statutes had been reauthorized by Congress, but most observers assumed that they will be renewed soon.)

The concept of ADR and the techniques of which it consists are a mixture of American inventions and processes developed in other countries. For example, the use of officials called ombudsmen to achieve resolution of controversies by negotiation featuring enhanced communications and mediation was an important early idea. It was borrowed from the Scandanavian countries, particularly Sweden. The most commonly employed contemporary ADR techniques include negotiation, mediation, and arbitration. Negotiation, of course, has become more common as the expense of litigation has spiraled upward. Neither agencies nor the people with whom they deal can really afford to go to court over every disagreement. If negotiations break down, though, there is always a recourse to the judicial forum. Mediation is a form of arm's length negotiation with a neutral third party who attempts to bring the first two parties together by facilitating communication. The mediator also works to clarify and, where possible, narrow the issues in dispute. Arbitration, by contrast, involves a third party who renders a decision in a dispute in which the parties agree to be bound by the ruling of the arbitrator. In the public sector, though, there are tensions around the use of arbitrators. Legislatures, for example, are often loath to be bound to appropriate money to pay obligations imposed by some outside decision maker.

ADR tools have been developed and refined over the past two decades. There have been combinations of techniques like mediation and arbitration called med/arb. Minitrials have been held in which parties try out their arguments in an abbreviated trial-type process to determine whether they really want to work harder to reach settlement or go to formal adjudication. Even if a case is filed in court, many judges now require what is referred to as *court annexed arbitration* before full litigation is available. Where the parties insist on moving into the courtroom, judges use pretrial conferences as negotiating opportunities to limit the disputes as much as possible.

Judicial Approaches

Despite all of the pressures to control and even reduce litigation, the seriousness of the consequences of administrative decisions, as well as their sheer number, ensures that judicial challenges will continue to be brought in an effort to control and maintain accountability over the bureaucracy. The most common actions are criminal prosecutions, judicial review, injunctive proceedings, and tort liability suits.

Criminal prosecutions are, fortunately, relatively rare. Moreover, they usually do not affect agencies' day-to-day operations extensively since some kind of administrative action is usually brought to separate a person suspected of criminal activity from an agency well before any prosecution, or even full-scale criminal investigation, is launched.[19] There are exceptions, and the U.S. Department of Justice has a unit pledged to protect "public integrity" and also has the option to call for appointment of an Independent Counsel under the provisions of the Ethics in Government Act. States and localities have prosecutors who may initiate corruption charges. Indeed, one of the justifications for having an independent attorney general's office represent state agencies is to provide an accountability check, both civil and criminal. Even so, all of these possible criminal law controls are exceptions to the norm.

Judicial Review. Many of the cases in which courts are called on to check administrative action come in the form of requests for judicial review. Under the applicable federal and state APAs, reviewing courts are to determine whether the agency has violated the federal or state constitution, relevant statutes, or procedural requirements. They are also to decide whether the agency reached a reasoned decision based on an administrative record which, when considered as a whole, contained substantial evidence in support of the agency conclusion. The agency need not always be correct, but its decision must be rational. The requirement is that a reasonable person *could have* reached the conclusion rendered by the agency, not necessarily that she *would have* reached the same judgment. Finally, the agency action must not be arbitrary and capricious or abuse its discretion.

Given the nature of the review, it is not surprising that agencies win many of their cases. Even if they lose, the usual result is to remand (meaning "to send the matter back") to the agency to correct errors and take further steps.

There are two other important issues apart from the more general question of how courts review. First, the court must decide whether to review. Second, the court must manage the deference problem. In regard to the first issue, judges will sometimes refuse to review administrative actions if the parties bringing the action cannot demonstrate legal standing to do so (meaning that they have been directly and seriously injured within the meaning of the law) or if the case does not meet the set of procedural requirements necessary to ensure that it is a proper case or controversy in which all alternatives short of court review have been addressed. Even if the parties and the case clear these hurdles, a court may nevertheless refuse to consider a dispute if it determines that the legislature intended to make the type of administrative decision in question unreviewable. In truth, however, the vast majority of administrative actions are reviewable and will face judicial scrutiny so long as the proper party brings a correctly prepared case.

The more complex question is how the court can carry out its obligation to provide a check against illegal behavior while granting the degree of deference that is due to expert and experienced administrators. Deference is the starting point for judicial review, but it cannot be an unquestioned deference or there would be no purpose to a review. For good or ill, the Supreme Court has directed federal courts to defer at least broadly to the interpretations of statutes by agencies if those interpretations are plausible.[20] The general bases for deference in particular cases are that: (1) agencies are often experts in a technical area, while judges are generalists; (2) administrators have considerable experience in the implementation of statutes in their particular field, while judges encounter disputes in any given area only sporadically; and (3) administrators must be able to have enough flexibility, so long as their actions are rational and not arbitrary, to make mistakes without fear that a disagreement will inevitably land them in court, or we risk the possibility of paralysis in agencies simply because of fear of legal actions. The other side of that debate, however, is that: (1) making a mistake is one thing, but violating the law is another; (2) precisely because they deal with a wide range of issues, courts are able to ensure that administrators do not become so focused on their own concerns that they lose sight of the larger set of legal rights and duties within which they function; (3) many of the decisions made by administrative agencies are not based on technological expertise; and (4) when it comes to matters of procedure and legal interpretation, courts are more expert than agencies. Hence, the tension between deference and the need for review is a continuing problem, and one constantly on the minds of judges.

Injunctive Relief. In few cases is the tension between courts and agencies greater than those in which the court is asked to intervene in ongoing administrative activities because of a charge of maladministration. Virtually every state has faced challenges to conditions in its prisons or mental health facilities.[21] In these situations, the court is not asked to review an administrative decision after the fact, but to determine whether the current situation presents a violation of law and, if so, to halt and remedy it.[22] In these cases, judges are asked to issue injunctions, orders requiring officials to stop some behavior or compelling them to do what the law requires. A judicial ruling that merely awards money to a mental health patient is of little value if the person remains confined in an unhealthy institution with no treatment. It is in such situations that injunctive relief is often used.

There are two problems confronting judges in such settings that compel them to issue injunctions they would just as soon avoid. The first is that an order to cease some illegal practice may be ignored. The courts have a long history of evidence on which to base such fears. Second, merely stopping illegal conduct does not repair the damage caused by that behavior over the years.

Despite the efforts by some commentators to picture the matter differently, administrators have not always been upset by suits to force reform of state institutions. In fact, many will admit that such improvements as have been made in the operation of prisons and mental health facilities were possible in large part because judicial orders gave administrators leverage to obtain the support necessary for the task. These cases have often been resolved by agreements reached between the litigants with the approval of the court through consent decrees, rather than simply through orders mandated by judges.

Still, it is no more positive an experience for judges to expend their time, effort, and meager resources wading through the morass of court-ordered change in administrative agencies than it is for the administrators to endure the burdens and disruptions in their operations brought about by litigation and judicial oversight of remedies. It is for these reasons that many judges have been less willing in recent years to approve consent agreements that appear to try to place the judge in the midst of a political battle. They have also been troubled by attempts to use the courts to leverage budgets for agencies. There have also been a number of strong statements by the U.S. Supreme Court discouraging trial courts from issuing remedial decrees. The Court has tried to limit the scope of those orders and has instructed trial courts to terminate their involvement in agencies as soon as possible.[23]

Even so, there will continue to be situations in which courts must intervene by injunction to stop illegal actions in administrative operations. For some time there appeared to be an emerging unspoken trend in which the Supreme Court was willing to constrain injunctive intervention while suggesting that the proper relief for abuse of rights was for the injured party to sue the government or the individual official for damages.[24] However, it is not at all clear that this alternative is better.

Tort Liability. The concept of tort liability assumes that government officials, like everyone else in the society, ought to be responsible for injuries caused by illegal actions. Of course, suits are often brought primarily against the government itself, rather than the individual officers. On the other hand, governments and government officials are not exactly like others in the society. They perform special tasks under a variety of legal and administrative constraints.

The concept of sovereign immunity, borrowed from British law and read into the U.S. Constitution by the Supreme Court, protects the national and state governments from damage suits unless they give their permission to be sued.[25] The Federal Tort Claims Act and many state statutes do give that permission for certain kinds of cases. The state statutes vary. Some authorize all suits except a particular list of types of cases, while other states prohibit all claims except those disputes specifically included in a list. Because of these restrictions, most suits tend to be brought against individual officers accused of legal violations or against municipalities which, as corporate entities, may be sued like a person.[26]

Suits against state and local officials or governments are brought in state courts under state laws or in federal courts, where citizens allege that the officers or local governments have violated their federal constitutional or statutory rights. Claims against federal government officials have traditionally been brought in the form of what are called constitutional torts, meaning a claim that an official has violated a right protected by the Constitution even though no specific piece of legislation authorizes a suit for damages.[27]

Juries tend not to like to return verdicts against individual public servants, but many are not as reticent about damage judgments against cities. The pressure of providing insurance plans to deal with such cases is an important fact of local government life in many communities.

Officials sued for damages can claim immunity on grounds that they could not reasonably have known they were violating a claimed right since it was not established in law at the time they acted.[28] On the other hand, officials are responsible to know the legal restrictions that apply to their jobs and can be held responsible for violating them.[29]

Efforts have been under way at the federal level and in some states over the past several years to write statutes limiting official immunity, but the process is still very much in flux. One of the difficulties with efforts to limit claims is that each time such a project is launched, there seems to be some kind of event, like the Rodney King beating in Los Angeles, that causes lawmakers to ask whether they really want to remove the threat of lawsuits from those who might otherwise abuse their authority.

Conclusion

Whether it comes from internal foundations, like ethical frameworks, or from external constraints, such as litigation and other kinds of limits that might be imposed through executive supervision or legislative oversight, accountability is a critically important fact of public administration life. However, while ethics and law may both be mechanisms of accountability, they are not the same.

Ethics provides an internal check. Law is external. They may be mutually reinforcing but they may also be contradictory in concept and in action. The tendency to confuse the two has led to a number of problematic ethics-in-government programs where it is not ethics but professional conduct that is in question, and where the laws seek to coerce public service ethics that may, in truth, only be elicited. Ethical foundations provide the beliefs, premises, processes, and, occasionally, principles that guide action, but law seeks to control and constrain forms of action. Many unethical actions remain lawful, and many ethical impulses may nevertheless lead to violations of law.

One can attempt to address both law and ethics effectively by retaining a sense of their differences. Over time, society may move to reconcile the two more closely and even perhaps eliminate some of the worst contradictions, but there will always be differences. Even if the statutes, administrative programs, and other policies are improved to make them as harmonious as possible with regime values, there will always be situational ethics problems and variations among officials as to matters of personal morality. These will ensure some degree of tension in any given case. Moreover, as administrators increasingly operate across national and cultural boundaries, it will become all the more important to learn how to work with others whose regime values, situational ethics, and personal norms are dramatically different.

One approach is to work with ethics in its own dialogue as a process of building understanding of regime values, situational concepts, and individual moral foundations, focusing on the need to reconcile competing tensions among the three. At the same time, it is possible, and not at all contradictory, to learn the legal mechanisms of accountability that constrain action. The broad effort to address potential and real conflicts will and must continue, but the more immediate task of establishing a framework for law and ethics is essential for every administrator.

Notes

[1] Ethics in Government Act, P.L. 95–521 (1978).

[2] Katy J. Harriger, *Independent Justice: The Federal Special Prosecutor in American Politics* (Lawrence, KS: University of Kansas Press , 1992).

[3] John Rohr, *Ethics for Bureaucrats,* 2nd ed. (New York: Marcel Dekker, 1989).

[4] See Harriger, *op. cit.*

[5] See Joel L. Fleishman, Lance Liebman, and Marck H. Moore, eds., *Public Duties: The Moral Obligations of Government Officials* (Cambridge, MA: Harvard, 1981).

[6] Herman Finer, "Better Government Personnel: America's Next Frontier," *Political Science Quarterly* 51 (December 1936): 569–599; Carl Friedrich, "Public Policy and the Nature of Administrative Responsibility," in C. J. Friedrich and E. S. Mason, eds., *Public Policy* (Cambridge, MA: Harvard, 1940); Herman Finer, "Administrative Responsibility in Democratic Government," *Public Administration Review* 1 (Summer 1941): 335–350.

[7] See Brian Chapman, *The Profession of Government* (London: Unwin University Books, 1971).

[8] See Ezra N. Suleiman, *Politics, Power, and Bureaucracy in France* (Princeton, NJ: Princeton, 1974).

[9] Frederick C. Mosher, *Democracy and the Public Service,* 2nd ed. (New York: Oxford, 1982).

[10] Rohr, *op. cit.*

[11] William Richardson and Lloyd Nigro, "Administrative Ethics and Founding Thought: Constitutional Correctives, Honor, and Education," *Public Administration Review* 47 (September/October 1987): 367–376.

[12] For a discussion of ethics based on the role of the public administrator, see Terry Cooper, *The Responsible Administrator* (Port Washington, NY: Kennikat, 1982).

[13] See John Rohr, "Ethical Issues in French Public Administration: A Comparative Study," *Public Administration Review* 51 (July/August 1991): 283–297.

[14] Cooper, *op. cit.*

[15] Richardson and Nigro, *op. cit.*

[16]See Albert O. Hirschman, *Exit, Voice, and Loyalty* (Cambridge, MA: Harvard, 1970).

[17]Alexander Hamilton, James Madison, and John Jay, *The Federalist* (New York: Mentor, 1961), No. 51.

[18]5 U.S.C.A. §706.

[19]Of course, if agency managers are asked to play a role in the prosecution, that process can consume a great deal of time.

[20]*Rust v. Sullivan,* 500 U.S. 173 (1991); *Chevron v. Natural Resources Defense Council,* 467 U.S. 837 (1984).

[21]Such situations are addressed in detail in Phillip J. Cooper, *Hard Judicial Choices* (New York: Oxford, 1988).

[22]See Robert Wood, *Remedial Law* (Amherst, MA: University of Massachusetts Press, 1991).

[23]See e.g., *Board of Ed. of Oklahoma City v. Dowell,* 498 U.S. 237 (1991); *Freeman v. Pitts,* 503 U.S. 467 (1992); *Missouri v. Jenkins,* 132 L.Ed2d 63 (1995).

[24]See e.g., *Rizzo v. Goode;* see also, David Rosenbloom, "Public Administrators, Official Immunity, and the Supreme Court: Developments during the 1970s," *Public Administration Review* 40 (March/April 1980): 166–173.

[25]This is discussed in greater detail in Phillip J. Cooper, "The Supreme Court on Governmental Liability: The Nature and Origins of Sovereign and Official Immunity," *Administration & Society* 16 (November 1984): 259–288.

[26]*Owen v. City of Independence,* 445 U.S. 622 (1980).

[27]*Bivens v. Six Unknown Named Agents of the Federal Bureau of Narcotics,* 403 U.S. 388 (1971).

[28]*Procunier v. Martinez,* 416 U.S. 396 (1974).

[29]*Harlow v. Fitzgerald,* 457 U.S. 800 (1982).

Chapter 4

The Intergovernmental Policy Structure and Action

If there is one thing on which civil servants and citizens in most countries around the world can agree it is that government has become much more complex than it used to be. Of course, they would hasten to add that the same is true of private sector firms and even many not-for-profit organizations that started life as volunteer groups. Complexity is quite simply one of the fundamental realities of modern life. That reality is not likely to change in the twenty-first century.

In fact, complexity has become such a difficulty in public administration that there is concern now with what is termed a *coordination crisis*. The coordination crisis is the difficulty of planning, coordinating, and operating the many organizations that are involved in the same area of activity simultaneously. Managers must think about how to understand the range and number of organizations in the public sector. In addition, they must manage across organizations at different levels of government and work with nonprofit groups as well as the private sector.

In the United States, the reality of administrative life in the twenty-first century will be very different from what the framers of the Constitution could have imagined in 1787. At that time one of the great debates was how to relate states (formerly colonies) to the new national government. When they began the preamble to the Constitution with the words, "We the People of the United States, in Order to form a more perfect Union . . . do ordain and establish this Constitution for the United States of America," they were making a very large statement in at least two important ways. First, unlike what had come before, this Constitution was not to be made by the states as such in a kind of treaty, but by the people themselves, making the state governments as well as the new national government subordinate to the new Constitution drawn by the people in constituent assembly. That was a very big step from the Articles of Confederation that had preceded the

Constitution and was very much a treaty among states. Second, the declared first purpose of the Constitution was to form "a more perfect union." The framers had seen quite enough of the feuding among states, and it was the abuses of state legislatures that precipitated the preparation of the new Constitution in the first place.

By the same token, there was great fear as to the nature and character of the new national government. Those who opposed ratification of the new Constitution, known as the Anti-Federalists, focused much of their attention on those fears. What emerged from all of this was a system of federalism that described the nature and operation of the division of powers among states and the national government. Local governments are creatures of the state constitutions and statutes.

Similar dynamics have emerged in many countries around the world, though in rather different forms from those most common in the United States. Many regimes are based on strong central governments, with regional or local agencies working directly for the central government ministries. Even so, decentralization has been a movement sweeping the globe over the past decade. Although decentralization has taken many forms in different places, it has to do with moving the governing function closer to the community. Often, it has meant something less than the ideal in which there would be more participation in decision making by people at the local level of government (both inside government and citizens) as well as greater responsibility for the implementation of public policy in the community. Too often it has involved the retention of policy making authority at the center and delegation of implementation responsibilities, frequently without adequate resources, to the state or local levels. Of course, the United States has its own version of that problem, referred to in contemporary political commentaries as the "unfunded mandates" debate.

As this picture implies, the reality of modern public administration is much more complicated than any simple picture of federalism in which there are three nice, neat levels of government with clearly defined roles, powers, and responsibilities. Indeed, a range of factors, from economics to international forces, have caused many to prefer the term intergovernmental relations to the older concept of federalism as a way to describe the structures and processes with which we govern.[1]

Intergovernmental relations (IGR) also emphasizes the idea that there is more at issue than formal constitutional powers. Indeed there are many types of relationships across jurisdictional boundaries based on a wide range of foundations, from money to expertise. At its core, intergovernmental relations is about connections, competitions, and interdependencies, forces that characterize the way public sector managers deal with one another and with the body politic.

This chapter considers the nature, function, dysfunctions, and likely future character of intergovernmental relations. It begins by discussing the changing structure of the formal/legal system of relationships, traces the development of what was once termed "fiscal federalism," considers the cross-cutting role of policy expertise, and returns ultimately to a discussion about the future of intergovernmental relations.

Building a Public Administration within American Federalism

In a period when so many parts of nations are breaking off into autonomous republics, it should not be hard to understand the forces at work in the early years of United States history. The colonies became states and were autonomous. Indeed, the initial problem was the existence of strong states and a weak central government. Once the basic problem was addressed, there remained the question of what the relationship between levels of government would look like, in practice as well as in terms of constitutional law. Finally, we saw a set of complex relationships that went beyond traditional notions of federalism into what we now call intergovernmental relations.

The Problem of Strong States

The early years of the American republic were filled with tensions among states. Even though we were at war, it took from 1776 until 1781 for the states to agree to any frame of government, and even then it was a weak and ineffective structure based on the Articles of Confederation. It was, in essence, a treaty among states without the ability to take serious action absent, in many instances, unanimous agreement among the states. Unanimity was not much easier to obtain then than it is today. There was no executive branch and no effective independent judiciary. During the Revolutionary War the new government lacked the ability to compel states to carry their full load in terms of troops or treasury. After the war, the unwillingness of states to work together was manifested in a plethora of areas. The inability to cooperate meant delay in the development of the infrastructure needed to construct a new nation. Indeed, it was disputes between Virginia and Maryland over just such issues that brought about the Mount Vernon Convention at which the two states worked out disagreements concerning the use of the Potomac River. Since Washington had hosted that meeting at his home in Virginia, the Marylanders reciprocated by inviting the other states to what became known as the Annapolis Convention to see whether it would be possible for all of the states to work out some of the many tensions between them. Though that conference was not well attended, it did serve as the occasion for the distribution of an invitation to a convention to be held in Philadelphia for the purpose of amending the Articles of Confederation in order to create a more effective governing arrangement.

Of course, at what is now known as the Constitutional Convention, the framers disposed of the idea of amending the Articles and proceeded to start over. While there were many long debates over the nature of the new central government to be created by the Constitution, there was agreement that the problems caused by abuses in the state legislatures had to be addressed and that means had to be found to prevent local prejudices from hindering the overall development of the nation.

The document that emerged contains several specific sets of provisions concerning those state issues. The preamble indicates that it is a document of the people and not a treaty among the states and that its purpose is to form a more perfect union. In Article 1, Section 8, the Congress was specifically given powers thought necessary to remedy the difficulties encountered under the Articles of Confederation, including the power to lay and collect taxes, the power to appropriate funds and pay debts, the authority to coin money, the ability to raise a military and control the militias (including the ability to mobilize malitias to deal with insurrection), and the powers to regulate commerce among the states, to set uniform rules of naturalization, and to lay the foundation for American infrastructure by building post roads and post offices.

The language in the Articles of Confederation that limited the national government to powers "expressly" enumerated by the document was eliminated and replaced by an authorization "to make all laws which shall be necessary and proper for carrying into execution the foregoing Powers, and all other powers vested by this Constitution in the Government of the United States, or in any Department or Officer thereof." The issue of inserting that limiting language came up again later in connection with what became the Tenth Amendment. The framers once again refused to place a restrictive reading on national powers. They avoided the "not expressly delegated" language and added that the powers "not delegated to the United States by the Constitution, nor prohibited by it to the States, are reserved to the States respectively, or to the people." Unfortunately, the document is often mistakenly interpreted to have said that the powers not expressly delegated by the Constitution to the national government are reserved to the states. That is obviously a misstatement of both the language and the history of the framing.

The framers were not content to concern themselves solely with what the powers of the national government should be. They also wanted to be certain to stop behaviors by the states that had been so problematic before the Constitution was created. Therefore, a last section was added to Article 1. It placed specific prohibitions on actions that states had previously taken, including issuing money, passing bills of attainder (a legislative determination of guilt and punishment), making *ex post facto* laws (making things illegal that had been lawful at the time they were done), interfering with the obligations of contracts, placing duties on imports or exports, barring states from entering into treaties or alliances, and attempting to hire mercenaries or raise a military.

The new Constitution made provision for an independent judiciary with the powers to decide "all cases, in law and equity, arising under the Constitution, the laws of the United States, and Treaties made, or which shall be made, under their authority." It was to have jurisdiction over disputes between citizens of different states or those involving federal questions to which states were a party. Just to make sure that there was no question on the matter, the framers added what is now known as the supremacy clause which states: "This Constitution, and the Laws of the United States which shall be made in Pursuance thereof; and all Treaties made, or which shall be made, under the Authority of the United States, shall be the supreme Law of the Land; and the Judges in every state shall be bound thereby, any Thing in the Constitution or Laws of any State to the Contrary notwithstanding."

In the years that followed, the Supreme Court added a host of interpretations that helped to establish the framework of federalism in its formal legal manifestation. As Chapter 2 indicated, since that time federalism has taken on a far more complex form to address the much more complicated world in which we now live. And despite the fact that efforts have been made to accommodate the many roles that state, local, and national governments play, there are still conflicts that require adjudication to settle. It is easy to assume that disputes among levels of government over who possesses which authority and which jurisdiction require that one unit will prevail and carry out whatever government function is in dispute. That is a dangerously deceptive picture. The situation is far more complex than such a zero-sum legal contest would suggest.

Layer Cake, Marble Cake, or Picket Fence

Morton Grodzins pointed out that the early twentieth century view of federalism that suggests a layer cake in which each level of government has exclusive powers and operations clearly distinct from one another is incorrect. The truth, he said, is that it more plainly resembles a marble cake in which one can still detect varying textures, colors, and tastes, but in which the elements are swirled together to produce the final confection.[2] The marble cake notion is more helpful than the layer cake, but by the late 1960s observers of federalism had come to apply a different metaphor, the picket fence. In this picture the rails represent levels of government and the individual pickets are policy communities like health, transportation, or public safety. At the heart of this picture of federalism were two very important assertions about modern federalism. First, the argument was that, for many purposes (perhaps for most), the jurisdictional boundaries between nation, state, and local government are extremely permeable, and officials from a variety of institutions move back and forth in conversations with their counterparts at other levels without regard to any kind of formal chain of command except for certain legal purposes. Second, picket fence federalism argued that the core of much of the activity that flows back and forth among government units at different levels is a common interest in a given area of policy. Thus, officials at a local hospital may not think much about the state legislature on a day-to-day basis and may consider themselves to be working more closely with federal agencies like the Centers for Disease Control (CDC) or the National Institutes of Health (NIH). The same is true of educators, librarians, law enforcement officers and many other types of participants in the public sector who worry much more about their particular field than they do about jurisdictional boundaries, except in a relatively technical sense.

From Federalism to Intergovernmental Relations

These contemporary pictures of a federalism that is far more complex, in which the parts are more interdependent and less oriented to formal layers in their interactions, came together with another important feature that caused many scholars and practitioners to make the shift from speaking in terms of federalism to intergovernmental relations. The other factor was the increasingly complex ways in which the taxing and spending powers of various types of governments were being used to knit the system together. The federal government's use of national taxing authority to serve as a collection point for revenue and its concomitant distribution of substantial portions of those funds to state and local governments or directly to citizens through what are termed transfer payments changed federalism. Indeed, the term *fiscal federalism* has sometimes been used as a shorthand term for intergovernmental relations.

There are many things that are unique about the experience of the United States with respect to federalism, but there are many features common to developments around the world as well. In particular, one of the dominant forces of recent history around the world is a move toward decentralization. However, when central governments decentralize, they encounter many of the same problems that one finds in American intergovernmental relations, particularly in developing countries where the central government is a long way from the capital. As a practical matter, lines of authority are regularly crossed by service providers who are more concerned about service to the citizens than they are about the niceties of legal jurisdiction.

Indeed, intergovernmental relations has come to include not merely subnational interactions, but supranational relationships as well, in part for reasons identified in Chapter 1. International agreements such as GATT, NAFTA, and Agenda 21 affect subnational units of government as well as the nations themselves. Moreover, the operations of the global economy affect decisions about local finances, such as construction of new facilities. Decisions made by international lenders about the value of the U.S. dollar and interest rates, quite apart from actions taken by the United States Federal Reserve system, all influence who buys government bonds. States and localities are now marketing abroad and concluding their own cooperative agreements with international partners. Border states find themselves in important international agreements such as the Great Lakes Compact that governs the use and protection of the lakes and involves Canada and states that ring the lakes. Southern border states are involved not merely in regular interactions with Mexico but also with the other nations of Latin America, including the island states of the Caribbean. A number of federal agencies like the Department of Agriculture and the Environmental Protection Agency (EPA) have international units and do not rely solely or primarily on the State Department for their international operation, mainly because their work clearly requires an ongoing presence in international matters.

Countries in Latin America, Africa, and Asia are experiencing similar phenomena. In addition, they are working to build public administration capacity in their own regions even as the availability of assistance from donor nations and international lending institutions shrinks.

It is increasingly common for there to be an international version of the picket fence model, as African medical officials dealt directly not merely with their own governments, but also with the World Health Organization (WHO) and the CDC in their attempt to fight back the Ebola virus. The U.S. EPA actually opened an office in Hungary to assist Eastern European nations in developing and operating environmental policy. It is increasingly common for officials of domestic organizations at all levels of government to interact with their counterparts around the world. That process has been well underway for more than a decade, but the advent of the Internet has dramatically increased supranational activity. It is no more difficult now for an official in Singapore to communicate with a colleague doing similar work in New York than it is to have the same interaction with another office across town in Singapore. Indeed, people doing related work in several countries can carry on a multiparty conversation in real time on the Internet in a manner that may in fact be easier to arrange than a meeting among the same number of officials in the same ministry at home simply because of the flexibility of e-mail and listserv technology.

The Framework of Intergovernmental Relations

For all these reasons, units of government often do not act alone. There are many incentives for cooperation among them. They can share technical expertise, offer mutual support in providing human resources to meet emergencies, realize efficiencies from economies of scale and from centralized revenue collection and distribution, and assure necessary political support to meet various challenges. Indeed, the implementation of a single policy may require resources and public administrators from all three levels of government.

This section describes the relationships that exist among governments, parastatals (units such as government corporations and other government-sponsored enterprises created by government but with independent status and operating characteristics), and nongovernmental organizations (NGOs), which often facilitate relationships among governments. First, however, it presents a brief overview of the intergovernmental framework within which public administrators live and work.

Intergovernmental relations (IGR) have been an intricate part of public administration for more than fifty years.[3] Intergovernmental relations is a concept used to include historic notions of federalism but also to go beyond federalism's traditional application to a sophisticated contemporary understanding of how the many units of government at all levels relate to one another.[4] Not only are the 3,043 counties; 19,296 cities, villages, and boroughs; 16,666 townships; 15,781 school districts; and 33,131 special districts included within the IGR framework, but so are the thousands of paragovernment and nonprofit organizations that play key roles in the delivery of public services.[5]

The IGR concept was popularized by Deil Wright, who argued that the IGR framework is like a new set of glasses: It makes visible the varied terrain and patterns of government that are obscure under older notions of federalism. It also facilitates an understanding of:

- the major actors involved in the delivery of public goods and services,
- the scope of public administration in the American political system,
- ever-changing administrative structure for addressing critical policy issues,
- the body of activities that commands the attention of public managers.[6]

The Structure of Intergovernmental Relations

Some of the relations between governments are voluntary while many others are the result of compulsion or mandates. Even those that are voluntary may arise because of enticements. In each instance, structures exist that serve as conduits for these intergovernmental relations.

One of the most common intergovernmental structures is that which permits cooperative arrangements between two or more governments. The federal government has agreements with state and local governments for the delivery of many services that are of national importance (i.e., education, national defense, and transportation). In these arrangements, the federal government provides funds to states to undertake various programs which, in order to be eligible for federal dollars, must meet minimum standards. States in turn have agreements with their subdivisions for the provision of services that have implications beyond a particular locale (i.e., social services, public safety, health). States allow their local governments to develop agreements with each other for services.

Relationships among governmental units, whether voluntary or mandated, are multi-dimensional. That is, a jurisdiction may have simultaneous relationships with other units at various levels of government around a single issue. For example, some twenty-eight federal, state, and local government agencies in Ohio, including education and service agencies, worked together in the Small Communities Environmental Infrastructure Group to help small communities address environmental infrastructure needs.[7] Each of the participants in the group, at any given time, may be working with individuals from local jurisdictions, state government, and the federal government. The multidimensional relationships possible through this group arrangement are typical of the structural framework for intergovernmental relations in the United States.

There are many ways in which state officials interact with each other. Formal interstate cooperative agreements have their origin in the constitutional requirement that "full faith and credit shall be given in each state to the public acts, records, and judicial proceedings of every state" and in the section permitting interstate compacts so long as they are approved by Congress. However, there are numerous interstate relations that are less about formal legal frameworks but are primarily based on the need by state officials for a more informal and flexible basis for cooperation.

Interstate relationships include those that develop as a result of:

1. interlocking structure of state institutions and state professional associations,

2. development of laws to cover concerns in which nationwide uniformity is desirable,

3. interstate compact.[8]

The interlocking structure of state institutions and professional associations is a result of memberships in national and regional state organizations. There is a national or regional professional organization for almost every group of elected and appointed officials. There are also numerous national professional organizations for state career civil servants. Table 4-1 contains a partial listing of these state organizations. Many of these organizations are interlinked through the work of the Council of State Governments.

The Council of State Governments is a nonprofit nonpartisan organization that serves the executive, legislative, and judicial branches of state governments. It fosters intergovernmental relations by "showcasing innovative state and regional actions; building partnerships within and among governmental entities, promoting multistate compacts and cooperations."[9] There are more than fifty-five state organizations that are affiliated with the Council. Through these affiliated organizations the Council works with nearly all state constitutional offices and many officials in functional areas of state government.

Another source of interstate relationships is the ongoing effort to develop uniform state laws. Such uniformity is often of concern to the legal community and to industries that do business in several states. It is also of interest to the federal government, which has imposed mandates on states requiring uniformity in several areas as a condition for receiving federal funds. Much of the cooperative effort by states to achieve uniformity has been through the National Conference of Commissioners on Uniform State Laws (NCUSL).

The NCUSL was created by the states in 1892. It is the oldest state organization and has representation from every state. Through the NCUSL, states are equipped with an intergovernmental mechanism that allows them to be active participants in the development of criteria for deciding legal matters relating to the economy, the family, and the elimination of interstate conflict. The most significant product from NCUSL has been the Uniform Commercial Code and its subsequent articles. However, it has developed more than two hundred model laws that have been submitted to states for enactment. Recent model laws were designed by NCUSL to help states:

1. Clarify and provide consistent procedures for terminating parental rights of putative and unknown fathers.
2. Simplify forms and procedures for creating power of attorney.
3. Provide criteria for determining legal parents when assisted conception has been used.
4. Permit detention without bail for a defendant charged with a violently committed felony.

Table 4-1
National Professional Organizations for State Officials

American Association of State Highway Officials
Association of State Correctional Administrators
Association of State Dam Safety Officials
Association of State Floodplain Managers
American Association of State and Interstate Water Pollution Control Administrators
Conference of Chief Justices
Conference of State Court Administrators
National Association of Attorneys General
National Association of Secretaries of State
National Association of State Agencies for Surplus Property
National Association of State Attorneys General
National Association of State Auditors, Comptrollers, and Treasurers
National Association of State Boating Law Administrators
National Association of State Budget Officials
National Association of State Civil Defense Directors
National Association of State Controlled Substances Authorities
National Association of State Departments of Agriculture
National Association of State Directors of Administration and General Services
National Association of State Election Directors
National Association of State Facilities Administrators
National Association of state Foresters
National Association of State Information Resource Executives
National Association of State Juvenile Correctional Agencies
National Association of State Land Reclamationists
National Association of State Mental Health Program Directors
National Association of state Telecommunication Directors
National Association of State Personnel Executives
National Association of State Purchasing Officials
National Association of State Treasurers
National Association of State Unclaimed Property Administrators
National Association of State Units on Aging
National Conference of Commissions on Uniform State Laws
National Conference of Lieutenant Governors
National Conference of State Legislatures
National Conference of State Fleet Administrators
National Conference of States on Building Codes and Standards
National Governor's Association

Source: *The Book of the States,* 1992–93 ed., (Lexington, KY: The Council of State Governments), 653. Copyright 1992 The Council of State Governments. Reprinted with permission from *The Book of the States.*

5. Provide alternative means ("living will" and a surrogate or "attorney-in-fact") for a competent adult to provide instructions to physicians concerning medical care.

The device known as the "interstate compact" is a unique constitutional entity that has been used to forge a variety of interstate relationships. An interstate compact has several distinctive characteristics. First, it has to be approved by Congress to become effective. Second, it has both the effect of a statute, in affected states, and, simultaneously, features of a contract. States that adopt a compact cannot renounce or leave it except by agreed-upon provisions. An interstate compact takes precedence over state laws or local ordinances that may be in conflict with its provisions. Finally, the interstate compact is the most binding form of intergovernmental cooperation between states. Nevertheless, it is used increasingly by states as a tool for solving common problems.[10]

Relations between states have been shaped in part by nearly two hundred formal interstate compacts. Some of these compacts are regional in focus and membership, and others national. In each instance, they promote interstate cooperation around such issues as education, water management, coastal development, energy, fisheries, and hazardous waste. Some of these compacts have evolved into ongoing interstate governmental agencies. Perhaps the most widely known interstate agency is the Port Authority of New York and New Jersey.

Interstate compacts were enacted in five areas during the early 1990s. In accordance with mandates of the Low-Level Radioactive Waste Policy Act, forty-two states had formed nine compacts by the end of 1992 for the disposal of commercial low-level radioactive waste. Also in 1992, the terms of an interstate compact were activated that provided for the coordination of state regulations for modular buildings. A compact between Alabama and Mississippi was activated that creates an authority to promote commerce, industry, and employment in the two states. All fifty states, the District of Columbia, Puerto Rico, and the U.S. Virgin Islands are participants in a compact for the supervision of parolees and probationers, which has provision for community protection and offender rehabilitation. In addition to these five areas, progress has been made on the Midwestern Higher Education Compact, the Environmental Compact of the States, and the Middle Atlantic Governors' Compact on Alcohol and Drug Abuse.[11]

Another area in which interstate compacts are generating considerable intergovernmental activity is the multistate effort to improve the enforcement of sales and use tax laws. The growing mail-order business is the object of these compacts. States and their subdivisions are losing an estimated two billion dollars annually because of unpaid taxes on out-of-state purchases. To minimize these losses, states have created regional compacts for the coordination of their revenue collection efforts. Millions in additional tax revenue have been collected.[12]

New York and New Jersey have a compact for the exchange of information gathered from vendors on purchases by residents of the other state. The Great Lakes Interstate Sales Compact, formed by Illinois, Indiana, Michigan, Ohio, and Wisconsin, requires states to encourage interstate vendors to register with member states for "use tax" collection. Iowa, Kansas, Minnesota, Nebraska and South Dakota developed an interstate compact that will make it easier for participating states to monitor purchases made by individual consumers from out-of-state vendors.[13] However, the United States Supreme Court has placed limits on the abilities of states to collect taxes on some kinds of out-of-state businesses, particularly mail-order operations, that will constrain some of the activities of this compact.[14] But since the ruling reinforced limits placed on individual states, it is likely to result in more cooperation among states in this area. Consequently, there is reason to believe that interstate compacts will continue to be a viable instrument for solving national and regional problems.

In addition to formal compacts, state relations have been fostered by a series of regional interstate commissions and agencies falling somewhere between formal compacts and informal associations.[15] Typical of this type of agency is the Appalachian Regional Commission. As pointed out in a study of multistate regionalism by the Advisory Commission on Intergovernmental Relations (ACIR):

> All of these commissions share certain common traits. They all are composed of one or more Federal representatives as well as gubernatorial members or designees. None formally includes local representation in their membership. . . . All have their own staff. All depend upon annual Congressional appropriations for a portion of their funds. All are charged with and engage in some type of broad gauge planning or priority setting as a major organizational activity.[16]

Intergovernmental Relations within The States

Of course, of the more than 80,000 units of government in the United States, the vast majority are local government entities such as counties, cities, special districts, and authorities. Thus, the web of intergovernmental relations is not merely about the relationships among states but also concerns the forces of competition and interdependence found at the local level. Considering the importance of substate regions as service-providing units and noting the prevalence of operating agreements among local government units and of multiunit contracts with nonprofit organizations, an argument can be made that local government is the most dynamic source of intergovernmental cooperation.

Local Government Cooperation

Cooperative agreements between local governments have historically dealt with "peak-load" problems or crisis situations in such areas as police and fire protection. These agreements have often been "mutual assistance" pacts that obligate cities to assist each other if either experiences a crisis situation.

In addition to these types of emergency cooperation agreements, however, there are substantial numbers of situations in which local governments become market participants in that they vend or purchase services from other units of government or private firms established to serve multiple government units. For instance, a survey of municipalities found that 63 percent had entered into agreements for the provision of services with other units of governments or private firms.[17]

Cooperative agreements among local governments usually have the following characteristics:

1. They are generally agreements between two governments concerning a single activity.
2. They pertain to services rather than to facilities.
3. They are not permanent and contain provision for future renegotiation or termination by either party.
4. They have stand-by provisions that come into effect only when certain conditions arise.
5. They are permitted by state legislation that authorizes cooperation among local governments in specific areas.[18]

For a period of time, given these constraints, local intergovernmental relations appeared likely to be limited in scope and time. However, the decades of the 1980s and 1990s saw encouragement for communities to increase contracted activities, both as a matter of management strategy and because financial pressures encouraged alternatives to direct service delivery by government units. Where communities felt they could sell services like police, fire, or emergency medical care to neighboring communities, efforts were made to take advantage of the opportunity (where state law permitted) in such a manner as to help offset high equipment and personnel costs for their own operations. Even though there are legal and political constraints, cooperative agreements continue to proliferate.

To this point much of the discussion of this kind of cooperative agreement has focused on municipalities. In most of the United States, for example, many of the important service functions ranging from medical care, to judicial operations, to education are carried out not by municipalities but by county governments. Many are quite large in size, encompassing literally hundreds of square miles of territory. With the growing numbers of telecommuters and residents residing in areas now termed *exurbs,* populations are shifting to make counties more important.

Surprisingly, counties have often been largely ignored in discussions of intergovernmental relations. Yet in many parts of the country the dynamics between cities and counties and between counties and the states are among the most important political and administrative facts of life. Indeed in some places, like Nashville, Tennessee, the relationship became so important that the city and county merged. Still, that is an exception and not the rule.

In fact, in many areas, it has only been recently that municipalities and counties have entered into cooperative arrangements, with more or less formality, for joint construction of such multiple-use facilities as school and municipal recreation centers. There have also been cooperative efforts at property tax and local option sales tax planning between cities and counties. With increased calls for decentralization and return of functions to local levels of government, these relationships between counties and cities will become increasingly important. The political dynamics of counties make them quite different from cities. For one thing, they often have a number of independently elected officials and may contain several municipalities with varying political alignments. They may also have large unincorporated areas that differ dramatically from the cities.

It is not at all clear how these local dynamics will look in countries that have traditionally had highly centralized governments and are now decentralizing. In some of these countries, regional governments take on the roles that are often the domain of counties in the United States, while in others the effort seems to be to move directly to a large number of municipalities to avoid multiple levels of government. Countries like Bolivia, Hungary, and Ghana may be very interesting laboratories of intergovernmental relations in the years to come.

The Increasingly Important Role of Not-For-Profit Organizations

In addition to direct relations with each other, intermediaries such as paragovernment and not-for-profit organizations are also participants in the complex interrelationships among local governments. It is not at all unusual, for example, to find communities contracting with the local chamber of commerce for economic development planning. Indeed, state governments and many local units rely on not-for-profit firms to provide services. This is done both by direct funding, as in the case of cities that pay hospitals to provide medical care for indigents or prison inmates, and through indirect means, as when communities cooperate with a nonprofit's grant applications for federal funding with the understanding that the organization will then use those funds to serve local residents in such areas as juvenile justice support programs, drug counselling, job training and placement, and many other types of activities.[19] Because state governments as well as localities often rely on not-for-profits to deliver many social services, they become part of the web of intergovernmental relations within states. That is all the more important in light of the fact that the nonprofit organizations are not limited by geographical boundaries that restrict the operations of local governments and may therefore be involved in service delivery on a multijurisdictional basis. These activities are not at the margins but rather at the center of public services (i.e., transportation, economic development, mental health, arts, and recreation).[20]

Many nonprofit organizations start small and begin their involvement as part of the intergovernmental system with a contract for service with a single governmental unit. The service area is then expanded to take advantage of economies of scale that come with wider delivery of services until they become regional providers. There have been situations in which a Catholic archdiocese has by contract essentially come to operate all the community juvenile justice programs.

This expansionary activity often occurs with the support of the contracting government, which sees this approach as a means of encouraging other governmental bodies to accept their fair share of the cost for providing a regional service. The inclination to expand is usually present when the service taken over has been consumed regionally, yet is provided by a central city. Thus, the cities lose their capacity to absorb the cost of providing regional services, and nonprofit organizations become a vital instrument for galvanizing intergovernmental support for alternative funding arrangements.

At some point the states, counties, and cities can become virtually dependent on contracted service providers. They may trim their own direct service operations to a point where they cannot break the relationships with the nonprofit organization, even if they want to do so, without suffering dramatic losses of services and incurring huge costs associated with rebuilding service delivery staff.

Political, economic, and social differences often make collaboration among central cities and suburban communities extremely difficult. Affluent suburban communities compete with the central city and each other in a variety of areas. Beyond the competition, though, are basic tensions such as racial division. As the Kerner Commission observed in the 1960s, the urban areas of America are frequently divided into two cities, one largely poor and Black or Hispanic and the other more often affluent and White. Justice Thurgood Marshall continued to remind the country of that problem during the 1970s and 1980s as many important cases came before the U.S. Supreme Court based on the tensions between urban and suburban development, housing, schools, and lifestyles.[21] Despite all of the civil rights efforts of the past two decades, it remains true that the tensions between cities and suburbs are very real and that a significant aspect of that tension has racial dimensions.

David Rusk, a former mayor and New Mexico state legislator, has explored these tensions between cities, suburbs, counties and what he refers to as exurbs in his book, *Cities Without Suburbs*.[22] Comparing a number of cities, Rusk concludes that the ability to escape the straitjacket of tight

President Lyndon Johnson meets in 1967 with members of the newly created Kerner Commission (chaired by then-Illinois Governor Otto Kerner). Johnson charged the panel with reporting on the causes of urban riots that had occurred earlier in the decade. The commission, officially called the National Advisory Commission on Civil Disorders, concluded the next year that the discord was a result of "two increasingly separate Americas," one consisting mostly of poor minorities and the other consisting of affluent whites.
(Photo courtesy of UPI/Corbis-Bettmann.)

boundaries is essential if metropolitan areas are to address the host of social and economic problems facing most of these areas. He highlights the successes of city/county consolidations in which the two units have merged to break down barriers and enhance service delivery, though he also notes that many tensions have blocked efforts even at cooperation in some communities, let alone a formal alliance. It should be understood that in some metropolitan areas there are in excess of one hundred local government units of various descriptions that may be involved with one or another type of service decision. Rusk points out that the politics of race are still very much at the heart of metropolitan stresses.

For all these reasons, it may sometimes be the case that units within a metropolitan area are more likely to establish relations through a process involving a nonprofit organization with an expanding revenue base rather than a city with financial difficulties. This is even more likely when the nonprofit organization is controlled by a well-established community group. The privatization of the Pittsburgh Zoo is an example of how a nonprofit organization can create a process for facilitating intergovernmental relations. An analysis of attendance at the heavily subsidized Pittsburgh Zoo showed that less than one-fourth (140,000) of its visitors (575,000) were residents of the City of Pittsburgh. Nearly 70 percent (400,000) were from the other 131 municipalities in Allegheny County.[23] After several unsuccessful attempts to secure state funding for several of its recreational facilities, the City decided to privatize the operations of its zoo, aviary, and conservatory.

The Zoological Society of Pittsburgh was hired to take over the city's operation of the zoo. More than a year before the society began operating the zoo, it had successfully organized a cross-section of intergovernmental support for the enactment of a "regional assets district" to help fund the zoo. To do this, it contacted municipal managers, lobbied state officials, and mailed letters to the seven hundred elected officials across Allegheny County. Thus, the Zoological Society was successful in generating regional support for the zoo even though other similar efforts by the city had been rebuffed.

The case of the Zoological Society of Pittsburgh demonstrates that intergovernmental activities facilitated by nonprofit organizations can result in the establishment of regional organizations for the provision of public services. Some nonprofit organizations become these regional entities themselves. In part for this reason, the roles that nonprofit organizations play in the intergovernmental arena are coming to be the focus of increasing attention.

Substate Regions

Ironically, the fact that some state legislatures were malapportioned led to the creation of complex sets of substate intergovernmental relations. For years state legislatures based representation partly on population and partly on other factors such as geography, historical community patterns, and economic similarities. As a practical matter, that meant that efforts by cities to get state action on important problems were often blocked in the upper house of most state legislatures by rural representatives. Of course, at about the same time, the United States Supreme Court struck down the old voting apportionment schemes and required that population be the basis for apportionment of both houses of the state legislature.[24] Those who assumed that the cities would be the winners failed to consider the fact that most of the population growth was occurring not in the cities but in the suburbs. Suburban representatives were in a position to vote with the rural representatives to block potentially costly programs to benefit cities, and could swing their support to the cities when development issues were on the agenda. In a nation experiencing violent confrontations over the problems of the cities, that ability of suburbs to deny help to the cities was untenable. That was one of the factors that led the federal government to try to find ways to get assistance directly to local governments and bypass the political logjams in the state governments. Thus, the number of categorical grants direct to local units of government from the federal government grew.

However, there was also concern that a proliferation of units, literally thousands of them, applying for more than four hundred types of federal grants, in addition to whatever state or local activities they may be pursuing were creating a crazy quilt system of finance and action. That led the federal government to attempt to facilitate creation of local and regional arrangements to enhance cooperation. Some of the most widely known are those created to implement requirements of the Office of Management and Budget Circular A-95, the document used by the federal government to attempt to rationalize the intergovernmental grant process. Provisions of Circular A-95 facilitated substantial cooperation between local governments by requiring:

1. all local governments to aid applicants in forwarding their proposals to an area-wide screening agency;
2. the screening agency to inform other governments in the area of the proposal's contents and to solicit reactions from those governments;
3. the local government to consider the responses received and to modify its own proposal if it chose to do so;
4. the screening agency to evaluate the proposal for consistency with existing state, regional, and local planning; and
5. the screening agency to forward the package of documents to the federal agency from which the requested grant would come.[25]

These requirements sparked development of regional structural arrangements that included councils of government, regional planning commissions, and economic development districts. The impact of Circular A-95 can be seen by the rapid increase in the number of councils of government (COG). In 1965 there were only nine COGs. However, by 1980 there were more than six hundred regional clearinghouses reviewing proposed projects within substate regions.

When federal requirements and financial incentives for substate regional coordinating bodies were eliminated in 1982, 10 percent of the bodies ceased to exist. The elimination of funding for COGs by Congress and the elimination of the A-95 process by executive order effectively withdrew the federal government from the business of encouraging substate intergovernmental cooperation. Nevertheless, not only have these organizations survived, many have expanded their role far beyond that required by the A-95 Circular. In recent years, the federal government has renewed encouragement for regional cooperation with such legislation as the Intermodal Service Transportation Efficiency Act, which is often referred to by an acronym that sounds like "iced-tea."

Regional Organizations as Service Providers

New service sharing arrangements and other forms of cooperation among local governments have been put in place, frequently using COG structures. This has been possible because many of the COGs created in the 1960s retained their vitality and are encouraging local officials to undertake new regional efforts. Some COGs have been transformed into regional service entities that amount to multipurpose special districts (such as water or fire protection districts) with real power.[26]

For reasons indicated earlier, regional cooperation historically has been a means through which local governments have shared the burden of tackling difficult problems that do not have well-defined boundaries. Regional arrangements for addressing these problems may include joint planning, financing, and management activities. Such regional arrangements offer a number of advantages, including:

1. consistency of local laws, regulations, policies, and practices across political jurisdictions;
2. efficient management of resources;
3. sharing of liability exposure;
4. political power through multijurisdictional cooperation; and
5. united front for building public support for regional programs.[27]

Services frequently provided on a substate regional basis include public safety, transportation, recreation, economic development, water, sewage, solid waste disposal, and other environmental activities. As Eileen Shanahan pointed out in her discussion of the resurgence of regionalism in the '90s:

> Public safety agencies lead the parade in service sharing. Police departments and sheriffs offices keep joint records, operate joint radio bands and 911 emergency numbers, share crime laboratories, do joint investigations, establish regional automated fingerprint identification systems, follow uniform rules for police pursuits when they cross jurisdictional lines and, in a variety of ways, share the cost of training law enforcement personnel. Jails are shared, or simply taken over by the jurisdiction with the healthier revenues.[28]

Transportation service has been another source of regional cooperation. The structural arrangement that facilitates intergovernmental relations in this area is the regional transportation authority. As Robert Smith points out in a discussion of these regional structures:

> From their conception, transportation authorities have stressed regional, or area-wide, organization. . . . Of the 361 transit systems listed in the Directory of the American Public Transit Association, some ninety have in their titles the words, Regional, Metropolitan, Area, and Greater, with Area predominant. Other words in titles imply unconventional boundaries: Valley, River, Bay, North Slope, Central, Suburban, and others.[29]

This regional focus for transportation authorities was encouraged by federal legislation. The Urban Mass Transportation Act of 1964 stated, in fact, that one of its purposes was to encourage the planning and establishment of area-wide urban mass transportation systems.

Regional authorities have been used as providers of water and sewage services over multijurisdictional areas for some time. Local governments are increasingly turning to regional approaches for carrying out solid-waste management activities. Four of these regional solid waste arrangements (Western Fingerlakes Solid Waste Management Authority in New York, Greater Portland Council of governments in Maine, the City and County of Spokane in Washington, and the Solid Waste Agency of Northern Cook County in Illinois) have been highlighted for their efforts by the International City/County Management Association.[30]

One of the main outcomes from these regional arrangements has been production efficiency derived through regional economies of scale. For instance, the Western Fingerlakes Solid Waste Management Authority, which encompasses a four-county, three thousand square mile area with a population of 250,000, is involved in planning and implementing elements of a long-term solid waste system for the region. The authority runs one of the largest recycling efforts in New York. It initiated regional curbside collection of recyclable and waste materials. The authority is currently negotiating for the development of a regional waste-to-energy facility to help finance other aspects of its solid waste operations.

The Greater Portland Council of Governments (GPCOG) has taken advantage of economies of scale through a voluntary association of twenty-one municipalities that represents a combined population of more than 200,000. Between 1960 and the late 1970s, the GPCOG's Regional Solid Waste Committee organized a regional landfill and formed Regional Waste Systems (RWS), a public intermunicipal solid waste authority. The landfill was replaced by a seventy-two million dollar regional energy-to-waste facility in the mid-1980s that burns five hundred tons of waste per day. The GPCOG is also involved in a landfill closure project, joint bidding for the removal of white goods and chemical wastes, and water testing for landfill sites.

The city and county of Spokane, Washington, which have a combined population of approximately 350,000, are collaborating on a regional solid waste management plan. The plan calls for the recycling of refuse and an eight hundred ton-per day waste-to-energy facility. The project includes the closing of a municipal landfill and a large county landfill.

Similarly, the Solid Waste Agency of Northern Cook County (SWANCC) was formed to take advantage of opportunities offered by a regional organization. It was formed by officials from twenty-eight local governments in the Northwest Municipal Conference. Municipalities in the Conference have a combined population of more than 800,000. The SWANCC has authority through the Illinois Intergovernmental Cooperation Act for implementing a balanced solution to the region's solid waste problem. This includes a recycling and composting program and a landfill on a strip-mine site in a sparsely developed area of the region.

As these examples illustrate, regional organizations have become valuable structures for addressing solid waste problems. Advantages derived from regional cooperation, however, have not been limited to the solid waste area. Infrastructure and economic development activities are others areas where local governments have benefitted from innovative regional policy structures and actions. Ohio has two innovative regional arrangements for intergovernmental coordination in these areas.

The state of Ohio has designated nineteen district committees, consisting of elected local government officials, to develop capital improvement plans on a region-wide basis. The state plans to raise $1.2 billion over ten years, and spend $120 million on transportation and environmental infrastructure each year. A jurisdiction requesting funds is expected to submit its capital improvement report to the district committee. The district committee integrates plans from local governments and develops district priorities. Using these priorities and criteria in the enabling legislation, the committee decides which projects to fund, subject to the approval of the state Public Works Commission.[31]

The district approach described above is a response to a state initiative. The regional economic development arrangement in Montgomery County, Ohio, is an example of local cooperative efforts. Under the leadership of the county, an innovative structural arrangement has been forged for funding economic development activities in twenty-three municipalities. The county has made a commitment to put five million dollars a year into a pot for municipal economic development efforts. The twenty-three municipalities must also put money into the pot, according to a formula based on the growth in their property and income tax collection since 1989. Municipalities must compete for these funds, which can be used for anything from infrastructure to an international marketing program.[32]

None of these regional initiatives for the cooperative delivery of public services, however, is more innovative than the arrangement that resulted in the establishment of Portland, Oregon's, Metropolitan Service District. This arrangement eliminated the existing COG and replaced it with a regional government, with multiple responsibilities, run by officials elected directly by the people. The Portland Metropolitan Service District is in charge of regional growth control, which allows it to enforce boundaries for urban development. It can require high-rise apartment buildings or shopping malls to be placed where they will be accessible from the regional light rail system. It does the transportation and water quality planning for the region; has a variety of environmental responsibilities; and operates the zoo, the coliseum, the convention center, and several recycling and solid waste facilities. The Portland Metropolitan Service District has been termed "a national model for the next generation of regional governments."[33]

Intergovernmental Mandates

Most of the intergovernmental relations described previously are voluntary in nature. Participation in interstate compacts, regional organizations, mutual assistance agreements, and other structural arrangements is usually optional. Many other intergovernmental relations are the result of mandates imposed through legislation, regulation, or judicial rulings.

These mandates imposed on governments are conditions that have the backing of law. Thus, action in response to mandates is involuntary. Mandated actions can be precipitated by direct orders, crosscutting requirements, crossover sanctions, and partial preemptions.[34]

Direct orders are statutory requirements, administrative regulations, or court decrees that are imposed on governments under threat of civil or criminal penalties. Crosscutting requirements are conditions imposed on grant programs to achieve policy goals not central to a particular grant. Crosscutting sanctions involve imposing requirements in one program area to influence policy outcomes in another. Partial preemption, addressed in greater detail in Chapter 2, is the enactment of national laws setting basic policies and the delegation of administrative responsibility for implementation to state and local governments.[35]

The use of mandates has increased steadily since the 1960s. As illustrated in Figure 4-1, twelve new federal legislative mandates were imposed on state and local governments between 1961 and 1970; twenty-two between 1971 and 1980; and twenty-seven between 1981 and 1990. These figures do not include many of the mandates that were created by imposing new regulatory requirements to existing programs or by court decree. For instance, new requirements have been added to Medicaid, and conditions have been attached to programs to aid families and children. Federal mandates, whether

Figure 4-1

The Growth of Regulatory Federalism

The number of federal mandates on state and local governments has grown steadily since the 1960s. These mandates are now often not accompanied by federal dollars and, therefore, impose additional costs on governmental bodies that must scramble to find new revenue or reduce other spending.

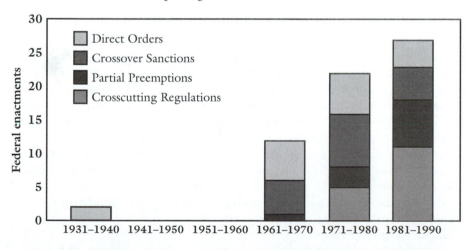

Source: U.S. Advisory Commission on Intergovernmental Relations, *Regulatory Federalism,* Appendix Table 1.

effectuated through regulation, new legislation, or changes in existing stat-
ues, can constitute a major burden for state and local governments. These
governments are forced to spend millions of dollars each year to comply with
federal mandates, with little or no financial assistance.[36]

The Congressional Budget Office estimated that new federal legislation
enacted between 1983 and 1990 may have imposed as much as $12.7 billion
in additional cost on state and local governments.

Twenty new federal legislative mandates enacted in 1991 were projected
to add seventeen billion dollars to state budgets alone over a five-year period.
These estimates would increase significantly if cost incurred because of mandates effectuated by judicial decree were included.

Judicial mandates arise when cases are brought challenging the legality of
the operation of public facilities or services such as school desegregation,
prison conditions, mental health program operations, education for children
with special needs, and other issues.[37] This is a complex area of mandates because courts are often called in when state or local governments refuse to address problems, many of which affect minorities within the community, like
segregated racial groups, handicapped children, mentally retarded citizens,
or prison inmates. By definition, a finding that the community has discrimi-
nated, violated the cruel and unusual punishment provisions of the Constitution, or been negligent in the operation of its facilities is likely to be rejected
by the community involved. Courts were, after all, designed in part to prevent majorities from breaking the law merely because some type of activity is
or is not popular and from denying "to any person within its jurisdiction the
equal protection of the laws."[38]

Because there has been a long history of resistance to court rulings by state
and local governments, and because these kinds of defendants often refuse
voluntarily to correct the conditions that gave rise to the violations, courts are
often forced to mandate specific actions. In so doing, the orders may be regarded as very intrusive in the operations of institutions and programs.

Moreover, judicial mandates, such as those involving jail construction, can
also be costly for local government. Allegheny County, Pennsylvania spent
$150 million on a new jail that was mandated by a federal judge whose rul-
ing that the conditions in the jail were unconstitutional was upheld by the
U.S. Supreme Court. After all, the Eighth Amendment prohibits cruel and
unusual punishment. If states and localities are going to operate prisons and
jails they must do so in conformity with that constitutional requirement. The
Constitution does not say that its mandates depend on whether they are considered too costly or not.

In addition to being forced to build the jail, many features in the Allegheny County jail are mandated by federal construction standards that
increase construction cost. Compounding this court mandate is a state

minimum-sentencing mandate that has aggravated the overcrowding problem. Minimum sentencing has increased the jail population in Allegheny fourfold; from 431 in 1980 to 1,750 in 1992. The County's criminal justice expenditures are expanding at a rate of 8.8 percent annually, driven largely by mandates. These expenditures make up one-third of the county's budget.[39]

Not all mandates are federally imposed. An increasing financial burden is placed on local governments by state mandates. Frustration with state legislated and judicial mandates on local government is widespread. State legislators and judges have mandated the closing of landfills, construction of storage sheds for road salt, new equipment for firefighters, special education classes for public schools, certification for code-enforcement officers, the hiring of civil defense officers, and many other services and programs. These mandates are usually unfunded.[40]

State mandates are also often accompanied by restrictions on local governments revenue generating capacities. For example, the Florida Legislature in 1991 enacted laws that contained fourteen mandates for local government. Eleven laws required new or expanded local services and four reduced the revenue generating authority of counties and municipalities. In response to these mandates, local governments in fourteen states have successfully pushed for constitutional amendments prohibiting their states from imposing unfunded programs on them.[41]

Conclusion

There is no doubt that governments have moved a long way from the original constitutional design of national, state, and local governments. There is now a complex web of intergovernmental relations that involves not only those traditional units, but also the many other types described in this chapter. Nonprofit organizations have come to play important roles as well.

What all of this means is that public administrators in the contemporary environment must be adaptable and capable of understanding government not as a simple overhead authoritative organization of institutions, but as a complex collection of different kinds of organizations performing a variety of functions in a number of ways. That level of complexity means that the challenges of coordinating and planning action are difficult. However, no amount of wishing will remove complexity from the modern world.

Along with these institutional and policy structures, however, there have emerged a variety of intergovernmental financial practices that have been central to making the web work and that are responsible as well for some of its failures. It is to these fiscal dimensions of intergovernmental relations that we will turn in the next chapter.

Notes

[1]Deil S. Wright, *Understanding Intergovernmental Relations,* 3rd ed. (Pacific Grove, CA: Brooks/Cole Publishing, 1988).

[2]Morton Grodzins, *The American System: A New View of Governments in the United States,* ed. Daniel Elazar (Chicago: Rand McNally, 1966).

[3]Wright, *op. cit.,* 13.

[4]*Ibid.,* 36–37.

[5]"Government by Type," *State Government News* 36 (April 1993), 30.

[6]*Ibid.,* 12.

[7]"Intergovernmental Digest," *Intergovernmental Perspective* 19 (Spring 1993), 23.

[8]Daniel J. Elazar, *American Federalism: A View from the States,* 2nd ed. (New York: Thomas Y. Crowell, 1972), 174–178.

[9]Council of State Governments, *The Book of The States,* 1992–93 ed. (Lexington, KY: The Council of State Governments, 1992), 651.

[10]Benjamin J. Jones and Deborah Reuter, "Interstate Compacts and Agreements," in *The Book of the States,* 1991–92 ed., *op. cit.,* 565–568.

[11]Benjamin J. Jones, "Interstate Compacts and Agreements," in *The Book of the States,* 1992–93 ed., *op. cit.,* 648–650.

[12]Jones and Reuter, *op. cit.,* 566–567.

[13]*Ibid.*

[14]*Quill Corp. v. North Dakota,* 504 U.S. 298 (1992).

[15]Deil Wright, *Understanding Intergovernmental Relations,* 2nd ed. (Monterey, CA: Brooks/Cole Publishing, 1982), 334.

[16]Advisory Commission on Intergovernmental Relations, *Multi-State Regionalism* (Washington, DC: Government Printing Office, 1972), 173.

[17]National Research Council, *Toward an Understanding of Metropolitan America* (San Francisco: Canfield, 1975), 21.

[18]Nicholas Henry, *Governing at the Grassroots: State and Local Politics* (Englewood Cliffs, NJ: Prentice-Hall, 1980), 186.

[19]David Schuman and Dick W. Olufs III, *Public Administration in the United States,* 2nd ed. (Lexington, KY: D. C. Heath and Company), 58.

[20]Judith R. Saidel, "Resource Interdependence: The Relationship between State Agencies and Nonprofit Organizations," *Public Administration Review* 51 (November/December 1991): 543–553.

[21]See e.g., *Memphis v. Greene,* 451 U.S. 100 (1981); *Arlington Heights v. Metropolitan Housing Development Corp.,* 429 U.S. 252 (1977); *Milliken v. Bradley,* 418 U.S. 717 (1974); *San Antonio Independent School District v. Rodriguez,* 411 U.S. 1 (1973).

[22]David Rusk, *Cities without Suburbs* (Baltimore, MD: Johns Hopkins University Press, 1993).

[23]*Pittsburgh Post-Gazette,* June 12, 1993, editorial, "Feed the Animals," B-2.

[24]*Reynolds v. Sims,* 377 U.S. 533 (1964).

[25]George J. Gordon, *Public Administration in America* (New York: St. Martin's Press), 142.

[26]Eileen Shanahan, "Going It Jointly: Regional Solutions for Local Problems," *Governing,* 4 (August 1991), 70.

[27]Milou Carolan, "Regional Approaches to Environmental Management," *Public Management,* 72 (March 1990): 15.

[28]Shanahan, *op. cit.,* 70.

[29]Robert Smith, "Reorganization of Regional Transportation Authorities to Maintain Urban/Suburban Constituency Balance," *Public Administration Review* 47 (March/April 1987): 172.

[30]Carolan, *op. cit.,* 16–20.

[31]"Ohio Funds Local Infrastructure," *The Public's Capital* 2 (Summer 1990): 8.

[32]Shanahan, *op. cit.,* 72.

[33]*Ibid.,* 73.

[34]Advisory Commission on Intergovernmental Relations, *Regulations, Regulatory Federalism: Process, Impact, and Reform* (Washington, DC: Government Printing Office, 1984), 265–269.

[35]William C. Johnson, *Public Administration:Policy, Politics, and Practice* (Guilford, CT: Dushkin Publishing, 1992), 127–130.

[36]Timothy J. Conlan and David R. Beam, "Federal Mandates: The Record of Reform and Future Prospects," *Intergovernmental Perspective* 18 (Fall 1992): 7–11.

[37]See Phillip J. Cooper, *Hard Judicial Choices* (New York: Oxford University Press, 1988).

[38]United States Constitution, Fourteenth Amendment.

[39]"Mandates: Major Drains on Local Government," *University of Pittsburgh Institute Report* 4 (Winter 1993): 6–7.

[40]Linda Wagar, "A Declaration of War: Local Governments Are Tired of Picking Up the Tab for State Programs," *State Government News* 36 (April 1993): 18–22.

[41]Joseph F. Zimmerman, "Developments in State-Local Relations, 1990–91," in *The Book of the States,* 1992–93 ed. (Lexington, KY: The Council of State Governments), 620–631.

Chapter 5

Fiscal Federalism and Its Constitutional Foundations

The last chapter sketched the basic structures and the overall framework of contemporary intergovernmental relations. We turn now to two sets of critical forces that are driving that framework in the United States. The first is what is termed *fiscal federalism,* the way that the flow of resources among and within units of governments operates. The second is the changing character of the constitutional infrastructure of intergovernmental relations, changes that are reshaping the economy and the ways in which state and local governments are experiencing the dynamics of the marketplace, both as market regulators and as market participants.

Fiscal Federalism: The Lifeblood of Contemporary Intergovernmental Relations

As Chapter 4 indicated, there are many ways in which officials at various levels of government work with one another to accomplish the wide variety of goals established by the nation, in state legislatures, and in local communities. Those efforts, of course, require resources, and the process by which those resources are accumulated in the form of taxes and various other kinds of fees, distributed in the form of grants and transfer payments, and expended in the form of direct services or contracting for the purchase of goods or services are critically important to the day-to-day life of the nation.

As other governments around the world implement various decentralization initiatives, even though they usually do so in a system far different from what Justice Hugo Black referred to as "Our Federalism," they have encountered problems and used tactics very similar to those employed in the United States. Even where governments are centralized, debate about how to channel funds to achieve the most efficient and effective program operations is an on-going discussion.

In many countries, the complaints by regional, state, or local governments are the same. They stem from the basic premise that the central governments make the key decisions and yield only the authority to do the difficult work of day-to-day implementation to the local authorities (almost always without sufficient funds to do the job). Unlike the developed countries, state and local units within developing nations must, in addition to responding to the mandates of the national governments, come to grips with the roles played by the so-called informal sector, community groups that provide education and other kinds of services outside the standard government programs, using volunteer labor and meager resources from external charities. Indeed, there is often a complex informal economy in many developing nations that is not subject to taxation and does not spend its revenues or other in-kind resources in accordance with government policies and regulations.

The Principles of Fiscal Federalism

While there are some common principles in intergovernmental relations that have been applicable in many settings, it is important to understand the context of American intergovernmental relations.

The Changing Context of Intergovernmental Relations. Deil Wright suggested that there have been several phases in the periodic reconsideration of relationships among the various levels of governments. These phases are as follows:

1. Conflict Phase (1890–1930s)
2. Cooperative Phase (1930s–1950s)
3. Concentrated Phase (1940s–1950s)
4. Creative Phase (1950s–1970s)
5. Calculative Phase (1970s–1980s)
6. Contractive Phase (1980s–1990s).[1]

Each of these phases evolved in response to particular problems like those outlined in Table 5-1. Each involved an associated set of behavioral characteristics and was implemented through a series of formal and informal intergovernmental mechanisms.

These phases also reflect significant changes in the fiscal and functional activities of various levels of government. For instance, the share of local government in total public expenditures was around 50 percent during the

Table 5-1
Phases of Intergovernmental Relations (IGR) and Fiscal Federalism

Phase	Main Problem	IGR Mechanism	Time Frame
Conflict	Defining boundaries	Statutes Courts Regulations	1800s–1930s
Cooperative	Economic distress International threats	National planning Formula grants Tax credits	1930–1950s
Concentrated	Service needs Physical development	Categorical grants Service standards	1940s–1960s
Creative	Urban-metropolitan Disadvantage clients	Program planning Project grants Participation	1950s–1960s
Competitive	Coordination Program effectiveness Delivery systems Citizen access	Grant aid entitlements Bypassing Loans Cost cutting Regulation	1970s–1980s
Calculative	Accountability Bankruptcy Constraints Dependency Federal role Public Confidence	General aid entitlements Bypassing Loans Cost cutting Regulation	1970s–1980s

Contractive	Borrowing
	  and deficits
	Federal aid cuts
	  and changes
	Judicial decision
	  making
	Managing mandates
	Fiscal bailouts
		Congressional
		  statues
		Court decisions
		
		Information sources
		
		Negotiated dispute
		  settlement
			1980s–1990s

Source: Deil S. Wright, *Understanding Intergovernmental Relations,* 3rd ed. (Pacific Grove, CA: Brooks/Cole, 1988), 67.

Conflict Phase (1890–1930). Federal expenditures were only about 36 percent. By the end of the Cooperative Phase the federal government constituted more than 66 percent of public expenditures and local governments' share had fallen to 19 percent. This significant change in the fiscal structure evolved in response to problems associated with the Great Depression and World War II, which developed during the Cooperative Phase.

State and local governments were unable to solve these truly national problems. The role of the federal system expanded during the Cooperative Phase, most of which took place during President Franklin Roosevelt's New Deal. The national government took the lead in efforts to alleviate widespread economic distress that came with the Great Depression and to respond to international threats, from the rise of Adolf Hitler in Europe to the growing tensions over Japan's demands in the Far East. On the domestic front, numerous new national policy initiatives were launched that included a joint-state unemployment compensation program; social security programs; expanded national electrical power programs, including the Tennessee Valley Authority; and public works projects of many kinds. "States and local governments were co-opted as third parties in major national efforts" during this period.[2]

This national dominance in the provision and finance of government services also involved efforts to address equity and quality-of-life issues that were important to many Americans. There were not only the initiatives to address the impact of the depression, but also the policies developed during World War II and those crafted to address the needs of postwar transformation into a peacetime economy. That overall effort to address national problems included needs for dramatic infrastructure development in the South and Southwest, regions that had been largely rural and with relatively small populations before the war. Many of the fiscal measures taken by the federal government during this period came in the form of formula grants (funds given to other units of government in a given area according to population or other standard criteria), many of which came as the national government sought to assist in the provision of services at all levels of government. By 1950, grants made up 14 percent of state revenues and nearly 30 percent of local revenues.

It is difficult to overstate the importance of postwar growth and change. Returning veterans married, and those families produced the baby boom that continues to shape American politics to this day. Those families and their children demanded opportunities to purchase homes and called for services from education to transportation. Earl Warren, then governor of California, complained that every Monday morning when he went to work, there was the equivalent of a new community in the state to be served and governed.[3] Moreover, it was an increasingly mobile society, with families moving frequently not merely from one community to another in the same state but regularly moving from one part of the country to another. They expected to find a minimum level of education and other services wherever they went and felt that the federal government was responsible to ensure that this national infrastructure existed for them.

The policies developed to address pressing problems on the public agenda between the Cooperative and Calculative Phases resulted in the continued enhancement of the national government's role in the federal system. The intense efforts of the Concentrated Phase resulted in the establishment of twenty-one new grant-in-aid programs during that period, but the period from the 1950s to the 1970s, which Wright called the Creative Phase, was the most substantial period of enhancement in the development and execution of policy by the national government. As Wright put it:

> The sheer number of grants alone is sufficient to set this period apart from all the others. In 1961 ACIR identified approximately 40 major grant programs that had been enacted prior to 1958 and were still in existence. By 1969 there were an estimated 150 major programs, 400 specific legislative authorizations, and 1,300 federal assistance activities. . . . In dollar magnitude federal grants jumped from $4.9 billion in 1958 to $28.9 billion between 1958 and 1970.[4]

The Creative Phase involved the extensive use of project grants. Unlike formula and categorical grants (funds made available for specific categories of action by recipients) of earlier phases, project grants were awarded based on applications from those who wanted to participate. As Chapter 4 indicated, part of the reason for the focus on projects was to get resources directly to where they were most needed without any kind of interference, to ensure that the funds got to specific priority targets rather than simply being allocated across the country, and to enhance accountability by giving the funds with a variety of conditions.

The Calculative Phase represented a period of grant consolidation and the development of new funding arrangements. It was also a period of immense competition for resources. Competition existed not only between officials from various levels and different units of government but from different functional areas as well. This competition helped to generate support for the reorganization of the federal grant-in-grant system.

The politics of backlash also played a role. President Richard Nixon rode frustration with violence in the streets into the White House in 1968. He played strategically to the anger in the suburban community against Great Society programs targeted to address city problems. One approach was a federalism argument that said that the current grant structure was too expensive and unwieldy. Therefore, the grant structure should be changed to eliminate the targeting and allow a wider range for local communities and states to make their own decisions with fewer federal government requirements and paperwork burdens attached. What resulted was the first round of "the New Federalism."

Once elected, Nixon and members of the Congress sought to reduce the number of categorical and project grants and created block grants as well as general revenue sharing. Block grants allowed more discretion and flexibility in programs and a wider range of activity in related areas like community development, law enforcement assistance, and health care. The object was to combine several related types of grant programs and then allow communities and states to apply resources more flexibly across several of these issue areas. Revenue sharing was simply a transfer of tax dollars from the federal government's income tax revenue to the states and the localities according to population with no significant attempts at accountability. Nixon wanted to use something called special revenue sharing to do the same thing as block grants but with even fewer restrictions than the block grants. He was not successful.

Michael Reagan criticized the Nixon administration on grounds that the real reason behind revenue sharing and block grants was to channel more of the funds away from cities and to the suburbs and states.[5] The argument was that, at the local community level, and without specific federal accountability requirements, local majorities would ensure that the funds would be not be used to address the needs of minorities and the poor. Indeed, there was support for those criticisms of Nixon's programs when it became clear that a number of cities were using Community Development Block Grant (CDBG) funds for all kinds of projects except to meet the kinds of low and moderate housing needs that were central to the purposes of the grant.

There was another side to the criticisms and changes during what Wright refers to as the Calculative Phase. There was a concern about the growth in government associated with the Great Society and a number of significant economic problems. While many of the social programs of the Johnson era were adopted during the mid to late 1960s, they began to have budgetary impacts a few years later. There were also new regulatory programs in the areas of health, environment, and consumer protection. Taken together, these expanded federal government activities made easy targets for opponents who argued for budget cuts.

In addition to these factors, the United States began to feel the inflationary effects of huge U.S. expenditures on the war in Vietnam. Although wartime expenditures have the initial effect of boosting the economy, there are, in the long run, costs to be paid, not only in terms of the high dollar costs themselves, but also because the assets generated by those expenditures are effectively dumped into the jungles and oceans. And none of these expenditures even begin to address the costs of postwar readjustment. Further, the heating up of the economy in a rapid fashion can foster inflation, particularly when the economy is already in a growth mode, as the stimulus of public spending is added.

The Nixon years saw the beginning of what was to be a decade-long stretch of serious economic stress. So volatile was the situation that President Nixon imposed a wage/price freeze in an effort to stabilize the economy. By 1975, President Gerald Ford was so frustrated by the economy that he encouraged the wearing of so-called WIN buttons, standing for "Whip Inflation Now."

President Jimmy Carter not only inherited the difficulties experienced by Presidents Nixon and Ford, but he also felt the impact of a 400 percent increase in petroleum product prices because of the OPEC price raises that brought inflation around the world, not just in the United States. The first major round of oil price jumps came in 1974, but its real effect took hold over the next two to three years as the increased costs of fuel drove up prices throughout the economy with increased prices for agriculture, manufacturing, and transportation. That, in turn, resulted in significant demands for increased wages. The economic uncertainties laid the foundation for the most dramatic increases in interest rates in years. On the other hand, there was serious inflation in housing markets, driving one of the fundamental family budget items into a much higher percentage of income. Indeed, the market factored in the fact that most households were now operating on two incomes. By the late 1970s, two incomes were essential for most American households that expected a middle class lifestyle. Of course, large numbers of families had only one parent in the home, often a woman who, because of historic inequalities in the marketplace, earned less than a similarly situated man. Pressures on family budgets and double-digit inflation frightened and frustrated many citizens, who demanded that government do something but also reacted against the idea of additional taxation. Despite the fact that Carter was able to move toward a balanced budget and was responsible for a wave of deregulation legislation, he was not able to realize significant improvements in the economy.

President Ronald Reagan ran for office on grounds that he would attack inflation and, in particular, that he would target government spending in the process. At the same time, the Reagan White House decided to dramatically increase defense expenditures. Despite the fact that Reagan was facing serious economic problems, the administration insisted upon a major tax cut. There are three arguments that have been made about the foundation for these decisions. The first was the influence of what was called *supply side economics,* which argued that by reducing taxes, particularly those taxes that prevented people with the resources from investing more of their money, there would be a dramatic impetus to inflation-free growth. The second argument was nothing so sophisticated, but merely a political contention that government was too big and would be trimmed only if the amount of resources it was given were reduced. The third argument was not publicly advocated but was made within Washington circles. It was that the spending priorities had been wrong for a long time. Defense spending had not kept pace with the need for Reagan's "Peace through Strength" campaign. On the other hand, domestic spending was, in Reagan's view, far too high, and particularly with respect to so-called entitlement programs in the social sphere. For a variety of political reasons, these programs seemed untouchable. There were those who argued that only by creating severe budgetary stress could that situation be broken and the outlays in social spending attacked.

Whatever the intention, the cuts in revenue from the tax reduction, along with the general efforts at budget cutting and the dramatic demands for revenue by the defense sector, created a crisis in support for domestic programs. While the Reagan White House called for a "New Federalism" (ignoring the fact that the tag had been used a decade earlier by President Nixon), and moved to send responsibility for programs back to the states and localities, it also moved to cut financial support for those programs. Thus, the administration consolidated many of the categorical grant programs, restructured the block grants, and eliminated all of the state and local government revenue sharing. Thus, federal grants financed 25 percent of state and local expenditures in 1980. However, by 1988, they were financing only 18.2 percent. To some observers, the Reagan administration got trapped in some of its own party's political rhetoric and pushed into more of a problem than it had anticipated. The problem emerged because of something called *bracket creep*. It had been possible over the years to address increasing expenditures without raising tax rates because inflation not only increased the dollar amount of taxes paid but also pushed many taxpayers into higher tax brackets, which also brought increased revenue. Thus, there was a vehicle for helping to keep the budget deficit under control without pitched national battles over new taxes or changing tax formulas. Because the federal income tax was the most progressive form of taxation, the bracket creep dynamic was redistributive in character, helping those most in need.

But supply side economics advocates were intent on attacking the progressive income tax on the theory that such a move would increase discretionary funds for those most able to invest. While the president was most interested in simply cutting taxes, others in the Congress and at the White House pushed for indexing to stop bracket creep. At the same time, the Federal Reserve was intent on wringing inflation out of the economy with a tight money policy. There was a dramatic recession with devastating results which, of course, meant increased demands for public services. The results were to eliminate the compensating stabilizing mechanism of bracket creep, reduce the tax rate, and make the tax less progressive. With dramatically increased military spending and significant social service needs, all of this led to a dramatic increase in the budget deficit.

> The Reagan administration had not originally intended to combine tax cuts with tax indexation. The president's advisers had in fact explicitly decided not to include indexation in the president's proposals. One of the political advantages to excluding indexation from the Reagan tax cuts was that such exclusion would have helped enable Reagan to realize sufficient government revenues and still fulfill his campaign promise to reduce taxes by 30 percent over the next three years. The advisers expected a relatively high rate of inflation-induced bracket creep to take away roughly half of the tax cut as fast as it was being implemented. But Senator Robert Dole, Republican majority leader in the Senate, saw the 1981 tax bill as an opportunity to enact tax indexation proposals he had long advocated. . . . Budget deficits ballooned.[6]

In terms of intergovernmental relations, the pressures were severe. The recession was felt quickly and severely at the local level as demands for social services grew. Revenue sharing disappeared. Overall federal assistance dropped, partly as a result of straight funding cuts and also because the administration led a move to consolidate a range of categorical grants and existing block grant programs into new block grants to states. They provided more discretion for states, but at a lower level of funding than had existed previously.[7]

While the actual dollars involved for many programs increased, the value in constant dollars and the pressures of increased demand for services meant that resources were severely strained. Apart from transfer payments, it was not unusual to find state and local governments operating at the same level of administrative expenditures even though inflation was affecting the costs of governing just as it was other participants in the economy. In actual effect, budgeting the same amount for administrative operations in the next year when inflation ran at 7 percent meant a 7 percent reduction in spending power, and that was the situation for many years in many jurisdictions.

These cuts continued during the Bush and Clinton administrations even though the many legislative mandates for program operation by states and localities were simultaneously increased. Thus, Wright refers to the 1980s and 1990s as the Contractive Period. Even though Congress adopted, with support from the Clinton White House, a law prohibiting so-called unfunded mandates, the legislation was not made retroactive.

The press for a balanced budget once again brought pressure on entitlement programs in the area of social services. Congress moved to eliminate the right to claim various kinds of benefits and return control of the programs in the form of block grants to the states. Of course, the states and localities braced for the increased responsibilities with even fewer federal dollars. State and local leaders have expressed concern that the decision to remove federal entitlements to social programs frees the federal government to begin cutting the present limited funding for the block grants over the next few years, effectively transferring complete responsibility for their operations to the state and local governments. That leaves those governments with the difficult task of either raising more funds or, if states and localities are unable to afford them, actually terminating badly needed programs.

The Fiscal Function of Government. In addition to the politics of intergovernmental relations, there are various theories that have been used to understand the nature of fiscal federalism as well. The arguments on economic grounds are complex and have their own political biases and significance. Thus, although the arguments are often phrased in terms of efficiency, that is not a neutral concept.[8] Indeed, for many, the only economically efficient decision is one made by the individual, meaning a market-type decision. Group decisions made in a political compromise context are by their nature not efficient to anyone adopting that definition of efficiency. Deil Wright warned against "monetary myopia and fiscal fixation."[9] Another long-time observer of federal/state relations, Daniel Elazar, suggested that the situation was one of "Fiscal Questions, Political Answers."[10]

With that in mind, it is nevertheless important to consider arguments on which the contemporary understanding of the system of intergovernmental fiscal relationships is constructed. Basically, that means deciding who obtains public resources, by which means they will be gathered, who will be permitted to expend them, and for what purposes they are to be used.

The Question of Taxation

The argument that has been used at least since the 1960s is that the national government is the best revenue collector, but that it is both more desirable and more efficient to have the actual expenditure decisions made by governments closer to home, preferably at the local level. The federal government traditionally relied primarily on a graduated income tax that taxed those most able to pay. That seemed to be the fairest and simplest way to collect a large body of resources that could be spent at the national level to meet national priorities. It would also allow the federal government to send funds to the states and localities to assist them in meeting their needs.

The states and localities relied principally on property and consumption taxes, like the general sales tax, to generate their revenue, with some states placing various degrees of reliance on income taxes. Property taxes are politically contentious and regressive. They are based on the value of one's property rather than on the ability to pay. A person who purchased a home twenty years ago may not have wages that grew nearly as rapidly as the value of the house in which she lives. The tax bill goes up because the value of the property has increased and is assessed at that current market value. In most situations, the owner can only realize the value of the house on sale, not while living in it. Except for senior citizens who may be able to qualify for a so-called "circuit breaker" provision of state law that protects them from increases in property tax bills, many people see only that their property taxes have increased, not that they possess greater wealth because of the value of their property.

Sales taxes are even more problematic. They plainly tax those with the lowest incomes for more of their income, since a larger percentage of their income must be spent directly on taxable items. That is especially true in the half of the states that still charge sales taxes on food and prescription drugs. There is a double hit for most of these taxpayers because they most often rent, rather than own their own home. They pay their landlord's property tax through their rent. The landlord can then take the tax advantages that come with property tax deductions, but the renters, in most states, have neither local property nor mortgage interest tax that they can deduct, which means that many cannot qualify for various benefits available to those who can itemize deductions on their federal tax returns.

It was also clear as the modern system of intergovernmental fiscal relations was being developed that there were inequalities in the abilities of some units of government to raise revenues. It became equally obvious that some states refused to tax themselves as necessary to provide services for all their citizens at the level considered essential by many Americans, even when they had the ability to do so. The classic example was the concern that some of the states in the rapidly growing south and southwestern portions of the country were simply not funding education at a level satisfactory to the many families moving into those regions as the national workforce became more mobile during the 1950s and 1960s. Beyond what families expected as national minimum standards in educational services, there were also the needs and expectations of growing national firms to be considered. In some small states around the nation, the problem was simply that there were not enough people to share the costs of the many things that needed to be done. In still other cases, the problem was not differences among states but tensions within states as cities, suburbs, and rural residents squared off in state legislatures over the types and limits of taxation. This resulted in the seemingly strange situation in which state legislatures put tax limits on how much city residents could vote to tax themselves. Hence, even cities that wanted to take on a heavier burden of taxation to meet educational and other needs were prohibited by their

REVENUE IN THE BAG

States and food taxes, 1996

Ala.	Yes	La.	Yes[4]	Ohio	No
Alaska	N/A[1]	Maine	No	Okla.	Yes
Ariz.	No	Md.	No	Ore.	N/A[1]
Ark.	Yes	Mass.	No	Pa.	No
Calif.	No	Mich.	No	R.I.	No
Colo.	No	Minn.	No	S.C.	Yes
Conn.	No	Miss.	Yes	S.D.	Yes
Del.	N/A[1]	Mo.	Yes	Tenn.	Yes
Fla.	No	Mont.	N/A[1]	Texas	No
Ga.	Yes[2]	Neb.	No	Utah	Yes
Hawaii	Yes	Nev.	No	Vt.	No
Idaho	Yes	N.H.	N/A[1]	Va.	Yes
Ill.	Yes[3]	N.J.	No	Wash.	No
Ind.	No	N.M.	Yes	W.Va.	Yes
Iowa	No	N.Y.	No	Wis.	No
Kan.	Yes	N.C.	Yes[5]	Wyo.	Yes
Ky.	No	N.D.	No		

Notes: (1) No state sales tax, (2) Voted to phase out by Oct. 1998, (3) Subject to 1% tax, (4) Voted to phase out by July 1998, (5) Reduced from 4% to 3% in 1996.

Source: National Conference of State Legislatures

A sales tax is often referred to as a regressive tax because its burden falls more heavily on the poor than on the rich. As a result, half of the states do not collect sales taxes on food, according to a survey in 1996 by the National Conference of State Legislatures. Those states will be joined by two more in 1998. Another five states do not levy a state sales tax on groceries but do allow local sales taxes.

Source: Reprinted with permission, © 1996, *Governing* magazine and Bob Lynch, illustrator.

state governments from providing the revenues they felt were necessary to address their own problems.[11]

Then there was the problem that came later in the 1970s and 1980s as the economy tightened, producing increased competition among cities and states to lure new businesses and the jobs that come with them. At the same time, they had to meet challenges from other communities attempting to attract existing businesses away. That was a newer version of a problem that had become apparent during the Great Depression in the 1930s. At that time, a number of states had wanted to experiment with unemployment insurance systems, but they were very much afraid that employers who faced a tax to support the plan might move to another state where there was no such tax. In at least one case, the state indicated that its plan would go into effect if and only if the adjoining states adopted a similar plan by the proposed date of implementation. The logjam was broken when the federal government adopted a policy that provided incentives for states to develop programs and eliminated the potential competition from other states.[12]

In more contemporary parlance, the effort by one community or state to undercut a competitor in the search for jobs was known first as "smokestack chasing" and, more recently, "chip chasing," because the effort is not only to attract businesses but to draw firms that are clean, high-tech, and profitable. The argument in these cases is not so much whether to create programs to be supported by taxes at all, though that debate does emerge from time to time, but whether to grant tax exemptions, abatements, or moratoria as incentives to potential businesses. There is considerable argument within the public administration community about these practices. The question is whether the benefits in the form of economic development and new jobs really offset the costs in terms of lost tax revenues and whatever infrastructure improvements are needed to get a deal with potential new businesses. The concerns are even greater where an existing business attempts to pit neighboring communities against each other by threatening to move. Then there are communities that have become frustrated by attempts by businesses to obtain multiple tax abatements. Even after a community takes these risks, there is no guarantee that the community will be able to recover any of these costs over the long term or even that the firm will actually remain in the community long enough to yield benefits to the city or town. Even so, it sometimes seems to community leaders that they have no real choice but to participate.

There is also a long-standing problem concerning the inability of communities to recover costs of services in the form of taxes or fees from the full range of people and organizations that benefit from those services. In the 1960s and 1970s, this dilemma became known as the *problem of municipal overburden*. Every business day hundreds of suburban commuters pour into cities or business parks at the edge of cities. Others move quickly into a city by air, shuttle about doing business in town, and then quickly leave the city to return to their homes. While these people are in the city, they need city services, from police and fire protection to water and sanitation. However, the city often cannot recover these costs since the suburbanites often pay their property taxes in another community and contribute whatever local option sales tax revenues they pay with their purchases not in the city but in suburban shopping malls. Indeed, while they are home in the suburbs, city police, fire, transportation, and other service providers are on the job protecting their offices and preparing for the next business day. When cities are walled in by surrounding communities and unable to ensure participation in city problem solving, the tensions and resentments increase.[13] The problem is that when people enjoy the benefits of the city but do not pay for them or participate in solving the other problems of the city, the stresses are apparent and real.

There is a variation on that idea that occurs in communities that are educational, medical, or governmental centers, areas with substantial amounts of tax exempt property. Probably the best known example is Washington, D.C., in which a very large percentage of property belongs to the federal government. However, the same kind of problem arises in most state capitals and many small- to medium-sized cities that are home to major state universities. There are no doubt benefits that flow from these institutions, such as the number of relatively high wage jobs that they bring, but there are also high service demands as well, particularly in such areas as police and fire protection. These debates over lost taxes are sometimes addressed through what are known as *payments in lieu of taxes (PILOTs)*. Still, the debate over the relative costs and contributions continue in many communities.

There are many variations around the world as to who pays taxes to which level of government and for what purposes. In Sweden, for example, most of the income tax is paid to the local government, which is the primary level at which services are provided. Most countries have strong central governments and do not regard American-style federalism as anything like their own arrangements. The primary taxing unit is the national government. However, many nations rely heavily on the so-called *value added tax (VAT)*, which is a form of consumption tax. However, current moves aimed at free trade and at regional integration like the European Union are forcing reexamination of those traditional modes of taxation. Thus, in Denmark and other Scandinavian countries, the move to join the EU meant abandoning reliance on their very high VAT to meet EU requirements. The problem becomes how to substitute for the lost revenue in societies that already face a very high tax burden.

In developing countries, there is also the risk that using property taxes or income taxes to increase financing for public activities may force small landowners to sell their property. There are twin risks at that point. First, there is the danger that the property will be sold at bargain-basement prices to international investors who will then be in control of substantial portions of the productive land in the country. Second, there is a danger that potentially regressive taxes will exacerbate existing inequalities and reverse progress that has been made in some places in terms of land reform.

All of these discussions about taxation are pinned to political dynamics or related questions of economic development. However, there are those who argue that issues of equity and equality as well as the other political considerations are fine, but they ignore important economic dynamics like efficiency. One can argue that revenue devices like those most often used at the state and local levels are more efficient precisely because they are closer to the forces of the marketplace. Particularly where there is an identifiable community that will both pay for and benefit from a particular service, there is the potential for adjusting both the taxing and spending to its most efficient form.

Moreover, there is also the question of efficiency in the manner in which decisions are made about taxation and expenditure. Thus, rational choice theorists have argued that the most efficient decisions are made where individuals who pay and benefit from public programs are allowed market-type choices, for the same reasons that markets attain efficient choice in the private sector.[14] The argument is that market forces can be used to attain both better efficiency and improved quality in service delivery.[15]

In developing nations, the arguments are often threefold. First, there must be sufficient centralization for rational decision making by the community, which is absolutely crucial to building a democracy. Then there must be capacity building so that local government administrators and service providers can prepare themselves to do more at the local level and develop a service orientation that provides the necessary backdrop for market-oriented service delivery systems. There is a third very difficult problem in that not all societies are culturally prepared to accept market-oriented devices in place of existing social services provided by the government.

This discussion of the question of the best fiscal organization for efficient provision of societal goods and services addresses the proper mix of centralization or decentralization of decision making and administration.[16] Allocative efficiency assumes that the costs of providing goods and services are shared in line with the incidence of benefits. The types and levels of services a jurisdiction provides should, in theory at least, reflect preferences of citizens within its geographical limits.

The efficiency argument, which emanates from the allocative function, leads to a theory of multiunit organizations for the provision and finance of government goods and services. However, as Richard and Peggy Musgrave observe: "While some services call for nationwide, other for statewide, and still others for metropolitan area-wide or local units, the argument so far does not call for an ordering of 'higher-level' and 'lower-level' governments."[17]

The efficiency argument extends to the question of how citizens within a given jurisdiction relate to one another on decision making for social services. It suggests that citizens would choose to live in jurisdictions whose public revenue and expenditure decisions best satisfy their own preferences. That approach to determining how citizens come together to make decisions may be interesting for theoretical purposes, but the assumptions that underlie it, namely that everyone has complete knowledge of the relative mix of goods and services in alternate jurisdictions and is fully mobile, are simply not true for the vast majority of people in most situations.

There are two things that seem clear. First, because of the nature and range of factors affecting decisions about how to tax, what to spend, and who should make those decisions, the decisions are becoming more complex and not getting any simpler. Second, these complexities argue for a variety of types of institutions and processes at all levels of government for making decisions on matters of revenues and expenditures both for one's own community and for the nation as a whole.

Intergovernmental Finance toward What End?

Consider the questions that are being raised here in slightly different terms for a moment. What are all these complex intergovernmental financial relations about and why do we care? At the level of the individual citizen, we care because they have a great deal to do with the question of who gets what and who pays. In more formal terms, and at the broad society-wide level, the government is involved in what are termed the *allocative function, the distribution function,* and the *stabilization function*. These functions include:

1. The provision for social goods, or the process by which total resource use is divided between private and social goods and by which the mix of social goods is chosen. This provision may be termed the *allocation function* of budgetary policy. . . .

2. Adjustment of the distribution of income and wealth to assure conformance with what society considers a fair or just state of distribution, here referred to as the *distribution function.*

3. The use of budget policy as a means of maintaining high employment, a reasonable degree of price level stability, and an appropriate rate of economic growth. There is also the objective of stability in the balance of payments. We refer to all these objectives as the *stabilization function.*[18]

It is not difficult to understand that sets of decisions must be made as to what should be provided by government in the form of public goods, rather than merely leaving those issues to the private markets. It is also obvious that there are times when the body politic decides, through its elected officials, that there should be a reordering of the costs and benefits of public activities with an intention to redistribute the burdens and rewards of the society. These are redistributive decisions that address inequities and needs of the poor or persons with special needs. Hence, progressive systems of taxation are intended to have a modest redistributive character to them in which it is quite clear that those who earn more are expected to carry an additional set of costs for social problems by paying higher tax rates. There are also various forms of assistance that are intended to help avoid a society in which the gulf between the rich and the poor is too severe and inflexible.

What is not so obvious to many people, however, is the stabilization function, in part perhaps because it is not so visible.

> The government intervenes to stabilize the imperfections in our economic system. . . . One simple illustration of government's stabilization function is our income tax system. When the economy is healthy, when the unemployment rate is low, wages tend to increase. As income goes up so do taxes. Conversely, when the economy declines, when more people become unemployed, the amount of income tax collected tends to go down. Also, when the economy declines, the federal government and state governments will automatically spend more for programs that put money into the hands of those people who are adversely affected by the worsening condition of the economy. These programs include unemployment compensation, AFDC, food stamps, and social security. Notice that income taxes automatically go down and government spending automatically goes up. These comprise stabilization functions of the government. They are designed to protect individuals from the severe hardships of economic fluctuations; they represent the recognition that our economy is not entirely self-regulating and that government must intervene to smooth out some of the side effects of economic change.[19]

That might seem a little confusing. The bottom line is that not all policies that help those facing hard times are intended only as social welfare programs. The debates over various income protection programs associated with the development of Social Security were not intended only to help people in need. Programs like unemployment insurance and various social security programs were also intended to help keep a floor under the purchasing power of the nation's citizens. Secretary of Labor Francis Perkins put the matter bluntly:

> This is truly legislation in the interest of the national welfare. We must recognize that if we are to maintain a healthy economy and thriving production, we need to maintain the standard of living of the lower income groups of our pop-

ulation who constitute 90 percent of our purchasing power. The President's Committee on Economic Security, of which I had the honor to be chairman, in drawing up the plan, was convinced that its enactment into law would not only carry us a long way toward the goal of economic security for the individual, but also a long way toward the promotion and stabilization of mass purchasing power without which the present economic system cannot endure.[20]

The jobs programs of the New Deal were viewed as help for the victims of the Great Depression, yes, but they were also seen as critical elements in the restoration of the marketplace and the economy it supports.

There continues, not surprisingly, to be serious debate about how all three functions—allocation, distribution (or redistribution), and stabilization—are carried out and whether government does too much or too little in each area. However, there is not really a serious question about whether they need to be done because few but the most extreme ideologues believe they could be abandoned altogether. Rather, the problem is to decide where in the inter-governmental system the decisions should be made, how the funds to support them should be raised, and how they should be spent.

Paul Peterson has argued that one way to approach this discussion is to posit a functional argument which runs as follows. The two primary tasks of government are redistributive and developmental. "Developmental programs provide the physical infrastructure necessary to facilitate a country's economic growth."[21] By contrast, "redistributive programs reallocate societal resources from the 'haves' to the 'have-nots.' . . . Most people regard at least a minimal level of redistribution as justifiable regardless of the developmental consequences. Most people also think that the higher the level of economic development, the more a society should redistribute some resources to the poor and the needy."[22] The task, then, is to determine which level of government is best able to meet these responsibilities.

Peterson asserted that local governments are best able to handle the development roles but that the national government is plainly the better choice to address the redistributive needs. For that reason, he cautioned against efforts to turn over welfare reform and other social welfare programs entirely to the states. While he plainly favored moving many of the developmental policies to the states and localities, he warned that this logic cannot be taken so far as to mean that the federal government no longer has an important role to play. After all, some states are far better able than others to fund developmental activities that are in the national interest. Besides, there are needs for some degree of national coordination in infrastructure development and problem solving.

If national mandates are deleted from developmental grants, then (unless they reduce fiscal disparities) there is hardly any justification for a national grant.

Put more strongly: a national grant should be made only when it is necessary to encourage state and local governments to cooperate in order to achieve some broader national objective, such as the reduction of environmental pollution or the achievement of a more coordinated transportation system. There is no reason why Congress should not fund mandates it thinks necessary, but a law banning any and all unfunded mandates could limit Congress's capacity to coordinate policy among the states.[23]

Alice Rivlin, former director of the Office of Management and Budget, wrote a book just as she was about to enter the Clinton administration in which she addressed many of the problems highlighted by Peterson. Although she agreed that a redefinition of intergovernmental relations with renewed attention to the importance of the roles of the state and local governments was critical, she started from somewhat different premises and had her own set of concerns about the conditions under which there could be a successful redefinition of fiscal federalism given contemporary realities.[24]

Rivlin identified at least five forces that must be understood in the contemporary economic and political environment. First, the globalization of the marketplace is a reality in a way that could not have been imagined in the days when the Great Society was created. Second, the pressure from citizens to have an economy that is providing an enhanced standard of living and quality of life has intensified. There is considerable frustration because there is a great deal of fear that this expectation will not be met and indeed that many people are sliding backward. Third, discussions of economic development must be considered in terms of the requirement for sustainable development. Sustainable development, of course, addresses social, environmental, and economic dimensions. In the economic arena,

Economic activity that fails to replace the capital it uses is also unsustainable. Accounting principles that apply to companies require recognition that capital assets wear out and must be replaced. However, public capital such as roads, bridges, schools, and government buildings is often allowed to wear out or fall into disrepair without people recognizing that the future national standard of living will be reduced by such shortsighted policies. The decay is often gradual and the cost spread widely.[25]

She also pointed out that development that is based on excessive debt and that prompts high inflation is equally unsustainable. Rivlin observed that the other essential reality of sustainability is that behavior that "damages the environment in ways that lower the standard of living in the future"[26] must be avoided.

Finally, Rivlin noted that there must be development of a sort in which all groups share. "The situation is especially worrisome if the people being left out of the general prosperity are clearly identifiable both to themselves and to others because of race, sex, ethnic origin, or some other visible characteristic."[27] She pointed out that whatever the cause, the economic and political reality was that while inequalities were declining up to the 1970s, the gap has widened in the 1980s and 1990s.

Like Peterson, Rivlin concluded that it is once again time to "divide the job" of governing and reconsider the responsibilities of the various levels. However, her prescription was somewhat more complex than Peterson's. She assigned tasks on a pragmatic basis. Thus, she would leave health care issues with the federal government on the argument that it is simply too large and pervasive a problem for any state to address. On the other hand, like Peterson, Rivlin argued that most of what she called the productivity agenda would be left to the states. The productivity agenda would consist of "reforms designed to revitalize the economy and raise incomes. These reforms would address needs such as education and skills training, child care, housing, infrastructure, and economic development."[28] She would move to the states from the federal government some of the many programs in the area of education and employment, but not all of them. For example, she would keep some higher education programs, particularly financing and research and development, and some other programs such as transportation at the national level, but most of housing policy and education would be left to the states. Other programs, however, like Aid to Families with Dependent Children (AFDC, commonly known as welfare) would remain a dual program, involving states and the federal government. Rivlin concluded that she could accomplish this move as well as balance the national budget by these changes, coupled with significant savings in the area of national defense, the development of health insurance taxes, and the movement of Medicaid to a "health insurance trust fund."

Assuming that these changes worked at the federal level, there is still the question of how the states would be able to address their increased burden. Rivlin called for the development of what she referred to as "common taxes," and then all states would share from the revenues among the states. The common taxes would address the competition among state and local governments that is currently based on driving down taxes to attract business and would provide a largely unrestricted pool of resources to finance the increased program responsibilities that come with devolving national programs to the state and local levels.

Rivlin recognized that there are differences in ability to pay, problems of inequality, and interstate competition. However, she argued that the shortcomings of the current system plus the attractiveness of having more resources to address new obligations would be attractive enough to entice states to support the common tax idea. She suggested that either the federal government could enact the taxes and then apportion them among the states or that states could come together and form interstate compacts, with congressional approval of course, that would invoke the common taxes.

Of course, none of these suggestions deal with the long-standing tensions between state and local governments or between the demands of larger cities and state legislatures dominated by rural and suburban legislators. That situation was not eased with the development of block grants to the states during the Reagan era since key decisions were left in the state capitols. After all, the prior experience with federal assistance had demonstrated the need to send some aid direct to the local governments without potential political roadblocks that had historically been posed by state legislatures.

The problems with all of these recommendations, however, are not merely economic but also political. We have no history that would suggest that states are prepared to give up their competitive struggles to advantage their own citizens. Indeed, the Constitution was written largely to address problems presented by competitive and discriminatory behavior by the states. There are those who contend that that is now ancient history, but recent behavior in the great battles over economic development do not suggest all that much change. One need only look at the way in which Nevada targeted California businesses during the 1990s and the manner in which the increasingly powerful sunbelt areas have resisted providing assistance to the so-called Rustbelt states to help rebuild their infrastructure in order to see clear examples of the continuing competition. The recent experiment under which states were to have solved the low-level nuclear waste disposal problem by interstate compacts does not give much confidence that interstate negotiations of compacts will be any easier or more effective than congressional debate as a way to address serious and divisive national issues.[29] Moreover, history and contemporary practice tell us that despite the many forces tending to homogenize state cultures into a more common national foundation, Daniel Elazar's conclusions that there are important differences remains largely true. States and localities around the nation may have many problems in common, but it is not at all clear that the same solutions are politically feasible in those different constituencies.

The contemporary effort in Congress and the White House is to think in terms of the use of block grants as the devices to move program responsibilities back to the states and to send some amount of financial support with them, while simultaneously shedding the budget burden of the federal government. In light of the growing momentum for renewed use of block grants, the U.S. General Accounting Office, in early 1995, reexamined the experience to date with the use of that device. It found a mixed history. On the one hand, the block grants initially offered states more flexibility in the use of funds, even if it was a somewhat smaller amount of money. Indeed, the

GAO found that the transition to block grants went relatively smoothly in those states that had operating programs that were a good match with the contours of the block grant.[30] There seemed to be some managerial efficiencies realized because of the flexibility available under the block grant. On the other hand, there were costs that could not be readily determined for the increased management effort required in the state agencies.[31]

There were some relatively obvious problems in the shift to block grants as well. First, the 1981 block grant reorganization resulted in a "12-percent overall federal funding reduction when the categorical programs were consolidated into the 1981 block grant programs."[32] In the initial years, the thirteen states studied by GAO met the reductions by transferring funds among block grants and by working to find state funds for short-term support. The difficulty is that overall aid to the states also declined dramatically during the decade, reducing the ability of the states to continue to meet the federal cuts. Another problem was the fact that block grants used funding formulas to determine which states got how much money. Initially, the 1981 block grants used the formulas from the preexisting categorical programs, but those formulas were not well suited to the economic conditions or the needs of particular states. Because the different block grants are designed to meet different needs and problems, each requires a unique funding formula, but those different formulas, when combined, can yield potentially inequitable funding arrangements for particular states. The other question that must be determined is whether the federal grants will say anything about substate distribution of funds.

Clearly, the major issue associated with block grants, apart from the overall level of funding relative to the tasks to be accomplished, is the question of accountability. By definition, increasing state discretion under the grant implied a loosening of accountability controls. Since there were fewer reporting requirements, there was little comparability of state data and it became quite difficult for Congress to conduct oversight over the programs. There emerged a certain irony in that state discretion led to more constraints by Congress.

> Paradoxically, accountability is critical to preserving state flexibility. When adequate program information is lacking, the 1981 block grant experience demonstrates that the Congress may become more prescriptive. For example, funding constraints were added that limited state flexibility, and, in effect, "recategorized" some of the block grants.[33]

There is one final lesson that states have learned from the experiences of block grants, revenue sharing, and categorical grants over the last twenty-five years. It is that it is both dangerous and difficult to plan on the basis of expectations of federal assistance. That problem is all the more complicated when, as the federal government has done on several occasions, the decision is made to change several variables at one time. Thus, most observers at the state and local level are viewing the present rhetoric about decentralization and reinvigoration of state and local government with some degree of skepticism. They know that, as in earlier "New Federalism" moves, the federal government is counting on the devolution of responsibilities to help cut federal spending. That means either that the states and localities will be picking up what the federal government drops or that they will have to take the political heat for terminating programs. They also know that there will be winners and losers as funding formulas are developed and modified.

States and localities are also aware of another critical fact the GAO pointed out in its block grant study. The broad-based program devolutions presently under consideration are very different from the earlier versions. Not only are the newer proposed block grant programs much larger and wider-ranging than their predecessors (they may amount to as much as $75 billion out of a current total of about $200 billion as compared to $6.5 billion out of $95 billion in the 1981 changes), but they are also very different in character.

> In addition, these block grant proposals include programs that are fundamentally different than those included in the 1981 block grants. For example, Aid to Families with Dependent Children provides direct cash assistance to individuals. Given that states tend to cut services and raise taxes during economic downturns to comply with balanced budget requirements, these cash assistance programs could experience funding reductions, which could impact vulnerable populations at the same time their number are likely to increase. In addition, some experts suggest that states have not always maintained state funding for cash assistance programs in times of fiscal strain.[34]

In developing countries, it has been extremely difficult to fashion intergovernmental aid systems in the senses described above. Instead, the aid often comes directly in the form of goods, services, or salaries for public employees. In some cases, there is little tradition of providing direct financial assistance to capitalize local efforts because the move to decentralization is relatively recent. There is also the stress of meeting international debt service obligations, burdens that drain off the available cash in many developing nations, leaving little to distribute internally.

New Stakeholders in the Changing Fiscal-Federalism Picture

The evolving nature of federalism is constantly generating new challenges for the financing and delivery of public services. New and creative intergovernmental arrangements of the kind described in Chapter 4 are developing in response to these challenges. Intergovernmental arrangements not only involve joint financing and production agreements with other jurisdictions, but often also include contracting-out for the production and delivery of public goods and services.

Joint production agreements include an expansion of arrangements for the intergovernmental provision of basic services such as fire protection, water, and sanitation. However, responses to market forces are leading to novel intergovernmental arrangements for pooling resources in the areas of debt management, investment, and risk management. Similarly, technological and knowledge utilization developments are fostering intergovernmental management activities in such areas as environmental protection and remediation, natural resource management, economic development, and tax base management.

Resource constraints are causing a proliferation of contract arrangements with nonprofit and for-profit organizations for the provision of government goods and services. In many instances, these organizations are jointly owned or controlled by several governmental bodies. More frequently they are independently chartered community-based organizations that have an interest in particular public services.

Both groups of administrative arrangements mentioned above have major implications for public administration. Technological advances not only affect the benefits incidence of many government goods and services but their tax bases as well. Advances in communication that have spawned such practices as electronic banking and investment, telemarketing, and home shopping make it extremely difficult to identify income and consumption. These advances can allow individuals hundreds of miles away to contribute to "congestion" and "crowding effects" that result as the consumption of government goods and services increases. New approaches to information sharing represent only one of many intergovernmental responses to these challenging issues.

Managing contract provision of public goods and services is another major challenge for public administrators. There are special management responsibilities that come with having commercial vendors or nonprofit organizations as providers of public services. In addition to the possibility of multiple vendors producing one service, a particular vendor may also be producing the same service for other jurisdictions, as is sometimes the case with solid waste collection or ambulance services. In either instance, the opportunity for benefit comparisons, whether intra- or interjurisdictional, represents a potential source of conflict. Contract management for providers of basic services requires more interactive involvement than those for auxiliary services. These contracts demand that special attention be given to issues of service equalization across service areas and among jurisdictions.

Issues of where individuals work and live will take on new dimensions in the twenty-first century. Questions of economies of scale and the definition of benefit regions will mean that administrators, and the elected officials they advise, will have to give more consideration to those who consume public goods and services. In that sense, the "reinventing government" movement and the "total quality management" movement have conditioned many state and local officials to think in terms of a consumer orientation to the delivery of services and to consider how contract arrangements can be employed to facilitate consumer satisfaction. There is an interesting question of what these dynamics will mean for intergovernmental relations as the uses of market tools tend to respond more to demand and resources rather than to the formal jurisdictional boundaries of communities.

The Importance of Changing Constitutional Infrastructure

Actually, many scholars of intergovernmental relations have seen the fiscal tools and approaches changing but more or less assumed that the constitutional foundations on which the contemporary system of intergovernmental relations is based is more or less fixed. Nothing could be farther from the truth. There are two reasons for the fact that the constitutional foundations are changing at the same time that other forces are in flux. First, because state and local government units are doing new things in new ways, there are new questions about how those activities relate to the constitutional bases of federalism. Second, although it seemed that the U.S. Supreme Court had definitively established the relationships among units of government and between the government and private sector, there have been new justices appointed over the past quarter century who take the position that these questions are far from settled. Consider some of the issues that can best be described as dynamic at the turn of the century.

For one thing, the constitutional situation is different when government acts as a market regulator as compared to situations in which government becomes a market participant. When state or local government is a market regulator, there are a number of questions that must be considered. They include issues of the taking of property versus regulation, the questions of how much authority is left when the federal government deregulates, the situations that arise when state or local governments try to address their own problems protected from national demands, the issue of taxation of contemporary businesses, and the question of the impairment of the obligations of contract.

The question whether the community is engaged in regulation or is it taking property is a critical distinction. The normal theory is that when government takes property, usually through eminent domain, it must compensate the owner for the loss. It can take property for many reasons, including aesthetics, and it can use its eminent domain powers for redevelopment projects even when a private developer is involved. "We do not sit to determine whether a particular housing project is or is not desirable. The concept of the public welfare is broad and inclusive. The values it represents are spiritual as well as physical, aesthetic as well as monetary. It is within the power of the legislature to determine that the community should be beautiful as well as healthy, spacious as well as clean, well-balanced as well as carefully patrolled."[35]

However, regulation is the price we all pay for being able to live together and maintain a quality of life. Thus, a local community can force owners to cut down diseased trees that could infect other trees in the area, and this action is not considered to be a taking of property. On the other hand, when there is no specific danger that rises to the level of what could be considered a nuisance, the Supreme Court has suggested that the regulatory intrusion may be sufficient to term the action a taking.[36]

There is an intense debate ongoing over just how much government may regulate before its actions interfere so much with the use of private property that there is really a taking. More recently, the Court warned that it would look carefully at the use of land use regulations that sought to make developers take a particular responsibility for the problems of community planning and services. Specifically, the Court determined that a Tigard, Oregon, community development code amounted to a taking of property. The code required a 15-percent open space requirement, a demand for developers to dedicate land for pedestrian pathways, and, in certain places, a requirement for a greenway adjoining the flood plain.[37] The Court warned:

> In evaluating petitioner's claim, we must first determine whether the "essential nexus" exists between the "legitimate interest" and the permit condition exacted by the city. . . . If we find that a nexus exists, we must decide the required degree of connection between the exactions and project impact of the proposed development.[38]

The dissenters pointed out that the Court's majority had shifted the presumption from the idea that government actions are assumed to be lawful to a situation under which local governments are faced with a very substantial burden of proof if they wish to be able to carry out essential land use planning efforts that will both serve the needs of the community and protect the community from the effects of a variety of problems from flood to earthquake.

These may seem like fairly arcane technical cases about when government has to pay a property owner to achieve state and local goals. They would be important even if they were no more than that, since there are many regulations at all levels of government that invariably affect the value of property. If state and local governments are required to pay for even a significant part of them, we will have an impossible situation. However, these cases have implications far wider than it may at first appear. Building permit requirements and zoning restrictions have a great deal to do with the value of the tax base in their communities. The planned nature of a community that ensures open space, guards against development that could cause flooding or traffic congestion, and protects residential sections from commercial encroachment all affect the value of the property in the community and therefore the kinds of tax revenue that the local governments can achieve. The quality of life in communities of a state also affect decisions by potential residents and businesses about whether to move to, remain in, or depart from a state. Decisions one way or the other affect the full range of intergovernmental decisions that can be made by the state and its subdivisions.

Of course, the range of decisions that states and localities can take is related to the powers of the federal government, for while there are areas of concurrent power, such as the ability to tax, there are plainly fields in which the national government can preempt decision making by state and local governments. Most of what the federal government does in domestic policy is based either on the commerce power and the necessary and proper clause or on the taxing and spending powers. While there had been a debate about just how far the federal government could go under the commerce clause, that discussion seemed to have been settled by the mid-1960s. In a case upholding the Civil Rights Act of 1964 on the basis of the commerce power, the Court sent word that Congress would be able to use that provision of the Constitution to reach most areas of national life. The Court said that the test for determining whether the commerce power had been abused was in two parts: "(1) whether Congress had a rational basis for finding that racial discrimination by motels affects commerce, (2) if it had such a basis, whether the means it selected to eliminate the evil are reasonable and appropriate."[39] Put in those terms, there seemed to be little one could imagine that could not be regulated within that standard. Congress made an argument that it should be able to adopt a criminal law covering the carrying of firearms in schools on the ground that it had the power to deal with the costs and other impacts of crime on the nation. That was more than the Court was willing to tolerate. In a 1995 ruling, the Court struck down the federal law.[40] It seems that there is at least a possibility now that states and localities may be able to keep the federal government out of some of their activities. On the other hand, it also means that Congress may be prohibited from adopting legislation that state and local administrators may find essential because the problems simply seem too large and complex to address without help. Certainly, the presence of guns in school seemed to many to be that kind of problem until the Supreme Court ruled otherwise.

Of course, the federal government has used the taxing and spending powers to reach matters that seemed to be beyond its commerce power jurisdiction in such areas as education and health. The frustration is that those federal dollars come to the state and local governments with a whole set of strings attached. Thus, when the federal government attached a requirement for a legal drinking age of twenty-one to federal highway funds legislation, there were challenges. The Court upheld the statute but set forth four requirements that must be met by such programs.[41] The programs must be "in pursuit of the general welfare"; conditions must be unambiguous so that the states "exercise their choice knowingly"; the program must be related "to the federal interest in particular national projects or programs"; and the act may not be barred by another provision of the Constitution.

If a decision is made at the federal level to move away from categorical grant programs, with many requirements, toward block grants, with few stipulations, there may very well be a change in the range of federal power. As the level of federal funding declines, the willingness of states and localities to challenge efforts at control from Washington are likely to increase, particularly in an era when the Supreme Court appears more favorably disposed to that kind of attack than at any time in modern history.

That willingness to challenge may extend to states who feel coerced in other respects as well. One such example is the case of the federal law governing the handling of low-level nuclear waste. In that case, states asked Congress to be allowed to address the matter by forming interstate compacts to solve the problem, states unwilling to enter such a compact being obligated to take care of their own waste. The Supreme Court struck down the law, finding that while the Congress might have regulated the waste directly, it could not force the states to use their regulatory authority to do so.[42] The irony is that the states managed to kill the precise policy that they had asked Congress to adopt.

Prior to these cases, few would have anticipated that limits would be placed on Congress in any of these areas. On the other hand, there remain many constraints on the states and localities. Some of these constraints have emerged recently in ways that some state and local officials did not anticipate and have found troublesome.

One of the important questions concerns what happens when the federal government deregulates and states wish to step into the breach. Thus, state attorneys general thought they had more than adequate authority to step in and regulate what they saw as deceptive trade practices in the sale of airline tickets. The Supreme Court ruled that they did not because, although it never said so in so many words, the comprehensive nature of the federal deregulation statute preempted the states from taking action even though the national government did not wish to take any action itself.[43] Given the range of commercial activities that have been undertaken—and the decision to deregulate many of those activities—state and local governments cannot be certain where and how they will be able to step in to protect their citizens and their markets.

A related problem came up when the national government deregulated natural gas.[44] The problem was that the state of Kansas both regulated sales of natural gas within the state and was itself a purchaser of gas. When the federal government moved to deregulate, the state followed by adjusting its own rules. However, some of those involved in pending contracts sued, challenging the state's action as an impairment of the obligations of contract. The Supreme Court found it necessary to engage in a relative complex analysis:

1. Is there "a substantial impairment of a contractual relationship?"

2. "The severity of the impairment is said to increase the level of scrutiny to which the legislation will be subjected."

3. "We are to consider whether the industry the complaining party has entered has been regulated in the past."

4. "If the state regulation constitutes a substantial impairment, the State, in justification, must have a significant and legitimate public purpose behind the regulation."

5. "Once a legitimate public purpose has been identified, the next inquiry is whether the adjustment of the rights and responsibilities of contracting parties [is based] upon reasonable conditions and [is] of a character appropriate to the public purpose justifying [the legislation's] adoption."[45]

What this means is that the state and local officials need to have federal officials give serious consideration to the intergovernmental implications of their decision about the marketplace. Even the decision to step away from regulation has important impacts on the states and localities.

State governments and localities have the ability to adopt policies affecting interstate commerce, but they may not attempt to wall themselves off from national problems in the process. That is important because it is very difficult to think of the market as local. Even many of the stores on Main Street are owned by firms in other states and sometimes even other nations. Therefore, when local governments seek to integrate business and community life in their decision making, they may find themselves confronted with a constitutional infrastructure that is interpreted as if the market still looked like it did a half century ago. Thus, the state of Alabama and a Michigan county were told that they could not restrict shipments into their waste facilities of solid or toxic waste from outside their state or community.[46] North Dakota was told that it could not tax a large mail-order office supply firm, even though it was one of the largest suppliers of office equipment in the state, because the firm did not have a warehouse or other physical facility in the state.[47] A state was told that it could not tax a corporation from another state that sold stock of a firm that operated within the state to finance an acquisition of a third firm.[48]

The questions about taxation are important and difficult in part because of what is called *tax migration* and *tax overlap*. The ability of taxes to migrate from one jurisdiction to another became a more pronounced concern in recent years because of developments in telemarketing, video shopping, home-based employment, and other commercial arrangements that transcend jurisdictional boundaries and normal methods of tax assessment and collection. In these settings, the identification of income generation and consumption is more difficult. Activities that result in income generation and consumption can migrate into and out of jurisdictions without notice. They may also be highly responsive to tax pricing. The prevalence of and opportunities for tax migration increase at the lower levels of government because they are limited to action within one jurisdiction and because they have few means by which to monitor and address these business flows.

State and national government tax bases are also vulnerable to the effects of migration. The geographic correlation between where individuals generate their income and where they live is decreasing. The same is true of consumption. These activities can take place via telephone and computer networks thousands of miles from where one lives. What applies to individuals is true for firms as well. Many American firms were incorporated under the laws of Delaware or New Jersey because they have historically had the weakest corporation control laws. It matters mightily where a firm is incorporated because that state retains considerable authority over the firm.[49] However, these firms operate all over the country as well as around the world, and there are limits to what those other jurisdictions can do with respect to corporations operating in their jurisdiction without running afoul of the commerce clause or other constitutional restrictions.

The issue here is not a detailed debate about the constitutional law behind these discussions, but rather the idea that states and localities have an interesting intergovernmental problem. They are attempting to operate their governments and to provide all of the infrastructure needed to support both public sector and private sector activities. Traditional ideas of taxation and business regulation assumed that there were ways that those state and local governments could obtain the resources needed and exercise sufficient regulatory authority to maintain their communities and their economies. But the economy is changing, and it is not clear just how the constitutional interpretations of recent years will affect the foundations of intergovernmental relations under modern economic and social conditions.

Finally, this set of questions about state and local governments in the future is made more complex because these governments are increasingly acting not merely as regulators of the marketplace but also as market participants. Relatively little consideration has been given to this growing phenomenon, but we have some indications of the kinds of questions that can be anticipated.

The Supreme Court has recognized a difference for some purposes between situations in which government units act as market participants rather than market regulators. In a Massachusetts case, the Court rejected a challenge under the interstate commerce clause to a city requirement that 50 percent of all employees on city construction projects had to be hired locally. The Court wrote that "when a state or local government enters the market as a participant, it is not subject to the restraints of the commerce clause. If the city is a market participant, then the Commerce Clause establishes no barrier to conditions such as those which the city demands for participation. . . . Insofar as the city expended its own funds in entering into construction projects it was a market participant."[50] Well, that would seem to settle the matter, but there is more. Camden, New Jersey, adopted a policy similar to the Boston requirement and was promptly challenged, but on different grounds. The Supreme Court, in that case, decided only a year after the Massachusetts matter, found that while the local hiring requirement did not violate the interstate commerce clause, it did violate the privileges and immunities clause.[51]

States have found themselves in similar quandaries. The state of South Dakota operated a cement plant and gave preference to in-state buyers. The Supreme Court rejected a challenge by an out-of-state firm brought on commerce clause grounds. Justice Blackmun wrote: "Here the state acts as market participant rather than as market regulator. Such policies, while perhaps protectionist in a loose sense, reflect the essential and patently unobjectionable purpose of state government—to serve the citizens of the State."[52] However, the Court put boundaries around that broad language in a later ruling. The case involved a challenge to an Alaska requirement, placed into timber contracts, that called for the initial processing of the raw lumber in Alaska before it could be removed from the state. The Court found that the Alaska contract requirement did violate the commerce clause.[53] The Court agreed that the state could attach some normal business conditions to the contract and yet remain a market participant outside the constraints of the commerce clause. However, the state was not allowed to disguise attempts at market regulation with the guise of market participation.

The question of government's role as market participant also arises with respect to the relationships of state and local governments to federal regulation. In a number of cases during the late 1930s and 1940s, the Court ruled that when a public organization engages in market-type activity, it is subject to taxation[54] and regulation[55] by the federal government in the same manner as a business. In the early years, the discussion was about the specific distinction between activities considered proprietary and those considered governmental. More recently, the Court rejected that distinction as the primary factor. In a case involving a federal tax to support air traffic control that was applied to state aircraft, the Court said: "[Where] the subject of tax is a natural and traditional source of federal revenue and where it is inconceivable that such a revenue measure could ever operate to preclude traditional state activities, the tax is valid."[56] The Court has held repeatedly that regulation could reach state and local activities as well.[57]

Then, in 1976, Justice Rehnquist was able to attract a shaky five person majority to suggest that even though an activity of state and local government might be within the commerce power of Congress, there are some limits on that power implied by the Tenth Amendment.[58] It was clear to anyone who read the concurring opinion of Justice Blackmun, who provided the pivotal vote, that the *Usery* decision limiting the reach of the Fair Labor Standards Act with respect to local government employees was in trouble from the day it was written. Over the next few years, the Court issued several rulings narrowing the idea of immunity of states and localities from the national government. Finally, in 1985, the Court reversed the *Usery* ruling, restoring the federal authority to regulate state and local government practices to where it had been prior to 1976.[59] It was, not surprisingly, a disappointment to many local government administrators, but not one that should have come as any surprise.

Thus, the Court has identified differences between government as market regulator and market participant for some purposes but not for others. However, these cases do not begin to address the wide range of issues that arise when government becomes both a purchaser and a vendor of services. Nor do they tell us very much about what changes may come through judicial interpretation in the constitutional framework of intergovernmental relations in the twenty-first century.

There are many other unanswered questions that concern both constitutional powers and their limits and constitutional rights and liberties when states and localities act by contract with private firms. Experiments with contract-operated correctional facilities and contract social service providers are raising issues about the point at which state or local cooperation with the private sector means that there is state action within the meaning of constitutional law. That is, at what point are contractors acting as state agents and to what degree are they covered by various accountability devices designed to be used with respect to public agencies? We have yet to hear much from the Supreme Court on this point.

The concern here is not that the interpretations rendered by the Supreme Court with respect to state and local governments are incorrect. Indeed, most of them follow long-standing principles rather than breaking new ground. Nor do most administrators care about the arcane debates among constitutional lawyers. For most public managers, the point should be that it is not enough merely to think about changing individual policies through legislation. It is not enough for Congress or the White House to move to "send programs back to the states," as the language is often framed. It is crucial to have leaders in Washington realize that there are constitutional constraints to what states and localities can do and how they can interact with each other and with the private sector.

Conclusion

Contemporary intergovernmental relations are a long way from the simplistic notions of federalism held by many citizens. It is not enough to speak only about the structures and processes associated with federalism. Rather, public managers must be concerned about the nature of the many relationships and interdependencies that exist among the different kinds of organizations that must work together in order for the public sector to deliver the high-quality services needed by its citizens at affordable prices. It must also be concerned with how those services are financed, which means not merely through the most common taxes but through a wide variety of sources of funding, a significant portion of which comes from the federal government.

What is also clear is that there are efforts under way to make major changes in the system of intergovernmental relations. Some of these changes are in line with the general international trend toward deregulation, while others are driven by the press to achieve a balanced budget and still others are motivated by ideological opposition to federal programs. It is crucial for public administrators to watch the shape of the legislation that is making the changes, but it is also important to think into the future about the funding stream that will be used to finance public programs once the federal government alters its current approaches to aid to states and localities. Finally, it is important as well to look back to the legal context of intergovernmental relations. First, we need to consider in greater detail the implications of increasing activity by states and localities as market participants as well as market regulators. We also need to understand what changes in the federal government will mean for the options available to state and local governments.

Notes

[1]Deil Wright, *Understanding Intergovernmental Relations,* 3rd ed. (Pacific Grove, CA: Brooks/Cole, 1988), 65–112.

[2]Deil S. Wright and Harvey L. White, *Federalism and Intergovernmental Relations* (Washington, DC: American Society for Public Administration, 1984), 1–22.

[3]Bernard Schwartz, *Super Chief* (New York: New York University Press, 1980), 18.

[4]Wright, *op. cit.*, 78.

[5]Michael Reagan, *The New Federalism* (New York: Oxford University Press, 1972).

[6]Paul E. Peterson, *The Price of Federalism* (Washington, DC: Brookings, 1995), 77–78.

[7]U.S. General Accounting Office, "Block Grants: Characteristics, Experience, and Lessons Learned," GAO/HEHS-95-74, February 1995.

[8]Dwight Waldo, *The Administrative State* (New York: The Ronald Press, 1948).

[9]Wright, *op. cit.*, 121.

[10]Quoted in *ibid.*

[11]See *San Antonio Independent School District v. Rodriguez*, 411 U.S. 1 (1973).

[12]This approach was upheld by the Supreme Court in *Stewart Machine Co. v. Davis*, 301 U.S. 548 (1937).

[13]David Rusk, *Cities Without Suburbs* (Washington, DC: Woodrow Wilson Center Press, 1993).

[14]See Vincent Ostrum, *The Intellectual Crisis in American Public Administration*, 2nd ed. (Tuscaloosa, AL: University of Alabama Press, 1989); James M. Buchanan and Gordon Tullock, *The Calculus of Consent* (Ann Arbor, MI: University of Michigan Press, 1962).

[15]David Osborne and Ted Gaebler, *Reinventing Government* (New York: Penguin, 1993).

[16]See generally Richard A. Musgrave and Peggy B. Musgrave, *Public Finance Theory and Practice*, 2nd ed. (New York: McGraw Hill, 1976), 613–636.

[17]*Ibid.*

[18]*Ibid.*, 6–7.

[19]Jeffrey Straussman, *Public Administration* (New York: Holt, Rinehart and Winston, 1981), 17–18.

[20]Francis Perkins, "The Principles of Social Security," in Howard Zinn, ed., *New Deal Thought* (Indianapolis, IN: Bobbs-Merrill, 1966), 280.

[21]Peterson, *op. cit.*, 17.

[22]*Ibid.*

[23]*Ibid.*, 189.

[24]Alice M. Rivlin, *Reviving the American Dream: The Economy, the States, and the Federal Government* (Washington, DC: Brookings, 1992).

[25]*Ibid.*, 39.

[26]*Ibid.*, 40.

[27] *Ibid.*, 38.

[28] *Ibid.*, 118.

[29] *New York v. United States,* 505 U.S. 144 (1992).

[30] GAO, *op. cit.*, 32.

[31] *Ibid.*, 34.

[32] *Ibid.*, 34.

[33] *Ibid.*, 42.

[34] *Ibid.*, 47.

[35] *Berman v. Parker,* 348 U.S. 26, 33 (1954).

[36] See *Lucas v. South Carolina Coastal Council,* 120 L.Ed2d 798 (1992).

[37] *Dolan v. City of Tigard,* 129 L.Ed2d 304 (1994).

[38] *Ibid.*, 317.

[39] *Heart of Atlanta Motel v. United States,* 379 U.S. 241 (1964).

[40] *United States v. Lopez,* 131 L.Ed.2d 626 (1995).

[41] *South Dakota v. Dole,* 483 U.S. 203 (1987).

[42] *New York v. United States, op. cit.*

[43] *Morales v. TWA,* 504 U.S. 374 (1992).

[44] *Energy Reserves Group v. Kansas Power & Light,* 459 U.S. 400 (1983).

[45] *Ibid.*

[46] *Fort Gratiot Landfill v. Michigan Department of Natural Resources,* 504 U.S. 353 (1992); *Chemical Waste Management v. Hunt,* 504 U.S. 334 (1992).

[47] *Quill Corp. v. North Dakota,* 504 U.S. 298 (1992).

[48] *Allied Signal v. Director, Division of Taxation,* 504 U.S. 768 (1992).

[49] *CTS Corp. v. Dynamics Corp.,* 481 U.S. 69 (1987).

[50] *White v. Massachusetts Council of Construction Workers,* 460 U.S. 204 (1983).

[51] *United Building Trades Council v. Cambden,* 465 U.S. 208 (1984).

[52] *Reeves v. Stake,* 447 U.S. 429 (1980).

[53] *South Central Timber Development v. Wunnicke,* 467 U.S. 82 (1984).

[54] *New York v. United States,* 326 U.S. 572 (1946).

[55] *United States v. California,* 297 U.S. 175 (1936).

[56] *Massachusetts v. United States,* 435 U.S. 444 (1978).

[57] *Maryland v. Wirtz,* 392 U.S. 183 (1968); *Fry v. United States,* 421 U.S. 542 (1975).

[58] *National League of Cities v. Usery,* 426 U.S. 833 (1976).

[59] *Garcia v. San Antonio Metro Transit* 469 U.S. 528 (1985).

Chapter 6

Public Policy in Administration

Among the many things that governments do, one of the most important is to make policy. Much of public administration is focused on the implementation of policy, a good deal of which is done by elected officials but a substantial amount of which is carried out by administrative agencies themselves. Public policy can appear to be a very simple statement of the intentions of the people expressed through their elected officials, but it is in reality considerably more complex. It could be legislation, but it could also be administrative regulations or an executive order issued by the president or a governor. It may be the result of a referendum campaign in which the citizens vote directly to create a specific policy. Policy can even come in the form of a consistent pattern and practice of behavior that may never have been reduced to a rule or a statute. It is the result of myriad decisions and actions that government takes as well as many positions and symbolic stances that the government assumes.[1]

Public policy is inextricably rooted in politics or power relations between the federal government, interest groups, local governments, states, regions, countries, and international organizations.[2] In that sense, the study of public policy is not only about the substance of the policies themselves, but also concerns the process by which policy choices are made. Since there are so many institutions, groups, and individuals who play important roles in the policy process, the study of it by definition requires some degree of care and a tolerance for ambiguity—both important qualities for any professional administrator in any country or international institution.

As with all of the subjects that have been addressed throughout the book, the internationalization of public policy making represents a set of unique challenges to traditional approaches.[3] Most of the policy literature has had a domestic focus, but, for reasons discussed in earlier chapters, that is not an adequate scope of reference for the situation confronting modern public managers. Policy choices taken in China, India, and other nations affect far more people than live in the United States. Policy problems facing decision

157

makers in Mexico City and Sao Paulo concern far more residents than even those complex situations confronting those who must govern New York, Los Angeles, Atlanta, or Chicago. Decisions made in Tokyo, Berlin, Dakka, Riyadh, and Brasilia affect life in the United States.

On the other hand, it is extremely important to consider not merely what happens at the international level or in a nation's capital, but also to think in intergovernmental terms. As Chapters 4 and 5 indicated, even in countries that have a centralized form of government, as compared with the federalism one finds in the United States, the task of public administration is truly one that crosses boundaries and involves cooperative and competitive interactions with a wide variety of public sector organizations, from the smallest local government to international institutions like the United Nations or World Bank. Even so, much of the public policy literature has tended to focus almost exclusively at the national level.

There is one other warning that is appropriate concerning the public policy literature. It has to do with issues of bias and perspective. Much of the modern version of public policy literature grew out of frustration in the 1970s with the fact that policies in operation seemed generally to fall short of the lofty goals stated when those policies were adopted. Thus, much of the emphasis has been on policy failures, and those failures have often been attributed to malevolent or manipulative public administrators out to undermine the political process.[4] Perhaps not surprisingly, such criticisms have often been levelled by commentators whose knowledge of public administration was, to be charitable, extremely limited and often based on little or no empirical inquiry into public administration issues. In short, there is a good deal of ideological and process bias in what is said about how policy is made and implemented.

Third, much of the public policy literature has the character of "Monday morning quarterbacking." Instead of looking at the situation confronting public managers as various decision points were reached and the policy in question was actually working its way through the process, there is a tendency to look backward with what is often referred to in the vernacular as "20/20 hindsight" and lambast administrators for the ultimate failures of policy. To be blunt, that sort of an approach tends to give us little useful knowledge that can help us, as administrators, do a better job in the future. Nevertheless, we must try to learn lessons about policy—as well as the processes by which it is developed and implemented—from the problems we see along the way from grand idea to day-to-day operations. It is to these tasks that we turn in Chapters 6 and 7. This chapter will emphasize the overall policy process and will consider in particular what takes place from the point at which a problem is identified and the policy process is triggered into action through the point at which a policy has been adopted by the legislature or whatever other authority ultimately issues it. Chapter 7 will emphasize the implementation and evaluation that takes place after adoption. These chapters examine these subjects with a particular concern for the perspective of the administrator acting in real time.

Public Policy: What Is It and What Is Its Relationship to the Rest of Public Administration?

Public policy is one of those terms that seems obvious enough until we take a close look at it, at which point it turns out to be relatively complicated. It should also not be surprising, therefore, that understanding the role of policy analysis, implementation, evaluation, and the like also require some degree of care. The first step is to be as clear as possible about the concepts most often used to discuss the subject.

The Central Concepts of Public Policy

What gives rise to a public policy decision is what we term an _issue_. An issue is merely a problem on the public agenda. A policy is an answer to the problem. It is _an_ answer rather than _the_ answer because there can be many possible answers for any given issue. Thus, when we speak of public policy with respect to homelessness, there is clearly no one single answer. The same is true of hazardous waste policy, education, health care, or child development.

Indeed, when a legislature adopts a policy in such complex fields, the legislation often has several different kinds of answers or policies as part of the overall package. We refer to this phenomenon as a policy mix. In the environmental example, the legislation might include regulations governing the handling of toxic waste; a permitting and tracking system for monitoring compliance with those regulations; a potential liability for toxic waste handlers who violate the law, which is both an enforcement tool and an incentive for possible violators to bring themselves into compliance; and it may even include the opportunity for grants to improve the handling and disposal of wastes. While we would often speak of this as a policy because it came from a single piece of legislation, it is in truth a mix of policy tools, all of which are related but each of which is intended to achieve a different specific purpose.

Policy mixes are constructed from a variety of policy tools. These tools include the full range of possible responses that a government can take to a problem.[5] They could involve legal prohibitions, regulation, taxation, a system of fees or fines, grants-in-aid, incentive systems, information disclosure and monitoring, direct government action such as the provision of services, or the use of government contracts to leverage action.

Of course, there are many different tools that can be combined in any number of policy mixes. Which seem most popular vary from problem to problem and over time. Thus, the contemporary policy world frowns on the use of regulation and encourages the use of market-oriented tools such as incentive systems.

Policies emerge over time in different packages of policy mixes. At any given time there are many issues that are the subject of action in the public policy process in a given field. In the field of education in recent years there have been issues associated with violence in the schools; multicultural sensitivity; inclusive education for all children, particularly for children with special needs; educational accountability issues concerned with ensuring learning outcomes; home schooling; religious activities in the schools; educational finance, including the use of voucher programs; and the reexamination of the respective roles of the state and federal government in educational operations. These are issues in what is called the *education policy space.*

A policy space is a field in which there are a variety of related issues and policies. There are two reasons why those involved in public policy use the policy space concept. First, the policies in a given space are related in one way or another and often have important effects on one another. Thus, decisions about the form of school finance dramatically affect not only responses to children with special needs but also accountability programs aimed at providing measurable learning outcomes. Taking action on one set of issues has consequences for the others, often quite direct consequences. Second, there are a variety of institutions, groups, and individuals who have interests in these kinds of issues and tend to remain involved with the policy process in that policy space over time. Thus, in the education arena, there are state government organizations, the U.S. Department of Education, associations of school boards, associations of school superintendents, teachers' unions, the parent groups, child advocacy organizations, textbook publishers, and education committees of Congress, all of whom have an ongoing interest in education policy. We refer to this set of stakeholders as a policy community.

Policy communities are also sometimes referred to as policy networks or policy subsystems, but, whatever they are called, the idea is the same. These people tend to remain involved in the education policy space over time, are considerably more attentive to policy making in that field than the public at large or even other players in the general public policy arena, and consequently tend to be more knowledgeable about activities in the field. Thus, by the time the news media begins to alert the public that there is a debate over a pending policy, the stakeholders in the relevant policy community have usually already weighed in with their perspectives and demands. Of equal importance is the fact that the people within a policy community tend to deal with one another regularly and over time. Therefore, members come to have understood patterns of interaction and even unwritten rules of the game as to how they should and should not behave. These members of a given policy community are not the only ones who can influence policy, but because of their ongoing involvement, knowledge, interest, and patterns of influence, they are most often extremely important.

Public Policy and the Public Interest

Finally, it is very important to consider the word *public* in public policy. There are many types of policies. Businesses have their own policies, and certainly not-for-profit organizations of all types make policies for their members governing their interactions with others. What makes public policy different is that it is an authoritative "choice made on behalf of other people."[6] Policies may be directed at private behavior, like unacceptable business practices, or at the operation of public organizations, but they presumably are aimed at achieving the public interest.

Of course, there is often a great deal of argument as to just which activities are purely private, which are public, and precisely how to define the public interest. Some critics have gone so far as to suggest that there is no such thing as the public interest, at least not in any meaningful sense.[7] Some economists contend that, since only individual choices are rational, the public interest cannot be determined by a group but only by the dynamics of the marketplace in which individual preferences are revealed and out of which broad social trends emerge. Of course, Charles Lindblom has argued that if one accepted that idea, then democracy is impossible, for it assumes that people can and should come together to make choices as to how they are to be governed and those choices must concern issues about which the market is often neither helpful nor informative.[8]

Still, the definition of what is in the common good is susceptible to debate.[9] Indeed, disputes over how to define the public interest with respect to particular issues and how to craft a policy to achieve it are the critical ingredients in the public policy formation process.[10] It is about competing sets of different values. It is at the very core of what we call politics.

Even so, it would be extremely difficult for one to be a professional public administrator and not believe that there is something called the public interest that is distinct from narrowly defined private interests. Certainly, the framers of most governments, including that of the United States, take that idea as the starting point for constructing constitutions and the laws that guide the governments they create.

When we speak of public and private policy, we often use the terms public goods and private goods. Private action is usually taken to achieve private goods, that is, results that have a special value for the person or organization involved, anything from money to having one's own way. Normally, that private good is exclusive in the sense that the benefits go to one or a few beneficiaries and not to everyone. Thus private business is not concerned with achieving the public good but with its own private good, the so-called bottom line. In making decisions, it is making private choices that govern no one else. The classic example is that the person who decides which kind of automobile to purchase is not making a choice for anyone else.

Of course such private choices can certainly have consequences for others. Thus, when a business decides that it can make more money by moving a plant from one state to another, the consequences in terms of unemployment and damage to the local economy of the community losing the facility may be so severe that some kind of concerted community action, a policy decision, may be called for by that community. Still, the decision by the business is a private decision, not a public policy. But when the decisions concern public goods—matters that affect many or all of us, such as clean air or public health, so that the results of decisions about these subjects are authoritative and nonexclusive in that we share the impact—these are matters of public policy.

Public-Policy Analysis

There is one other concept that should be understood because it is used in so many different ways by very different people. Policy analysis is a field of study, an activity, and a way of referring to a political process.

We can trace policy analysis, or policy studies as it is sometimes called, back many years. In the United States it began to emerge in common political parlance in the late 1940s and early 1950s.[11] The contemporary field of policy studies really emerged from the late 1960s into the 1970s. In the U.S. and elsewhere scholars began to express frustration with the fact that social scientists had been so busy trying to be scientific (meaning objective, theoretical, empirical, and methodologically sophisticated [read quantitative]) that they had become irrelevant with respect to many of the most important problems affecting society.[12] There was a growing desire to use the best of social science, including its systematic and rigorous techniques of inquiry, to produce useful answers to real problems.[13] Efforts were undertaken to build centers for the study of policy and to design graduate education programs to train students in policy studies. On the academic side, a group of scholars at the University of California at Berkeley led by Wildavsky, Pressman, and others launched ambitious studies into the implementation of policy to learn why such positive policies as were developed during the late 1960s did not seem to produce the expected results.[14]

There were three component parts of the policy studies movement. First, there was the study of the policy process itself. Indeed, the Berkeley group focused on the implementation portion of that process. The second element of the field was policy analysis techniques. Thus, several universities, such as the University of Michigan and the Kennedy School of Government at Harvard, moved away from public administration and designed new units to launch public policy programs with a strong focus on analytic techniques, with particular interest in the use of tools of economic analysis. The third aspect of the field is the study of particular policy spaces. Thus, clusters of people developed whose principal interests were in transportation, environment, health care, and education, to name but a few.

As is often true of third party movements, as soon as they are fully developed and appear popular, the more established parties tend to absorb them. Indeed, both political science and public administration moved rapidly to take over the policy studies movement. The momentum was so strong that, by the late 1970s, some argued that the core of public administration had been transformed by it.[15] Many other fields, from education to anthropology, focused on policy issues relevant to their fields and moved to develop policy analysis specialties in their areas. So powerful was the lure of working with the design and assessment of policies that some fields, like education, found policy coming to take a dominant role in their field.

The point of the reinvigoration of policy studies was not, however, merely to create more scholarship but to transform knowledge into action or at least to inform action with analysis. According to Dubnick and Bardes, public policy analysis is "the application of problem solving techniques to questions concerning (1) expressed intentions of government in relation to a public problem, and, (2) those actions government officials take (or avoid) in attaining those objectives."[16] The demand for policy analysts to advise policymakers was so high that, by the late 1970s, there were real concerns about whether policy analysts had become important players in the political arena in their own right by virtue of the expertise they claimed to possess.[17] Some interest groups shifted their emphasis from standard lobbying techniques to policy analysis, in part to make their arguments seem more scientific and objective but also to counter the analyses that were being prepared in the executive departments and congressional staff operations. In the late 1970s and 1980s this trend changed somewhat as the emphasis moved more specifically to policy analysis as economic analysis.

President Carter provided the seeds for this important shift as he brought more economists into government, in part because of his move toward deregulation and partly because of an interest in the use of microeconomic decision tools like cost/benefit analysis. In fact, Carter, for the first time, mandated that all executive branch agencies that were about to issue new regulations had to undertake cost/benefit analyses. His successor took the movement even further, demanding that in order for a new rule to be issued by an executive branch agency there had to be a demonstration of a significant benefit over cost. In Executive Order 12291, Reagan required that:

> In promulgating new regulations, reviewing existing regulations, and developing legislative proposals concerning regulations, all agencies, to the extent permitted by law, shall adhere to the following requirement:
>
> (a) Administrative decisions shall be based on adequate information concerning the need for and consequences of proposed government action;
>
> (b) Regulatory action shall not be undertaken unless the potential benefits to society for the regulation outweigh the potential costs to society;
>
> (c) Regulatory objectives shall be chosen to maximize the net benefits to society;
>
> (d) Among alternative approaches to any given regulatory objective, the alternative involving the least new cost to society shall be chosen; and
>
> (e) Agencies shall set regulatory priorities with the aim of maximizing the aggregate net benefits to society, taking into account the condition of the particular industries affected by regulations, the condition of the national economy, and other regulatory actions contemplated for the future.[18]

The Clinton administration argued that the Reagan administration burdens on administrative agencies had resulted in environmental damage and deterioration of health and safety programs, but the Clinton White House immediately launched its own attack on regulatory processes through the National Performance Review, headed by Vice President Al Gore. Clinton issued a string of executive orders mandating a range of complex analytic techniques to be accomplished by administrative agencies. To the earlier notions of cost/benefit analysis, the Clinton administration added a requirement for risk analysis.[19] While it is a complex topic in its own right, reduced to its minimum characteristics risk analysis states that a cost/benefit calculation cannot be meaningful unless it is clear what the acceptable range of possible actions can be. Thus, the costs of action are to be evaluated against the probability of unacceptable risks.

Of course, just what constitutes unacceptable risk is far more than a scientific or economic conception. It is a political issue. For instance, consider the implementation of the Medical Waste Tracking Act, a statute passed because of concern about the appearance of medical waste in surprising places, such as nationally televised revelations about used hypodermic needles washing up on beaches. An official responsible for the effort indicated that the approach to implementation would be relatively low-key since there was no medical evidence that the risk to a child who might step on a syringe on a beach was any greater than would be posed by stepping on a tin can on the same beach. The official failed to understand that, in a nation frightened by AIDS and hepatitis outbreaks, the public was not about to be convinced that their children had nothing in particular to fear from used hypodermic needles. The issue is not about science, but politics.

That brings us to the third dimension of policy analysis—policy as a process at the heart of politics by which we respond to issues on the public agenda. There are two dimensions to this aspect of the study of the policy process. First, who makes policy decisions and how are they accomplished? Second, what are the elements of the policy process and how do they work together?

Decision Processes: Who Decides and What Kinds of Decisions Are Made?

Political scientists have promoted the notion of competing theories about the distribution of political power in the United States. However, an understanding of how policy choices are made requires attention not only to who has power, but also a sensitivity for the nature of the decisions and constraints on decision making. There are a number of accepted explanations for policy decisions.

Rational Actor. The rational actor model of policy making is the approach we all like to think we use. In this model the analyst defines a problem, considers and evaluates all available options, selects the most rational alternative according to objective criteria, and carries out the policy chosen as efficiently and effectively as possible. The process is linear, objective, comprehensive, and efficient. Of course, there are very real difficulties with any attempt to take this model seriously as a prescription, and few careful observers of decision-making behavior would conclude that it is an accurate description of how most people solve most problems most of the time. Among other things, because we cannot know all of the possible options and all possible consequences that each option might entail, we can only expect to be able operate with what Herbert Simon has termed "bounded rationality."[20] Even if we did not face such limits, we have neither the time nor the resources to investigate even all of the options and consequences of which we are already aware. As a result of these forces, Simon said, we do not attempt to optimize, but instead seek to "satisfice," to find an acceptable answer to our problems.

Even if these barriers to fully rational calculation were not present, the idea that we can develop purely objective techniques with which to analyze options is a myth. Even the most sophisticated analytic techniques are no better than the set of assumptions on which they are based. The idea that all of the values that matter in a decision process can be incorporated into a cost/benefit calculation without making controversial and debatable assumptions is simply untenable, and the attempt to argue the contrary has bred considerable cynicism toward policy analysts. It led some members of Congress to publish a report entitled *Cost-Benefit Analysis: Wonder Tool or Mirage?*[21] Excessive claims for analytic capabilities undermine the legitimate need for the use of such techniques as are available as adjuncts to the political decision process. But, in the end, most major policy judgments are political and not simply or even primarily analytic calculations.

We would do well to remember the example of President Roosevelt's comments to Luther Gulick while the Social Security program was under consideration. When Gulick came to the president's bedroom to report that he had found serious actuarial difficulties with the proposal as an insurance program, the president lauded his analysis. After doing so, however, he added that he did not want the Social Security program to be based on an insurance model because of its actuarial soundness, but because once every Tom, Dick, and Harry had his own account in his own name, Republican Party leaders would not be able to do away with the program!

Incremental. Indeed Charles Lindblom has argued that not only is it impossible to have a true rational actor model of policy making, it is not even particularly desirable.[22] Lindblom argued that the general tendency in decision making is to look for marginal changes to the status quo that provide an acceptable, though usually not the best possible, solution to the problem. Most of us, most of the time, seek the solution to a problem that brings as little disruption to our present lives as possible. He referred to the search for incremental solutions as a process of "successive limited comparisons."

Not only, Lindblom said, is the incremental approach how we actually make decisions most of the time, it also has a number of advantages. For one thing, small steps can be retraced more easily than large leaps in the event that a choice proves problematic. It also causes less disruption to fewer people and organizations. It is therefore much more likely to be implemented than a major change. For these and other reasons, Lindblom argues that in our attempt to be sophisticated about decision making, we ought not be so ready to abandon incrementalism.

Pluralist. Many commentators have argued that the basis for policy making is not about the method of analysis or the design of modes of change, but about a set of political judgments. Those political judgments are not choices about some clear idea of the public good, but are the result of a political process. That process involves groups who bargain amongst each other to achieve agreement on decisions, a process referred to as *pluralism*.[23] It focuses on group interaction because individuals need organizations to be effective and to make themselves heard in the modern political arena. As long as the process is open, so that various groups can enter the discussion, and so long as those debates take place within the constitutional rules of the political game, the result is the best approximation of democracy that a large modern complex state can expect to achieve.

Pluralism accepts that decisions made under its strictures may very well be wrong if judged by some scientific criteria, but it prefers the democratic values over claims of scientific accuracy. Pushed to an extreme, it assumes that the public interest in any given situation is whatever the solution happens to be that emerges from the pluralist process at that time. In a pluralist system, power distribution patterns are the result of competing interests that win by increasing their numbers and resources and indeed through publicizing the nature of reality that is consistent with their perceptions of what should be.

Power Elite. Of course, critics charge that pluralism is itself a myth that has some elements of truth to it, but is far from an accurate representation of how decisions are made. In the first place, most people do not participate often or actively in the political process apart from occasionally voting in a presidential election. Fewer and fewer take active roles in interest groups beyond possibly paying annual dues and receiving the organization's magazine. Moreover, such critics are fond of citing E. E. Schattschneider who said that "the pluralist choir sings with a distinctly upper class bias."[24] Most working-class people with two breadwinners often working multiple jobs have little time, education, inclination, or opportunity to play active roles in the civic life of their communities beyond perhaps cooperating with church or youth groups in which they or their children have a connection.

These critics argue from an alternative perspective known as *power elite theory*.[25] They maintain that the decisions made by government in the public interest are not really subject to debate in a real sense. This, according to power elite theorists, is because the elites, that is the economic and hence political leadership of the country, determine to the greatest extent the nature of public policy. Further, some power elite commentators hold that this leadership strata is cohesive. The same people and groups tend to be key players in the political game over time. They have interests in common that are not necessarily widely shared with others. The most common version of this theme, less extreme than some commentators would use, is the tendency of presidential candidates to run as outsiders against the "Washington establishment." Candidates of both parties beg voters for the opportunity to go to Washington to throw the rascals out and break down "business as usual" in which special interest groups have taken over and, using illicit campaign contributions, have managed to hijack the public interest. It is an argument made by radical conservatives on the one end of the spectrum and Marxists on the other. There is perhaps a special irony when that argument is used by people of wealth and influence like Steve Forbes or Ross Perot.

The power elite argument has an obvious attractiveness to frustrated people who would like to find a simple explanation for the fact that there are so many problems that seem so intractable. The problem, of course, is that simple explanations often sound fine but do not hold up well when applied in a given setting. An example is the problem of the iron triangle argument.

For years political scientists were fond of explaining policy choices as the result of iron triangles made up of interest groups, the administrative agencies with which those groups most often worked (such as arms manufacturers and the Pentagon), and the principal congressional committee with control over that policy space. It turns out, however, that there are often several agencies active in a given policy space, sometimes with competing missions, and competing interest groups whose arguments are anything but consistent. Moreover there are at least six different congressional committees that are potentially critical in any set of policy choices. There are, in each house, authorization committees that write the basic legislation administered by the executive branch, appropriations committees that add a host of requirements and restrictions to those policies in the process of appropriating money for their implementation, and oversight committees that seek to influence the ongoing operation of policies during implementation and evaluation. These committees often vie for control over a given policy, and each is generally chaired by a senior member with a strong ego operating in legislative bodies that do not have a history of strong party discipline. Moreover, even if there was a time when life within Washington or the state capital was self-contained, that has long since ceased to be the case. Modern press and communications have made that kind of insularity all but impossible to maintain over time.

Organizational (Structuralist). In fact, one of the interesting questions is whether the basic unit of decision is a set of individuals who are part of some kind of elite or whether it is in fact organizations that are essential focal points of policy choice and action. Graham Allison, in his classic analysis of the Cuban missile crisis, pointed out some crucial factors that make organizations central players in the policy process.[26] Allison emphasized the fact that what tends to happen when a problem comes to government, or any organization for that matter, is that it is broken down into functional categories and parcelled out to the parts of the organization with expertise in those respective areas for action. Those units have repertoires, sets of possible responses to problems that they have developed over time. They tend to select one of their responses from the existing repertoire and offer that to the headquarters of the organization. The headquarters then reassembles the possible answers and makes choices from among them. Thus, Allison argued, the Air Force came forward with a bombing plan for air strikes on the Russian missiles in Cuba that was based on a plan that had been designed to support an invasion because that is what was available immediately. The Navy proposed to run its blockade of Soviet ships during the Cuban missile crisis in the traditional way because that was how the Navy knew how to run a blockade, despite the fact that both the Navy and Air Force responses were singularly inappropriate to the situation.

Moreover Allison argued, this role of organizations and their behaviors are not limited to ultimate policy choices but to less dramatic, though nevertheless important, actions as well. The Russian missiles in Cuba were spotted by U.S. spy planes in part because Russian air defense units set up their surface-to-air missiles in the traditional pattern dictated by their strategy books, though that pattern stood out like a neon sign to reconnaissance aircraft. American intelligence officers had passed definitive information on the presence of the Russian missiles and their crews into their normal intelligence channels, but that information never reached top decision makers until long after the crisis was already well under way. The information was delayed as it worked its way through the Central Intelligence Agency.

The argument is that policies are in many ways the result of organizations and cannot be otherwise. Individuals act through organizations, both in fashioning policies and in implementing those chosen. The character, culture, and behavior of those organizations, therefore, affect every aspect of the policy process. That includes the tendency of those organizations to protect themselves. Many of those organizational characteristics remain over time, regardless of the individuals who come and go in leadership positions.

This phenomenon is not limited to separation of powers countries like the United States. Defense establishments in many countries, finance ministries, tourist departments, agricultural ministries, and social welfare ministries share many common behaviors and often play comparable roles in policy debates in very different governments, notwithstanding frequent changes of the governing political parties.

The same is true of international organizations. There are relatively distinct cultures in the World Bank, International Monetary Fund, World Health Organization, Organization for Economic Cooperation and Development, and the United Nations Development Program. These cultures affect the way their officials behave and the kinds of policy decisions that will come from and be advocated by them.

Bureaucratic Politics. Other observers of the policy process, though, find that the character of organizations themselves is only a part of the calculation. Francis Rourke, for example, found that the real force is the mix of key people who know how to function within and across organizations and the nature and strength of the organization those people head that explains policy outcomes.[27] For Rourke, it is important to understand both how leaders come to have power within their own organizations and then why it is that one organization has greater power than another in a given situation.

Rourke's answer to the question about power differentials is that players in the policy process have more power than others as a result of their own expertise and the amount of external support they can marshal. Those, like Arnold Meltsner, who emphasize the role of policy analysts in the process, add that the analysts have added new dimensions to the idea of expertise over the past two decades, sets of analytic skills to accompany the technical skills and work experience that administrative agencies have possessed for many years.[28] It is this combination of key people and particular organizations that explains why some well known figures do not have good experiences in some organizations but succeed very nicely in others. The individual characteristics of manager and organization matter, and so does the particular match of the two in any given policy arena.

Another reason why the bureaucratic politics argument is popular is that it speaks to the fact that important changes often come when key stakeholders step outside the routine modes of interaction across organizations to make new things happen in creative ways. In more stressful situations, the bureaucratic politics approach considers the common phenomenon that occurs when a crisis hits and special groups of key people are brought together into ad hoc problem-solving groups. In those settings, traditional lines of interaction within and among organizations are abandoned in favor of some kind of crisis group that seems to offer fast response and flexibility.

Exchange Theories (Market or Public Choice). Since the late 1960s, however, there has been a strong effort to explain the policy process—and a normative effort to reshape it—in terms of what have variously been referred to as exchange theories or market approaches. At root, exchange theories represent a kind of combination of pluralist politics with market logic.[29] This approach argues that policy choices operate on the basis of exchanges among stakeholders. These trades may be of political goods and bads (support and threat) much like economic trades. Smart participants in this political market will seek non-zero sum solutions, agreements in which one does not seek to win completely and inflict losses on others but arrangements in which everyone wins something. In achieving such so-called win/win arrangements, all participants will be amenable to future opportunities for cooperation. The minimization of conflict will also achieve policy choices without a loss of energy or resources to major political battles. The necessary assumptions that must be present to support this approach, of course, are those of the market, including the idea that participants in these exchanges have perfect knowledge and perfect competition.

There are many variations on this theme that rest along a continuum on one end of which is the position that what is important is the manner by which participants in the political marketplace achieve satisfactory exchanges sufficient to produce consensus. At the other extreme is the argument that there is no issue of consensus. Rather, the political marketplace, like the economic version, has no need of consensus but functions instead merely as a collection of individual choices expressed in market terms. Whatever emerges from that set of choices represents collective action or public choice. In such a model, whatever policy option allows the greatest individual choice is by definition the best alternative.

Underlying much of this approach to policy is the philosophy that private sector logic needed to be shared with the public sector to strive for efficiency and effectiveness. Indeed, the technical methods often employed by policy analysts have as their roots a combination of political methodology and quantitative techniques borrowed from the field of economics. But quite apart from these forces, there are more fundamental factors that brought such attention to the exchange or market approach.

Vincent Ostrum and others argued vigorously in the early 1970s that what explained the various crises in modern government was that they had ceased to be democratic and had become so centralized that they had lost the advantages that come with decentralized decision making.[30] Ostrum contended that the best model for this notion of decision making was economics. Therefore, he argued that efforts should be made to use a range of policy tools that were most responsive to immediate political market reactions such as the contracting out of public services or voucher programs.

But just as there were criticisms of the rational actor school, which was in some respects the polar opposite, there were also attacks on the emerging public choice school. For one thing, Ostrum's argument was heavily ideological, though it was cast in historical language. One of the reasons why some of the policy decisions had moved to Washington, indeed one of the basic forces that brought about the Constitution in the first place, was conflict and jealousy within and among the states.[31] Furthermore, it was clear that local decision making had led to policies that did not serve minorities, whether the group in question was a racial minority or another kind of group, such as children with special needs or poor women. Market forces had never addressed their concerns, nor was there any reason to believe that "political markets" would either. It was not merely a matter of market failures, but basic political issues that had led the framers of American government and other governments around the world to adopt not pure democracy but a republic, representative government designed precisely to filter and check the passions of majorities.[32] In a more contemporary vein, it was precisely those difficulties that had led the national government to create policies that sent financial aid and services directly to the cities and the needy rather than filtering them through state governments.

Of course, the advocates of these approaches knew those things, but public markets became the language needed by an emerging new right in the political arena that was working to articulate an argument against the Great Society programs and the government bureaucracy that was developed to administer them. Just as the rational actor whiz kids of the 1960s had used the logic of their arguments to justify centralized elite decision making by basing their ideas in cutting-edge scientific analysis, so the new right of the 1970s and 1980s used their radical view of the logic of democracy to justify dismantling the post—New Deal positive state.

Conflict Models. There is a sense in which some of these systems of decision making have come full circle with the reemergence of an old idea. That old notion is the view that policy decisions do not seem to be made, at least the most significant ones, because they are dictated by the logic of the marketplace, because they represent an effort to achieve non-zero sum solutions by groups operating in a pluralist game, or because they are the most rational choices based on rigorous systematic analysis. They appear, and indeed increasingly appear, to be the result of plain old-fashioned political conflict.

E. E. Schattschneider attacked the pluralists in the early years of the development of that approach on grounds that political decisions are not about agreements and how to achieve them but about conflict over issues.[33] And when people disagree over important issues, they want to win. In fact, he said, the best metaphor for understanding such decisions is not a debating society or a trading floor but a street fight. The initial participants in the fight do their best to bring the bystanders into the melee on their side.

Increasingly, observers of policy fights are coming to realize that even though it is not a very pleasant reality, Schattschneider's view of the world of policy contests seems to be a much better explanation of disputes over abortion, education, health care, and tax policy than the more genteel middle class picture of pluralism. When Schattschneider indicated that the pluralist choir sings with a distinctly upper class bias, he was addressing both the fact that such an approach is largely available only to the wealthier and better educated among the population and the reality that the policy outcomes of pluralist decision making will most often favor that group.

Of course, while the conflict approach injects some realism into what can sometimes seem to be intentionally naive and sterile presentations of the policy process, it is only part of the picture. Just as most people walking down the street do not tend to devolve into street brawlers, so most policy choices on a day-to-day basis do not elicit the level of conflict of which Schattschneider spoke. On the other hand, the more the political and economic systems are stressed, as they have been in recent decades, the more likely it is that we will see reversion to conflict rather than alternative models.

The Policy Process: Lines and Loops

These models of how decisions are made tell us something about the forces driving the participants in policy making, but they do not tell us much about the institutions and processes that are the settings in which the decisions are made. While many scholars of policy making offer variations on what those institutions and processes look like, what follows is a fairly standard synthesis.[34] The basic approach is of a systems model that follows the path of decisions as they flow through the process, recognizing that this system operates within a larger political environment that is continually changing.

Agenda Setting. The first element of the policy making process is agenda setting. That begins with problem identification, the attempt to specify as clearly as possible what the problem really is. Because issues are often interrelated and because advocates often want not discrete and narrow decisions but large policy statements, it is often difficult to untie the knots and separate the strands in order to determine just how to view the specific problem that is in need of attention.

That last matter involves determining whether the kind of problem presented is one that should be on the public agenda as opposed to being resolved elsewhere. It also entails determining what priority this particular problem should have as compared to other issues already pending on the agenda.

It has been argued that modern governments have not been very successful in domestic policy. What may appear to be dismal results may not necessarily be a consequence of the approach, but rather of the fact that the problems were impossible to solve and the current level of amelioration is all one could realistically expect. Thus, when President Lyndon Johnson declared a war on poverty, the best we could hope for was a relative decline in poverty, an expansion of the middle class, a general improvement in the availability of equal opportunity, and progress in providing young people with the tools to take advantage of those opportunities. The forces that give rise to poverty were never likely to capitulate in unconditional surrender. A set of limited victories that kept poverty in some kind of check was probably the only realistic resolution of the war. Yet perhaps because of the terms in which the task was stated, the war on poverty is generally thought to have failed from today's perspective.

Another related argument about expectations is that there are many problems that should be left to private decision or resolution at the local level rather than finding a place on the national agenda. That may be either a function of an ideological view that national governments are doing too much or simply a suggestion that the issue in question really is not something national governments can address very effectively. Thus, despite the fact that being tough on crime is a popular campaign theme for national officials, crime control is really a problem that is necessarily addressed at the local level or the states (in some countries the regions). National criminal laws in the United States affect a very limited amount of what is called crime. Providing funds to add a few police officers here and there for a limited period of time is a symbolic gesture, particularly when the national government has eliminated revenue sharing, which was a means that local governments could really use and count on to assist in their battles against crime. Congressional passage of draconian federal criminal punishments reaches very few of those who actually commit crimes, and such an approach is particularly ineffective if at the same time the legislature is cutting funding programs that local officials argue are indeed working.

Thus, the argument is that there are some problems that simply do not belong on the policy agenda, or, if they do, should be the agenda of states or local decision makers rather than the national government. A refusal to make those choices can result in unrealistic expectations and inevitable policy failures.

Of course, implicit in the suggestion about what does not belong on the agenda is the decision not to decide. The determination of what is nonproblematic or not serious enough to reach the public policy agenda is one of the greatest challenges facing decision makers. If a problem is ignored or dismissed, there may not even have been an effort to collect information about it. When a problem begins to surface and groups begin to coalesce around it as a policy issue, its importance may be difficult to understand. For example, it took a relatively long period for governments to recognize the seriousness of the AIDS threat and begin to mobilize forces to combat it.

Sometimes it takes a major event to engender enough pressure to move a problem onto the agenda. John Kingdon refers to the idea that such a dramatic event may open a policy window. Those who are promoting policies may then seek to push their policies through that window.[35] An example is the development of the Superfund program to clean up abandoned toxic waste sites. Attorneys at the Environmental Protection Agency had begun in the late 1970s to explore ways they could us the Resource Conservation and Recovery Act (RCRA), the regulatory program governing the handling of toxic chemicals, to address the problem of the hundreds of abandoned toxic dumps around the nation. Some time thereafter, the nation awoke to headlines about the Love Canal dump site near Buffalo, and a national demand for action followed. The furor that resulted gave those who had been at work on the issue an opportunity to push their idea for a solution forward. It was adopted in 1980, and the Superfund program was launched.

However, even when people become mobilized around the need to address the problem as part of the public agenda, it remains to be determined just what priority this problem will have relative to other pending issues. Thus, there have been debates among groups who advocate more effort on research for various diseases. Just how much should be spent for AIDs research as compared to cancer research or efforts to find the causes and cures of heart disease? When the available resources increase, the competitive pressures among policy advocates are manageable. When the resources shrink to the point where whole programs must be targeted for elimination, however, that competition heats up dramatically.

Policy Formulation. The fact that a problem reaches the public agenda and even prompts a decision to make it a high priority issue does not mean that any particular policy will be easily formulated and adopted. The first question arising in these situations is, What type of a policy should be employed?

There are several general categories of policy that have been used for many years.[36] Typical of modern arrays of policy options are the categories described by Fred Frohock,[37] including regulatory, distributive, redistributive, capitalization, and ethical policies. Regulatory policies may control entry into a field and may set controls on professional practices within that field. Thus, physicians are required to be licensed and are subject to a variety of checks on their behavior. In addition to whatever civil suits may be brought against them for malpractice, they are subject to regulatory penalties like the revocation of their licenses. While much of the policy literature has concentrated historically on major national regulatory programs, local governments are often involved in regulation ranging from control of taxicabs to health code enforcement for restaurants and medical facilities. Indeed, national governments often depend on state or local officials to do the day-to-day enforcement work for their agencies.

A second category is distributive policy. These policies target a group (veterans, for instance), and provide it with a particular type of service or support. These programs are sometimes referred to as entitlement programs, since anyone who fits the definition of the beneficiary category is entitled to the support.

Redistributive policies are "aimed at rearranging one or more of the basic schedules of social and economic rewards."[38] One of the long-standing examples of redistributive policies is the graduated income tax. In many nations, people who earn more are asked to shoulder a higher tax burden. Such a tax has a deliberately redistributive effect but has generally been justified on equity grounds and on the humanitarian premise that for those who earn less, virtually all of their income is required merely to obtain the necessities of life. Another example is the Food Stamp program under which lower income persons get a subsidy in the form of food stamps that enables them to leverage their own limited food budget into an amount of food more likely to meet the needs of the family. Of course, one must take care not to assume that all programs that have redistributive effects were solely designed to assist the poor. Food stamps and school nutrition assistance programs, for example, have historically also been supported by agricultural interests as a means of increasing market strength for commodities and reducing surpluses.

Though they are rarely discussed in these terms, a host of policies are designed as capitalization policies. They either assist with capital formation or are designed to maintain the financial base under important enterprises or fields of activity. These policies make use of subsidies, tax credits, tax abatements, contracts, or grants to assist in a wide variety of activities from enhancement of plant and equipment to the maintenance of the family farm. On some occasions capitalization policies can be extremely large in scope, as in the case of the use of postal subsidies to help in the development of the airlines or the even larger effort to provide the financial infrastructure under the residential real-estate market with the establishment of guaranteed loans and tax deductions for mortgage interest and state and local taxes. But capitalization policies need not be particularly large. For example, the Department of Women and Culture in Fiji has a program to assist women to launch microenterprises. Along with the loans, the recipients receive business training and other assistance to help make their businesses succeed and, not incidentally, to enhance the likelihood of payback on the loans made to them.

There is some degree of irony, and not a little hypocrisy, in our tendency to speak of redistributive assistance as entitlement programs that burden the society but to ignore the scope and significance of capitalization policies, which may be even more costly entitlement programs.

Frohock made an interesting point by observing that there are also ethical policies. These vary from programs intended to advocate some values with no sanctions to policies like the Ethics in Government Act, which are intended to work through moral suasion but also carry a regulatory punch if the ethical pressures are not sufficient to encourage the desired behavior. At some point, for reasons discussed in Chapter 3, that kind of policy is not really about ethics but is really a legally oriented regulatory policy.

A different kind of ethical policy relates to the need to address injustices in the manner in which other policies have been designed or implemented. Thus, the Clinton administration created a policy on environmental equity that grew out of findings that toxic waste and other kinds of environmental problems had often been addressed by approaches that placed a greater burden on minority, and often low income minority, communities.[39] The White House, by executive order, mandated the EPA to consider the problem and attempt to avoid more such inequalities in the future.

Remember, it is often the case that the legislature will elect to use several different kinds of policies together in a policy mix to address an issue. Similarly, there are several types of policy tools that can be used as the basis for a particular kind of policy. Thus, financial incentives and disincentives can be used to build a regulatory policy or a capitalization policy. Various kinds of tax tools are often used for these types of policy. Of course, when tax incentives are provided as tools for a particular policy, the revenue lost as a result of those tax breaks must be obtained from some other source. Since some taxes are more regressive than others, there can be disproportionate impacts from the use of tax measures as policy tools.

There has been more attention to policy tools in recent decades, in part to move away from what are commonly called *command and control mechanisms* and toward more sophisticated and less heavy-handed devices.[40] In fact, decentralization has become an important policy tool in many countries. For many types of policy, the effort has been to move the policy closer to the local community for action.

In particular, there has been a tendency to use market-oriented tools to take advantage of self-interest to encourage the targets of the policy to behave as the policy makers intend.[41] On some occasions these are techniques that are used within government, but there is also the effort to move policies out into the private sector to take advantage of the competitive pressures that are present with such techniques as contracting for services. Sweden, for example, has adopted the increasingly popular approach of contracting out some of its social service delivery activities while retaining some functions within government units and then putting them into competition in an effort to determine where the better service and lower prices can be found. In a way, this technique involves the creation of a market as a policy tool, a tactic that has also been used in the environmental arena where markets have been created that involve the trading of air pollution effluent allowances. Thus, investors can purchase or sell these allowances on the Chicago Board of Trade. The idea is that clean businesses can sell their permits for needed cash and society can make polluters pay for increased emissions by bidding up the price of the permits. Other techniques include the use of labelling and disclosure as means to provide incentives to producers and sellers of various products, from food supplements to home products, to produce and market their wares in ways that will attract buyers to labels that can boast healthy or environmentally friendly contents or processes.

Even where regulatory tools are used, there is an increasing effort to use alternative dispute resolution techniques, rather than litigation, to resolve disputes.[42] Thus, the U.S. government adopted the Alternative Dispute Resolution Act and Negotiated Rulemaking Act in an effort to avoid more adversarial approaches. Related alternatives to dispute resolution are the use of probabilistic tools such as comparative risk-based negotiations. In this technique, there is an attempt to avoid pushing a company against an absolute standard and a move to negotiate toward a more flexible goal chosen on the basis of the particular circumstances. One of the better known examples is the effort to rewrite the Superfund program to negotiate cleanup of toxic sites based on the anticipated use of the site.

It would be a mistake to assume that the use of market-based tools means that regulatory devices are avoided. There are many forms of behavior that are simply considered too dangerous or damaging to permit or to leave to the vagaries of incentives. However, the trend has been to move away from specific engineering standards that tell someone precisely what they must do and how they must do it to performance standards that delineate the results that must be achieved but leave to the regulated party the decision as to exactly how to meet those requirements. An increasingly popular approach in some quarters is what can be called a *tracking* or *manifest system*, under which regulated parties are required to establish what amounts to a paper trail of their activities such that any resulting damage can be traced to the door of the responsible party, where restitution may be obtained.

In fact, as Chapter 2 explained, administrative agencies or ministries often administer a complex collection of different kinds of policies that employ a wide variety of policy tools. This portfolio of policies contains decisions made by a wide variety of policy makers over a long period of time. They can sometimes be contradictory, presenting administrators with the difficult task of reconciling these varying mandates.

The tendency, when selecting a type of policy and a set of tools for that policy at any moment in time, is to concentrate on the particular issue on the table and the specific question at issue. Unfortunately, that may be mean a lack of sensitivity to just how the solution to today's problem will fit with the existing body of policies already extant. And while that is a problem for policy makers at the point at which the new policy is adopted, it should also be a question for the policy analyst during the policy formulation process.

Policy Adoption. The choice of policies and the particular tools that will be used in them is constrained by the need to move them through the people and institutions that must adopt them. That range of choice is not limited only by the politics, institutions, and processes of a particular government but also by bilateral, regional, and international agreements.

In considering the adoption process, it is important to recall that it is a political rather than an analytic process. Given the tendency in the contemporary policy arena to speak in terms of market analogies, it is also important, as James Q. Wilson points out, to remember that policy choices are political rather than economic decisions. The difference matters. He wrote:

> First, politics concerns preferences that do not always have a common market measuring rod. In an economic market, we seek to maximize our "utility," a

goal that substantively can be almost anything but in practice involves things that have, or can easily be given, money values. . . .

In nonmarket relationships, such as in voluntary associations or in legislatures, we may also behave in a rationally self-interested manner—but we do so in a setting that does not usually permit monetary (or quantitative) values to be assigned to our competing preferences in any nonarbitrary way. . . .

Second, political action requires assembling majority coalitions to make decisions that bind everyone whether or not he belongs to that coalition. When we make purchases in a market, we commit only ourselves, and we consume as much or as little of a given product as we wish. When we participate in making decisions in the political arena, we are implicitly committing others as well as ourselves, and we are "consuming" not only a known product (such as the candidate for whom we vote) but also a large number of unknown products (all the policies the winning candidate will help enact). . . .

The third and most important difference between economics and politics is that whereas economics is based on the assumption that preferences are given, politics must take into account the effort made to change preferences.[43]

It is therefore crucial to know not only who must approve a policy proposal but something of who the stakeholders are and how a policy proposal originates. As a rule, proposals usually emerge from within the policy community that retains an ongoing interest in the policy space in question. It may emerge as a legislative or rulemaking proposal from an administrative agency. It may also come from negotiations among stakeholders within the policy community and may very well draw opposition from others in that same policy community, particularly if they feel as though they were left out of the policy formulation process. Interest groups are often advocates for a particular proposal. When regular stakeholders with knowledge, experience, and resources develop proposals, they can often bring well-developed plans forward for consideration. These are resources that some legislators do not have.

One of the subjects of continuing interest to all participants in the process is just where the government will look for policy advice. John Halligan, an Australian examining trends in several countries, observed that the role of civil servants is changing but that it is at this point unclear just where that change will be taking us.[44] He noted that the policy advising role had been on the increase but had suffered when governments led by ideologically committed leaders came to power in the 1980s and 1990s. More recently, the trend has been toward varying policy advice systems, depending on the kind of issue and the situation at hand. At the end of the day, Halligan argues, there are three principles "central to the good advisory system. The first is the provision of multiple sources of advice. The second is flexibility; to be able to choose a mix of adviser(s) and processes appropriate for satisfying the needs of particular policy issues."[45] Advice is one facet of the process, but only one.

Of course, one of the important aspects of the adoption process is the evaluation of who will win and who will lose. Indeed, Wilson points out that the type of political behavior that we see during this stage can be dictated by the question of who pays and who benefits. He argues that where both benefits and costs of a proposal will be widely distributed across the population, we find "majoritarian politics." "Interest groups have little incentive to form around such issues because no small, definable segments of society (an industry, an occupation, a locality) can expect to capture a disproportionate share of the benefits or avoid a disproportionate share of the burdens."[46] He concluded that where both the benefits and the costs are narrowly distributed, "interest group politics" predominate. By definition there are clear winners and losers who have strong incentives to organize and lobby.[47] Where the costs are widely distributed but the benefits are narrowly concentrated to a particular group or locality, the tendency is toward "client politics." The beneficiaries have strong incentives to organize and attempt to influence decision makers, but others do not see themselves as clear losers and therefore lack the incentive to act. He points to a regulated industry as an example. Finally, he argues that where the benefits are widely distributed but the costs are relatively concentrated, we tend to see what he refers to as "entrepreneurial politics."[48] He points to Ralph Nader, the consumer advocate, as an exemplar of this kind of political behavior.

The political dynamics are somewhat different in parliamentary regimes, particularly those based on the Westminster model as compared to governments based in separation of powers like the United States. Because the policy offered on the floor of the Parliament is not merely the proposal of the ministry involved, but is also the position of the government, by definition it carries a majority in the House of Commons. Conversely, the separation of powers governments provide more veto points—opportunities to kill a proposal—than are available in a parliamentary regime.

The dynamics are different, too, at the local level of government, where governments have a decentralized system. First, the context of a policy discussion is often constrained by the mandates issued by the national and state governments. Second, the range of choice available to a city council varies depending on whether the community enjoys home rule powers or must take any decision of significance to the state legislature for approval. It differs as well in the nature of bodies approving the policy. Since local councils often play a role in the implementation of the ordinances they adopt, the discussion of consequences and exceptions can sometimes be very different from what one finds in a state or national legislature.

Of course, none of these dynamics provides any assurance that the concerns of minority communities will be addressed. Indeed, because of the relationship between race or ethnicity and economic status in many countries, the tendency of national and even local politics is to emphasize those who are able to mount effective efforts to influence decisions and not necessarily to consider the impact of possible policy choices on all segments of the community.

Apart from these broad considerations, there are more specific problems that must be addressed before a policy will move through this phase of the process. What organization will be assigned to administer the new policy? Where will the money come from to finance it? Who will conduct oversight over its operations? The answers to these questions are important not only because the ability to get such a policy adopted can often depend on the answers to them, but also because they have a great deal to do with the problems that will be encountered in the implementation of the policy and the expectations for positive outcomes during the evaluation stage.

Conclusion

The character and operation of the policy process is a central fact in the life of every public administrator. It is not all that public managers deal with, but it is critical. Policy analysis is not merely a broad term for talking about policy, but a subfield with a set of important concepts, approaches, and purposes that must be understood. It emphasizes decision processes, a range of methods for policy development, the elements of the policy-making process, and substantive foci on particular policy spaces.

The policy process begins with agenda setting and moves to policy formulation and adoption. These facets of the process seek to find the right type of policy and specific kinds of policy tools to address the specific issue that is on the agenda. But the choices that are ultimately made during policy adoption are political decisions rather than analytic resolutions to a well-defined problem. They produce winners and losers.

Those decisions made at the time of policy adoption shape what will happen during implementation and evaluation phases of the process. It is to those facets of the process that we turn in Chapter 7.

Notes

[1]A number of works discuss public policy making and the role of government. Among these are Charles S. Bullock III, et al., *Public Policy in the Eighties* (Monterey, CA: Brooks/Cole, 1983); Guy B. Adams, ed., *Policymaking, Communication, and Social Learning* (New Brunswick, NJ: Transaction Books, 1987); Frances Castles, ed., *The Comparative History of Public Policy* (Cambridge: Polity Press, 1989); R. Lance Shotland and Melvin M. Mark, eds., *Social Science and Social Policy* (Beverly Hills, CA: Sage, 1985); Michael Hill and Glen Bramley, *Analyzing*

Social Policy (Oxford: Basil Blackwell, 1986); and Robert Formaini, *The Myth of Scientific Public Policy* (New Brunswick, NJ: Transaction, 1990).

[2]Charles W. Anderson, *Statecraft* (New York: John Wiley and Sons, 1977), discusses the political implications and interactions of various actor involvement in the policy-making process. Also see Melvin J. Dubnick and Barbara A. Bardes, *Thinking about Public Policy* (New York: John Wiley and Sons, 1983).

[3]Curtis Ventriss, "The Pedagogical Implications of the Internationalization of Public Policy," in Peter J. Bergerson, ed., *Teaching Public Policy* (New York: Greenwood Press, 1991).

[4]Eugene Bardach, *The Implementation Game* (Cambridge, MA: MIT Press, 1977).

[5]Frederick C. Mosher, "The Changing Responsibilities and Tactics of the Federal Government," *Public Administration Review* 40 (November/December 1980): 541–548; Lester M. Salamon, ed., *Beyond Privatization: The Tools of Government Action* (Washington, DC: Urban Institute, 1989).

[6]Anderson, *op. cit.,* 12.

[7]Glendon Schubert, "The Public Interest: Theorem, Theosophy, or Theory" in Carl Friedrich, ed., *Nomos: The Public Interest* (New York: Atherton Press, 1962).

[8]Charles Lindblom, Gaus Lecture, Meeting of the American Political Science Association, Chicago, August, 1995.

[9]See J. H. Hegeman, *Justifying Policy* (Amsterdam: Free University Press, 1989).

[10]See Richard I. Hofferbert, *The Reach and Grasp of Policy Analysis* (Tuscaloosa, AL: University of Alabama Press, 1990).

[11]See Daniel Lerner and Harold D. Lasswell, eds., *The Policy Sciences* (Stanford, CA: Stanford University Press, 1951).

[12]See Yehezkel Dror, *Public Policymaking Reexamined* (San Francisco: Chandler, 1968) and Dror, *Design for the Policy Sciences* (New York: American Elsevier, 1971).

[13]Peter deLeon, *Advice and Consent* (New York: Russell Sage Foundation, 1988), 62–63.

[14]Jeffrey L. Pressman and Aaron Wildavsky, *Implementation* (Berkeley, CA: University of California Press, 1973).

[15]Emmanuel Wald, "Toward a Paradigm of Future Public Administration," *Public Administration Review* 33 (July/August 1973): 466–472.

[16]Dubnick and Bardes, *op. cit.,* 3.

[17]See Arnold J. Meltsner, *Policy Analysts in the Bureaucracy* (Berkeley, CA: University of California Press, 1976); Robert A. Goldwin, ed., *Bureaucrats, Policy Analysts, Statesmen: Who Leads?* (Washington, DC: American Enterprise Institute, 1980); and deLeon, *op. cit.*

[18]E.O. 12291, Section 2, 46 Federal Register 13193 (1981).

[19]See Executive Order 12866, June 1, 1994.

[20]Herbert Simon, *Administrative Behavior,* 3rd ed. (New York: Free Press, 1976).

[21]U.S. House of Representatives, Report of the Subcommittee on Oversight and Investigation of the Committee on Interstate and Foreign Commerce, 96th Cong., 2nd Sess. (1980).

[22]"The Science of Muddling Through," *Public Administration Review* 19 (Spring 1959): 79–88.

[23]See Robert Dahl, *Who Governs* (New Haven, CT: Yale University Press, 1961).

[24]E. E. Schattschneider, *The Semi-Sovereign People* (New York: Holt, Rinehart and Winston, 1960).

[25]See C. Wright Mills, *The Power Elite* (New York: Oxford University Press, 1956); Eric Domhof, *The Higher Circles* (New York: Random House, 1970).

[26]Graham Allison, *Essence of Decision* (Boston: Little, Brown, 1971).

[27]Francis E. Rourke, *Bureaucracy, Politics, and Public Policy* (Boston: Little, Brown, 1968).

[28]Meltsner, *op. cit.*

[29]Robert H. Salisbury, "An Exchange Theory of Interest Groups," *Midwest Journal of Political Science* 13 (February 1969): 1–32.

[30]Vincent Ostrum, *The Intellectual Crisis in American Public Administration*, 2nd ed. (Tuscaloosa, AL: University of Alabama Press, 1989). (Originally published in 1973.)

[31]Alexander Hamilton, James Madison, and John Jay, *The Federalist* (New York: Mentor, 1961), No. 48.

[32]*Ibid.*, Nos. 10 and 51.

[33]Schattschneider, *op. cit.*

[34]See James E. Anderson, *Public Policymaking* (Boston: Houghton-Mifflin, 1990); Charles O. Jones, *An Introduction to the Study of Public Policy*, 3rd ed. (Monterey, CA: Brooks/Cole, 1984).

[35]John W. Kingdon, *Agendas, Alternatives, and Public Policies* (New York: Harper Collins, 1984).

[36]See e.g., Theodore J. Lowi, "Public Policy, Politics, and Political Theory," *World Politics* 17 (July 1964): 677–715.

[37]Fred Frohock, *Public Policy* (Englewood Cliffs, NJ: Prentice Hall, 1979).

[38]*Ibid.*, 13.

[39]Robert D. Bullard, *Dumping on Dixie* (Boulder, CO: Westview Press, 1990).

[40]Salamon, *op. cit.*

[41]Organization for Economic Cooperation and Development, *Economic Instruments for Environmental Protection* (Paris: OECD, 1989).

[42]Jon Martin Trolldalen, *International Environmental Conflict Resolution: The Role of the United Nations* (Oslo: World Foundation for Environment and Development, 1992).

[43] James Q. Wilson, "The Politics of Regulation," in Wilson, ed., *The Politics of Regulation* (New York: Basic Books, 1980), 358–363.

[44] John Halligan, "Policy Advice and the Public Service," in B. Guy Peters and Donald Savoie, *Governance in a Changing Environment* (Montreal: McGill/Queens University Press, 1995).

[45] *Ibid.*, 162.

[46] Wilson, *op. cit.*, 367.

[47] *Ibid.*, 368.

[48] *Ibid.*, 370–372.

Chapter 7

Policy Implementation, Evaluation, and Termination

Why is it that policies do not look the same in practice as they did when they were adopted? There are few questions that have been more vexing to legislators, policy analysts, and administrators than that one. Of course, there are two related questions that have also become hearty perennials. How do we know how well a policy is working, and what will happen if we determine that it is either not working well or is no longer serving a useful purpose?

Taken together, these questions form the basis for the other stages of the policy process that come after policy adoption. They are generally termed policy implementation, evaluation, and termination, respectively. This chapter considers each of these questions from the perspective of a number of participants and stakeholders. It concludes with a discussion of some of the limits that arise in connection with traditional concepts of policy process.

Implementation

At its simplest, policy implementation is the translation of a policy statement into action. But like most elements of the policy process, this stage requires some care in establishing premises. It is important to consider just who the implementers are, to contemplate the conditions under which they operate, and to establish the mind set they bring to the task.

Who Are the Implementers?

The assumption is that when a legislature (whether Parliament, Congress, or state legislature) adopts a policy, an administrative agency assumes responsibility for the policy's implementation. However, the reality is that there are often as many participants in the implementation process as were involved in the earlier stages, and sometimes more.

The policy may: (1) create a new agency charged with its implementation and operation; (2) delegate responsibility to an existing ministry; (3) parcel out responsibility for implementation to a variety of agencies, each of which is expected to integrate the new policy into its existing operations; or (4) it may even decide not to assign implementation responsibility to any particular agency. The first model is clear enough. If a new ministry is created, then its primary focus and energy are dedicated to the success of the new policy. The advantages are obvious, but it also means that policy makers face the dreaded charge that they are "creating more bureaucracy."

Thus, policy makers tend to try to assign responsibility to an existing agency. Of course, adding one more policy task to the Environmental Protection Agency, for example, runs the risk of having the new program get lost in the host of existing policy operations. Moreover, in times of fiscal scarcity—which has been the case for a very long time now—those charged with implementing new policies must compete for resources with advocates of well-established policies. This is particularly true if, instead of creating a new unit within the agency, the new responsibilities are merely assigned to an existing office.

Parcelling out responsibilities for the implementation of a new policy to all agencies avoids the problem of one embattled unit. For example, assigning environmental responsibilities to all organizations in the executive branch relieves one organization of the whole task, but, by definition, fragments the process of implementation and, potentially at least, reduces the ability to focus responsibility in one place. And, if there was a chance that the new policy would get buried in existing units of one ministry, that risk is much greater when the new program is parcelled out among a number of agencies. Not surprisingly, therefore, policy advocates often prefer a hybrid model in which responsibilities are distributed among all appropriate organizations, but primary responsibility is vested in one agency that is then given sufficient political and legal "clout" (a colloquial but well-understood term in many countries) to enforce action and face accountability for success or failure.

Of course, it sometimes happens that no specific institution is given responsibility. Thus, in the case of the Americans with Disabilities Act, the Congress employed a civil rights model in which the assumption was that the act would be primarily self-implementing. Individuals would bring court actions to enforce their rights to reasonable accommodation for their disability in employment or public facilities. The difficulties with that kind of model are legion, starting with the fact that those who should comply with the law must wait for a tedious and lengthy process of litigation to establish the meaning of terms like "reasonable accommodation," and they face the risk of losing a good deal of money and time in the process. Moreover, it is extremely difficult to know how to assign responsibility for implementation and how to evaluate success.

In cases such as the ADA, the Courts become important participants in policy implementation. That is, however, but an extreme case of a more common phenomenon. Courts are normal participants in the policy implementation process and have been for many years. And despite the fact that they are sometimes seen as a threat to administrators, the fact is that while they may overturn some administrative decisions that are found to be unconstitutional, in violation of a statute, or arbitrary and capricious, they more often support administrative decisions. In so doing, they support the authority of unelected officials who are exercising considerable discretion in important matters. With those decisions, the courts assist in establishing the legitimacy of the many important decisions that must be made during policy implementation. But whether they serve as supporters or checks on administrative discretion, they remain expected and important players in the implementation process.

Beyond the courts, the members of the policy community continue to be important after policy adoption. In fact, they remain even after the general public interest that comes while a major policy is moving through the legislative process declines, since they know that policies can be reshaped during implementation. They seek to influence rulemaking proceedings as the detailed regulations needed to move from legislation to action are drafted. They lobby the agencies on issues ranging from enforcement priorities to competition for contracts to provide services. They are present when the legislatures undertake oversight activities to assess the performance of the implementers. In parliamentary systems, of course, the legislative proceedings take different forms, sometimes a parliamentary inquiry or creation of what may be termed a *royal commission*. At all these stages, the interest groups, state and local organizations, and affected agencies are actively involved.

Indeed, with the increasing use of decentralized policies and contracted operations, the role of the many stakeholders in the policy community has increased. Because policies are often adopted that allow subnational units of government to prepare their own regulations and service standards—so long as they are at least as rigorous as the national program—and permit them to implement the policy with an attention to local sensitivities, there is an important shift of action and responsibility. Of course, such delegations of authority and responsibility to many different subnational governments mean that policies may look very different in implementation from one jurisdiction to another than they appeared when they were originally adopted at the national level. There are two important tradeoffs that come with decentralization of this sort.

First, there is an inevitable change in accountability, usually a reduction. That is one of the reasons that the use of block grants has been so hotly debated in the United States. In both major rounds of block grant activity, first during the Nixon years and later during the Reagan administration, there were significant accountability issues, ranging from health care to community development, that arose during implementation of the block grant programs.[1]

The second risk of decentralized administration is that as decisions move closer to local majorities and away from the filtering action of representative bodies, the more likely it is that there will be a loss of attention to the needs of minority groups. Indeed, there may even be outright discrimination. The level of problem varies from community to community or state to state, but it has historically been a significant issue in everything from education to environmental protection.[2] Thus, it is not surprising, though certainly unfair, that children with special needs have been singled out in the blame game of local politics as the effort is made to identify culprits behind recent tax increases. One of the difficulties of expanded use of contracting as a mechanism for the implementation and operation of policy is that it becomes less clear and more difficult to address both the issues of accountability and the problems of inequality.

Implementation, Crisis Management, or Normal Administration?

In assessing the implementation process, however, it is important to understand that the circumstances are often very different at different times for the public managers responsible for the effort. There is a tendency in the public policy literature to assume that everything that happens after a policy is adopted until it reaches evaluation is implementation. On the other hand, the public administration literature often speaks in terms of administration but not implementation. In fact, there are at least three conditions that public managers confront.

First, when a policy is adopted, administrators face the task of putting it into action, including building whatever organization is needed to make it happen, establishing the rules under which those operations will be conducted, setting up the processes required so that the intended beneficiaries of the policy may present their requests, and undertaking whatever service provision is needed. At the point at which policy is adopted there is often significant interest and support as well as considerable pressure to move rapidly to implement the policy. After all, policies are often not adopted unless they address a problem serious and imminent enough to have put the issue on the agenda and assist in the adoption process. The level of energy is high and perhaps growing.

Once the basic apparatus and processes for implementation are developed, and the capacity has been built to deliver the services, things begin to level off and transition from an implementation approach to a standard operating mode. The tendency is to regularize operations and establish standard operating procedures that enhance efficiency and effectiveness. Management values become particularly important, and the level of operations moves along at a more or less routine level of energy with limited or moderate levels of stress.

In most cases, however, one can be certain that that standard operating scenario will be radically challenged by some kind of crisis. The shift from normal operations to a crisis mode comes with a dramatic increase in tension and demand. It may come from a financial crisis, a political attack, a natural disaster that places major demands on service providers, or an organizational upheaval created by internal forces such as significant leadership changes. When that happens, standard operations are forgotten, at least by the concerned managers, and the thoughts are less about policy implementation and more about crisis management. Standard organizational patterns may be ignored and crisis teams assembled. The tendency is to rapidly centralize decision making. As the crisis subsides, organizational life adapts to the new situation, the stress level declines, and there is a slow movement back toward the direction of standard operations, though with the changes that came as a result of the challenge.

There are two key lessons that come from this reality. The first is that much of a policy's life exists what is termed the implementation phase, but this important phase consists of at least three very different and dynamic types of activity. Second, these phases come and go over time and are to be expected.

From Compliance to Cooperation to Creativity

Whoever the players may be and whatever the nature of the environment within which they operate, there is always the question as to the proper approach or orientation that should be taken to achieve the purpose of a policy. Over the years there has been a movement in the dominant frame of reference from compliance to cooperation to creativity.

One of the forces driving the study of policy implementation in the United States was the concern during the 1950s and 1960s that the civil rights rulings issued by the Supreme Court, most notably *Brown v. Board of Education*,[3] met with so little compliance. Many of the studies were about why such authoritative policy decisions seemed to have so little effect and were focused on the question of impact where impact was principally defined in terms of compliance with directives of government.[4] Over time, however, scholars began to realize that there was a range of reaction not only by those expected to respond to policy decisions but also on the part of the government itself. That range included coercion to comply (often called enforcement) on one end of the continuum to action based on consensus at the other, with compliance based on compromise somewhere in between.[5]

As the policy implementation literature matured during the 1970s and 1980s, it moved away from a top-down perspective focused on policy mandates from top-level decision makers.[6] It became clear that successful implementation required not merely compliance but active cooperation, not only from the agencies involved but from the clients intended to benefit from the policy. For one thing, it became obvious that there are so many veto points, places where one or more participants in the process can frustrate the implementation efforts,[7] that cooperation is essential.

More recently, analysts have realized that resource constraints, limits on government capacity, desires for increased efficiency, effectiveness, and economy, and a need for flexibility call for more than cooperation. These conditions require active creativity among members of the policy community if there is to be successful policy implementation. In this setting, government seeks the active involvement of not-for-profit organizations as contract service providers, invites greater stakeholder participation, and offers accountability in the form of service standards to clients.[8] Even in the regulatory arena, efforts are made to avoid adversary procedures in favor of alternative dispute resolution techniques like negotiation, mediation, or arbitration.

At the end of the day, all of these mind sets are required for successful policy implementation and operation. They work side by side. There are situations where compliance is needed, others where cooperation is useful, and others in which great flexibility is needed to take advantage of the creativity that is available in the policy community.

Standard Models of Implementation: Top-Down Bottom-Up, and Something In-Between

Those who have studied the process have emphasized the issue of why policy implementation efforts fail.[9] Particularly in the early years, they tried to identify causes of failure and suggested strategies needed to overcome them. Daniel Mazmanian and Paul Sabatier, in fact, advocated a number of principles of successful policy implementation that included:

1. clear and consistent objectives,
2. adequate causal theory,
3. an implementation process legally structured to enhance compliance by implementing officials and target groups,
4. committed and skillful implementing officials,
5. support of interest groups and a "fixer,"
6. changes in socioeconomic conditions that do not substantially undermine political support or causal theory.[10]

Fourteen years after he had originally advocated these principles, Sabatier looked back on some twenty empirical studies testing them and found that while some of the principles had been supported, others were more problematic. He found that all but the first point concerning clear and consistent objectives were important in many of the real cases studied. However, he concluded that while it was a useful checklist, there was a danger of taking too much of a top-down perspective and encouraged the use of the checklist in combination with lessons from the bottom-up perspectives offered by people like Lipsky, who wrote of the importance of "street level bureaucrats" in the life of a policy.[11] Those people at the line level make critically important decisions every day, whether they are police officers deciding who to arrest or social workers making critical judgments about service coordination.

Policy Evaluation: Well, Does It Work?

Of course, any discussion as to whether a particular policy design worked or whether there were implementation failures assumes that we know how to evaluate policy decisions and actions. It is therefore no surprise that policy evaluation developed as a field of study and consultation as policy analysis became more popular, and hit a high point in the 1970s and early 1980s.[12] At the same time, there is probably no aspect of public policy study that has been more hotly debated and criticized. The controversy concerns a number of important questions. What kind of a process is a policy evaluation? How do we know what success means? Who determines success?

Politics, Analysis, or Advocacy for Hire?

Charles O. Jones characterized policy evaluation as a process of "specification, measurement, analysis, [and] recommendation."[13] So defined, evaluation is a rational process of assessment performed using precise tools that produces judgments. Indeed, the very idea of policy evaluation assumes a rational actor model of policy making which is, for reasons discussed in Chapter 6, a very problematic assumption. In fact, relatively few students of public policy outside of evaluation analysis assume that the rational actor model describes reality. Some have gone so far to say that the tendency of policy evaluation to move toward economic styles of analysis and to claim precision in measurement ignores the fundamental fact that policy choices are political decisions. What constitutes success is determined politically and not mathematically or economically.[14]

Those criticisms of policy evaluation have been made more poignant by the evidence that the techniques of evaluation analysis have so often been used as tools of advocacy rather than neutral analysis. The suspicion that many who hold themselves out as evaluators are essentially hired guns ready to justify or attack whatever policy they are paid to address, depending on who is paying, has led to considerable doubts about the validity of evaluation claims. To those tensions are added the frustrations of people involved in the operation of programs who rarely ever see positive outcomes from evaluations. Instead, they often receive a great deal of criticism from people who parachute into a situation, pronounce success or more often varying degrees of failure, make those judgments within very limited time frames, and then leave, accepting no responsibility for the ultimate consequences of their judgments.

On the other hand, there is always the danger that if policy evaluation is rejected because the analysts are often unpopular messengers carrying bad news, the alternative may be the kind of empty ideological judgments about policy that too often characterize political decisions. If the answer to that problem is merely to let market choices take the place of policy judgments, then there are significant social consequences that will follow just as they did at an earlier time in history. At a time when hard decisions must be made among programs serving worthwhile ends, there must be some way to determine how well, albeit perhaps in relative terms, any given policy is doing and how it can be improved.

How Do We Learn the Meaning of Success?

Essentially, policy evaluation asks how well a policy is working. What are the actual costs as compared with the anticipated costs of the policy? What are the unanticipated consequences, either positive or negative, that have come from the policy? To these more general questions, Peter Rossi and Howard Freeman add:

- What is the nature and scope of the problem requiring new, expanded, or modified social programs? Where is it located, and whom does it affect?
- What feasible interventions are likely to ameliorate the problem significantly?
- What are the appropriate target populations for a particular intervention?
- Is the intervention reaching the target population?
- Is the intervention being implemented in the ways envisioned?
- Is it effective?
- How much does it cost?
- What are the costs relative to its effectiveness and benefits?[15]

To answer these questions, it is essential to decide what counts as success and how to assess it. There are several different kinds of measures that have been used over time. They provide different perspectives on a policy and call for different kinds of measurements at different points and times in the policy process. Robert Behn provides examples of the differences as they might appear in connection with a hypothetical health program intended to help pregnant women and their children.

[handwritten: • base line measure as starting point for evaluation.]

- *Input measures* include the number of public health clinics providing this service, the number of public health nurses working in these clinics, and the dollars spent on the program.

- *Output measures* include the number of women who participated in the program, the number of visits these women made to the clinics, and the prenatal instructions they followed.

- *Outcome measures* include the number of healthy (and unhealthy) babies born to women who participated in the program.

- *Impact measures* include the difference between the number of healthy babies born to women who participated in the program and the number of healthy babies who would have been born to these women had they not participated in the program.[16]

There has been considerable criticism of evaluations that focus on outputs from agencies, and a demand from legislators and constituents to increase the measurement of outcomes and impacts that flow from policies. Only in this way can we know how well a policy is being implemented and understand its real consequences. But sometimes the outcomes and impact assessments can lead to problems of interpretation as to success. Thus, there is the classic case of the so-called THOR program based on the idea that labelling possessions and putting out warning signs to potential robbers would reduce burglaries. On evaluation, it was determined that there had been no significant reduction in the number of burglaries, but, because of the fact that property was marked, the successful return of stolen property to its owners improved dramatically. Was the policy successful? There are two answers. The first is that the policy was not successful but did have a positive externality, an unanticipated benefit or at least an underappreciated result. The other is that it was successful but in a different way from that which was originally intended.

When analysts try to assess relative benefits and costs, the situation becomes much more complex. Sometimes the costs and benefits come in terms of political value or in terms of behaviors that are difficult to characterize. Thus, it becomes very difficult to assess fully the benefits associated with health and nutrition programs for pregnant women and their children. While the costs are relatively easy to measure, the estimate of benefits is extremely complex and difficult to capture and quantify.

Who Determines Success?

These difficulties raise the question of who sets the criteria by which success or failure is to be determined. Policy evaluation as a field faced some of the same criticisms as policy implementation in that it was often a top-down activity in which national or state-level organizations contracted with evaluators to go out and make assessments of policy success or failure. That kind of activity is often sporadic and, frankly, a somewhat arbitrary process. It often gives a snapshot that may or may not be a good picture at any given moment in time. Public administrators have had difficulty with it in part because it is so often in the form of a judgment rather than assistance.

These frustrations have led to improvements in policy evaluation, but they have also encouraged the development of a different approach to evaluation that is quite separate from the accepted policy evaluation literature. Flowing out of the Total Quality Management literature borrowed from the private sector, the attempt is to engage those involved in the day-to-day operation of policies at the service-delivery level in a continuing conversation about program improvements.[17] In theory at least, if those administrators and service delivery officers can be encouraged to spot problems and work together to develop solutions, the result will be far more effective and valuable than any top-level policy assessment performed in an agency. Moreover, because these people are at the point of service, they are in a position to see outcomes much more directly and to value both outcomes and impact much more than the kinds of input or output measures that are so often used at the top levels of a ministry or agency.

Related to that is a desire to engage the recipients of public services, the targets of policy, in the assessment process. This effort has taken various forms and names in different countries over the last several years, from the British Citizens' Charter, setting forth certain levels of service that a citizen has a right to expect from a ministry, to the Customer Service Standards developed in the United States by federal agencies under the reinventing government initiative of the Clinton administration. There are also those who advocate taking the process several steps further and using voucher programs to allow clients to choose the services and organizations in which they wish to participate, and letting these market-type decisions judge service quality.

There are, unfortunately, a range of problems associated with these efforts, starting with the fact that citizens are far more than customers.[18] Moreover, there are many kinds of policies that cannot really be evaluated in that way, particularly in regulatory areas or law enforcement activities. Additionally, the kinds of responses one obtains may be of value in some aspects of evaluation but not others. They may be less indicators of the policy or its administration than of the operation of a particular office. At the very least, the argument runs, one cannot ensure continuous improvement in the implementation and operation of a policy, nor can one assess the overall effectiveness of a policy at any particular moment in time without involving both the people who operate it and the perspectives of those affected by it.

Policy Termination: Quick Death, Reincarnation, or Long-Term Hospice Care?

The question that often arises, however, is what to do if a decision is made that a policy is ineffective, inappropriate to the current situation, or too costly. In terms of the stages of public policy, this is often termed policy termination or transformation. It is somewhat surprising that of all of the facets of the policy process, policy termination has received the least attention.[19]

One of the reasons it has been difficult to draw attention to this process is that it represents a kind of failure and brings with it a host of consequences, most of which are negative. The metaphor is that of a physician who concludes that she has a terminally ill patient. It is very difficult for someone trained to heal to accept the inevitability that the patient will die despite the doctor's best efforts. Having once accepted that reality, however, it is even more difficult to go on treating the patient, because each contact is a continuing reminder of the physician's limitations. Those feelings for the clinician do not, however, affect the fact that the patient needs and deserves the best care that can be provided during this most difficult phase of life. There are similar sensations for public administrators called to preside over the death of a policy. Like the physician, the decision to declare a policy terminal is out of the administrator's hands, a matter normally within the province of elected officials.

Should the Policy Be Terminated or Transformed?

There is another metaphor that has become increasingly popular in discussions of this phase of the policy process. It does not assume that the answer is necessarily to kill a policy. It is a picture more like that of the corporate troubleshooter who is brought in from the outside to pare down, reorganize, reshape, discipline, and straighten out a troubled firm. The corporate ramrod may decide that a merger or sell-off is in order or that a wholesale dismissal of the management team is required. The idea is to cut through the normal forces of organizational life, straighten things out, tighten things up, and move forward.

Within public management, this model gained popularity in the 1980s with the rise of what is often termed "cutback management." Charles Levine, the best known scholar of cutback, was trying merely to convince public administrators that it was possible to live with pressures on public agencies and even to use those pressures to achieve changes that might not be possible during normal times.[20] However, his ideas were applied in a much more ambitious fashion. Whereas in an earlier time the mark of political success for a public manager might be the expansion in the size of his or her organization and the growth of the agency's authority or jurisdiction, the mark of success in the past twenty years has often been how effectively one could pare down the organization, get rid of people, and reduce the scope of agency operations. Cutback became an end in itself, with the successful cutback manager anticipating an opportunity to move on to more influential positions.

The medium ground was an effort to say that many policies had been understandable and appropriate when adopted, but that circumstances had changed over time. Now the policies should either be terminated or transformed to meet the new conditions. Indeed, throughout the 1970s there was expanded use by many governments of sunset provisions in legislation that required a program to be reauthorized by a fixed date or go out of existence. Unfortunately, because of the press of business, or for political reasons, sunset reviews have been extremely uneven in quality and sporadic in timing.

What Are the Implications of Termination?

One of the reasons that decisions about transformation or termination of policy are so difficult is that the consequences are so significant. Clearly, there is the loss of service to the clients, but there are also losses of jobs to service providers and the impacts that brings to communities where those offices are located. This problem was seen in most dramatic form with the wave of military base closings of the 1990s. It is all but impossible for individual members of Congress to decide to terminate facilities in their districts, which is why the legislature created a commission to recommend base closures, relieving members of the individual responsibility.[21]

These consequences are reasons why policies are often not terminated as such, but are bled dry over time and eventually fade from the scene, though perhaps retaining a shell in the form of a weak organization. At some point they may be terminated. The problem in the contemporary context is that the fiscal stresses are so severe that many governments cannot afford to have a large number of weak programs: They require the resources those programs are wasting for new policies. The short-term solution has often been to encourage weak organizations to become more entrepreneurial, but that is often a relatively limited option that only holds off the inevitable for a time.

The Shortcomings of the Traditional Policy Process Models

It may be these new circumstances that have called for a realization of the weaknesses in our understanding of the policy process and have encouraged a more realistic appraisal of the forces shaping it. There are several lessons that have emerged.

First, the policy process is not linear. It is perhaps better characterized by loops rather than by lines on a systems diagram. It is iterative in the sense that as a policy moves into implementation it triggers new problems that are fed back into the problem-definition and agenda-setting stages for further policy action. The same is true of evaluation. Indeed, if evaluation is working well, it should change implementation and improve program performance. The lessons learned in the termination of one policy should inform the policy formation process for another policy, and so on.

Second, studies of policy implementation and evaluation have too often failed to produce lessons about how to produce and operate better policy and have instead focused on what not to do. The level of complexity needed to understand the problems of implementation can lead to a sense that it is only possible to find out what was wrong with the patient by performing an autopsy after he dies rather than finding out in time to save him. For example, the "Garbage Can Model" developed by Michael D. Cohen, James G. March, and Johan P. Olsen,[22] has been widely favored by implementation scholars in the past decade, but it has a number of problematic implications. March and his colleagues begin from the proposition that decision makers operate in "organized anarchies" characterized by "problematic preferences . . . a variety of inconsistent and ill-defined preferences," "unclear technology" in which "its own processes are not understood by its members," and "fluid participation" in which "participants vary in the amount of time and effort they devote to different domains; involvement varies from one time to another. As a result, the boundaries of the organization are uncertain and changing; the audiences and decision makers for any particular kind of choice change capriciously."[23] Although these authors were speaking of organizational choice, commentators on policy have applied this approach to policy choice as well. To evaluate what goes on in the policy process, they suggest, it is possible to envision

a choice opportunity as a garbage can into which various kinds of problems and solutions are dumped by participants as they are generated. The mix of garbage in a single can is dependent on the mix of cans available, on the labels attached to the alternative cans, on what garbage is currently being produced, and on the speed with which garbage is collected and removed from the science.[24]

Analysts who view the policy process from this perspective tend to look back to examine how the various unanticipated problem streams flowed together to produce what actually happened as compared with what had been expected to take place under a particular policy. While there is much that can be learned from this approach, it is not especially helpful to public administrators who must deal with policy in real time from within the process rather than after the fact and looking backward.

One answer has been a revival of focus during the 1990s on policy formulation with an emphasis on designing policies that are as self-implementing as possible. Hence, we find market tools attractive on the theory that they are driven by their own dynamics. Sadly, that is taking us back in the direction of fantasies about the possibility of rational actor policy making, something that many years of experience have proven illusory. The third lesson we have learned with regard to successful policy choices is that there is a need to learn from the international community and to acknowledge the effect at all stages of the policy life cycle of global realities on what may appear to be domestic policies. That global view should also produce an awareness of the importance of issues of equality and fairness that are so often lost in the dynamics of the policy process. Hence, the Brundtland Commission report entitled *Our Common Future* (discussed in Chapter 1) observed that without a sensitivity for these issues of equality and equity, it will be impossible to achieve the critical synthesis of social development, environmental protection, and economic development essential to our survival together in the century ahead.

Conclusion

It is clear that the formulation of a policy is only a part of an ongoing process that is influenced by a wide range of factors, including lessons learned from the implementation and evaluation of previous policies. For public administrators, in fact, the primary emphasis is on policy implementation. Of course, implementation is not a task that is enclosed within a single agency but is an effort to manage within one's own organization, coordinate with other agencies at several levels of government, and cooperate with nonprofit and private sector organizations as well. It is not merely a top-down activity concerning the issuance of regulations and guidelines, but, in many respects, a bottom-up activity that requires not merely compliance, but cooperation and even active creative partnerships if the policies that legislatures design are ever to realize their purposes in the streets. It is often at the street level where some of the most important implementation decisions are made on a day-to-day basis.

Indeed, one of the major transformations of policy evaluation has been to attempt to refocus. Rather than overly simplistic top-down measures of policy success or failure, recent efforts to determine how we are doing have, like implementation perspectives, moved to a bottom-up approach. Emphasis is on the need to have administrators at the point of service be willing to identify problems and be rewarded for communicating with superiors so that problem-solving efforts can begin. The task is to get rid of the old attitude that superiors only want to hear of successes. In fact, the effort is to move beyond internal techniques of evaluation to involve the people who are the recipients of the government's services, where appropriate, in the assessment of policy performance.

The most complex questions continue to be what to do if a policy is judged to be ineffective, no longer feasible, or outmoded. There continues to be a need for creativity by public managers in policy termination or transformation. The difficulty is to convince administrators that the goal is not simply to determine who can cut the most people or reduce budgets the most as a goal in itself. Rather, the challenge is to feed back the information collected during evaluation and use it to reshape policies and their implementation to fit the new circumstances and solve existing problems. Making such changes, of course, requires attention to organizational theory and behavior, human resources management, and budgeting, which are the subjects of the chapters to follow.

Notes

[1] See e.g., U.S. General Accounting Office, *Block Grants: Characteristics, Experience, and Lessons Learned* (Washington, DC: General Accounting Office, 1995).

[2] See Robert D. Bullard, *Confronting Environmental Racism* (Boston: South End Press, 1993).

[3] 347 U.S. 483 (1954). See generally Charles S. Bullock III and Charles M. Lamb, *Implementation of Civil Rights Policy* (Monterey, CA: Brooks/Cole, 1984).

[4] See e.g., Charles Johnson and Bradley C. Canon, *Judicial Policies: Implementation and Impact* (Washington, DC: Congressional Quarterly, 1984); Bradley C. Canon, "Courts and Policy: Compliance, Implementation, and Impact," in John B. Gates and Charles A. Johnson, *The American Courts: A Critical Assessment* (Washington, DC: Congressional Quarterly, 1991); Theodore L. Becker and Malcolm M. Feeley, *The Impact of Supreme Court Decisions,* 2nd ed. (New York: Oxford, 1973); and Stephen L. Wasby, *The Impact of the United States Supreme Court: Some Perspectives* (Homewood, IL: Dorsey Press, 1970).

[5]Howard Ball, Thomas Lauth, Dale Crane, *Compromised Compliance* (Westport, CT: Greenwood Press, 1982). Ball, Lauth, and Crane also relied on the important work by Harrell R. Rogers and Charles S. Bullock III, *Coercion to Compliance* (Lexington, MA: D.C. Heath, 1976).

[6]Paul Sabatier, "Top-down and Bottom-up Approaches to Implementation Research: A Critical Analysis and Suggested Synthesis," Paper presented at the XIIIth World Congress of the International Political Science Association, Paris, July 15–20, 1985.

[7]See Eugene Bardach, *The Implementation Game* (Cambridge, MA: MIT Press, 1974).

[8]See B. Guy Peters and Donald Savoie, eds., *Governance in a Changing Environment* (Montreal: McGill/Queens University Press, 1995).

[9]Jeffrey L. Pressman and Aaron B. Wildavsky, *Implementation* (Berkeley, CA: University of California Press, 1973); Donald Van Meter and Carl Van Horn "The Policy Implementation Process: A Conceptual Framework," *Administration & Society* 6 (Feb. 1975): 445–488; Robert T. Nakamura and Frank Smallwood, *The Politics of Policy Implementation* (New York: St. Martin's Press, 1980); Daniel A. Mazmanian and Paul A. Sabatier, *Effective Policy Implementation* (Lexington, MA: D.C. Heath, 1981).

[10]Paul Sabatier, *op. cit.,* 3–4

[11]Michael Lipsky, *Street-Level Bureaucracies* (New York: Russell Sage, 1980).

[12]See Peter H. Rossi and Howard E. Freeman, *Evaluation: A Systemic Approach,* 4th ed. (Newbury Park, CA: Sage Publications, 1989).

[13]Charles O. Jones, *Introduction to the Study of Public Policy* (Monterey, CA: Brooks/Cole, 1984), 196.

[14]Deborah A. Stone, *Policy Paradox and Political Reason* (Glenview, IL: Scott Foresman, 1988).

[15]Rossi and Freeman, *op. cit.,* 18.

[16]Robert Behn, "The Three Big Questions of Public Management," *Public Administration Review* 55 (July/August 1995): 319.

[17]See generally Peters and Savoie, *op. cit.*

[18]See Jon Pierre, in Peters and Savoie, *op. cit.*

[19]See Peter deLeon, "Public Policy Termination: An End and a Beginning," *Policy Analysis* 4 (Summer 1978): 369–392.

[20]Charles H. Levine, "Organizational Decline and Cutback Management," *Public Administration Review* (July/August 1978): 316–325.

[21]See Eugene Bardach, "Policy Termination as a Policy Process," *Policy Sciences* 7 (1976): 123–131

[22]Michael D. Cohen, James G. March, and Johan P. Olsen, "A Garbage-Can Model of Organizational Choice," *Administrative Science Quarterly* 17 (March 1972): 1–25.

[23]*Ibid.,* 1.

[24]*Ibid.,* 2.

Chapter 8

Managing Public Organizations

Few things in, around, or about organizations survive or persist for long periods of time unless they serve useful purposes. Politicians and citizens alike may thoroughly enjoy engaging in "bureaucracy bashing," but bureaucracy as we know it remains the dominant form of government (and business) organization in the United States, as it has for nearly two hundred years. This chapter is about the techniques of organization that public administrators use to manage and change the organizations within which we live and work. Bureaucracy is one of those types of organization. Before moving on to consider the different kinds of organizations we employ, it is useful to clear away some of the underbrush that has been piled onto this term, *bureaucracy,* and to consider why it has persisted. After examining this concept, one that all the world seems to love to hate, we will turn to a basic discussion on historical assumptions about organizations and some of the problems that arise from the sometimes uncritical continued use of those assumptions.

Bureaucracy's Advantages

While a number of the advantages of the large-scale, bureaucratic form of organization are examined later in this chapter, it is useful to introduce them now. Bureaucracy is the single best form of organization yet devised for providing consistency, continuity, predictability, stability, deliberateness, efficient performance of repetitive tasks, equity, rationalism, and professionalism.[1] It is a way of organizing that is well suited to the task of minimizing the influence of politics and personality on organizational decisions. It helps, for example, to support hiring and promotion of employees based on job skills and knowledge rather than "who you know" or political patronage.

In addition, bureaucracy is based on the need to provide well-defined lines of individual accountability, authority, and responsibility. These characteristics are ones that are particularly desirable—and necessary—for maintenance of a representative democracy. In government organizations, bureaucracy provides accountability to higher authorities, ultimately to authorities who are elected by the public, through unambiguous chains of command. This accountability works because bureaucracy defines distinct boundaries of authority for individuals and offices. Chapter 2 explained that officials can be asked to provide evidence that they rightfully possess the authority they are asserting by producing the legal delegation that empowers them. Thus, bureaucracy is the best organizational form yet devised for allowing elected officials (and others) to identify and control who in government is responsible to whom for what.

This brief overview of bureaucracy's advantages, however, contrasts sharply with the image most people have of bureaucracy. How can we possibly claim that government bureaucracies are: (1) efficient; (2) ideally suited for minimizing the influence of politics and personality on organizational decisions; or (3) the best form of organization yet devised for allowing elected officials (and others) to identify and control who is responsible to whom for what?

Dissatisfaction with the performance of government bureaucracies is rampant. For many of us, our frustration has advanced into cynicism, anger, and perhaps even alienation from the organizations of our own governance. This does not, however, refute claims about the advantages of bureaucracy. There are two fundamental reasons for the disparity between the asserted advantages of bureaucracy as a form of organization and our frustration with government bureaucracies, our collective sense that they are totally unable to deal with important issues.

First, there are flaws in the ways that government bureaucracies are structured and managed. Few government agencies are set up or run precisely as prescribed in the theory of bureaucracy. We bend, fold, and mutilate our public organizations, management systems, and policies every time a politician alleges fraud, inefficiency, mismanagement, or nonresponsiveness to policy initiatives. We modify them more whenever a business-dominated blue-ribbon task force, for instance the Reagan administration's Grace Commission, issues recommendations about how government should be run more like a business. We tinker with them if a citizens' group complains about its treatment at the hands of the bureaucracy. It is much easier to reorganize or make other symbolic shufflings than it is to ferret out and fix the root causes of problems. Government bureaucracies have been altered endlessly to fit political demands. It should come as no surprise, therefore, that most presidents of both political parties appoint groups to recommend reforms of the bureaucracy. And it is equally obvious why all of those appointed commissions recommend greater authority for control by the president of administrative agencies and the civil servants who staff them.

Although this problem is large and aggravating, it reflects the realities of democracy. We do not live in a world of organization theory, but in political reality.

Second, bureaucracy's advantages are also becoming its greatest weaknesses. As the prevailing form of large-scale organization, however, bureaucracy faces an even more serious, long-term problem. Many of the advantages that cause bureaucracy to be a desirable form of organization are losing or have already lost importance. Even if our public bureaucracies were perfectly run, they would still be inadequate for administering government in the environment that emerged in the 1990s and that we will face in the twenty-first century. What we expect from our government agencies is changing. Fine tuning or learning how to manage hierarchical organizations better[2] will not suffice.

Bureaucracy's Advantages as Weaknesses

Consistency, continuity, predictability, stability, deliberateness, efficiency in performing repetitive tasks, equality, and rationalism are without doubt important criteria, but they will not be adequate standards for the challenges of the twenty-first century. The environment in which government agencies operate and the methods of administering them are undergoing fundamental change. Organizational structures, forms, procedures, and concepts need to change as well.

A number of the changes that will continue to have the greatest impact on public organization theory are discussed in this chapter. They include technological change, the accelerating rate of overall change in the environment, the complexity of our social problems, increasing use of third-party management, and changing demographics. These changes are interconnected and interactive. Their effects are cumulative. While it is important to understand them individually, it is necessary to visualize each as a component of a larger composite picture, rather than merely as distinct developments.

Technological Change

Although many varieties of technological change can influence government structures and functions, advancements in information systems will have the most dramatic impacts. In *The Age of the Smart Machine: The Future of Work and Power,* Shoshana Zuboff[3] observes that we are moving beyond "automating, . . . replac(ing) the human body with a technology that enables the same processes to be performed with more continuity and control." Zuboff continues, saying that we are moving on to "informating, . . . using the same technology of automation to simultaneously generate information about the underlying productive and administrative processes through which an organization accomplishes its work."[4] Information that is needed to coordinate, operate, and control organizational processes can be accessed easily at the work site through computer technology.

Informating is already requiring us to make important choices. Zuboff proposes two contrasting scenarios. In the first, intelligence will reside in smart machines at the expense of human critical judgment. Managers will attempt to control access to information in order to maintain their traditional authority. Employees will become "ever more dependent, docile, and secretly cynical."[5] At worst, the new technology may be used for surveillance purposes, to coerce employees into submission and conformity. Already business telephone messages tell the client that the call may be monitored by supervisors.

Zuboff's contrasting scenario is more optimistic. It pictures an environment where workplace behavior is transformed. Relationships are more collaborative. As old supervisory functions become unnecessary, hierarchical distinctions disappear. "Authority comes to depend more upon an appropriate fit between knowledge and responsibility than upon the ranking rules of the traditional organizational pyramid."[6] New forms of information and social exchange yield a new level of shared responsibility.

Both of Zuboff's scenarios are plausible. Obviously, most of us hope the optimistic version will emerge, but we need to do more than passively hope. People who are accustomed to having power will not relinquish their hold on it easily. At the same time it is very difficult for most people, supervisors or workers, to conceive of organizations without hierarchical layers of power and authority. Although information technology may eliminate the need for many of the coordinating and controlling functions that supervisors and managers have performed for generations, it will be very difficult to throw off our mental images. Organizations resemble pyramids to most of us. Managers seem traditionally to have possessed almost a divine right to manage, direct, and control those beneath them in that pyramid.[7]

Information technology is already changing the shape, form, nature, and rules of bureaucracies as we know them. This is not a futurist's scenario, but today's reality. In the past several years, numerous major corporations have been laying off thousands of middle-level managers, largely because of information technology. The assumption is that many of the functions performed by those managers can be accomplished by first-line employees equipped and educated to work with information technology. They can be monitored by top managers who can simply sample the network to check up on operations.

The concepts of organizational hierarchy, accountability, authority, and responsibility will never return to their pre-1990s' meanings. Informating is forcing basic change. The questions we face are not whether change will occur or when. They are, rather: In what ways can we adapt? What can we do to steer through the currents of change to take our organization in the directions we desire to go?

Accelerating Change in the Environment

This chapter examines how bureaucracy is designed to buffer and protect government agencies and citizens against sudden, potentially damaging changes in values, fads, and fancies. The price we have been paying, though, has been a lack of flexibility. The bureaucratic form of government is designed to produce efficiently within a known set of rules. Bureaucracy is not designed for and should not be expected to deal with rapid changes that are beyond rule changes.[8] Since 1990, we have been confronted, with little or no advance notice, with numerous electrifying changes in Eastern Europe, Asia, and Central and South America as well as within the United States. These developments have amounted to much more than rule changes. They are changes in the "game" of government. The depth and scope of these transformations will continue to accelerate. Will bureaucracies be rendered impotent or irrelevant? Will agencies be able to operate government programs and services? Will governments as we know them be able to survive if administrative agencies are not able to meet these challenges?

More Complex Social Problems

While the rate of basic change in society continues to accelerate, the challenges that confront government organizations daily are becoming even more complex. And, as earlier chapters have stressed, important issues and forces will not stop at organizational or jurisdictional boundaries. The economy, international debt, crime, pollution, global warming, national security, productivity—nothing that is truly important—will remain neatly within the boundaries of the public or private sector, or within the public sector at the national, state, or municipal level. In addition to requiring interpersonal and organizational competence, agencies will need interorganizational and intersectorial competence. Bureaucracy, which needs clear lines of accountability, authority, and responsibility, has great difficulty with these permeable boundaries.

Third-Party Management

As the issues with which government is expected to deal grow more complex and cross sectoral and jurisdictional boundaries, programs to manage and eliminate problems must address those two characteristics. The trend is already evident. Goods and services that used to be produced by single units of government are being contracted, franchised, granted, vouchered, and divested in favor of for-profit companies, nonprofit organizations, or interjurisdictional agreements. Countless newly established quasi-governmental/ quasi-nongovernmental districts and authorities have appeared on the horizon.

Our current organizational forms are not adequate for coping with a proliferation of multiorganizational and blurred-jurisdictional service delivery and financing systems. An organizational form designed to provide stability and consistency through layered levels of formal authority and direct accountability cannot be expected adequately to implement public policy in the complex environment of the twenty-first century.

Changing Demographics

The changing demographics of the workforce will continue to cause radical transformations in the values, attitudes, expectations, and behaviors of public employees, administrators, service recipients, and taxpayers. The population is visibly aging. The U.S. workforce is becoming more multicultural and more feminized. White male authority–oriented values and behaviors are undergoing unprecedented challenges inside organizations, in courts, and in legislative hearings. A different reality is needed and is only just beginning to emerge. It will not be adequate to our needs merely to recruit non-Whites and women who are encouraged to think and act like White males.[9] Public and private organizations are beginning to understand the need for new forms of organizational structures, policies, methods of doing business, and styles of interpersonal behavior.

There is a danger that some of those who are looking to the changing demographics in their own countries, including the United States, will miss the fact that public sector organizations are competing for talent and creativity in a global marketplace. As Chapter 1 noted, the United States represents a small minority of the world's population. While it is economically powerful, that strength can be matched by international competitors for available talent.

Challenges to Public-Organization Theory

For all these reasons, it is clear that government programs in the twenty-first century will be substantively different than they are today. Public sector organizations and the multiorganization systems that administer them will have different structures, reporting relationships, and forms of accountability. The processes of administration and service delivery will be different. The people who administer, deliver, and receive public services will look, see, think, and act fundamentally differently than the people we have become accustomed to encountering in the past.

The challenge for students of public organization theory is to devise organizational forms, styles, processes, and behaviors that can do more than accommodate and adapt to these changes. They must be designed so that they thrive on the new realities while simultaneously protecting and advancing the basic values set forth in the foundations of the political culture such, as the Constitution. At the same time, we need to be able to recognize that the colleagues with whom we deal from agencies in other countries face similar challenges in their own political and cultural contexts.

Thus far, the challenge has exceeded our ability to respond with adequate creativity and sensitivity. We cannot remain locked into bureaucratic organizations, technology and patterns of thought.

The Classical-Structural Organization Model

Before leaping into that complex future, let us take a step back in time to understand the forces that have influenced our contemporary management practices. Organizations have existed since humans first found that it was advantageous to work together for hunting, safety, and successful family life. Much of what is now known about organizations is grounded in the ancient and medieval great civilizations, including those of the Chinese, Egyptians, Indians, Hebrews, Greeks, and Romans. Most analysts, though, define the beginnings of the factory system in Great Britain in the eighteenth century as the birth point of complex economic organizations and, consequently, the study of them as organization theory. For example, centralization of equipment and labor in factories, division of specialized labor, management of specialization, and economic paybacks on factory and equipment all were primary concerns of the Scottish economist Adam Smith in *An Inquiry into the Nature and Causes of the Wealth of Nations,* published in 1776. Smith is widely known as the father of the academic discipline of economics, but he also revolutionized thinking about organizations.

It was not until the twentieth century, however, that the formal study of organizations began to expand and take shape as a field of study for academicians and managers. Prior to then, the need for knowledge of and insights into the workings of organizations simply had not been urgently needed, so the study of organizations largely lay dormant. The situation changed markedly when national industries began to supplant local businesses as the dominant institutions of production and commerce. The problems of managing large-scale organizations, public and private, brought the newly developing field of organization theory to center stage. Colonial powers took their emerging models of organization and management into the developing world.

Throughout history, the basic elements and functions of organizations have remained rather stable. Organizations have purposes, attract participants, acquire and allocate resources to accomplish goals, use some form of structure to divide and coordinate activities, and rely on certain members to lead or manage others. On the other hand, their purposes, structures, processes, and methods for coordinating activities have always varied, because organizations are complex open systems that are influenced by the world around them. Organizations are an integral part of the culture and environment in which they exist and function.

Likewise, theories of organization do not develop in a vacuum. They reflect what is going on in the society around them. Therefore, there is no such thing as *the* theory of organizations. Rather, there are many theories that attempt to explain and predict how organizations and the people in them will behave in varying organizational structures, cultures, and circumstances. Some groupings of theories share common assumptions about humans and organizations and also the aspects of organizations that are believed to be most important for understanding and predicting the actions of organizations. These groupings of theories are usually called *models, perspectives,* or occasionally *schools of organization theory.*

It should not be a surprise, then, to know that each of the major perspectives on organization theory is associated with a period in time and a particular cultural context. Thus, the late twentieth-century movement to break down barriers to trade has not alone resulted in allowing access to some markets. The difficulties that American organizations have in Asia have as much to do with cultural patterns governing how organizations interact as it is a matter of formal trade policies. In order to understand and appreciate public organizations as they exist and are viewed today, one must appreciate the historical contexts through which they developed and the cultural milieus during and in which important contributions were made to the body of knowledge about them.

The classical-structural organization model is associated with the advent of the factory system in Great Britain. The experiences of World War II and the postwar economic and social recovery led into the neoclassical organization theory. The "flower child"/anti-establishment/self-development era of the 1960s coincided with the rise of the organizational behavior perspective, or human resource organization, model. Finally, the computer-led information era of the 1970s and pervasive uncertainties of the 1980s substantially influenced the evolution of organization theory through the systems model, the organizational power perspective, the organizational culture perspective, and what have been variously called the post-systems and post-modern perspectives.

The classical-structural organization model was the first major organizational model. It dates back to the turn of the twentieth century. Despite its age, it continues to serve as the foundation, the base from which all other perspectives of organization theory have evolved. The classical-structural model developed during harsh times. The advent of power-driven machinery and the modern factory system presented managers, indeed societies, with unprecedented new challenges. Factories and equipment were more expensive than laborers, so it made economic sense to keep the machines busy. Thus, workers were not valued as individuals. People were treated as interchangeable parts in organizational machines whose parts were made of flesh only when it was impractical to make them of steel.

Foundations of the Classical Model

The classical model was virtually the only theory of organization until about 1940, and it remains highly influential today. Its basic tenets are rooted in the industrial revolution and the professions of mechanical engineering, industrial engineering, and economics. Organizations, it was thought, should be modeled after machines, using people, capital, and machines as their elements. Thus, classical organization theory is concerned primarily with the anatomy or structure of formal organizations, control of employees, and the flow of work through them. This was the milieu, the environment, the mode of thinking that shaped and influenced the enduring principles of classical-structural organization theory.

Lee Bolman and Terrence Deal have listed the basic assumptions or tenets of the classical model:

1. Organizations exist primarily to accomplish production-related economic goals.
2. There is one best way to organize for production, and that way can be found through systematic, scientific inquiry.
3. In order to function effectively, organizations need rationality. Thus, they need to shield their internal workings from environmental turbulence and develop norms of rational behavior.
4. Production is maximized through specialization and division of labor.
5. People and organizations act in accordance with rational economic principles.[10]

If we wanted to learn about a particular public agency from the classical perspective, our quest would start with Bolman and Deal's basics. First, we would examine its mission and primary functions as they are stated in the statutes that created the agency and modified its obligations over the years.

Second, we would study the organizational chart that graphically identifies the span of authority (the right to give directives and the power to exact obedience), lines of accountability and responsibility, mechanisms of support and advisement, and that suggests how important some functions may be. Third, we would ask for annual reports that had been prepared for the chief executive or the legislature. Annual reports describe the goals that were accomplished during the past year, give reasons why other goals were not fully achieved, and discuss plans for the future. The annual reports also document successful efforts to improve the efficiency and effectiveness of operations. Finally, we would peruse performance studies or audits conducted by outside evaluators such as the U.S. General Accounting Office (GAO). That agency produces studies of ineffective programs, inefficient operations, waste or fraud caused by inappropriate or inadequate structure, work processes, management procedures, and systems of accountability and control. Usually studies and audits recommend changes to strengthen management accountability, clarify responsibilities, streamline processes and practices, and tighten policies and procedures. The excerpt from a letter that accompanied a 1990 GAO study, which appears on page 211, provides an example.

There are five focal issues for classical-structural organization theory. First, organizations have *formally established purposes, goals, and activities* which, if accomplished, will benefit the citizenry or particular population the agency was created to serve. Second, they have an *organizational structure* that arranges offices and people in a logical set of formal reporting relationships. The organizational structure needs to provide clear lines of authority, responsibility, and communication among the individuals, branches, offices, bureaus, divisions, and departments of an agency. Third, they have *written policies and procedures* that specify what work is to be performed, using which processes and technologies, when, by whom, according to what quality and quantity expectations, and within what cost limits. Fourth, the organization has an agency *mission defined by elected officials* through legitimate political processes. Finally, an organization's structure, policies, processes, methods, controls, and responsibilities should be established through *rational, systematic, scientific analysis.* They should not be influenced by politics, personalities, or the preferences of individuals or interest groups.

How these characteristics would play out in an agency can be described using the themes of three pioneering groups of classical-structural giants, Frederick Winslow Taylor, Max Weber, and Henri Fayol. Consider briefly their three themes and then apply them to a hypothetical current-day government agency.

Theme 1, from Frederick Winslow Taylor and His Associates. There is one best way to structure an organization, to flow work through an organization,

General Accounting Office
Washington, D.C. 20548

B-222859

March 26, 1990

The Honorable Richard B. Cheney
The Secretary of Defense

Dear Mr. Secretary:

In January 1990, the Comptroller General identified the Department of Defense's (DOD) inventory management as an area of particular risk for mismanagement, fraud, and abuse. The Office of Management and Budget has also identified this as a vulnerable area. Over the last 20 years, we have issued more than 100 reports dealing with specific aspects and problems in DOD's inventory management. In May 1986 (1), we issued a summary report of over 300 prior DOD and GAO reports discussing problems in accountability and security of DOD inventories which showed that most of the systemic problems identified have existed for years.

DOD promised corrective actions in response to our recommendations, and it has made improvements in some specific areas, such as improving or amending policies and procedures for following up inventory inaccuracies. However, these corrective actions have not been effectively implemented, and the basic problems in DOD's inventory management remain. . . .

Although DOD officials say that economy is part of its goal, performance measures used throughout the system belie that statement. Little management attention has been focused on economy and efficiency. . . .

To meet the demand of a rapidly changing environment and decreasing dollars, DOD needs to change its mindset and reform the way it manages its inventory. This means requiring and rewarding efficient management practices while still satisfying customer demands. It also means top management involvement to effect reform. . . . DOD has often agreed with our report recommendations and has published revised policies and procedures which call for better controls. What was missing, however, was the next step—to follow up to ensure that the policies and procedures were being implemented.

Source: United States General Accounting Office, Report to the Secretary of Defense. *Defense Inventory: Top Management Attention Is Crucial* (Washington, DC: GPO, 1990), 1–2.

and to conduct any particular task. Starting about 1900, Frederick Winslow Taylor,[11] Frank B. Gilbreth,[12] and a group of their followers were spreading the gospel that factory workers could be much more productive if their work was designed scientifically. Scientific management, or Taylorism, was a series of methods and organizational arrangements designed by Taylor and others to increase output by discovering the fastest, most efficient, and least fatiguing production methods. This was a classical notion of efficiency. Indeed, the term "Therblig" (Gilbreth spelled backward) was coined as a unit for the measurement of efficiency.

Once the "one best way" was found, the job of the manager was to ensure that people used it. The classical model was a natural outgrowth of this line of thinking. If there is one best way to accomplish a particular production task, then there must also be one best way to accomplish tasks of social organization, including the design of organizational structures.

Theme 2, from Max Weber.[13] Bureaucracy is the best way to structure a large-scale organization. The single most influential statement, and the point of departure for all further analyses on the subject of bureaucracy, was written by the brilliant sociologist Max Weber (1864–1920). Weber communicated his notion of bureaucracy by describing an ideal type bureaucracy. The term *ideal type* does not mean ideal in the sense of perfect or desired. Instead, it means a simplified model of an idea taken to its extreme. It is an extrapolation from the real world of organizations to the central features that are characteristic of the most fully developed form of organization; in Weber's case, to the most fully developed form of bureaucracy. Weber's ideal bureaucracy includes the five characteristics defined earlier in this chapter.

Theme 3, from Henri Fayol[14] *and Luther Gulick.*[15] Scientific study of organizations and management will yield general principles of management and organization that can be applied to most large-scale organizations. During the same period when Taylor and Gilbreth were tinkering with time and motion studies of individual work places, Henri Fayol (1841–1925), a French engineer, was wrestling with the broader set of elements necessary to organize and manage a large corporation. Although Fayol's major works were published from 1910 to 1920, his contributions were almost ignored in the United States until *Administration Industrielle et Generale* was translated into English in 1949.

In the United States, the best known statement of the general principles approach to managing organizations is Luther Gulick's 1937 essay, "Notes on the Theory of Organization," in which he introduced the famous mnemonic, POSDCORB, which stood for the seven major functions of executive management (Planning, Organizing, Staffing, Directing, Coordinating,

Reporting, and Budgeting). Gulick's principles included, for example, unity of command (every employee should report to one supervisor) and span of control (the maximum number of people who should report to a single supervisor).

There is no agency of which we are aware that exactly fits the parameters of the classical model. However, many public agencies that have been described in the literature come quite close. An example might be the U.S. Forest Service, as described by Herbert Kaufman.[16] For present purposes, we will descibe in the next few paragraphs a hypothetical government agency—a police department—that faithfully adheres to the tenets and prescriptions of the classical-structural organization model and the three themes. How would such an organization look and work?

First, we would shape our police department like a pyramid, with a clearly ordered hierarchical system of supervisors and subordinates (Figure 8-1). Following Gulick, every employee would report to one supervisor. For example, each officer would report to only one sergeant, each sergeant would report to one lieutenant, and so forth up through the department to the chief.

Formal lines of authority would be established through which sergeants, lieutenants, and captains would be permitted to issue commands. There would be clearly documented rules for granting and limiting their authority to issue commands (as in Weber).

Again following Gulick, we would not permit more than seven subordinates to report to the same supervisor, which would very quickly guarantee that the organizational chart would be a tall pyramid (see Figure 8-1). For each officer, we would determine the responsibilities, tasks, and the best way to perform each task through scientific analysis (derived from Taylor and Gilbreth). Tasks would be divided into their smallest elements, and each officer would be assigned to perform a limited number of those elements. For example, some officers would specialize in investigating convenience store robberies and others in fast-food robberies. Some would become experts in working with youth, while others would specialize in providing court testimony in specific types of traffic cases. We would document the specific methods they are to use for doing each task element and train the officers to do them correctly. As employees repeatedly perform the same task elements, they will become highly proficient and the tasks will therefore be performed efficiently (taken from Taylor, Gilbreth, and Gulick).

In 1912, Frank Gilbreth articulated five important benefits that could be gained through the use of time studies. His somewhat timeless list includes:

1. To obtain all the existing information about the art or trade being investigated that is possessed by the present masters, journeymen, and experts of that trade. . . .

Figure 8-1
Organizational Hierarchy Shaped Like a Pyramid

In a classically structured hierarchy—such as a hypothetical, large-city police department—the lines of authority are in a rigid pyramid shape. Each person in the organization reports only to one person on the step above.

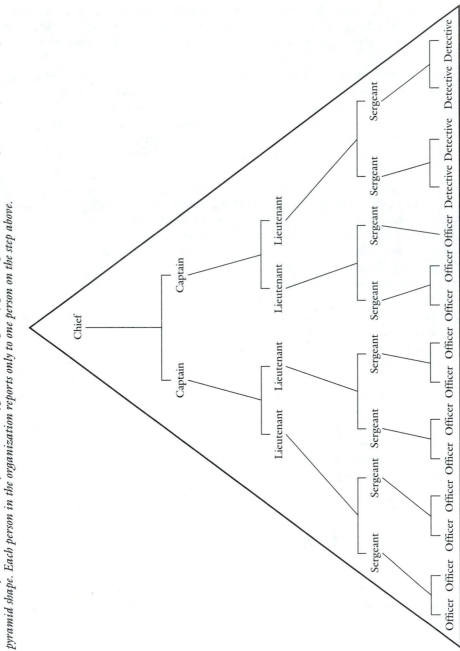

Source: J. Steven Ott.

2. To get the most exact information regarding the time required to perform each smallest element of the operation, so that in building up the standard method synthetically the quickest elements and motions may be selected, in order that the workman can, other things being equal, use a method consisting of elements requiring the least time to perform.

3. To determine which motions and elements are the least fatiguing, that the worker may be caused no unnecessary fatigue in his work, nor any fatigue outside of his work of actually producing output.

4. To determine the amount of actual rest that each kind of work requires.[17]

We would institute incentives that would motivate our police officers. They would be paid for the quantity and quality of their performance. Once they have been trained in the best way to perform their tasks, we would reward those who produce the most (again relying on Taylor and Gilbreth). Financial rewards might be given, for example, to officers who close difficult cases, do not lose cases on "technicalities," or negotiate through a hostage crisis without injuries. Taylor explained why the workers, not management, would be the chief beneficiaries of pay-for-performance incentives.

> Without any question, the large good which so far has come from scientific management has come to the worker. To the workmen has come, practically right off as soon as scientific management is introduced, an increase in wages amounting from 33 to 100 percent, and yet that is not the greatest good that comes to the workmen from scientific management. The great good comes from the fact that, under scientific management, they look upon their employers as the best friends they have in the world; the suspicious watchfulness which characterizes the old type management, the semi-antagonism, or the complete antagonism between workmen and employers is entirely superseded, and in its place comes genuine friendship between both sides.[18]

New police officers could only enter the organization at the bottom of the pyramid. All sergeants, lieutenants, and captains would be career officers, promoted and appointed from within based on their qualifications and knowledge of the department's policies, procedures, and rules (from Weber).

Systems and procedures would be established to ensure the accurate and rapid flow of information and decisions downward through the organization—from the chief and captains who have the most comprehensive knowledge to "beat cops" with the least knowledge. Requests, questions, and other types of communication with offices in other areas of the department (horizontal communication) would have to work their way up through the bureaucracy and then back down to the recipient. Employees would not be allowed to communicate outside of their chain of command (as in Weber).

Finally, all employees would receive never-ending training that would enable them to perform tasks in the best way and to know the policies and procedures. The training will also help prepare them for eventual promotion to a higher position (again from Weber).

Our hypothetical police department would be a tightly run ship, with strong centralized leadership. Its mission and purpose would be stated definitively in statute. Any lack of legislative clarity would be handled through administratively established rules documented in the policies and procedures manual. There would not be any ambiguity or uncertainty about what the department is expected to accomplish or where it fits into the broader government of the jurisdiction.

Likewise, there would not be any uncertainty about who in the department has the right to issue directives, the extent or limits of each position's authority and responsibility, or who is accountable to whom for what. All rules, rights, responsibilities, and work procedures would be documented in the policies and procedures manual. Executives (captains) would work their way up through the ranks over the course of a lifelong career, and in many instances, they would be the people who wrote the policies and procedures. They would be expected to have a complete grasp of the department's purposes and goals, technology and processes, policies, and rules. There would be integrity of purpose and policy, as well as consistency of practice from the top to the bottom of the department.

Our police department would have a large division of work analysis staffed by industrial engineers, systems analysts, and operations researchers. The division would analyze all positions, tasks, and the flow of work through offices and positions. Using the latest technology, all tasks and work flows would be broken down into elements, then studied intensively to determine how they could be performed most efficiently and with least employee fatigue. New equipment would be purchased whenever it can be justified through cost/benefit analysis. The division of work analysis would document its findings for each position, task, and flow of work in the policies and procedures manual. These would then be used in training programs and incorporated in exams to determine which officers qualify for promotion. Standardization of practices across the department would result, making it easy to locate qualified replacements for empty positions.

Well-analyzed tasks, disseminated through extensive employee training programs and the policies and procedures manual, would allow the department to offer financial incentives to its high producers. Once again, ambiguity would be minimized. Employees at all levels would know precisely what they are expected to accomplish and would be trained in the best methods for doing it. They would have the best equipment the department could provide. All employees who perform the same tasks would have an equal opportunity to raise their production. Those who do the best job of raising productivity would share financially in the gains.

Our hypothetical police department would pride itself on being absolutely consistent and equitable in its dealings with the public. If citizens with the same problems and circumstances came to different offices of the department, they would be dealt with identically. The policies and procedures manual, ongoing employee training programs, qualifications for promotion, and monitoring-control systems ensure that everything is decided and done the same way, by different officers, in different office locations, on different days.

Although employees know that promotions will not come along rapidly because there are few positions in the upper levels of the department's hierarchy, they also know that they will not have to compete with outsiders. We would appoint to higher positions only from within the department. No one from the outside could shortcut the lifelong process of learning needed to understand and appreciate our department. Job security is very high. Our people have made what amounts to a lifelong career decision; there is no need to rush. Besides, the department's rules and technology are complex, and the longer people stay in their present positions, the more time they have to master the intricacies of their next higher position.

When an employee is approached with a problem that is not documented in the procedures manual and, for example, requires our police department to coordinate with another office, agency, or level of government (such as a city, county, state, or national government), the employee knows to send the information in writing up through the bureaucracy until it reaches the appropriate level for a decision or for horizontal communication. The decision is then communicated down to the employee for implementation. Unanticipated incidents will cause new procedures or rules to be developed and implemented through the policies and procedures manual and incorporated in the department's training programs. Although our employee probably could have dealt with the issue (perhaps with assistance from a peer or supervisor), it is important to preserve the integrity of the policies, procedures, and hierarchical authority. If employees are permitted to make decisions that are not prescribed in the policies and procedures manual, the department will lose its ability to be consistent and equitable. It will make mistakes, the chain of command will be violated, authority will break down, and employees will be deprived of the opportunity to learn the best way to deal with future similar circumstances.

The roles and functions of department administrators would be quite clear. Know the policies and procedures, adhere to them faithfully, train and direct subordinates to adhere to them, and monitor subordinates to ensure that they are adhered to. When confronted with situations, decisions, or actions that are not addressed in the policies and procedures manual or are not within the scope of the administrator's responsibility or authority, pass them up the chain of command for resolution. Accurately communicate directives, information, and new policies and procedures received from above to employees.

Our hypothetical example of a police department is not very hypothetical. Many government agencies (and more than a few private companies) have been organized and run in essentially this way. This model makes a lot of sense. How else could a government agency, such as a police department, be structured and managed? The classical-structural model of organization is indeed a logical and rational way to run government. Does it matter that the model reflects thinking from the turn of the twentieth century? Does "old" necessarily mean that it is wrong?

The Classical Model in Twenty-First Century Management

In many respects, this hypothetical example of the classical model describes how many citizens believe most government agencies look, act, and should be managed. This is the model we have been raised to expect. There are exceptions, of course. For example, most people know that few government agencies have pay-for-performance or gain-sharing plans in place. For the most part, though, our model represents the pervasive public belief and expectation. Particularly if we listen very long to politicians on the campaign trail, it is easy to start believing that the model does indeed describe how government works—or should work—today.

As a general statement, military, law-enforcement, public safety, and other uniformed agencies tend to be organized and to operate more like our hypothetical police departments than other types of government agencies. Even the most militaristic agencies, however, deviate substantially from aspects of the model. We know, for example, that police officers in the street make a host of important decisions every day that call upon them to exercise judgment in situations so complex that no policy and procedures manual could possibly anticipate them.[19]

Indeed, the classical-structural organization model is a myth. The myth persists, however, because it feels right and appears to be rational. It fits our collective image of rational, purposeful, government agencies where administrators and employees know precisely what needs to be done and how, and what they personally can and cannot do or decide. When an administrator is promoted, dies, or resigns, one of several employees who has been groomed carefully for years to move into this position is appointed. There is, according to the myth, no break in continuity or change in policies and procedures. The agency rolls on, doing its work with precise efficiency.

The Limited Applicability of the Classical-Structural Model in the 1990s

The reality is that too many of the model's tenets, assumptions, and design characteristics simply are not applicable in today's world. Maybe they never were, but, without question, they are not now. Consider some of the most important gaps.

Modern Employees are Different. *People, at least in contemporary American culture, do not think or behave on the job in ways that the model assumes and requires that they will.* Individualism is a cherished value in the United States. People are not robots. They do not stop thinking when they go to work in the morning. They are not content when ordered to learn detailed procedures for performing a limited number of tasks and to perform those tasks repetitively. Specialization may increase the rapidity with which new tasks are learned, but people become bored, need challenges, and want to exercise a degree of control over their working environment. Except in unusual circumstances, they also are not willing to follow directives from on-high, blindly and passively. Government employees are thinking, feeling humans who often have access to more accurate information and may have a better understanding of circumstances and problem solutions than their superiors.

Although most people want more money than they currently earn, pay-for-performance plans have not been as successful, even in private enterprise, as might be expected. Taylor's "two-dollar-a-day man" attempt to explain motivation in simple economic terms does not usually work. Obviously, they are widely used in some occupations, most notably sales. Numerous studies over many years, though, have found varied effects of incentive pay on individual employee output. Despite the complexities and qualifications contained in the myriad research studies on the subject, their findings can be summarized as follows:

1. Motivation is something that happens *inside* individuals.
2. Different people are differentially motivated by different things.
3. Individuals are differentially motivated by different things under different circumstances and at different stages in their lives.

4. Money tends to get people's attention, but it does not always motivate and sometimes decreases motivation.

5. Many things that are not financial in nature affect motivation.

A Dynamic Open-System World. The classical model is designed for consistency and continuity in a stable, closed-system environment, but the context in which public sector organizations operate is neither stable nor a closed system. The greatest strength of the classical model organization is also its greatest flaw. In order to maximize efficiency, control, and consistency, it assumes that an organization is minimally affected by changes in its external environment. This assumption is, in fact, a requirement for organizational survival. It allows the organization to shield everything within it from externally imposed change, including its mission, policies, procedures, requirement to communicate through the chain of command, rule-based decision making, and management succession only from within. Inability to cope with unexpected change is the price the classical model pays for continuity and consistency. No agency can afford this price.

> For sheer tactical idiocy (during World War I), however, nothing could match that of the generals who clung to their "Attack" schema long after it had been rendered clearly obsolete by the machine gun. Time after time, wave after wave of troops proved that direct frontal assault was a futile exercise in carnage. Everyone knew it but those in command. It took a few years and millions of casualties for this idea to trickle upward in a convincing fashion to those who found explanations for failure everywhere but in their own planning. In fact, it probably never would have made it on its own but was carried along with field officers as they gradually were promoted to staff officers with the passage of time and then could make their views known.[20]

The environment fundamentally influences organizations in two ways: the need for timely, accurate information about the environment and how it is changing; and the need for resources from the environment. Agency employees at all levels and in all areas must know about what is occurring in the environment in order to manage and cope with change.[21] The classical model, however, carefully channels information about the environment to decision makers who interpret it and issue directives through the chain of command. Access to important information is restricted in order to retain control at the top of the pyramid, and thereby maintain consistency. By so doing, a classical-structural model agency is guaranteeing that it will become an organizational dinosaur.

Further, all organizations need to obtain resources from the environment for their survival and growth. Private firms sell products and services to customers in exchange for financial resources. In contrast, the primary sources of government agency revenues are taxes set by the legislature and allocated among agencies through the budgetary process. Agencies that do well in attracting resources are responsive to the public, the legislature, and the chief executive officer's ever-changing interests.[22] Agency entrepreneurial behavior is needed to persuade not only the officials who prepare the president's or a governor's budget request but also the program and appropriations committees of Congress or a city council. Career bureaucrats need to have access to legislative committee staff people, lobbyists, and budget analysts.

Access provides opportunities to learn about change as well as to influence the allocation of resources. Responsiveness to the changing desires of multiple interest groups and entrepreneurial behavior require both the willingness and the ability to adapt rapidly—to thrive on innovative and creative change. No organization can do so without the means to accumulate and interpret information rapidly. These organizational characteristics are diametrically contrary to the assumptions, tenets, structural design principles, and process rules of the classical model.

The classical model is a closed-system model of organization designed for efficient, tightly controlled production-type functions and employees suited to them in a relatively stable and certain environment. Today's government requires open-system models, designed primarily for complex information-based functions performed mostly by professional employees[23] in an uncertain, unstable environment.

Appointed Executives and Career Employees. *The highest ranking officials in government agencies do not work their way up through the ranks, learning the intricacies of an agency over years.* At all levels of government—city, state, and national—the highest-ranking officials in agencies are appointed by the elected chief executive officer—the mayor, governor, or president. These politically appointed administrators serve at the pleasure of chief executive officers for the express purpose of carrying out their particular policy agendas.[24] It is not at all unusual for the agenda of elected officials (and thus their appointees) to be contrary to an agency's ongoing mission and purpose. Permanent employees of an agency, employees who are not appointed by elected officials but instead are hired and promoted under the rules of a merit-based civil service system, consider themselves responsible professionals, the protectors of the agency's programs and values. It is naive to expect them to carry out directives dutifully and unquestioningly, particularly when they believe a directive would be detrimental to the agency's long-term interests. Besides, there will be another election in a few years, and the current officials may be gone. President Ronald Reagan's appointment of Terrel Bell as secretary of education provides a good example. Bell was appointed with the

Although President Ronald Reagan named Terrel Bell as secretary of education with a mandate to close the department, Bell did not do it.
(Photo courtesy of George Tames/NYT Permissions.)

clear charge to close down the U.S. Department of Education. It did not happen.

Permanent employees do not often resist initiatives from political appointees at the top. But it does happen, particularly when the agency's identity or professional stature is in jeopardy, such as when Reagan appointed Bell. When resistance occurs, it is rarely overt. That would be foolish. However, there is an old saying, unspoken but often thought, among civil servants: "I will be here long after you are gone." Many business executives who receive government appointments leave in frustration because they are not able to make things happen. That is in part because government and its permanent employees do not always behave as the classical-structural model—and political appointees from private business—assume. Some comments from former Secretary of the Treasury Michael Blumenthal are illustrative of the issue and the frustration it can cause for political appointees.

> The head of a government department or agency is not like the chief executive of a large corporation who has control over the personnel system, who can change it, can instill a certain spirit, can hire and fire. In government that kind of control does not exist. . . . So, even though I'm technically the chief executive of the Treasury, I have little real power, effective power, to influence how the thing functions. . . .
>
> Most of the people who work for you are not selected because they have administrative ability. They are selected because they have substantive knowledge in particular areas, and they get their jollies, their kicks, out of trying to have influence over those areas, not trying to become the best administrators of their particular bureaus.
>
> Out of the 120,000 people in the Treasury, I was able to select twenty-five, maybe. The other 119,975 are outside my control. And not only are they outside my control in terms of hiring and firing—they're also virtually outside my control in terms of transferring.
>
> So it's hard to talk about running something. If you wish to make substantive changes, policy changes, and the department employees don't like what you're doing, they have ways of frustrating you, or stopping you, that do not exist in private industry. . . . The main method they have is the Congress. . . . They can also use the press to try to stop you. . . .
>
> In private industry you have many ways of motivating people. . . . That's impossible in the government, because if I do it with one, all the others . . . say, what about me? If you say well, you're not as good, you may quite possibly be sued. So it just cannot be done. You have almost no control over selection. Hiring goes off a list. And to go outside that system involves more bureaucratic footwork than it is worth. . . .
>
> Therefore, to control the development of a policy, to shape out of that cacophony of divergent interests and dissonant voices an approach that eventually leads to a consensus and can be administered in a coherent fashion is an entirely different task in the government than it is for the chief executive of a company. . . . So you have to learn to become one of a large number of players in a floating crap game, rather than the leader of a well-organized casino that you're in charge of.[25]

Formal and Informal Dimensions Are Critical. *In government, most things are accomplished through a combination of formal authority and informal* *influence, not through the exercise of formal authority and directives alone.* One of the reasons so many businesspeople fail in the government or get frustrated and quit is that they cannot take this system. They dislike the fact that so many people get involved in decisions, so much is open, and there are virtually no secrets. Wallace Sayre[26] and Douglas Yates, Jr.[27] communicate this point effectively in diagrams (see Figures 8-2 and 8-3).

A few of the reasons why attempts to get things done often do not work through formal authority alone, without also using informal influence, have to do with the complexity of the context in which government agencies work. In the early pages of this chapter, we asserted that important problems and issues that governments are expected to solve seldom stop at organizational or jurisdictional boundaries. In many instances, government agencies (or jurisdictions) do not have authority over each other. Either they solve problems collaboratively—through informal influence—or the issue probably will not get solved.

Implications of the Problematic Classical Model

Almost anything a government manager undertakes involves trade-offs between competing values and goals. The structural and functional design of government organizations is not an exception. Effective public administrators must maintain a balance between the useful principles of the classical model and the realities of the twenty-first century. The classical model remains the single best organizational design that has ever been devised for such fundamental government purposes as unity of command (particularly useful purposes when an agency is responding to human- and nature-caused disasters) and unambiguous accountability for its actions (to an elected chief executive officer and legislature). The model cannot be ignored or discarded.

On the other hand, the ideal-type classical model must be adapted to current realities. Citizens expect more than the model is able to provide from their city, state, and national governments. Employees do not behave as that model requires. Even though military and para-military agencies have historically leaned toward classical-type models, even they have had to make major concessions to the changing times and expectations.

The structure and processes of public organizations present an ongoing dilemma. How can a public administrator take advantage of the strengths inherent in the classical model without falling victim to its weaknesses? Public officials must use professional judgment and skills to weigh advantages and problems, and select among alternative structural and functional designs.

Public agencies today are vastly different from the organizations that were described by Henri Fayol, Max Weber, Frederick Winslow Taylor, and Luther Gulick near the turn of the twentieth century. The differences, however, are

Figure 8-2
The Wallace Sayre Decision-Making Model

Based on Wallace Sayre's model, it is little wonder how any decision maker in the federal bureaucracy can make a decision. The model clearly illustrates the range of pressures applied to the bureaucrat.

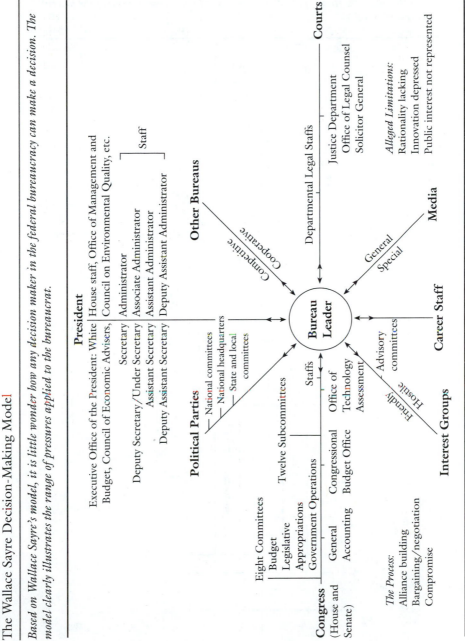

Note: The presidential and congressional lines of influence have been modified to reflect organizational changes since the Sayre model was developed.

Source: Walter G. Held, *Decision Making in Federal Government* (Washington, DC: Brookings Institute, 1979). Reprinted with permission.

Figure 8-3
The Douglas Yates Model

Unlike Wallace Sayre's model, Douglas Yates has constructed a management model emphasizing the influence that a public manager may have on other parts of the federal government and beyond.

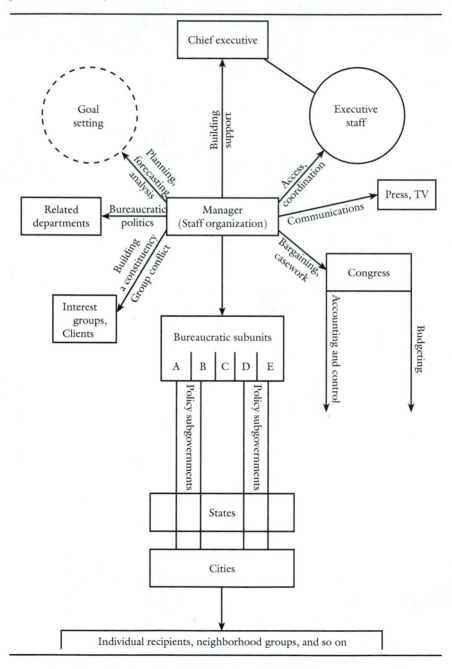

Source: Figure 1, "The Public Manager and the Management Environment" in Douglas Yates, Jr., *The Politics of Management.* (San Francisco: Jossey-Bass), 36. Reprinted with permission.

more than cumulative, normal changes over ninety to one hundred years of history, as seen with hindsight. The search for replacement models is the topic of Chapter 9. Before moving on to alternative models, however, we also need to look at the limits of this model from an entirely different vantage point: the technological perspective, with particular focus on information technology. Information technology limits the applicability of the classical model.

The classical model's technological flaws reflect society's leap into the information age. Technological advancements, particularly in information and control technology, have reduced the need for classical-model structures and procedures. For example, supervisors used to spend a large part of the working day telling employees what they needed to know, giving instructions, coordinating assignments so that jobs were done on time, checking work for accuracy, and making an almost infinite variety of workaday decisions. These functions were absolutely essential if the job was to get done efficiently and effectively.

The classical design is characterized by layers upon layers of supervisors who perform these information and control tasks. The shape of an organizational pyramid reflects the span of control—the number of people who report to each supervisor. A smaller span of control requires a higher pyramid. A larger span of control creates a flatter pyramid. Classical-structuralists since Henri Fayol and Luther Gulick have been concerned with the maximum number of people who should report to a supervisor, not the smallest number. In Gulick's words:

> *The Span of Control.* In this undertaking we are confronted at the start by the inexorable limits of human nature. Just as the hand of man can span only a limited number of notes on the piano, so the mind and will of man can span but a limited number of immediate managerial contacts. . . . The limit of control is partly a matter of the limits of knowledge, but even more is it a matter of the limits of time and of energy. As a result the executive of any enterprise can personally direct only a few persons. He must depend upon these others to direct others, and upon them in turn to direct still others, until the last man in the organization is reached.[28]

Three categories of limitations are evident in Gulick's analysis that collectively support the principle of narrow span of control; information limits, limits of human cognition, and control limits. Together, they virtually guarantee that large organizations, including most government agencies, will be tall pyramids.

Information Limitations

Information technology now performs many tasks that used to fill a supervisor's day. For public administrators, the most important information-technology advancements of the last decade have been in the actual use at their own workstations of computers and information technology by employees who are not computer or EDP (electronic data processing) specialists. Technological breakthroughs and equipment cost reductions have helped fuel these advances. Many organizations have abandoned their rigid, centrally controlled, preprogrammed, mainframe-based, management information systems of the 1970s in favor of flexible database systems. Database information system technology permits, and even encourages, people to structure and restructure information into patterns that fit and support their own particular needs, cognitive patterns, and problem-solving approaches. The technological breakthroughs, however, represent only part of the story. We have also experienced dramatic advances during the past decade in the willingness of public administrators and frontline workers to accept, use, and even experiment with computers and data systems.

Even though computers obviously have not and will not totally eliminate the need for supervisors, they have greatly reduced employee dependence on supervisors for some things, including much of the information needed to perform their jobs. Desktop and notebook computers with direct access to databases through network or modem communications provide more information, faster, more accurately, and in more usable forms than the best supervisors ever could. It is possible for line personnel in some agencies to access information as specialized as a client's history of missing scheduled meetings, the expected availability of a specialized hospital bed, the probability that a client will meet the eligibility rules for a program or service, the current location of a herd of bison, the best route to an emergency scene during inclement weather, when a "job-shadower" will be available for a supported job placement, the snow depth on specific stretches of highway, reported incidents and locations of a highly communicable disease, the percentage of drivers exceeding the speed limit on a particular stretch of interstate highway this morning, or which client a case manager should take on next.

Cognitive Limitations

The usefulness of the organization design principles espoused by Luther Gulick and Henri Fayol is constrained by limits on the amount of information the human mind can hold, process, and recall efficiently. "Just as the hand of man can span only a limited number of notes on the piano, so the mind and will of man can span but a limited number of immediate managerial contacts. . . . The limit of control is partly a matter of the limits of knowledge, but even more is it a matter of the limits of time and of energy."[29]

Fayol, Taylor, Gilbreth, Gulick, and other proponents of the classical model were committed to the maximization of efficiency through division of labor and close coordination of employees by supervisors with narrow spans of control. Tasks are analyzed scientifically and reduced to their smallest elements. Each employee is trained to do a few task elements very well and is assigned and paid to perform these elements only. Supervisors maximize efficiency by closely coordinating, supporting, and controlling the people who perform these highly specialized task elements. Frank Gilbreth explained these principles eloquently in 1911.

> *Description and General Outline of Motion Study: Necessity for Motion Study.* There is no waste of any kind in the world that equals the waste from needless, ill-directed, and ineffective motions. When one realizes that in such a trade as brick-laying alone, the motions now adopted after careful study have already cut down the bricklayer's work more than two-thirds, it is possible to realize the amount of energy that is wasted by the workers of this country. . . . Our duty is to study the motions and to reduce them as rapidly as possible to standard sets of least in number, least in fatigue, yet most effective motions.[30]

Since the early 1900s, the United States has moved from a production-based economy to a service economy and, increasingly, to an information-based economy. Highly repetitive and physically demanding jobs that are suitable for the old model are dwindling in both the private and public sectors. The activities carried out in government agencies have largely changed from the production of goods and services to the provision of information and regulation. These changes in the types of work done in public agencies have created the need for a more highly educated and trained workforce, for people who can collect, process, and disseminate information to others or use information to make decisions.

It is almost trivial to observe that today's information technology is able to relieve humans of lower-level mental tasks such as memorization and routine calculations. Computers and systems thereby play important direct roles in reducing cognitive limitations and the need for supervisors, and, by extension, for hierarchy. This does not necessarily mean, however, that supervisors, managers, and hierarchical organizational structures will disappear in the near future. Edgar Schein explains that our minds and emotions may not be able to cope with the notion of organizations that are not hierarchical.

> Our thinking about these matters is hampered by one major, deeply embedded cultural assumption so taken for granted that it is difficult even to articulate. This is the assumption that all organizations are fundamentally *hierarchical* in nature, and that the management process is fundamentally hierarchical. We need new models, but we may have difficulty inventing them because of the automatic tendency to think hierarchically. . . .

What may well happen is that *management as a traditionally conceived, hierarchical function will disappear altogether,* to be replaced with concepts that we have not yet developed. If that happens, of course, our traditional concepts of educating and developing managers will disappear as well, to be replaced with models that do not yet exist. . . .

I believe we take hierarchy for granted and that we have failed to realize how the assumptions underlying hierarchy pervade our thinking both in schools and in the workplace. If it is true that organizations will be flat networks in the future, then we must give serious thought to the following questions.[31]

The combination of changing government functions; rising education, training, and computer-literacy levels of employees; and the burgeoning growth of workplace information technology are collectively reducing cognitive limitations. Government employees know more, have more access to needed information, are more cognizant of their organizational and functional connectedness with others, and are expected to be less dependent on positions above them in the hierarchy for information, coordination of work activities, and in many cases, for decision making. The classical model's drive for efficiency through reductionism and analysis has largely been replaced by the drive for effectiveness through information integration and inference.

Actually, the difficulty today is not so much the availability of information that can be processed, but the danger of information overload. There is so much material that comes across a computer screen today that the difficulty is often finding ways to control the torrent. Hence the oft-repeated expression that trying to decide what to do with all the information on the World-Wide Web is like trying to take a drink of water from a fire hose.

Control Limits

The third category of limitations that supports the principle of narrow span of control is control limitations. Controls and control systems are the tools and methods that an organization uses to be certain that plans are executed as intended. They are used to monitor behavior and make corrections when behavior or results veer from expectations. They represent the maximum number of people and operations that a supervisor can have enough information about, understand well enough, and have enough time to control. Control limitations are being reduced by information technology as well as by recent trends in management technology.

The ability to control requires an ability to identify, understand, and gain access to information about the cause-and-effect relationships between activities and results. It is dependent on knowledge, and knowledge is dependent on information.[32] Under classical-model assumptions, information and control flow down through the bureaucracy to supervisors and their subordinates. Increasingly in today's world, information flows directly to employees (individuals or small work teams) who transform it into the knowledge and self-control needed to make corrections and meet expectations.

The leap from control by a supervisor's human judgment to self-control by employees and small work teams is not complex technologically. Any management-control system consists of five functions:

1. establish performance expectations (in other words, quality and quantity standards);
2. measure or observe performance;
3. identify deviations (in other words, possible problems) by comparing actual performance with expected performance;
4. take corrective action when actual performance deviates from expected performance by predetermined levels; and
5. adjust standards to reflect experience.

Three of these functions (2 and 3) are ably performed by information systems. Functions 1, 4, and 5 are measurably aided by computer systems but still require human decision making.

The impacts of developments in information technology on control limitations are profound. We have entered a period of exciting management-technology change that emphasizes self-control by individuals and work teams. Organization development (OD),[33] participatory management or employee involvement (EI),[34] Japanese management,[35] excellence in management,[36] total quality management (TQM),[37] and even management by objectives (MBO)[38] are part of the developments discussed in the next chapter. We introduce them here because all of these management movements share a tenet that is central to control limitations. All of them stress increased individual responsibility with decreased dependence on control imposed from higher in the bureaucracy. Although all of these management movements may share this tenet, each has its own vision about how that should look in operation.

Conclusion

We have introduced in this chapter the orderly, mechanistic tenets and assumptions of the classical-structural organization model and presented a hypothetical police department to demonstrate how they would play out in the design and processes of a Weberian ideal-type government agency. We have also explained what the classical model does well and, thus, why it continues to be the most pervasive model of organization. On the other hand, we have identified the major weaknesses that limit the model's usefulness in today's environment.

Even flawed models of organization serve useful functions, or they do not survive. The distinctive aspects of public agencies are a primary reason why the classical model has not quietly withered away into obscurity. Despite its weaknesses, the classical model remains better able than other models for coping with the organizational implications of public agencies legal-political contexts and their political accountability.[39] For example, people in government agencies are accountable to external entities to an extent and in ways that are alien to all except a very few private businesses.

A complex web of externally imposed influences and controls, accountability that does not include clearly defined rules or protections, and the necessity for appointed and elected executives to control the actions of career administrators, have resulted in the establishment of elaborate government agency structures, processes and controls. Even though classical model bureaucracies can be enormously frustrating, everyone who works directly in or with them benefits in some way. Layers of political appointees review what others have already reviewed to ensure agency consistency, fairness, and accountability to elected officials. The same multiple layers of review buffer, shield, and protect career administrators and programs from arbitrary, politically motivated, and capricious actions by elected officials and their appointees. Everyone gains from the same characteristics of bureaucracy organization about which they complain.

Thus, despite nearly universal criticisms of rigid, inhumane, inflexible, government bureaucracies, the classical model has proven to be difficult to eradicate. Not as a result of government ineptness, but because it is the single best organizational model for some purposes. The challenge is to realign the model with today's realities. Unfortunately, two fundamental requisites must be met before we can change to an alternative model of organization. First, we need to change our basic assumptions about human nature and the nature of relationships between people and organizations.

Second, a better model has to be available for adoption. Other interesting organization models exist, but none are free of flaws. Two alternative models, with their strengths and weaknesses, are the subject of Chapter 9.

Notes

[1]See Jay M. Shafritz and J. Steven Ott, "Classical Organization Theory," in Shafritz and Ott, eds., *Classics of Organization Theory*, 4th ed. (Belmont, CA: Wadsworth, 1996.)

[2]Elliott Jaques, "In Praise of Hierarchy." *Harvard Business Review* (Jan.–Feb. 1990): 127–133.

[3]Shoshana Zuboff, *In the Age of the Smart Machine: The Future of Work and Power* (New York: Basic Books, 1988).

[4]*Ibid.*, 9.

[5]*Ibid.*, 5.

[6]*Ibid.*, 6.

[7]Edgar H. Schein, "Reassessing the 'Divine Rights' of Managers." *Sloan Management Review* 30 (Winter 1989): 63–68.

[8]Will McWhinney, *Paths of Change: Strategic Choices for Organizations and Society* (Newbury Park, CA: Sage, 1992).

[9]H. Cox Taylor, Jr., *Cultural Diversity in Organizations: Theory, Research & Practice* (San Francisco: Berrett-Koehler, 1993).

[10]Lee G. Bolman and Terrence E. Deal, *Reframing Organizations: Artistry, Choice, and Leadership* (San Francisco: Jossey-Bass, 1991), 49.

[11]Frederick Winslow Taylor, *The Principles of Scientific Management* (New York: Norton, 1911); and F. W. Taylor, "The Principles of Scientific Management," *Bulletin of the Taylor Society,* December 1916. An abstract of an address given by Dr. Taylor before the Cleveland Advertising Club, March 3, 1915, two weeks prior to his death.

[12]Frank B. Gilbreth, *Motion Study: A Method for Increasing the Efficiency of the Workman* (New York: D. Van Nostrand, 1911); and F. B. Gilbreth, *Primer of Scientific Management* (New York: D. Van Nostrand, 1912).

[13]Max Weber, "Bureaucracy," in H. Gerth and C. Wright Mills, eds., *Max Weber: Essays in Sociology* (Oxford, England: Oxford University Press, 1946).

[14]Henri Fayol, *General and Industrial Management* (trans. by C. Storrs, 1949) (London: Pitman Publishing, 1916).

[15]Luther Gulick, "Notes on the Theory of Organization," in Luther Gulick and Lyndall Urwick, eds., *Papers on the Science of Administration* (New York: Institute of Public Administration, 1937).

[16]Herbert Kaufman, *The Forest Ranger* (Baltimore, MD: The Johns Hopkins Press, 1960).

[17]F. B. Gilbreth, *Primer of Scientific Management, op. cit.*

[18]Frederick Winslow Taylor, *The Principles of Scientific Management, op. cit.*

[19]Michael Lipsky, *Street-Level Bureaucracy* (New York: Russell Sage Foundation, 1980).

[20]James F. Welles, *Understanding Stupidity: An Analysis of the Premaladaptive Beliefs and Behavior of Institutions and Organizations* (Orient, NY: Mount Pleasant Press, 1986), 146–147.

[21]James D. Thompson, *Organizations in Action* (New York: McGraw-Hill, 1967).

[22]Francis E. Rourke, *Bureaucracy, Politics, and Public Policy,* 3rd ed. (Boston: Little, Brown, 1984).

[23]Frederick C. Mosher, *Democracy and the Public Service,* 2nd ed. (New York: Oxford, 1982).

[24]Patricia Ingraham, "Building Bridges or Burning Them? The President, the Appointees, and the Bureaucracy," *Public Administration Review* 47 (1987): 425–435.

[25]W. Michael Blumenthal. "Candid Reflections of a Businessman in Washington," *Fortune,* January 29, 1979.

[26]Walter G. Held, *Decision Making in the Federal Government: The Walter S. Sayre Model* (Washington, DC: The Brookings Institution, 1979).

[27]Douglas Yates, Jr., *The Politics of Management* (San Francisco: Jossey-Bass, 1985).

[28]Luther Gulick, "Notes on the Theory of Organization." In Luther Gulick and Lyndall Urwick *op. cit.,* 7.

[29]*Ibid.,* 7.

[30]Frank B. Gilbreth, *op. cit.,* 2–3.

[31]Edgar H. Schein, *op. cit.,* 63–68.

[32]J. Steven Ott, Albert C. Hyde, & Jay M. Shafritz, Chapter V in Ott, Hyde, & Shafritz, eds., *Public Management: The Essential Readings* (Chicago: Nelson-Hall, 1991).

[33]For example, Richard Beckhard, *Organization Development: Strategies and Models* (Reading, MA: Addison-Wesley, 1969); Warren G. Bennis, *Organization Development: Its Nature, Origins, and Prospects* (Reading, MA: Addison-Wesley, 1969).

[34]For example, Edward E. Lawler III, Susan Albers Mohrman, and Ferald E. Ledford, Jr., *Employee Involvement and Total Quality Management* (San Francisco: Jossey-Bass, 1992).

[35]Notably, William G. Ouchi, *Theory Z: How American Business Can Meet the Japanese Challenge* (Reading, MA: Addison-Wesley, 1981); Richard T. Pascale and Anthony G. Athos, *The Art of Japanese Management: Applications for American Executives* (New York: Simon & Schuster, 1981).

[36]The best example is Thomas J. Peters and Robert H. Waterman, Jr., *In Search of Excellence* (New York: Harper & Row, 1982).

[37]See W. Edwards Deming, *Out of the Crisis: Quality, Productivity and Competitive Position* (Cambridge, UK: Cambridge University Press, 1988); Joseph J. Juran, *On Planning for Quality* (New York: Collier Macmillan, 1988); Mary Walton, *The Deming Management Method* (New York: Dodd Mead, 1986).

[38]Dale D. McConkey, *MBO for Nonprofit Organizations* (New York: AMACOM, 1975); George S. Odiorne, *Management by Objectives* (New York: Pitman, 1965).

[39]See, for example, Jay M. Shafritz and J. Steven Ott, *op. cit.,* Ch. 1.

Chapter 9

Organization Development, Participation, and Culture

This chapter introduces two alternative models of organization that represent major departures from the classical-structural model. These are only two of many alternatives that have been proposed over the years.[1] Alternative models supplement the classical model but also challenge it. The two alternative models that are examined here are the organizational behavior (OB) perspective and the organizational culture perspective.

These alternative perspectives incorporate important advances in knowledge about human behavior in organizations, advances that were unavailable to the classical-structuralists. They include useful insights from many fields, including sociology; individual, social, and industrial psychology; cultural anthropology; and political science. However, none of these disciplines can provide absolute answers about how to organize or explain the behavior of organizations. There is no such thing yet as the one best theory of organization. The demands on public agencies to be responsible and accountable are too urgent, government organizations are too complex, and our understandings are still too limited. We need several perspective and multiple theories to help us understand how organizations—and the people in them—will behave in varying organizational structures, cultures, and circumstances.

Why not incorporate the strengths of each model into a single theory of organization? This question is an important one that keeps many organization theorists busy. The search for compatibilities and linkages among diverse theories is never-ending. As we saw in Chapter 8, however, the barriers are formidable. Each major theory of organization is built on a different set of assumptions and reflects profoundly different values, beliefs, and understandings about what is important. Only rarely is it possible to merge the best of each model into a unified theory. At least for now, we must work with multiple theories of organization, even though we know that each is partially accurate but also partially inadequate.

The Organizational Behavior Perspective

The first alternative model in this chapter, the organizational behavior perspective, also known as the human resource perspective, has its own assumptions. It also has two different meanings. First, OB is the actual behavior of people and groups in and around purposeful organizations and the study of that behavior. Thus, OB is the application of the theories, methods, and research findings of the behavioral sciences to understanding the behavior of individuals and groups in organizations.

For our purposes, though, the more important definition of OB is as a model of organization and management. The OB perspective was the first comprehensive challenge to the legitimacy of the classical model. Managers and researchers have been interested in the behavior of people in organizations for a very long time. Before the mid-1950s, however, students of organizations who were interested in the behavior of people in organizations saw employee behavior through the lenses of the classical model. Except for a few pioneers, organizational psychologists and theorists continued to regard people in organizations as replaceable parts in the machinery of organizations. Their primary interest was in learning what an organization could do to get people to perform in the ways that the classical model assumed they would. The idea was that managers need people in order to achieve organizational goals. The task was to find them and shape them into effective members of the organization.

Thus, from the late 1800s until well into the 1950s, the role of behavioral scientists in organizations was to serve as agents of management in finding, selecting, and shaping people who would be replacement parts in the organization machine. The field of industrial/organizational psychology (or simply I/O psychology) was in the forefront. For more than sixty years, the military and private industry supported myriad I/O studies into how organizations could match new employees with job and organizational requirements, shape employees' attitudes toward their work and the organization, and understand how to maneuver workplace variables so as to impact positively on employee productivity.[2] The classical-model assumptions were evident. The ghosts of Frederick Winslow Taylor, Max Weber, and Henri Fayol lived on. Pioneering OB theorists such as Mary Parker Follett,[3] Elton Mayo,[4] Roethlisberger and Dixon,[5] and Chester Barnard[6] remained interesting anomalies until late in the 1950s.

The OB perspective could not emerge until cultural assumptions about people, organizations, and the relationship between them changed. As a society, we simply did not believe that codependence was the right relationship between organizations and employees. Employees ought to be beholden to their employers. These assumptions began to shift slowly in the 1950s and literally exploded into revolutionary change in the tumultuous environment of the 1960s. In the 1950s, most citizens agreed with a pronouncement from the White House: "What is good for General Motors is good for the United States." Less than ten years later, the messages of the 1960s were: "Resist authority," "big" suppresses, people first, "small is beautiful," "no one over thirty can be trusted." Classical structuralism and "the establishment," which was the term used to describe corporate America and government, was thrown into a state of shock. The mood and consciousness of society had been altered. It was now possible for the OB perspective to emerge.

Early Pioneers of the Organizational Behavior Perspective

The earliest of the pioneering organizational behaviorists, the people who laid the foundation for the emergence of the OB perspective of the 1950s and 1960s, were accidental converts from Taylorism. In 1924, a team of researchers led by Elton Mayo, a professor at Harvard University, began a multi-year investigation into methods for improving productivity at the Hawthorne, Illinois, plant of the Western Electric Company. The Mayo-led team spent its first several years in a futile search for ways to increase worker productivity, using assumptions from the classical model. They experimented with many variables in the work environment, including, for example, the level of illumination, speed of the materials flow, and alternate wage-payment plans. They were unrelenting in their search for independent workplace variables that could cause desired changes in their study's dependent variables—workers.[7]

As long as productivity was defined as the problem, a problem that it was thought could be solved by altering aspects of the work environment until workers performed as the organization desired, productivity was affected only marginally. It was not until the Mayo team redefined employee productivity as a social-psychological question that profound breakthroughs were achieved and the Hawthorne studies became a legendary contribution to understanding people at work.[8]

The Hawthorne studies are legendary because they represented a new level of learning. They opened previously unrecognized vistas. For example, if we want to learn about the behavior of people in organizations, the organization is the wrong unit of analysis. People and groups of people should be the focus. Organizational factors are not the independent variables and human behaviors the dependent variables. People do not respond like machines. Instead, organizations need to be understood as the environment in which human behavior occurs. Although environment obviously does affect behavior, the basic equation needs to be reconstructed. Organizations and employee behaviors are simultaneously independent and dependent variables. Employee feelings and behaviors shape the behaviors of other employees and the organization, just as organizations influence human behavior. Employees are thinking and feeling people who do not respond to stimuli like rats in one of B. F. Skinner's experimental mazes.[9] Employee behavior affects and is affected by factors such as interpersonal relations in groups, group norms and pressures, control over one's own environment, and personal recognition, as well as the formal rules and directives that are the focus of the classical model.

People in organizations often behave in accord with economic rationality, but certainly not always. Other realities that may or may not have anything to do with organizational goals also affect employee behavior and cannot be ignored. If a youngest child is about to leave home, a physician gives a guarded warning, a parent or significant other becomes seriously or terminally ill, or a person achieves a level of accomplishment or recognition in an outside activity that warrants a significant investment of time and energy (perhaps an offer of a leadership position in a professional or service organization), it affects behavior on the job.

Several other pioneering works also appeared about the same time as Mayo's and Roethlisberger's. Their ideas remain enormously influential today. For example, Mary Parker Follett's 1926 chapter, "The Giving of Orders"[10] was the first definitive statement about workplace leadership that reflected the OB perspective's tenets. "The Giving of Orders" introduced what Follett termed the "law of the situation," a participatory approach to problem solving where employees and employers collaboratively assess situations and decide on courses of action. According to Follett, functional leadership should be determined "by the situation."

Likewise, *Functions of the Executive* by Chester Barnard,[11] a brilliant 1938 book about leadership in industrial organizations, argued that the most important functions of an executive are: (1) to balance the needs of an organization with the needs of its employees, and (2) to create a "moral tone" or "vision" for the organization and communicate it effectively to all who work there. Barnard's thesis was that an executive who successfully accomplishes these two functions will not need to "waste time" directing, monitoring, and controlling employees.

The pioneering works of Mayo, Roethlisberger, Follett, and Barnard from the 1920s and 1930s provided important insights into the essence of the OB perspective. Table 9-1 presents its assumptions explicitly. They are displayed next to the classical-model assumptions for comparison. The depth and breadth of the differences are striking and cannot be overlooked.

Table 9-1
Basic Assumptions of Two Models or Perspectives

The Organizational Behavior Model	The Classical-Structural Perspective
1. Organizations exist to serve human needs (rather than the reverse).	1. Organizations exist primarily to accomplish production-related and economic goals.
2. Organizations and people need each other. (Organizations need ideas, energy, and talent; people need careers, salaries, and work opportunities.)	2. There is one best way to organize for production, and that way can be found through systematic, scientific inquiry.
3. When the fit between the individual and the organization is poor, one or both will suffer: Individuals will be exploited or will seek to exploit the organizations or both.	3. In order to function effectively, organizations need rationality. Thus, they need to shield their internal workings from environmental turbulence and develop norms of rational behavior.
4. A good fit between individual and organization benefits both: Human beings find meaningful and satisfying work, and organizations get the human talent and energy that they need.	4. Production is maximized through specialization and division of labor.

Sources: Oganizational Behavior model from Lee G. Bolman and Terrence E. Deal, *Reframing Organizations.* (San Francisco: Jossey-Bass, 1991), 121. Classical-Structural Perspective adapted from Bolman and Deal, 1991, p. 48. Bolman and Deal use the label "Structural Frame" rather than the "Classical-Structural Organization Model."

The OB Perspective's Challenge to the Classical Model

In Chapter 8, we introduced a hypothetical example of an "ideal-type" government agency, a police department, that epitomizes the classical model. According to Douglas McGregor's classic 1957 book, *The Human Side of Enterprise,*[12] management's task in the hypothetical agency would be to harness human energy to organizational requirements. McGregor generated a list of management propositions about people in organizations that become self-fulfilling prophecies—beliefs that self-perpetuate simply because they exist. He labeled the classical model–type propositions Theory X. These are presented in Table 9-2.

Table 9-2
A Manager's Propositions under McGregor's *Theory X*

1. Management is responsible for organizing the elements of productive enterprise—money, materials, equipment, people—in the interest of economic ends.
2. With respect to people, this is a process of directing their efforts, motivating them, controlling their actions, modifying their behavior to fit the needs of the organization.
3. Without this active intervention by management, people would be passive—even resistant—to organizational needs. They must therefore be persuaded, rewarded, punished, controlled—their activities must be directed. This is management's task. We often sum it up by saying that management consists of getting things done through other people.
4. The average man is by nature indolent—he works as little as possible.*
5. He lacks ambition, dislikes responsibility, prefers to be led.
6. He is inherently self-centered, indifferent to organizational needs.
7. He is by nature resistant to change.
8. He is gullible, not very bright, the ready dupe of the charlatan and the demagogue.

*Some readers may conclude that the use of "man" and "he" in propositions 4 through 8 meant that McGregor was describing the basic nature of *men*. In 1957, however, "he" often meant gender-neutral "person" or "individual."

Source: Douglas McGregor, "The Human Side of Enterprise," *Management Review* 22 (November 1957): 88–92.

McGregor's contribution to the understanding of management and organizations is a self-fulfilling prophecy. In reality, some employees do behave as Theory X describes, but not because Theory X describes human nature accurately. Quite the opposite is true. When employees in an agency behave as Theory X describes them—when they are indeed indolent, lazy, lacking in ambition, indifferent to organizational needs, and resistant to change—it is because management believes this is human nature. Public executives and legislators who hold Theory X assumptions about employees create the behaviors that they believe are inherent or natural through their own actions. Legislators and government executives implement classical-model structures, policies, and tight systems of control to deal with lazy employees. They talk to and about employees as though this is simply the way they are. Employees are told rather than asked, directed rather than invited to problem solve, bribed with rewards and threatened with punishments rather than involved, and placated paternalistically rather than listened to sensitively. Executives eat in separate dining rooms and wash their hands in separate restrooms with locked doors.

Implications of the OB Perspective: What Does It Take to Be an Administrator?

Theory X propositions assume there are two distinct classes of people in organizations: managers and employees. Each class thinks, talks, acts, and is motivated differently. An effective manager utilizes structure, processes, and controls to induce employees to maximize productivity. A Theory X manager who seeks consulting assistance would love to call Frederick Winslow Taylor or Hugo Munsterberg.

Even if the old perspective and its assumptions are becoming less and less useful, however, they could not be discarded until an acceptable alternative model was found. McGregor was the first OB theorist to forge a comprehensive argument and package it in language acceptable to government and industry leaders. If managers would internalize a different set of assumptions about the human nature of employees, he argued, the management and organizational implications would be revolutionary. A new perspective could and should be developed to challenge the Theory X classical model. McGregor called the propositions of his social sciences–based model Theory Y (see Table 9-3).

The implications of Theory Y for organizations extend far beyond changing organizational structures, processes, and controls. If managers would change their assumptions about the nature of people to the Theory Y propositions, then the OB perspective could possibly challenge the classical model.

Table 9-3
A Manager's Propositions under McGregor's *Theory Y*

---

1. Management is responsible for organizing the elements of productive enterprise—money, materials, equipment, people—in the interest of economic ends.
2. People are *not* by nature passive or resistant to organizational needs. They have become so as a result of experience in organizations.
3. The motivation, the potential for development, the capacity for assuming responsibility, the readiness to direct behavior toward organizational goals are all present in people. Management does not put them there. It is a responsibility of management to make it possible for people to recognize and develop these human characteristics for themselves.
4. The essential task of management is to arrange organizational conditions and methods of operation so that people can achieve their own goals *best* by directing *their own* efforts toward organizational objectives.

Source: Douglas McGregor, "The Human Side of Enterprise," *Management Review* 22 (November 1957): 88–92.

Organizations and management could enter the era of modern behavioral sciences. Employees could be recognized, accepted, and dealt with as creative, responsible, thinking people who care about their organizations accomplishing their goals. The ideas of Follett, Mayo, Roethlisberger, and Barnard could become mainstream organization theory. The barriers are the attitudes and assumptions of people in power. That includes legislators and city councilors as well as elected and appointed executives. After all, it is extremely difficult for a manager to use OB approaches within a structure created by legislators who operate on Theory X assumptions.

The reasons for wanting to work past the classical model and toward the OB perspective are persuasive. Government could stop wasting time, money, and effort on rules, procedures, and control systems. It could tap into the huge reservoir of underutilized employee energy and creativity, since employees have more firsthand knowledge about how to improve internal operations than anyone else in the organization. Government could take advantage of employees' knowledge and insights to reduce costs and improve efficiency, effectiveness, and client satisfaction with public sector services. It could be more flexible and adaptive to the agencies' external environments and constituencies by listening to the environment and reducing internal rigidities. Public managers could allow employees to define how they can best achieve their own goals by directing their own efforts toward agency objectives. Employees could decide how to develop themselves as individuals and as employees, in their present agency or potentially for any other employer. Classical model agencies could at least be reshaped into more responsive, responsible, and energetic organizations where employees work hard because they are respected and valued.

Roles, Functions, Requirements, and Characteristics of an OB-Perspective Public Administrator

Managers with an OB perspective perform different functions and do old tasks in new ways. The behavioral changes needed to breathe life into the OB perspective are not mechanistic or procedural. They cannot be memorized from a checklist. The OB attitudes and beliefs must be internalized before an administrator's behavior can be consistent. If the OB-perspective assumptions are not brought to life, the self-fulfilling prophecy phenomenon will cause administrators inexorably to revert to the classical model.

Unless administrators regularly test their behaviors, roles, functions, and skills against McGregor's Theory Y propositions and the tenets of Bolman and Deal's "Human Resource Frame," they will trigger continuing spirals of unwanted causes and related effects. Until administrators have truly accepted

Table 9-4

A Hypothetical Example of a Communication—
But Not the Message that Administration Wanted to Communicate

---

As you know, all of us in management are looking forward with great enthusiasm to our first quality circles. We have very high hopes for them. Many private companies and other agencies have benefited greatly from the circles, and we expect the same results here. It will be an excellent experience to work shoulder-to-shoulder with our employees, identifying and solving problems collaboratively. Remember, our employees are our most important assets.

Unfortunately, a few employees who have created some problems in the past for us, may try to use the quality circles to re-raise old gripes about how we didn't listen to their complaints before installing the new reporting system last year. They will try to embarrass us because the system isn't giving us all of the information. We will not permit the quality circles to degenerate into gripe sessions. The reporting system decision and resulting unfortunate problems are "water over the dam."

Each of you is responsible for starting the first quality-circle sessions. Please announce that the new reporting system is off limits in the circles. It would be a waste of valuable time. We have too many important issues to work on. If any troublemakers try to raise the subject, remind them of our rules. If anyone persists, I will have a talk with them. If all of the time and money we are putting into these quality circles are going to pay off—save us money—we must get them off to good, solid, constructive starts. We want to work with our employees to make this great agency even better. Remember, the great majority of our people want to work with us. We can't let a few rotten apples spoil the works.

---

the OB assumptions, their discrepant underlying assumptions broadcast contradictory messages by employees. The same words can communicate very different messages. For example, "I love you" may communicate a sincere message of deep affection or serve as a disguise for an attempt to manipulate. Likewise, administration may tell employees that "we are going to be one big happy family as we manage participatively here from now on." If, however, classical-model assumptions persist, employees will quickly read the inconsistencies. Classical-model messages will overpower the OB-perspective words. Table 9-4 provides an example.

Management's assumptions (see example in Table 9-4) will actually cause Theory X–type employee behavior. These assumptions will overpower and defeat the official message, "come join us in participative management." The assumptions are:

- "We are going to manage participatively, but administration will exercise its right to control the quality circles. Administration will set the agenda. Anything subject that management does not want to be discussed will be off-limits. If employees do not respect this, disciplinary action will be initiated."

■ "The purpose for the quality circles is to save money. If money isn't saved, they are a waste of time and will be discontinued (in fact, probably rather quickly)."

■ "A few chronic gripers will want to waste time talking about the reporting system fiasco. These troublemakers want to embarrass or "get" administration. They are rotten apples. We would fire them if we could."

The reporting system may have been a major blunder. Management may very well have resisted employee attempts to voice concerns or suggestions while the system was being designed. Now, by telling employees that the reporting system is not open for discussion in the quality circles, a setting where administrators and employees supposedly solve problems collaboratively, administration will destroy the credibility of the quality circles. It will ensure that participative management fails, now and for a long time to come. The secondary messages are too strong. No employee with common sense will leave the first quality circle session thinking, believing, or feeling what administration hoped. Instead, water-cooler conversations will sound something like the following: "Here we go again. I told you the quality circles would amount to nothing more than a gimmick to let administration cover their butts while they try to get more work out of us for no more money."

Administrators will sense employee doubts and resistance to the quality circles quickly. They, in turn, will start doubting Theory Y assumptions—if they ever accepted them in the first place. Some variation of the paragraph that follows has been heard too often in many organizations.

> We did our share. We went more than half-way. We went out of our way to involve the employees. The quality circles cost us a lot of money. Unfortunately, the OB perspective doesn't work here. Our agency is different from those (hundreds) (thousands) of other places that we were told and read about. They don't have to contend with _____ like we do. Our employees are wonderful, but they are a different lot. We have to keep things a bit more under direct control here, set tighter limits. Of course, we value our employees. For the most part, they are wonderful. They are our most important assets. On the other hand, we have to be realistic. We can't just turn the shop over to the employees. The (congress) (legislature) (council) expects us to _____ .

Undoubtedly, years later an administrator will suggest starting a total quality management (TQM) program or the like. Other managers will smile knowingly and respond: "We tried that, but it isn't right for our agency." Employees will say, "here we go again." Meanwhile, administrators and employees alike will be wishing things could be different, that the agency could be a more vital, involving, and innovative place to work.

Thus, OB perspective administrators perform many of the same functions and fill many of the same roles as classical-model administrators, but they do them in different ways. They also emphasize different things and fill different roles.

Developers of People and Work Teams. Managers must be coaches who believe the organization benefits when all employees from diverse backgrounds grow as people and organizational members.[13] Employees are more than willing to learn, expand their capabilities, and take on new responsibilities. They can become genuinely excited. When employees are dealt with fairly as responsible adults, they will develop in ways that benefit the organization as well as themselves.

Empowerers. Managers must be organizational stage-setters who remove barriers to employee growth and development, whether they are male, female, white, or purple.[14] The task of empowerment requires both the need to provide support for employees in their creative efforts and also an obligation to remove barriers that the organization placed in the way of creativity.

Leaders. Managers must be leaders whose ability to influence others is largely independent of the formal authority granted to them by virtue of their hierarchical position. People accept their leadership because of demonstrated interpersonal and professional competence and because they possess credibility and legitimacy.[15] They have reputations for getting things done well, and also ethically.

Collaborative Problem Solvers. Managers are people who believe problems should be solved and decisions made by the people who are closest to the issue. They trust their people's input and judgment, and will support them when the going gets tough.[16] That is why it is important for management to accept bottom-up problem solving.

Visionaries. Managers must have a clear picture of an agency's identity and the directions it should be taking. They communicate that vision to others clearly and effectively, thereby providing a values-based framework that is accepted and incorporated into day-to-day decisions. The integration of individual needs and goals with organizational vision is one of the manager's most important challenges.

Effective Communicators. Managers must listen and absorb information as carefully as they disseminate it. They hear people's emotions as well as task-related data and questions. They communicate directly and honestly when things are going well and when problems are developing. Differences of opinion are dealt with straight-on, up-front, but always with respect for the person.[17]

Organization Development: Managing Change from the Organizational Behavior Perspective

The process of introducing change into organizations provides an excellent stage for examining the OB perspective's impacts on the functions, roles, and requirements of administrators. The management of organizational change from the OB perspective requires an administrator to understand and use both theoretical and practical knowledge about organizations, their needs, directions, and context, in addition to knowledge of human motivation, leadership, group behavior, intergroup dynamics, the interplay between individuals and the organizational environment, power, and influence.

Organization development (OD) is the subfield of organization behavior that focuses specifically on planned change in organizations. It is the full range of assumptions, values, and beliefs of the OB perspective. Although definitions of OD vary, most agree that it is not a program or project. It is a top management–supported, long-range, planned, organization-wide effort to increase organizational effectiveness and improve problem solving and self-renewal processes. Organization development relies on theory, knowledge, and techniques derived from research in the applied behavioral sciences.[18]

Since the 1960s, OD has represented the mainstream of organizational change. This perspective's interests have been centered on the strategies, tactics, and tools that are used to design, introduce, and implement change. Its substantive focus of change is not the issue. In contrast, the classical model focuses on change strategies that will directly improve organizational outcomes, such as the quantity and quality of output, or lower costs.

Organization development is not interested in unplanned, piecemeal change, what might be termed evolutionary change. Neither is it concerned with revolutionary change, radical change that is imposed on an organization. Thus, OD is about planned, ordinary change, change that occurs without seriously violating pivotal organizational norms. The concluding section of this chapter concerns the Organizational Culture perspective. It introduces transformational change or radical change, change that consciously violates existing organizational norms and mores.

In order to understand fully how OD conceptualizes and approaches organizational change, it is necessary to reflect first on one other construct. Specifically, it employs the OB perspective's premise that organizational effectiveness is a process. This belief causes the OB perspective to avoid the classical model's pursuit of organizational improvement through the use of extrinsic variables such as rewards and punishments. Instead, organizational effectiveness is defined as an ongoing process analogous to a holistic definition of organizational health.

Warren Bennis lists four criteria of organizational health and thus of organizational effectiveness:[19]

1. adaptability—the ability to solve problems and to react with flexibility to changing environmental demands;

2. a sense of identity—knowledge and insight on the part of the organization of what it is, what its goals are, and what it is to do;

3. capacity to test reality—the ability to search out, accurately perceive, and correctly interpret the real properties of the environment, particularly those that have relevance for the functioning of the organization; and

4. integration—a state of integration among the subparts of the total organization, such that the parts are not working at cross-purposes.

The outcome of a planned OD change strategy is ongoing renewal. It is a set of processes for self-initiating, organization-wide, and sustained organizational introspection and regeneration. This set of processes itself is defined to be organizational effectiveness. Success, for OD, is the achievement of total organizational commitment to never-ending, pervasive, well-integrated improvement.

Those who have attended workshops or read about total quality management (TQM) should recognize many familiar notions. Although some words are different, the base concepts and beliefs of OD are quite consistent with TQM philosophy and its approaches. Indeed, TQM borrowed important ideas and strategies from management movements that preceded it. Total quality management, however, has blended them and created a more comprehensive package. Organization development is only one of its sources. Others include[20] statistical quality control (or process quality control),[21] entrepreneurial government that is driven by a commitment to customer or client satisfaction,[22] Japanese management,[23] and visionary leadership.

On the other hand, some OD strategies and tools for improving organizations have not been adopted widely by TQM practitioners. For example, OD interventions usually are facilitated by change agents. Typical OD strategies include organizational diagnosis, process consultation, team building, action research, data feedback, job enlargement, job enrichment, and dispute management. More specifically, the tools of an OD change agent might include training and education, process consultation, mentoring, coaching, support groups, communications meetings, data feedback, goal setting, problem-solving task forces, flexible scheduling, and job redesign.[24]

Organization development is not a prescribed set of activities. Rather, it is the application of knowledge, values, assumptions, and beliefs about people, organizations, and the relationship between them. However, the fact that OD approaches are flexible foes not mean they lack power or direction. For example, Chris Argyris's assumptions for OD interventions are decidedly normative:

1. Without valid, usable information (including knowledge about the consequences of alternatives), there cannot be free informed choice.

2. Without free informed choice, there cannot be personal responsibility for decisions.

3. Without personal responsibility for decisions, there cannot be deep commitment to action.[25]

Organization development is perhaps best characterized by the action research model of organizational change (see Figure 9-1). This model is a structured process for identifying needs for organizational improvement and creating strategies that convince the people in the organization to take psychological ownership. It assumes that they must accept both the need for change and change strategies and tactics. First, action research collects diagnostic data, usually by questionnaires or interviews. Second, it provides feedback to the people who provided input, but it does so in group settings. Third, the task is to discuss the interpretations and implications of the feedback. In so doing, the challenge is to be certain the diagnosis is valid and that the process creates psychological ownership of the need to make improvements. The fourth step is to create action plans for organization improvement, using the knowledge and skills of a change agent as well as the insights of organizational members.

Everyone who works in an OB-oriented agency needs to have attitudes and abilities useful for working with people. In contrast with the classical model, employees in OB organizations are expected to be responsible, committed, learning individuals who function effectively in teams as well as on individual assignments. Administrators are expected to lead by competence, develop resources, create and communicate a vision for members of the organization, but also to actively solicit, hear, and use information and the

Figure 9-1
The Organization Development Action Research Model

Initial Diagnostic and Planning Phase

Preliminary conceptualization of organizational problems by management and consultant
↓
Consultant gathers diagnostic data through, for example, questionnaires, interviews, and observations
↓
Consultant prepares the data for feedback to organization members
↓
Consultant feeds back diagnostic data to organization members
↓
Joint interpretation of the meaning and implications of the data by organization members and the consultant
↓
Joint action planning by organization members and consultant
↓

Implementation Phase 1 ←

Organization members implement action plans with assistance from consultant as desired or needed
↓
Consultant collects data on progress and effectiveness of action plan implementation
↓
Consultant feeds back data to organization members
↓
Joint interpretation of the meaning and implications of the data by organization members and the consultant
↓
Joint action planning by organization members and consultant
↓

Implementation Phase n

Organization members implement new action plans with assistance from consultant as desired or needed
↓
Repeat steps in Implementation Phase 1

Source: J. Steven Ott, "Organizational Change" in J. S. Ott, ed., *Classic Readings in Organizational Behavior,* 2nd ed. (Belmont, CA: Wadsworth, 1996), 441.

judgments of others. The skills that make for effective administrators and employees in the classical model can sometimes be counterproductive in the OB perspective.

Criticisms of the Organizational Behavior Perspective

The organizational behavior perspective virtually exploded onto the organizational scene in the 1960s. It reflected the mood and values of the time. People, it was insisted, are as important as the organization itself. Knowledge and capability are spread throughout an organization. There are not two classes of employees. Although employees sometimes act in Theory X ways, the argument ran, it is because a self-fulfilling prophecy, a reflection of management's assumptions about the nature of employees, causes the behavior.

Thus, OB entered the organizational scene with a humanistic fervor and a near-religious sense of mission. The zeal of its proponents was enviable, but it also has caused problems. Too often, for example, OB and OD have been oversold. More has been promised than could be delivered. In some instances, the evidence is that we simply did not know as much about human nature as we thought we did, and not nearly enough to be effective with new OB-oriented management innovations. In other instances, the zeal of OB practitioners and consultants has proven to be naive and overly optimistic. Our belief in the tenets of OB have sometimes led to implementation based more on hope than on knowledge. The deepest criticism that has been aimed at OB, however, goes to its very nature. It was the charge that OB has been used as a set of highly manipulative social pressures and psychological tools through which management can maneuver employees to desired ends. Chris Argyris, one of the most ardent advocates of what is sometimes called the neohumanist school of organization theory and behavior was, surprisingly, one of the critics. He argued that the key is to value the individual's needs for self-actualization as such and not simply to use OB as a tool to get increased productivity.[26]

There have been other criticisms as well. The first is that OB works best when people in the organization are at a level such that their basic needs are being met and they can be concerned about self-actualization. As Abraham Maslow argued, people who are busy trying to meet their basic needs, and those of their families, for food, shelter, and security are in no position to engage with others on the kind of psychological level that is often assumed in OB social interchange.[27] That does not mean that they do not wish to be valued as people and to be included in problem solving, but it does mean that expectations must be related to the conditions in which the people in the organization find themselves.

Another challenge to the OB perspective is its lack of attention to the cultural determinants of human behavior. As we have noted above, OB was very much the product of a social context that had very definite assumptions about human nature and behavior. More than that, it was very much an American and to some extent European set of cultural assumptions, a set of processes clearly designed for developed countries. It did not reflect the realities of the developing world. To the degree that the assumptions were applied by consultants in Latin America, Asia, or Africa, it was an attempt to implement a set of assumptions that often violated religious or political norms and ignored indigenous values that simply did not fit the Western premises.

But even if we stay with the developed countries, there are difficulties. The social, political, and even cultural context of those countries is very different at the turn of the century than it was in the 1960s. Whereas the OB perspective tends to emphasize intangible benefits to individuals from cooperation, the competitive orientation of the marketplace tends to encourage individual competition over social cooperation. While the attack on materialism was very much at the heart of the cultural movements that supported OB, the societies of the 1980s and 1990s have celebrated materialism to an unprecedented degree. Insofar as public sector organizations are increasingly drawing on market-oriented techniques in a materialistic society, there are potentially serious difficulties for the application of OB-related techniques.

Thus, Patricia Ingraham has argued that there is a tension between aspects of TQM and reinventing government initiatives. The basic problem is that much of the reinventing government work, in the several countries where such reengineering experiments have been undertaken, is focused on downsizing of organizations in search of budget cuts.[28] On the other hand, TQM approaches are aimed at providing a level of support for people in organizations that is needed to release creativity and encourage risk taking. It has not been surprising, in the contemporary context, to see that many employees have been unwilling to invest themselves fully and take substantial risks where they see a substantial possibility of losing their jobs.

Clearly, the organizational behavior perspective and OD are not the culmination of organization theory's evolution. Obviously, OB, like all other management perspectives, has flaws. Even so, it has provided managers with a valuable and useful alternative to the classical model. It is an alternative that opens the way for humans to use their full range of capabilities more fully and satisfactorily at work. "A good fit between individual and organization benefits both [humans and organizations]: human beings find meaningful and satisfying work, and organizations get the human talent and energy that they need."[29]

The Organizational Culture Perspective

Since about 1982, a sizable and rapidly growing cadre of critics has been expressing dissatisfaction with the mainstream perspectives of public and private organizations, including the classical model and the OB perspective. The essence of the criticism has been that the mainstream perspectives overlook important alternative ways of seeing organizational phenomena. The more traditional perspectives are unable to produce substantive answers, or even ways to find answers, to many pressing contemporary questions in and about organizations. Thus, in recent years, several "new wave" perspectives have been struggling to emerge.[30] Since about 1982, however, proponents of the organizational culture perspective, or symbolic management approach, have been the most visible and vocal advocates for their alternative to mainstream organization theory.

Organizational Culture as a Social Construction

As with the term organizational behavior, organizational culture also has two different meanings. First, it is the culture that actually exists in any organization. Second, it is another way of perceiving organizations, yet another alternative perspective with its own tenets and assumptions. The organizational culture perspective defines the classical model's and the OB views of organizations as too limited and restrictive. The organizational culture approach views organizations as mini-societies made up of complex patterns of social constructions. (Although organizations are indeed "mini-societies," in today's world of organizational giants "mini-" is only a relative term. Many organizations are larger and more complex societies with larger budgets than some nations.) Although these social constructs are never absolutely consistent across all functional areas and levels in any organization, common beliefs, values, and ways of doing things are shared throughout an organization. These common threads make up the culture of an organization. In some respects, they are an organization's distinctive identity.

In 1923, William I. Thomas wrote: "If people believe things are real, they are real in their consequences."[31] It is in this sense that the organizational culture perspective makes its claim that reality and truth are social constructs. These shared truths and realities, including assumptions, beliefs, ideologies, and values, are constructed by the people who have been socialized into a culture, whether it is a particular society, a community, or an organization. They are shared assumptions that are often arrived at implicitly and subconsciously as members work together and learn how to overcome problems. Over time, and with repeated use, these assumptions slowly recede into members' subconscious where they exist unquestioned and influence behavior. Yet, they are rarely spoken or written explicitly because they are so basic, such elemental truths, that they are virtually forgotten.[32]

People who are new to an organization learn the assumptions, beliefs, values, and realities through an organization's jargon—stories and myths that are told over—and over again, as well as through nonverbal signals and symbols. The holistic composite of these interwoven, socially constructed assumptions, beliefs, ideologies, values, truths, and realities is the organizational culture.[33]

Functions of Organizational Culture

An organizational culture serves several important purposes. It provides organization members with a way to understand and make sense of uncertainty, events, and symbols. It stands as a source of guiding beliefs, communicating what is expected of members, including how they should deal with different types of circumstances and problems. Organizational culture defines what is right and wrong, particularly when issues appear in shades of gray. Indeed, an organization's ethical system is a product of the culture. A well-integrated organizational culture can reduce the need for the use of authority, rules, and controls and thus is a powerful mechanism that guides actions by approving or prohibiting different patterns of behavior. When the organizational culture is strong, control of employee behavior can be achieved and maintained without resorting to authority. It can be elicited through use of the culture's norms, mores, ideologies, sanctions, and taboos.

The organizational culture perspective assumes that organizations are complex societies in environments characterized by uncertainties and unknowns. Organization members regularly are confronted with questions to which there are no definitive answers, problems for which there are no right solutions, and cause-effect relationships that are not understood and cannot be managed. In these regards, organizational cultures are similar to societal cultures, where traditions, rituals, and religions arise to provide answers to unanswerable questions or at least provide comfort in the midst of uncertainty. Because an organizational culture is partially shaped by the culture of the society within which it operates, the organizational culture perspective also is helpful for understanding differences among organizations across state and national boundaries.

Organizational culture, however, can also have negative impacts. It literally can put blinders on organization members, causing people to stop asking important questions. That is dangerous because unquestioning acceptance of historically based premises can lead to inflexibility and rigidity. If an organization's recruitment and socialization processes work too well, they pose a potential danger. They may produce clones who think, talk, and act like current and past administrators. An organizational culture thus can function to exclude people who are from different backgrounds or genders.[34] Organizational culture teaches people to look back in time for answers, solutions, and precedents rather than to look forward into the future. A culture tends to protect the status quo, but in so doing may prevent an organization from instituting changes needed to adapt to a dynamic environment. Thus, organizational cultures can foster deeply ingrained habits of mind (ruts, to use the colloquial term) that can not be easily or quickly changed. If an organization's culture is truly understood, its patterns of behaviors and decisions become predictable.

Symbols and Symbolic Management

In all cultures, people create and use symbols to create certainty from uncertainty and meaning from confusion or mystery. Symbols carry a deeper and usually a more emotional meaning than their extrinsic content. A flag is a symbol that embodies values, history, traditions, and emotions. In times of conflict, the emotions become very strong. Symbols, however, are not limited to tangible things. Words, anthems, phrases, salutes, organizational structures, closed office doors, and partially accurate stories about organizational heroes are all symbols.

Cultural values are communicated through their symbols. The more complex, confusing, or uncertain life is in an organization, the more important symbols are for providing members with a sense of meaning and direction. Because most government agencies have multiple and often conflicting goals, uncertain technologies, and diffuse or unclear outcomes, the organizational culture perspective and symbols serve particularly important purposes. They are a part of the reality of the nation's capital, state capitals, and city halls.

The basic assumptions or tenets of the organizational culture perspective are:

1. The importance of an event is its meaning.
2. Events and meanings are loosely connected. Things have different meanings for different people.
3. In complex organizations, it is often difficult to understand what has transpired, why, or to predict what will happen.
4. When ambiguity and uncertain reign, rational, linear, cause-and-effect logic will not work in planning or decision making.
5. People like to understand. They create symbols to help make sense out of confusion or uncertainty and to create a sense of direction.

6. Organizations are not rational, goal-driven, structures. Often in organizations (and particularly in government organizations), the communication of meaning through events and processes is more important
   than the actual accomplishment of stated goals. Myths, rituals, cere-
   monies, stories, and sagas help members and nonmembers deal with
   complexities. They allow people to reduce uncertainty by creating new
   and comforting realities.[35]

Usefulness of the Organizational Culture Perspective

The organizational culture framework has numerous applications, particularly in government agencies. It is perhaps most useful for intentionally
changing the character or identity of an organization. Thus, organizational
culture analysis goes beyond the normal change with which OD advocates
are comfortable. A decision to alter radically an organization's identity may
be made for any of many reasons. Alternatively, organizational culture can
provide effective approaches for perpetuating an existing culture in the face
of external threats. For example, the culture of a bureau would be threatened
by a reorganization into another division or department with a very different
set of values. In 1992, the U.S. Government Accounting Office (GAO)
completed a study entitled *Organizational Culture: Techniques Companies
Use to Perpetuate or Change Beliefs and Values*,[36] designed to learn how to
modify aspects of the culture of the Department of Defense. The GAO concluded:

> According to several experts we spoke with, an organization's decision to
> change its culture is generally triggered by a specific event or situation. A
> change in the world situation, international competition, or a severe budget
> reduction are some events that could provide the impetus for an organiza-
> tional culture change. For example, the oil shocks of the 1970s and the in-
> crease in international, particularly Japanese, competition spurred Ford's
> change in culture.
>
> The experts generally agreed that a culture change is a long-term effort that
> takes at least five to ten years to complete. . . .
>
> The experts noted that these techniques could be used to perpetuate as well
> as to change an organizational culture.[37]

Organizational culture is not something to be toyed with carelessly. It
is not a useful tool for short-term gain or to initiate a quick fix to a problem. Because organizational cultures are deeply embedded in the minds,
habits, and assumptions of people, it takes a long time and total commitment
to alter an organizational culture. Most serious students estimate that an

organizational culture cannot be truly changed in less than five years, and it often could require considerably longer.

One of the best known attempts to change a large organizational culture was undertaken by Lee Iacocca when he took over leadership of Chrysler Corporation.

> Lee Iacocca (1984) faced a similar problem [of needing to radically change the culture] . . . when he took over leadership of the Chrysler Corporation. Chrysler was a "loser" in just about every way imaginable—in the eyes of employees, potential employees, investors, car dealers, financiers, suppliers, and car buyers. It was simply *assumed* that Chrysler could not compete head-on. Iacocca had to change not only an organizational culture but also just about everybody's perception of that culture. Chrysler needed and got in Iacocca what Bennis (1984), Bennis and Nanus (1985), Tichy and Ulrich (1984), and Tichy and Devanna (1986) have called a *transformational leader.* A transformational leader is a person who can literally transform an embedded organizational culture by creating a new vision of and for the organization and successfully *selling that vision* by rallying commitment and loyalty to transform the vision into a reality.[38]

Organizational Culture and Total Quality Management

Most proponents of total quality management (TQM) are strong supporters of the organizational culture perspective. Total quality management requires administrators and employees to abandon old ways of thinking about and doing things and to accept new workplace realities. The old ways of allocating resources, setting priorities, controlling processes, rewarding employee performance, assuring product quality, and relating with workers are not the problem *per se.* These are the artifacts and symbols of the old organizational culture. The old ways and systems, however, are the reality. They reinforce and are reinforced by the organizational culture. Any one or two old ways can be altered without significantly affecting overall quality. Significant, deep, long-term changes, changes of the nature and magnitude envisioned under TQM, can be achieved only if the organizational culture is changed.

> Leaders beginning a TQM effort should bear in mind that to realize the full potential of TQM requires a fundamental cultural change. When this transformation has occurred, everyone in the organization is continuously and systematically working to improve the quality of goods and services, and the processes for delivering them, in order to maximize customer satisfaction. TQM becomes a way of managing that is embedded in the culture and environment of the organization, not simply a set of specific management techniques and tools.

It follows that a successful approach to quality improvement requires a long-term commitment and recognition that the effort is an unending journey. Although some early successes can be achieved, a cultural transformation to full use of the TQM approach will occur only gradually.[39]

When the GAO analysts asked officials of nine major corporations that had been attempting to address their organizational cultures what two key techniques were of most importance for successful culture change, they were told: "Top management must be totally committed to the change in both words and actions," and "Organizations must provide training that pro-

Table 9-5

Techniques that Organizations Use to Perpetuate or Change Their Culture

Degree of Importance	Technique
Very Great	Display top management commitment and support for values and beliefs.
	Train employees to convey and develop skills related to values and beliefs.
Great	Develop a statement of values and beliefs.
	Communicate values and beliefs to employees.
	Use a management style compatible with values and beliefs.
	Convey and support values and beliefs at organizational gatherings.
	Make the organization's structure compatible with values and beliefs.*
	Set up systems, procedures, and processes compatible with values and beliefs.*
Moderate	Replace or change responsibilities of employees who do not support desired values and beliefs.*
	Use stories, legends, or myths to convey values and beliefs.
	Make heroes or heroines exemplars of values and beliefs.
Some	Recruit employees who possess or will readily accept values and beliefs.*
	Use slogans to symbolize values and beliefs.
	Assign a manager or group primary responsibility for efforts to change or perpetuate culture.*

*Company officials' views about the importance of this technique varied markedly.

Source: U.S. Government Accounting Office, *Organizational Culture: Techniques Companies Use to Perpetuate or Change Beliefs and Values* (Washington, DC: GAO, 1992), 3.

motes and develops skills related to their desired values and beliefs."[40] But GAO also was warned that successful culture change requires the use of a combination of many techniques.

> Other techniques of varying importance include distributing a written statement of the desired values and beliefs to employees; creating a specific management style that reinforces the desired values and beliefs; offering rewards, incentives, and promotions to encourage behavior that reinforces these beliefs; holding company gatherings to discuss these beliefs; developing an organizational structure that is compatible with these beliefs; using systems, procedures, and processes to support organizational values; and using stories, legends, myths, and slogans to communicate these values and beliefs.[41]

The GAO report presented the lessons learned about that array of techniques.

An administrator does not need to abandon all tenets and management approaches of the OB perspective in order to make use of the organizational culture. Some remain applicable. A movement from the OB perspective to the organizational culture perspective is a major step. It advances the levels of complexity and subtlety in organizational understanding that is required of an administrator. Organizational culture provides another set of tools for use by administrators that is particularly useful for working with major organizational change. Holistic change, total change, requires new realities.

Conclusion

The search for an ultimate framework for understanding and managing organizations continues. The further we seem to get in understanding organizations and the people in them, the more distant the ultimate seems to be. The classical model continues to dominate, particularly in government organizations. The organizational behavior and organizational culture perspectives, however, have forced changes in the classical model. The old model can never return to its ideal type. It has been irreversibly humanized.

Organization behavior research has provided public managers with new understandings of employees, their needs, and the ways that their own wishes to play creative roles can be unleashed to enhance the organization. The organizational culture perspective has added an additional set of dimensions by working to relate individual behavior with the unique properties of the particular organizations in which those people work. Both of these approaches have required public administrators to accept new realities for administration in the twenty-first century.

Notes

[1] See e.g., Jay M. Shafritz and J. Steven Ott, *Classics of Organization Theory,* 5th ed. (Belmont, CA: Wadsworth, 1996). They include discussions of neoclassical theory, systems and population ecology theory, organizational economics theory, power and politics theory, and postmodernism.

[2] Hugo Munsterberg, *Psychology and Industrial Efficiency* (Boston: Houghton Mifflin, 1913).

[3] Mary Parker Follett, "The Giving of Orders," in H. C. Metcalf, ed., *Scientific Foundations of Business Administration* (Baltimore, MD: Williams & Wilkins, 1926).

[4] G. Elton Mayo, *The Human Problems of an Industrial Civilization* (Boston: Division of Research, Harvard Business School, 1933).

[5] Fritz J. Roethlisberger and William J. Dixon, *Management and the Worker* (Cambridge, MA: Harvard University Press, 1939).

[6] Chester Barnard, *The Functions of the Executive* (Cambridge, MA: Harvard University Press, 1938).

[7] J. Steven Ott, "Introduction," in J. S. Ott, ed., *Classic Readings in Organizational Behavior* (Belmont, CA: Wadsworth, 1996).

[8] Roethlisberger and Dixon, *op. cit.*

[9] B. F. Skinner, *Science and Behavior* (New York: Macmillan, 1953).

[10] Follett, *op. cit.*

[11] Barnard, *op. cit.*

[12] Douglas M. McGregor, *The Human Side of Enterprise* (New York: McGraw-Hill, 1960), 22–28.

[13] Taylor H. Cox, Jr., *Cultural Diversity in Organizations: Theory, Research & Practice.* (San Francisco: Berrett-Koehler, 1993).

[14] See Taylor H. Cox, Jr., and Stacy Blake, "Managing Cultural Diversity: Implications for Organizational Competitiveness." *The Executive* 5 (3 August 1991): 45–56. See also Renee Blank and Sandra Slipp, *Voices of Diversity* (New York: AMACOM, 1994).

[15] See Sally Helgesen, *The Female Advantage: Women's Ways of Leadership* (New York: Doubleday Currency, 1990); Ann M. Morrison, *The New Leaders: Guidelines on Diversity in America* (San Francisco: Jossey-Bass, 1992); Judy B. Rosener, "Ways Women Lead," *Harvard Business Review* (Nov./Dec. 1990): 119–125; and Virginia Schein, "Would Women Lead Differently?" in William Rosenbach and R. Taylor, eds., *Contemporary Issues in Leadership* (Boulder, CO: Westview Press, 1989), 154–160.

[16] Judy L. Rogers, "New Paradigm Leadership: Integrating the Female Ethos." *Journal of the National Association of Women Deans, Administrators, & Counselors* 51 no. 9 (1988): 1–8.

[17] See Camilla Stiver, *Gender Images in Public Administration: Legitimacy and the Administrative State* (Newbury Park, CA, Sage Publications, 1993).

[18]Adapted from Richard Beckhard, *Organization Development: Strategies and Models* (Reading, MA: Addison-Wesley, 1969); Wendell L. French and Cecil H. Bell, Jr., *Organization Development: Behavioral Science for Organization Improvement,* 5th ed. (Englewood Cliffs, NJ: Prentice Hall, 1994); and J. Steven Ott, *Classic Readings in Organizational Behavior, op. cit.*

[19]In Edgar H. Schein, *Organizational Psychology,* 3rd ed. (Englewood Cliffs, NJ: Prentice-Hall, 1980), 232.

[20]Mary Walton, *The Deming Management Method* (New York: Dodd, Mead, 1986).

[21]See e.g., W. Edwards Deming, *Out of the Crisis: Quality, Productivity and Competitive Position* (Cambridge, England: Cambridge University Press, 1988); Joseph J. Juran, *On Planning for Quality* (New York: Collier Macmillan, 1988); Ellis R. Ott and Edward G. Schilling, *Process Quality Control,* 2nd. ed. (New York: McGraw-Hill, 1990).

[22]Two of the best examples are Michael Barzelay, *Breaking through Bureaucracy* (Berkeley, CA: University of California Press, 1992); and David Osborne and Ted Gaebler, *Reinventing Government* (Reading, MA: Addison-Wesley, 1992).

[23]William G. Ouchi, *Theory Z: How American Business Can Meet the Japanese Challenge* (Reading, MA: Addison-Wesley, 1981); and Richard T. Pascale and Anthony G. Athos, *The Art of Japanese Management: Applications for American Executives* (New York: Simon & Schuster, 1981).

[24]Strong similarities also should be evident between the assumptions and philosophies of OD and the literature on the feminist perspective of organization and management from the late 1980s and early 1990s. See e.g., Helgesen, *op. cit.;* Rogers, *op. cit.;* Rosener, *op. cit.;* and Virginia Schein, *op. cit.*

[25]Chris Argyris, *Intervention Theory and Methods* (Reading, MA: Addison-Wesley, 1970).

[26]Chris Argyris, "Some Limits of Rational Man Organization Theory," *Public Administration Review* 33 (Mar./Apr. 1973): 263–267.

[27]Abraham Maslow, "A Theory of Human Motivation," *Psychological Review* 50 (July 1943): 370–396.

[28]Patricia Ingraham, "Quality Management in Public Organizations," in Peters and Savoie, *Governance in a Changing Environment* (Ottawa: Canadian Centre for Management Development, 1995).

[29]Lee G. Bolman and Terrence E. Deal, *Reframing Organizations: Artistry, Choice, and Leadership* (San Francisco: Jossey-Bass, 1991), 121.

[30]Including critical theory—Jurgen Habermas, *Toward a Rational Society* (translated by Jeremy J. Shapiro) (Boston: Beacon Press, 1970); emergence theory—Frederick K. Thayer, *An End to Hierarchy and Competition,* 2nd ed. (New York: Franklin Watts, 1981); Karl E. Weick, *The Social Psychology of Organizing,* 2nd ed. (Reading, MA: Addison-Wesley, 1979); and Orion F. White and Cynthia J. McSwain, "Transformational Theory and Organizational Analysis," in Gareth Morgan, ed., *Beyond Method: Strategies for Social Research* (Beverly Hills, CA: Sage, 1983), 294; inter-

pretive theory—Ralph P. Hummel, *The Bureaucratic Experience,* 4th ed. (New York: St. Martin's Press, 1994); and David Silverman, *The Theory of Organizations* (New York: Basic Books, 1971).

[31]William I. Thomas, *The Unadjusted Girl* (New York: Harper Torchbooks, 1923. Reprinted in 1967.)

[32]This argument is presented most persuasively by Edgar H. Schein in *Organizational Culture and Leadership,* 2nd ed. (San Francisco: Jossey-Bass, 1992).

[33]See J. Steven Ott, *The Organizational Culture Perspective* (Belmont, CA: Wadsworth, 1989).

[34]Cox, *op. cit.*

[35]Bolman and Deal, *op. cit.,* 244.

[36]United States Government Accounting Office, *Organizational Culture: Techniques Companies Use to Perpetuate or Change Beliefs and Values* (Washington, DC: General Accounting Office, 1992).

[37]*Ibid.,* 2.

[38]Ott, *The Organizational Culture Perspective,* 5.

[39]Federal Quality Institute, *Introduction to Total Quality Management in the Federal Government* (Washington, DC: United States Office of Personnel Management, 1991), 14.

[40]United States Government Accounting Office, *Organizational Culture: Techniques Companies Use to Perpetuate or Change Beliefs and Values* (Washington, DC: General Accounting Office, 1992), 2. The nine companies were AT&T, Corning, DuPont, Federal Express, Ford, IBM, Johnson & Johnson, Motorola, and 3M.

[41]*Ibid.,* 2.

Chapter 10

Personnel Policy
and Human-Resource Management

In 1978 Congress passed the Civil Service Reform Act (CSRA), legislation designed to overhaul the federal personnel system. Even though this was only the second time since the founding of the republic that such major civil service reform had been legislated (the first was in 1883), calls for reform have been incessant. In fact, less than a decade after the passage of CSRA, the federal personnel system was being criticized again. Now that it has been nearly twenty years since CSRA, that round of "reform" seems like ancient history. Similar patterns can be found around the world.[1] What is it about a process of matching people to the needs of an organization that should be in such constant need of revision?

Part of the answer has to do with the evolving nature of what is valued in civil-service systems. When the first major civil service reform act, the Pendleton Act, was passed in 1883, the goal was to curb the abuses of the "spoils system" (the appointment of individuals to positions based on patronage). Congress and the president recognized the need to create and maintain a professional civil service by ensuring that jobs were awarded to the most qualified candidates based on fair and open competition. Some cities and states followed the federal example and reformed their personnel systems at the same time, although greater progress was made following the progressive era of the early 1900s.[2]

Over the years, in the name of accountability and uniformity, additional laws and regulations were been added until the system became cumbersome. The National Performance Review (NPR) described the federal human-resource management system in its report "Reinventing Human-Resource Management" this way:

> Today, the system's functional operating components present a burdensome array of barriers and obstacles to effective HRM [human-resource management]. Hiring is complex and rule-bound; managers can't explain to appli-

cants how to get federal jobs. The classification and pay systems are inflexible. The performance management system is not adequately linked to the organization's missions and goals. The labor relations program is adversarial. The federal workplace is not family-friendly, with overly restrictive leave practices and limited implementation of available programs.[3]

The problem is not just that the processes for managing employees are complex and cumbersome, but that they run headlong into an emerging set of values that emphasize flexibility, simplicity, cost-effectiveness, customer service, and a quality work environment. These concerns are not present only at the federal level. Researchers analyzing state and local personnel systems for the National Commission on State and Local Public Service (also known as the Winter Commission) noted that when they presented their initial findings at a planning conference for the commission, the comment was made that the civil service system was so unwieldy that it was not salvageable. The commission, in its report published under the title *Revitalizing State and Local Public Service*, also stressed the importance of valuing deregulation, a customer orientation, and management discretion and flexibility.[4] Indeed, many countries that have emerged from authoritarian or military regimes have been attempting to adopt progressive reforms to attack corruption while seeking to avoid the burdensome complexities that have plagued developed countries.

In other words, whether at the federal, state, or local level, public personnel systems are continually confronted by challenges. Changes in social values, workforce demographics, technology, and the legal environment all deal forceful blows to the personnel system in any organization. In the public sector, organizations face an additional set of challenges because personnel systems are often expected to achieve conflicting goals. The civil service is expected to be professional and neutral, and yet it operates within a political setting. Managers must be able to discipline employees who are not performing their jobs, and yet employees need to be protected from reprisal for "blowing the whistle" on waste, fraud, or abuse. Tension exists between the need to ensure that members of an often large workforce are treated on a principle of equality, and the unique requirements of a diverse array of agencies that have special personnel requirements and for whom the uniform system may not be effective. Fiscal constraints can create a gap between public and private sector pay for comparable jobs, thus limiting efforts to motivate and reward exceptional accomplishments with performance awards. The situation is even more complex in some developing countries where gender roles and other social cleavages have not yet achieved working understandings or where cultural issues cause concepts of hierarchy and accountability to be even more problematic than they are in some developed countries.

Since the late nineteenth century, the idea that public sector employees should be hired, promoted, and rewarded based on merit has come to be widely accepted in the United States and a number of other countries. At the same time, enforcement of merit as a fundamental employment principle has often collided with other goals of effective management. These conflicts will become clear as this chapter examines how the personnel office attempts to serve the organization and the principle of merit at the same time.

After defining what is meant by a merit system and how it looks today, this chapter describes the processes that have traditionally characterized personnel management. It then discusses some of the ongoing challenges to the coherence of those processes, including the need to ensure optimal employee performance and organizational productivity, an ever-shifting legal environment, and the need to maintain good relations between labor and management. It concludes with an assessment of emergent demands confronting public sector human resource management that have led to calls for rethinking management of the person-organization fit.

What Is a Merit System?

Prior to 1883, jobs in the federal government and most state and local jurisdictions in the United States were based on patronage. That is, they were given to people supporting elected officials. By 1883 the excesses of this system, culminating in the assassination of President Garfield by a supporter who was not given the job he believed he deserved, led to the passage of the Pendleton Act. The Act called for a civil service system based on merit, although its merit provisions initially only covered about 10 percent of the civil service. At the heart of the system was the requirement that those who wanted government jobs would have to participate in an impartial and open examination process. In addition, the civil service was to be politically neutral and able to serve any party in power. An independent, bipartisan Civil Service Commission (CSC) was established to oversee the system at the federal level, and in many states and large cities as well.

Even as the new principles were developed, two sets of expectations strained the doctrine of selection based on pure merit in the federal sector: (1) veterans were to be given preference in hiring, and (2) the civil service was to be geographically representative; that is, civil service jobs were to be "apportioned among the several States and Territories and the District of Columbia."[5] Veterans' preference in the late nineteenth century meant that, other things being equal, honorably discharged soldiers and sailors were to be given preference in hiring and were not to be discharged during a reduction in force if their record was good. Veterans' preference is still in effect today, though its provisions have been modified to add points to their examination score or, in some cases, give qualified veterans absolute preference when applying for jobs.[6] As the issue of civil rights grew in importance in the latter part of the twentieth century, representation of women and minorities replaced the tenet of geographic representation. The same is true in many state systems.

For the next century, successive legislation and executive orders expanded the scope of the merit system in the federal government until, by the late 1970s, more than 90 percent of federal employees were covered by its rules and procedures. All U.S. states and cities with a population of at least 250,000 now have at least some provisions for a merit system on the books.[7] At the same time, multiple overlapping legislative development brought with it confusion and created a variety of exceptions to the merit rule. That same problem could be found in local and state governments, particularly those with a long history of machine politics.

President Jimmy Carter proclaimed in 1978 that there was "no merit in the merit system" and made the passage of the Civil Service Reform Act (CSRA) a centerpiece of his domestic policy.[8] The Act's reforms were designed to make the system, which had become increasingly rigid and complex, more flexible and decentralized. Not incidentally, it was also designed to give the White House greater control, particularly with respect to senior careerists. Carter hoped that the concept of merit would be strengthened through recognition of high-caliber performance and elimination of poor performance. The chief executive, acting through subordinates, could then reward excellence and punish poor performers. In addition, nine merit principles were written directly into the law (see Table 10-1).

The CSRA abolished the CSC and created three new agencies. The Office of Personnel Management (OPM) was to be the personnel management arm of the president. The OPM's job was to set government-wide standards for personnel management, audit agencies to ensure compliance with those standards, and then delegate many aspects of personnel management to agencies to perform. In so doing, OPM would maintain uniformity and accountability, while allowing for more flexibility. The OPM was also to conduct research to develop better methods of personnel management. The Merit Systems Protection Board (MSPB) was to safeguard the merit system through

1. hearing appeals from employees who charged that their agencies acted against them for "nonmerit" reasons,

2. reviewing OPM's regulations, and

3. performing oversight of the merit system.

Table 10-1
Merit Principles

1. Recruitment should be from qualified individuals from appropriate sources in an endeavor to achieve a workforce from all segments of society, and selection and advancement should be determined solely on the basis of relative ability, knowledge, and skills after fair and open competition which assures that all receive equal opportunity.
2. All employees and applicants for employment should receive fair and equitable treatment in all aspects of personnel management, without regard to political affiliation, race, color, religion, national origin, sex, marital status, age, or handicapping condition, and with proper regard for their privacy and constitutional rights.
3. Equal pay should be provided for work of equal value with appropriate consideration of both national and local rates paid by employers in the private sector, and appropriate incentives and recognition should be provided for excellence in performance.
4. All employees should maintain high standards of integrity, conduct, and concern for the public interest.
5. The federal workforce should be used efficiently and effectively.
6. Employees should be retained on the basis of the adequacy of their performance; inadequate performance should be corrected; and employees should be separated who cannot or will not improve their performance to meet required standards.
7. Employees should be provided effective education and training in cases in which such education and training would result in better organizational and individual performance.
8. Employees should be
   (A) protected against arbitrary action, personal favoritism, or coercion for partisan political purposes, and
   (B) prohibited from using their official authority or influence for the purpose of interfering with or affecting the result of an election or nomination for election.
9. Employees should be protected against reprisal for the lawful disclosure of information that the employees reasonably believe evidences—
   (A) a violation of any law, rule, or regulation or
   (B) mismanagement, a gross waste of funds, an abuse of authority, or a substantial and specific danger to public health or safety.

Source: Federal Statutes, 5 U. S. C. 2301(b)

Within the MSPB, an Office of Special Council was created to investigate abuses and protect whistleblowers (employees who speak out to disclose fraud, abuse, or waste in their agencies). The Federal Labor Relations Authority (FLRA) was given responsibility for overseeing labor-management relations in the federal sector.

State and local jurisdictions, as well as other nations, have also found it necessary to reevaluate the structure of their civil service systems from time to time. In 1989, the Canadian prime minister undertook an initiative called "Public Service 2000" that was intended to find ways to give public sector managers more flexibility, ensure greater accountability, and put greater emphasis on customer service.[9] This effort culminated in the enactment of The Public Service Reform Act in 1993.

In addition to creating new structures for implementing and safeguarding the merit system, the CSRA created a Senior Executive Service (SES) of top managers in the government. The new system gave agency heads more flexibility to reassign executives and remove them for poor performance without appeal. It also gave the president more power to make appointments to executive positions within agencies, although no more than 10 percent of senior executives can be political appointees. The SES currently consists of about seven thousand men and women.

Because of its size, the federal government has often set precedents in administrative practices that are followed by state and local governments. The evolution of the merit system and many of its current components are examples of such federal leadership. In other cases, because of their smaller size, state and local units are able to be the innovators.

Beginning in the late nineteenth century, state and local jurisdictions followed the federal example in establishing merit systems overseen by commissions, although many still remained under a patronage system until well into the twentieth century. These changes occurred in part because of the need to upgrade personnel practices in order to more efficiently carry out the growing responsibilities of government at all levels and to comply with federal laws such as those requiring equal employment opportunity.[10] Many states have established agencies equivalent to the Office of Personnel Management and the Merit Systems Protection Board. In many cities, the personnel system is under the jurisdiction of professional city managers who are generally insulated from politics with employment contracts providing for protections against political interference in the operation of their departments. The federal government, in the late 1930s, also began adopting a variety of means to coerce state and local jurisdictions into adopting merit systems by making compliance a condition for receiving federal funds.

The Civil Service Today

Nevertheless, the merit system continues down a rocky road. The CSRA did not quell criticism of rules and procedures that often appeared at odds with the effective and efficient management of federal agencies. Although support for merit principles continues, the system itself is often criticized. Less than twelve years after CSRA became law, a personnel officer was quoted by Patricia Ingraham and David Rosenbloom[11] in a paper prepared for the National Commission on the Public Service as saying, "The system is beyond repair; it needs to be totally rethought." Similar sorts of complaints were heard in Ottawa, London, and Canberra. They were emerging as well in developing countries that had concluded that personnel systems left over from colonial days, even with reforms, simply did not respond to contemporary needs.

By 1978, the federal personnel system had not only lost credibility as a merit system, but had become unwieldy. When the Civil Service Commission was established in 1883, its primary concern was the development of procedures for merit hiring. During the first half of the twentieth century it grew into a full-scale personnel agency and in the process took on conflicting roles. The CSC was to be both a management agency focused on efficiency, economy, effectiveness, and accountability and a regulatory body focused on evaluation of management practices, defense of the merit principles, and procedural fairness for employees.

As previously mentioned, the CSRA abolished the Civil Service Commission and created new agencies in its place (see Table 10-2). The Office of Personnel Management (OPM) now performs the central management functions required by the merit system. The Merit Systems Protection Board (MSPB) oversees the merit system, adjudicating employee appeals and performing reviews of merit systems and the significant actions of OPM. Within MSPB, the Office of Special Counsel (OSC) was created to investigate allegations of personnel abuse and prosecute violators of civil service regulations.

Table 10-2
Agencies Created by the Civil Service Reform Act

Agency	Headed by	Approximate Size of Staff
Office of Personnel Management	Director appointed by the president	6800
Merit Systems Protection Board	Bipartisan, three-member board	320
Office of Special Counsel*	Special counsel appointed by the president	90
Federal Labor Relations Authority	Bipartisan, three-member "authority"	250

*Created as part of MSPB; became independent in 1989.

Source: Katherine Naff

(In 1989, OSC became an independent agency). Finally, the Federal Labor Relations Authority (FLRA) was established to govern federal labor-management relations.

While these are the agencies with primary responsibility for the federal personnel process, other agencies have a role as well. The CSRA transferred oversight of equal employment opportunity in the federal government to the Equal Employment Opportunity Commission (EEOC). The General Accounting Office (GAO), the investigatory arm of Congress, also oversees the civil service system and reports to Congress annually on the performance of OPM. In addition, the Senate Committee on Governmental Affairs and the House Committee on Government Reform and Oversight have jurisdiction over issues pertaining to federal employment. Hence, there is considerable scrutiny of the management of the government's human resources, and the personnel agencies can be sure that their actions are watched very closely.

Public sector workforces today are large and diverse. According to the Office of Personnel Management, over three million civilians were employed by the federal government in 1992 (see Table 10-3). Of those, about one million work for the Department of Defense, and another 800,000 work for the U.S. Postal Service.

As large as the federal civilian workforce seems to be, it has declined from 135 employees per 10,000 population in 1960 to 125 per 10,000 population in 1990. The trend was the opposite for state and local governments, which grew from 356 per 10,000 population in 1960 to 614 per 10,000 population in 1990. Census data indicated that full- and part-time state and local employment grew by 200,000 from 1990 to 1991 for a total of 15.5 million in 1991.[12]

It is no wonder that, with large, diverse, and in some cases growing workforces, public sector jurisdictions have needed to find a way to manage their employees. It is the traditional role of personnel in performing this function to which we now turn.

Table 10-3
Federal Civilian Employment, July 1992

Total civilian employment	3,116,397
Legislative branch	40,585
Judicial branch	27,744
Executive branch	3,048,068
White collar (GS and other)	1,946,335
Blue collar (wage system)	378,076
Postal service	791,986

Source: Office of Personnel Management, 1992.

Traditional Personnel Functions

Traditionally, personnel management has been defined in terms of a specific set of processes or functions that "fit" the employee into the organization. The responsibility of the personnel officer begins with conducting a job analysis to identify the critical components of a job and the skills required to perform it. The position is then classified (matched with a predefined set of job titles and ranks or grade levels). Applicants are sought, and the most qualified among them is selected for the job. The personnel system also ensures that training is provided to maximize employee job performance. More recently, most personnel operations have recognized that positions need to be changed from time to time and for a variety of reasons. This redesign process feeds back into the entire process (see Figure 10-1).

Figure 10-1
Personnel Management

Managing personnel, in both the private and public sectors, has become more complicated. More weight should be placed on training and development of the employees, as well as on redesigning jobs for the future.

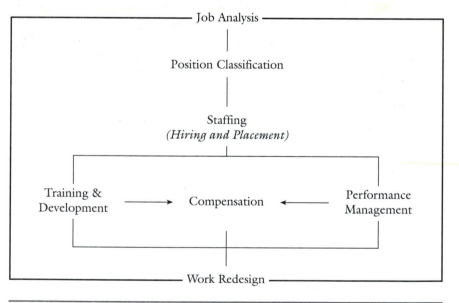

Source: Katherine C. Naff.

Job Analysis

Job analysis refers to the process of gathering information about a specific job in order to determine its responsibilities and qualification requirements. It is a means for ensuring:

1. that the job classification is valid;
2. that the recruitment and selection process can be based on an accurate understanding of the knowledge, skills and abilities required for the job; and
3. that training programs can be developed to enhance performance of the job.

In many public sector systems, including that of the federal government, job analysis and its products (qualification and classification standards) have been centralized. While part of the reason has to do with economies of scale, avoiding duplication in evaluating what may be similar jobs across agencies, there also has been a desire to ensure uniformity and objectivity in the manner by which qualifications and compensation are determined. Historically, there has been an underlying belief that allowing managers flexibility would lead to abuse of the merit system. However, the recent report of the National Performance Review on human-resource management makes it clear that there has been a marked change in views toward centralization and flexibility. Centralization, rather than protecting the merit system, has become a principal impediment to the hiring and retention of the most meritorious candidates. The report calls for much greater managerial involvement in the staffing process and holding those supervisors accountable for the success of their programs rather than just ensuring adherence to a particular process.[13]

Position Classification and Compensation

Traditional position classification can really be seen as an outgrowth of scientific management movement of the early twentieth century. As Chapter 8 emphasized, this movement was based on the notion that there was one best way to perform a task and that all work responsibility and division of labor within an organization could be so organized. Classification can also be seen as responsive to merit principles. It is a way to ensure that job duties are assigned based on the needs of the organization, and not on favoritism or individual preferences.

The fundamental principles of position classification were codified in the Classification Act of 1923. The primary principle is that positions are classified, not people. Once the job duties are determined, the job can be assigned to a job classification and grade level. Grade levels, in turn are associated with specific pay ranges.

Since 1949, white-collar federal employees at the same grade level have been paid the same across the country (although an extra stipend is allowed for employees working in expensive areas of the country). For example, a grade 5 engineering technician working for the Army Corp of Engineers in Oregon performs approximately the same duties, and receives the same pay, as a grade 5 engineering technician working for the Department of Interior in Kentucky. In the federal government, salaries are set by statute, and classification standards are generally issued by the Office of Personnel Management, leaving little discretion to an individual manager to determine the rank or pay of an employee.

More recently, it has been precisely this uniformity and objectivity that has been criticized as too rigid. Where the classification system was designed to promote fairness and prevent favoritism, an inadvertent consequence has been to tie management's hands. Particularly in an era of rapid technological advancement, classification standards have often lagged behind so that it is difficult to match a job to an existing job title. Supervisors are often frustrated with an inability to upgrade employees who may be performing duties beyond what was originally required by their job descriptions. This has been a source of tension between management and personnel officers who see it as their responsibility to limit costs by preventing "overgrading" (assigning a higher grade to a job than is warranted by its duties). As a result, many agencies have adopted a "manage to budget" or "manage to payroll" approach. Managers are permitted to classify their own jobs as long as the salary levels do not exceed the total budget allotted for their office.

In addition, evidence of federal pay lagging behind pay for equivalent jobs in the private sector has challenged the position classification system. During the 1980s, several studies spoke about a "quiet crisis" in the federal civil service whereby the government was increasingly unable to recruit and retain the best and brightest employees due, in large part, to this pay gap.[14] Since managers do not have the flexibility to raise an employee's pay (except, to a very limited extent, through the performance management system), they often resort to finding ways to upgrade employees jobs. This obviously severely tests the neutrality and uniformity of the position classification system.

A recent solution to the quiet crisis at the federal level was envisioned with the passage of the Federal Pay Reform Act of 1990. The Federal Pay Reform Act maintains the classification and grading system but, beginning in 1994, allows for the salaries of employees at the same grade level to vary according to location. Once the pay gap is reduced, it is hoped that some of the pressure on the classification system will be alleviated. It should be noted, however, that, as of yet, budget constraints have kept locality pay increases below what was envisioned by the legislation.

Another proposal to make the classification system more flexible is to replace it with what is termed "pay banding." This ideas groups separate grade levels into broader categories called pay bands, which allow managers wider latitude in setting pay. In addition, the nearly 450 white-collar occupations and nearly 350 blue-collar occupations that employees must be classified into would be replaced with simpler occupational categories.

Pay banding has been tested in the federal government with two demonstration projects. Title VI of the CSRA authorized OPM to conduct such projects in which certain civil service rules could be waived for a limited number of employees, and for a limited time period, in order to test new methods of personnel management. The first such project was developed in 1980 at the Naval Weapons Center in China Lake, California, and the Naval Ocean Systems Center in San Diego. Evaluations of the pay-banding experiment have generally been good, though there is some concern that one byproduct of increased pay flexibility has been an increase in salary costs.[15]

The current classification system is as much of an anathema to state and local governments as it is to the federal government. In their evaluation of state and local personnel systems for the Winter Commission, Ban and Riccucci noted that "[t]he tendency for classifications to proliferate and to become over-specific hampers management flexibility in both the hiring process and the assignment of work."[16] While some state and local jurisdictions have made efforts to simplify the classification system by reducing the number of job titles, there is a countervailing pressure to classify jobs more narrowly and specifically to ensure that qualification and pay reflect specialized skill requirements.

For its part, the National Performance Review recommended legislative change to remove the classification criteria that have remained in place in enactment of the Classification Act of 1949. It further suggested that OPM work with agencies to develop standard broadband patterns and work with agencies to test unique broadband systems under a more flexible demonstration project authority. The NPR also encourages OPM to submit proposed legislation to Congress to allow agencies more flexibility in setting base pay rates.[17] Again, the National Performance Review's recommendations are evidence that the classification system originally designed to achieve internal equity and fairness through precision has gone overboard, resulting in a lack of flexibility, credibility, and a perception by managers of a need to circumvent the system to achieve results.

Staffing

Like classification, the process of recruiting, examining, and selecting employees has been developed to be free from bias and personal whim. Recruitment and selection in the ideal merit system require a process for ensuring that all are able to apply for a job, and the most qualified is selected.

In addition, the federal government has another, sometimes competing, objective: to be representative. In 1944, J. Donald Kingsley, writing about the British civil service, coined the term "representative bureaucracy."[18] He argued that "for bureaucracies to be democratic, they must be representative of the groups they serve." Moreover, a representative bureaucracy shares social responsibility among people with diverse views, which generates acceptance for the bureaucracy's programs and policies. Thus, the bureaucracy should not consist entirely of white, upper-middle-class men, but include individuals from all of the diverse groups who make up its constituency. The Civil Service Reform Act included a call for a system "representative of the nation's diversity" and established the Federal Equal Opportunity Program (FEORP). FEORP requires federal agencies to establish affirmative recruiting plans designed to correct the underrepresentation of women and minorities at all grades in all occupations.

The need for representative agencies has also long been recognized at the state and local level. In its first report, the Winter Commission stated "There is a very legitimate question as to whether a government that does not reflect the demographic makeup of the governed can operate effectively over the long haul, or in the face of widespread hostility or resentment on the part of disenfranchised groups."[19] Thus, it is incumbent on federal personnel operations to ensure that they are recruiting for entry-level jobs and for promotional opportunities from a broad and diverse range of sources so that qualified women and minorities are included in the applicant pool. At the same time, the merit system requires that candidates are considered based on objective, job-related criteria.

The process for examining job candidates sometimes involves the administration of a written test. The test must be shown to accurately measure the candidates' likely performance on the job. In other cases, the examination is "unassembled," based on consideration of past work experience, education, and other relevant qualifications according to a previously specified crediting plan. In both cases, candidates are given a score, and the selecting official is required to select from among the three top-scoring candidates. In the federal government, veterans receive an extra three to five points added to their examination score, and must be selected in favor of a nonveteran whose name follows the veteran's name on the list. All state civil service systems provide some kind of veterans' preference, though the degree to which veterans are advantaged varies considerably among them.

Examination processes also have been the source of tension between managers, who would like to have a greater voice in selection of their employees, and the personnel office, which is responsible for seeing that the process remains objective and merit-based. In addition, veterans groups have successfully opposed efforts to end the veterans preference, leaving supervisors in many cases believing they have even less authority in choosing their employees than they would have if selection were based entirely on examination scores.

Selection processes have been challenged by minorities and by unions. For example, for several years OPM administered a single examination for most federal entry-level professional and administrative jobs called the Professional and Administrative Career Examination (PACE). The exam provided an efficient way of screening nearly 300,000 applicants a year for less than 15,000 jobs. But in 1980, the exam was challenged in a lawsuit representing African Americans and Latinos citing significant differences in the pass rates for Whites, African Americans, and Latinos.[20] The OPM agreed in a consent decree to stop using PACE and develop an alternative.

By 1990, OPM had developed a new series of six exams called the Administrative Careers for America (ACWA). At the same time, OPM implemented the Outstanding Scholar Program (OSP), which permits agencies to hire college graduates with a grade-point average of 3.5 or better or who are in the top 10 percent of their class for ACWA-covered jobs. (These graduates do not need to take an ACWA exam.) Agencies have found the OSP to be a quick and effective way to hire students they meet when recruiting on college campuses, and some complain the ACWA process is more cumbersome and time-consuming. Unfortunately, OSP has also been challenged. While it was intended to give greater opportunity to minorities than they might have under ACWA, the plaintiffs in the original lawsuit have argued that OSP has benefitted more nonminority candidates than minorities, and has asked the court to abolish it.

Efforts to ensure that women and minorities are adequately represented in employment through affirmative action programs have also come under attack recently. In a 1995 decision, *Adarand v Peña,*[21] the Supreme Court ruled that racial classifications must be narrowly tailored to further a compelling governmental interest. This suit challenged the means by which the government awarded contracts rather than its employment policies, and the full ramifications of the decision are yet to be understood. However, it does suggest that any program where the government tries to take race, national origin, or gender into account will be subject a greater degree of scrutiny than such programs had been subject to in the past.

At about the time the decision came down, there was a flurry of activity at all levels of government to try to strengthen or weaken affirmative action programs. For example, Governor Pete Wilson of California signed an executive order prohibiting all programs that provide preferential treatment based on race or gender. Meanwhile, in a speech given a month after the *Adarand* decision was issued, President Clinton reaffirmed his support for affirmative action, stressing that it remains a useful tool for widening economic opportunities for women and minorities. Some Republicans in Congress did not agree, and they introduced legislation in the U.S. House and Senate (HR 2128 and S 1085) to eliminate virtually all preferential programs within the federal government.

Thus, like the classification system, the public sector staffing system is subject to a variety of pressures. Its size and visibility put tremendous demands on the balance that must be maintained among multiple goals and competing interest groups. Not surprisingly, recommendations for reform at the local, state, and federal levels have called for increasing flexibility. The Winter Commission's proposals in the area of hiring included greater use of internship programs and reduced use of veterans' preference and seniority.[22] While the National Performance Review shied away from addressing the issue of veterans' preference, it recommended the abolishment of central registers and standard application forms, and the creation of more flexible qualification standards.[23]

Training and Development

Until World War II, little training was offered to federal employees because Congress and many managers believed the excess of applicants for jobs meant that an employee with the required skills could always be found. A shortage of personnel during the war changed this attitude, but it was not until the 1950s that civilian employee training gained real impetus with issuance of a federal training policy statement by President Eisenhower. In 1958, the Government Employees Training Act (GETA) authorized agencies to determine, manage, and fund their own training needs.

Since then, the training function has expanded greatly in the public sector. The OPM estimates that in 1989, the federal government spent nearly one billion dollars on training its employees. Reasons for the expansion include increasing job specialization, technological change, and an increasing understanding of the need to treat employees as a long-term investment. Technically, training involves giving employees new knowledge or skills, while development refers to the growing package of knowledge, skills and abilities acquired during one's organizational tenure.

Training can include a wide range of activities, such as teaching an employee a new skill on the job, offering a one day workshop in how to use a word-processing program, encouraging attendance at a professional conference, or providing a two-year, multifaceted, managerial-development program. As new technology becomes available, an increasing array of options is available for imparting new knowledge and skills to employees. For example, training courses that used to be offered to a limited number of employees can now be offered by satellite to anyone with access to the broadcast technology.

However, training is also the most vulnerable personnel function in times of fiscal constraint. While it is generally understood that for organizations to remain effective, they must continually invest in upgrading the knowledge and skills of their employees,[24] the benefits of training are often not easily visible or directly measurable. Training is often the first expenditure that is sacrificed when budgets get tight. This problem with the vulnerability of training programs has been a dilemma around the world as budget cuts have forced more work to be done by fewer people, making training time appear to be a luxury. There has also been the confounding argument that organizations can avoid high personnel costs by using short-term or part-time specialist contractors, seemingly rendering money spent on training programs even more unnecessary and inefficient.

One result of the desire to drive accountability into the training process has been to force managers to pay for the costs of training their employees from their own budgets rather than funding the costs through a central training budget. This can be seen on a large scale in OPM's relationship with federal agencies. For years OPM offered hundreds of training programs all over the country, from basic secretarial skills to a four-week, residential, executive-development program, but received no appropriation from Congress to do so. Instead, it operated with a revolving fund whereby agencies reimbursed OPM for training their employees. Recently, OPM decided it should not be involved in the training business at all and allowed a quasi-governmental agency to assume its training operation with some minor exceptions.

Personnel operations at all levels of government are relying to an increasing extent on outside vendors for meeting the training needs of their employees. Shopping around can save the agency money by taking advantage of market competition and economies of scale. Of course, agencies also run the risk of confronting poor quality vendors and ill-designed training courses. Nevertheless, training has become more decentralized and results-oriented, with a wide variety of venues and technologies available for offering training.

This is not to say that training and development, like other personnel functions in the public sector, has not come under criticism. In its assessment of the federal civil service, the National Commission on the Public Service (also known as the Volcker Commission) noted:

> Federal training is suffering from an identity crisis. Agencies are not sure what they should train for (short-term or long-term), who should get the lion's share of resources (entry level or senior level), when employees need additional

education (once a year or more often), and whether mid-career education is of value. . . . At both the career and presidential level, training is all too often ad hoc and self initiated.

While OPM, in response to such criticisms, began in 1992 to take some steps to take a stronger leadership role in the development of training policy, the National Performance Review suggested additional change was needed. It urged increased flexibility in the use of training by calling for the amendment of GETA to link training to the mission of a department or agency rather than to the official duties of an employee, and suggested removing the distinction between government and nongovernment forces to make the skills development more responsive to market forces. The NPR further suggested that agencies be allowed to invest their savings from other "reinvention" efforts in the training and development of their employees.[25] Many of these provisions were, in fact, enacted into law as part of the Federal Workforce Restructuring Act of 1994. For its part, the Winter Commission, finding it "utterly self-defeating . . . for governments to cut training money the instant that budgets get tight,"[26] called for the creation of "a learning government" by restoring training and education budgets, creating a new skills package for all employees, and basing pay increases on skills rather than tenure.

Given the stresses on the public service, the private sector has been known to wait until a training investment has been made by the public sector and then hire people away. This has been a particular problem in certain technical fields, like environmental and health administration. It has also been a particular problem for smaller or poorer developing countries.

Performance Management and Productivity

Once employees are selected, placed in their jobs, and provided with training, it is expected that they will effectively perform the requirements of the position. It follows from merit principles that employees are to be given objective standards for their performance. Dismissals, promotions, or rewards should be based on their accomplishments vis-a-vis those standards. Typically, performance appraisals are designed to serve such a purpose. In the federal government, supervisors are required to give their employees a written list of critical elements for the jobs they perform, and a set of standards that identify the conditions under which performance would be considered as meeting the requirements. In addition, other performance levels are specified to indicate when performance exceeds expectations or is unsatisfactory.

For example, a public relations specialist might be told that a critical element of her job is to respond to inquiries from the press. The standard for fully satisfactory performance of that task is if all calls are returned in a timely manner with the correct response to the inquiry. Her performance exceeds this standard if she also anticipates press inquiries and has the information prepared in advance. Her performance would be unacceptable if the press makes repeated calls to the agency with no response.

At least once a year employees receive performance appraisals from their supervisors. Unsatisfactory performance can be the basis for withholding a pay increase, demotion, or dismissal. Employees who receive outstanding performance ratings are often given cash awards, or, less commonly, an increase in pay. In the federal government, the salary of executives in the Senior Executive Service (SES) is always determined, in part, by their annual appraisal.

One of the major expectations of CSRA was that it would provide a more effective system than had existed in the past for motivating employees to exceed expected performance and for removing employees who had fallen short. In practice, it has been this feature of the current personnel system that has probably received the most criticism. Most agree with the need for a performance management system, but there is little agreement on the best mechanics for such a system.

A system for linking the pay of supervisors and managers in grades 13 through 15 in the federal government called the Performance Management Recognition System (PMRS), for example, was put in place in 1984 when the merit pay system for supervisors and managers established by the CSRA was found to be unworkable. It was to be in place for five years and then would expire if legislation were not passed to extend it. Although the system was extended twice with the hope that it could be made workable, it was terminated in 1993.

Problems with Performance Management

One of the most significant criticisms of the performance management system is that it does not effectively distinguish among employees. While the expectation would be that the majority of employees should receive a rating indicating that they fully satisfied the requirements of their job, this is not the case. In 1991, 41 percent of white-collar employees and 22 percent of PMRS supervisors and managers received fully satisfactory ratings. Nearly all the rest received ratings above full satisfactory. Less than 1 percent of employees in each category receive unacceptable performance ratings.

The performance management function epitomizes many of the conflicts inherent in our civil service system. The appraisal system is supposed to be uniform across government, but there is no means for ensuring that it is implemented uniformly across organizations. Some agencies give more than half of their managers top ratings, while others give less than 10 percent of their managers such evaluations. It is not likely that the former agencies really have several times as many outstanding managers as the latter agencies. But to impose uniformity would require a quota system which could well mean that some managers would receive ratings below what they merit.

Furthermore, rewards, promotions, and disciplinary actions need to be based on standards clearly communicated in advance. Civil service jobs, however, often exist in rapidly changing environments where job requirements shift frequently and written performance standards cannot keep pace. Finally, many jobs do not involve the kind of tangible, measurable output or distillable tasks that objective appraisals really demand.

The quest for a performance management system that can meet the objectives of a merit system will undoubtedly long continue. Not surprisingly, the National Performance Review was as critical of the federal government's performance management system as it was of other traditional personnel functions, stating, "The current approach promotes competition with winners and losers, rather than cooperation and cohesion, which are important elements in most successful government programs"[27] The NPR recommended that agencies be given authorization to develop their own incentive programs with the participation of employees and managers. The Winter Commission was somewhat more pessimistic in its evaluation of state and local performance management programs, suggesting that they are costly and cumbersome with few funds available to disburse as performance incentives. The commission's recommendation was to drop such programs where they are not perceived by employees as fair or are underfunded.[28]

Underlying much of the emphasis on performance appraisal in public sector organizations is a desire to ensure that taxpayers are getting what they pay for from public employees. Although concerns about productivity are not unique to the public sector, the CSRA set productivity improvement as a major objective for government. Former president Jimmy Carter ran on a platform that promised to put an end to an inefficient and unproductive federal bureaucracy.[29] Drafters of the CSRA focused a great deal of attention on ways to improve productivity as well as develop a performance management system that would encourage good performance and weed out poor performers.

There have, however, been many challenges. A serious program intended to to improve productivity requires an effective measurement system, and productivity in public sector agencies is often no easier to measure than employee performance. For example, how does one measure the productivity of a unit of the National Institutes of Health that is working on a long-range project to find a cure for AIDS? Productivity improvement also requires sustained leadership, and leadership has been anything but sustained in the federal government. Although the CSRA handed responsibility for overseeing productivity improvement to OPM, the agency's efforts were terminated less than four years later during the change in presidential administrations. It also requires a system of incentives, or at least a lack of disincentives. Yet the budget process has historically penalized agencies by taking away any savings the organization may have incurred through productivity improvement rather than allowing it to be reinvested.

The same dynamic operates in states, except that the situation is made more complex by efforts at the national level to move tasks out of federal agencies and down to states or localities without resources. Similarly, even countries that have a centralized government have been involved in a global effort to decentralize, but many have been guilty of sending operating responsibilities to subnational levels without adequate resources and often without adequate means for participation by local governments in decision making. Recognizing this dilemma, both the Winter Commission and the National Performance Review recommended the use of productivity gain-sharing programs whereby increases in productivity would be measured and a portion of the savings would be shared by employees and the organization.[30]

The concern for productivity and the conventional wisdom that public sector bureaucracies are inherently nonproductive has fueled the movement toward privatization or contracting of services previously performed by governmental entities. The federal government, over thirty years ago, established a policy that it would rely on the private sector for the provision of commercial goods. The policy shifted in 1967 to become one of encouraging competition between government-operated commercial activities and the private sector so that the entity that could provide the good for the least cost would do so. Contracting reached its height during the 1980s, in part because of the Reagan administration's ideological commitment to shrinking government and promoting private enterprise. Similarly, the tax revolts of the late 1970s gave state and local government new impetus to privatize. One dilemma in privatization is that the functions that the private sector is most interested in acquiring tend to be those that are the easiest and most profitable. An example can be found in mail delivery, where Federal Express and others moved in to take over the premium overnight delivery service, leaving high-cost and low-return daily mass delivery to the Postal Service.

The government has yet to meet its goals for productivity improvement. Budget deficits continue to pressure administrations to increase productivity and to try to perform functions with a smaller workforce. President Clinton's campaign platform in 1992 once again called on federal agencies to increase productivity by 3 percent per year, and to develop performance standards and measures for evaluating outputs in every office. The report of the National

Performance Review, released the following year, promised savings of $108 billion from fiscal 1995 to 1999.[31] Much of these savings was expected to come from the elimination of 252,000 employees, a target Congress raised to over 272,000 when it passed legislation in 1994 authorizing the use of monetary incentives to encourage employees to resign from their jobs (the Federal Workforce Restructuring Act).

Public sector bureaucracies, particularly when budgets are slim, are expected to maintain high levels of productivity and employee performance. Actually, there is considerable evidence that despite the national pastime of bureaucrat bashing, productivity in many public sector organizations is at least as high as many private sector organizations.[32] However, maintaining the balance among conflicting goals such as accountability, flexibility, uniformity, and fairness in the face of a lack of consensus and leadership on the best way to proceed is probably the greatest challenge facing the civil service system.

Employee Discipline and Grievances

Written performance appraisals have become a standard contract between employees and supervisors representing agencies. The employee promises to meet job requirements, and the organization promises to treat the employee fairly. Over the years, merit systems have also developed courses of action for agencies and employees who believe that the other has not fulfilled their part of the contract.

Most public sector organizations have a means of taking disciplinary action against employees whose conduct or performance is unsatisfactory. These actions can include poor performance ratings, letters of reprimand, temporary suspensions, or removals. But just as staffing processes were developed to prevent the hiring of employees based on political whim, protections have also been developed to prevent firing employees based on political whim. As a result, civil service systems are generally characterized by strong protection of employee rights. This protection generally takes the form of the right of employees to appeal actions taken against them to independent third parties. The burden rests with the supervisor to document the employee's poor performance or misconduct, and any efforts he or she has taken to help the employee improve performance.

The development of employee protections in the twentieth century are rooted in the same abuses that led to the creation of the merit system in the nineteenth century. The Pendleton Act had sought to free the civil service from partisan influences by regulating the recruitment and selection process. By the early 1900s it was clear that partisan considerations were still affecting discipline and removal of employees. The Lloyd LaFollette Act of 1912 stipulated that federal employees could only be removed for justifiable cause. It actually took several decades for the mechanisms for enforcing this principle to be put in place, culminating in their codification in the CSRA.

However, there has been the additional dynamic of significant labor union activity. Unions for police, firefighters, teachers, and others have had varying degrees of success at structuring protections for employees. Complicating the issue for managers is the fact that a single jurisdiction may have contracts with a half dozen or more unions, each of which is negotiated separately. Although such governments try to engage in pattern bargaining, under which the attempt is made to treat unions similarly, the task is difficult. Where governments cannot really bargain on pay issues, work rules, including disciplinary processes, become a focus of attention.

At the federal level, certain employer actions are appealable by the employee (within specified time limits) to the MSPB. These actions include removals, suspensions of more than fourteen days, reductions in grade or pay, furloughs of thirty days or less, and certain OPM determinations in retirement matters. Actions not appealable to the MSPB are often appealable to OPM or covered by grievance procedures within the agency itself. About one-third of the full-time civilian workforce, including political employees or those who work in the intelligence agencies, do not have appeal rights to the MSPB.

At virtually all levels of government, employees must elect either to operate under the terms of a negotiated agreement or to take the formal civil service appeal options. Once a path is chosen, however, the grievant cannot switch.

Sometimes employees believe that actions were taken against them as a result of discrimination based on race, color, religion, sex, age, national origin, handicapping condition, or marital status. In this case, the complaint is handled initially within the agency, and then appealed to the Equal Employment Opportunity Commission (EEOC) if it cannot be resolved within the agency.

Unfortunately, many countries, including many with large populations, have little or no history of protecting civil servants from either inappropriate political pressures or the temptations of corruption. As our fate is more closely linked to one another by the phenomenon of globalization, all of us have a stake in the professionalization of the public service, including encouraging mechanisms for its protection.

This high concern for employee job protection has a negative side, as well, as anecdotes about incompetent employees who appear immune from sanction feed the public's concern about inefficient bureaucracy. Moreover, supervisors are frustrated with the time-consuming process required for removing a problem employee. The employee may remain on the rolls for months pending resolution of his or her appeal, and the employee may win based on a narrow technical legal issue.

The National Performance Review recognized the frustration that federal managers have with the disciplinary aspect of the performance management system but had few concrete suggestions for how to improve it. Other than suggesting that the required time for notice of termination be reduced from thirty days to fifteen days, NPR simply suggested that agency heads hold supervisors accountable for dealing with poor performers and give them training in how to use the system.[33] Similarly, the Winter Commission acknowledged that many state and local managers are so stymied by the process required to terminate a public employee that they would rather promote a poor performer into a new, useless job than initiate termination proceedings. However, the commission simply recommended that a speedier means for resolving the issue be put in place.[34]

Once again, the merit system poses two goals for the civil service which call for seemingly conflicting responses. In order to maintain a neutral, nonpartisan civil service, employees must be protected from unjust reprisal or dismissal. But these protections also make it more difficult for supervisors to rout poor performance, and sometimes inadvertently contribute to the image of the bureaucracy as inefficient and rigid.

Traditional Personnel Functions Face a New Set of Demands

All of the traditional personnel functions outlined in Figure 10-1, from staffing to performance management and training and development, continue to be important components of human resource management. But over the decades the underlying objectives for these functions has changed. It is the new set of demands that underlies the frustration the National Performance Review and Winter commissions expressed with how these functions operate at all levels of the public sector. At one time, these functions were geared toward protecting employees and the integrity of the systems from management abuse. Now management is viewed as the customer whom personnel functions should serve so that the manager can in turn serve the public. Where there was a need for control, now there is a need for flexibility. Where there was an emphasis on adherence to process, there is now an emphasis on achievement of outcomes. Personnel is no longer to be the protector but the facilitator. As suggested by Figure 10-2, these personnel functions have not been replaced but rather subsumed under a new set of principles. It is possible that the desire for reform will result in a complete transformation of these personnel functions sometime in the future. But in general such reform is a slow process because it must be accomplished within an already established legal environment. It is to an overview of that legal context to which this chapter now turns.

Figure 10-2

Reinventing Human Resources Management

Personnel function in the governmental work environment is evolving beyond the traditional outlines presented in Figure 10-1. Even the title has changed from "personnel management" to "human-resources management," reflecting both the fact that employees are viewed as valuable resources for the organization and that they are human beings, not just workers.

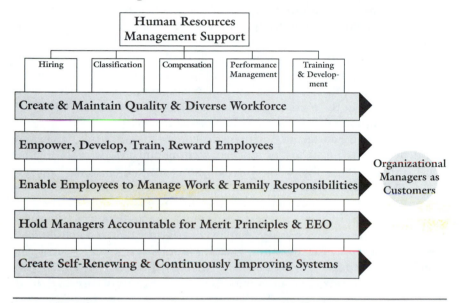

A Process Perspective—Processes that Enable

Source: Katherine C. Naff.

The Legal Environment

As should be clear from much of the preceding discussion of personnel functions, protection of employee rights has taken on ever-growing importance in the public as well as private sectors during the twentieth century. In an effort to protect the rights of employees, Congress has passed legislation and created agencies to regulate various aspects of the personnel process. Some of these laws, such as the CSRA, are intended only for federal employees. Others, such as those pertaining to equal employment opportunity, apply to both public and private sector employees. The courts are also playing a greater role than ever before, as those who believe their interests have been harmed by the implementation of the laws or regulations have sought to protect their rights through litigation.

For decades, the courts have struggled with what has been called the "right/privilege dichotomy." During the 1950s, the courts tended to view benefits provided by the government, including employment, as a privilege so that no rights of employees were violated should benefits or jobs be taken away from them. By early 1970s the scope of government employment had grown so large that the courts rejected the notion that employees had no rights with respect to their employment with the government.[35] However, balancing employees' constitutional rights with the need for the government to most efficiently and effectively serve the public interest is not always an easy task.

One area of continuing contention is the applicability of the right of due process to situations in which public employees are threatened with removal from their jobs. While the practical implementation of due process rights were discussed in the preceding section on Employee Discipline and Grievances, it is appropriate to review the legal issues involved.

The Fifth and Fourteenth Amendments convey that the government cannot deny citizens life, liberty, or property without due process of law. During the 1960s and 1970s the courts ruled in a series of decisions, culminating in *Board of Regents v. Roth*,[36] that public sector employees were entitled to due process rights wherever actions were taken that would infringe on their liberty, future employability, or where they would lose a job in which they had tenure. The due process accorded employees was their right to appeal the decision. However, by the time the Supreme Court issued its 1976 decision in *Mathews v. Eldridge*,[37] it became clear that the justices had shifted their thinking from insisting that a hearing was required to ensure fairness to holding that a hearing was required only to ensure accuracy, and that the benefit of such a hearing had to be weighed against the burden to the agency of providing one.[38] In a later decision, *Cleveland Board of Education v. Loudermill*,[39] the Supreme Court required that tenured public employees be given notice of any charges against them and an opportunity to present their side of the story.[40]

Two laws known as the Hatch Acts also treat employment in the public sector differently from the private sector. These laws, passed in 1939 and 1940, prohibit federal employees—and state and local employees whose jobs are at least partially federally funded—from engaging in partisan political activity. The acts were intended to ensure the political neutrality of the civil service. As the threat of a partisan civil service has receded during recent decades, there has been growing pressure for reform of the Hatch Acts in order to allow public-sector employees the same opportunity for political involvement that other Americans enjoy. In 1993 Congress passed, and the president signed, legislation which removed some of the restrictions, although retaining the principle that public employees cannot run for a partisan office nor solicit political contributions on the job (see Table 10-4).

Perhaps the best example of regulation of personnel functions affecting both private and public employment is equal employment opportunity. The EEO considerations come into play in all of the personnel functions previously discussed. Title VII of the Civil Rights Act of 1964 bars discrimination based on race, color, religion, sex, or national origin. (The Equal Employment Opportunity Act of 1972 extended its provisions to public sector employees.) Although this sounds simple, the interpretation of this law has been the subject of extensive litigation with a variety of outcomes.

In *Griggs v. Duke Power Company*[41] the Supreme Court interpreted Title VII to mean that employment practices cannot have an unequal impact on minorities and nonminorities. The power company had required applicants to have a high school diploma and a passing test score to be hired. Although the policy seemed neutral, it had an adverse impact on African Americans, who were much less likely to have a high school diploma or pass the test than Whites. A prima facie case could be established if the number of minorities selected was less than 80 percent of the number of nonminorities selected (also called the "4/5ths rule"). Had the employer been able to prove that those who could not pass the test and did not have a high school degree would be unable to perform the job, the company would have been off the hook. In other words, for the employer to justify use of the test, he or she would have to demonstrate that there was a "demonstrable relationship to successful performance of the job," commonly called a "business necessity." The power company could not do this. Hence the Court found the requirements to be constituting an artificial barrier that was perpetuating a situation of racial imbalance in the workplace.

This was not the final interpretation of Title VII, however. In *Wards Cove v. Antonio*[42] a more conservative Supreme Court shifted the burden of proof from the employer to the plaintiffs, and rejected the establishment of a prima facie case with the 4/5ths rule. Wards Cove was a packing company that used unskilled workers who were primarily minorities, and skilled workers who were primarily nonminorities, in their operation. The minority unskilled workers were paid less, lived in separate dormitories, and ate in separate dining rooms. This time the Court ruled the plaintiffs must show how the employer's practices actually caused disparities between the percentage of minorities employed by the company and the percentage in the qualified labor force. Moreover, the Court watered down the business necessity standard, holding that the test need only serve the legitimate goals of the employer rather than be essential to the employer's needs.

After several attempts, Congress passed the 1991 Civil Rights Act, which its proponents hoped would restore the *Griggs* standard to employment discrimination cases. However, most commentators agree that the two years of

Table 10-4
Hatch Act Restrictions on Federal Employees

Federal employees may:

- Register to vote
- Express their opinions as individuals, publicly or privately
- Wear a political badge or button, or display a bumper sticker on their private automobiles
- Make campaign contributions
- Accept appointment to public office, provided the service will not interfere with efficient discharge of their federal duties
- Participate in a nonpartisan election either as a candidate or in support of a candidate and, if elected, serve in that office provided it doesn't interfere with their federal duties
- Be politically active in connection with an issue not specifically identified with a political party, such as a constitutional amendment or referendum
- Be a member of a political party or other political organization
- Attend a political convention, rally, or fund-raising event
- Sign petitions, including nominating petitions
- Express their opinions on issues to members of Congress.

In addition, employees covered by the 1993 Hatch Act* reforms may engage in the following activities that were not allowed previously:

- Hold office in political parties
- Distribute literature, solicit votes, and otherwise actively work for partisan candidates or causes as long as it is away from the workplace and on the employee's own time

Employees may not:

- Use their official authority to influence or interfere with an election
- Collect political contributions unless both the donor and solicitor are members of the same federal labor organization or employee organization and the one solicited is not a subordinate
- Knowingly solicit or discourage political activity of any person who has business before their agency
- Engage in political activity while on duty, in any government office, or in an official uniform or government vehicle
- Solicit personal contributions from the general public
- Be a candidate for a partisan public office

*Certain employees, primarily in security and law enforcement agencies, remain covered by the more limiting restrictions of the original (1939) Hatch Act.

Source: Federal Employees Almanac, 1994.

political bargaining required to secure enactment of the law left the language with regard to business necessity and the burden of truth open to debate. It will be left to the courts to determine what constitutes illegal employment discrimination. Some of the major and more clearly defined provisions of the Civil Rights Act of 1991 are summarized in Table 10-5.

The Court has also become involved in issues of affirmative action in the public sector. In a decision that is still cited by the EEOC in its guidance to federal agencies, *Johnson v. Santa Clara County,*[43] the Supreme Court found it permissible for public sector employers to consider more than just who received the highest examination score when evaluating candidates in order to increase the representativeness of the workforce. Factors such as gender or minority group status can be equally important considerations in a public sector agency that is attempting to achieve a workforce demographically representative of the local labor force. The *Johnson* case involved a promotion decision for the position of road dispatcher in Santa Clara County. Diane Joyce had received a score three points lower than Paul Johnson in competing for the position. The director was given the names of all seven applicants with a passing score to choose from and, in part because of affirmative action considerations, selected Joyce. Johnson sued, and initially prevailed after convincing the Court that he was better qualified, and that she was promoted based on her

Table 10-5
Some Important Provisions of the Civil Rights Act of 1991

- Racial discrimination includes not only discrimination in hiring or promotion, but also racial bias in any other employment decision, such as harassment or termination (in response to *Patterson v. McLean Credit Union*).
- Challenges are allowed for Title VII cases where a seniority system is believed to intentionally discriminate (in response to *Lorance v. AT&T*)
- Discrimination is prohibited even if the employer can show that the same decision would have been made if no discriminatory motive were present (in response to *Price Waterhouse v. Hopkins*).
- Challenges to consent decrees are prohibited when they are not made in a timely manner if the parties had notice of the judgment when it was made and had a reasonable opportunity to present their objections (in response to *Martin v. Wilks*).
- Victims of intentional discrimination may sue on grounds of intentional bias based on gender, religion, or disability, and both compensatory and punitive damages may be sought. Punitive damages may be sought where the employer's actions involve "malice and reckless indifference" toward the plaintiff (expanding the scope of the Civil Rights Law of 1866).

Source: Based on Gullett, 1992.

sex. He lost the appeal, however. When the Supreme Court finally ruled on the matter in 1987, it noted that "there is rarely a single, 'best qualified' person for the job," and therefore other considerations, such as achieving a representative workforce, may be taken into account without violating the law. However, the Court specified fairly narrowly the conditions under which race or gender could be considered in employment decisions. In writing for the Court, Justice Brennan noted that a jurisdiction interested in implementing such a plan must consider whether:

- there is a "manifest imbalance" as reflected in a comparison of minorities or women in the employer's workforce with the percentage in the area labor market, or among those in the area with relevant qualifications if the job requires special skills;

- the manifest imbalance relates to a "traditionally segregated job category";

In 1987, Justice William J. Brennan, Jr. authored the majority (6 to 3) opinion in Johnson v. Transportation Agency, Santa Clara County, California. *A staunch supporter of affirmative action who served on the bench from 1956 to 1990, Brennan died in July 1997 at age 91.*
(Photo courtesy of Ken Heinen/Collection of the Supreme Court of the United States.)

- the plan "unnecessarily trammel[s] the rights of male employees or create[s] an absolute bar to their advancement" by establishing a rigid quota system or earmarking of positions; and whether
- the plan is temporary, intending only "to attain a balanced workforce, not to maintain one."

As noted in an earlier section of this chapter, the recent *Adarand* decision suggests that the Court will subject affirmative action plans to greater scrutiny in the future. However, given the rather narrow confines of the Court's approval of an affirmative action plan in the *Johnson* decision, it may be possible that a plan implemented within such constraints today might also be held to be constitutional under the *Adarand* decision. Clearly, this remains a volatile area, under continuous redefinition by the courts as well as by executives and legislatures.

Thus, personnel managers must be aware of the constant stream of legislation and case law that can dictate many aspects of personnel operations and how employees are to be treated. Some of these laws are designed to ensure that social values, such as the elimination and alleviation of the harm caused by discrimination, are extended into the employment process. Other laws are based on a concept of the civil service as a unique employment situation requiring special regulation.

Labor-Management Relations

Thus far, personnel management has been discussed largely from the perspective of how management works with individual employees. However, employees do not always act individually. As the personnel system has developed in the public sector, so have employee organizations and unions. Even while union membership overall in the United States has dropped, unionization in the public sector grew from 900,000 in the late 1950s to over six million in 1987.[44]

Although public sector unions have existed since the early 1880s, they did not gain the right of collective bargaining, comparable to the private sector right, until the 1950s. The first official recognition of these rights in the federal sector occurred with the issuance of two executive orders by President Kennedy in 1962. These and subsequent executive orders were codified into the federal labor relations statute (FLRS) with the passage of the CSRA in 1978. About 60 percent of the nonpostal, federal workforce is now covered by collective bargaining agreements, a percentage that has remained fairly stable since 1975.[45] Largely because unions are required to represent employees in a bargaining unit regardless of whether they are dues-paying members, the number of federal employees who actually belong to unions is much smaller. It has been estimated that less than 22 percent of federal employees represented by unions pay dues.[46] Wisconsin became the first state to allow public sector employees to bargain in 1960, followed by thirty-two other states in the following two decades.[47] In 1990, 40 percent of state employees and 47 percent of local employees belonged to unions.[48]

In the federal sector, and in many state and local jurisdictions, unions do not enjoy the same rights as their private sector counterparts. They cannot bargain over many traditionally basic issues such as wages and benefits, nor are any matters that are set by government-wide laws, rules, or regulations open to negotiation. They cannot be involved in discussions about how jobs are classified, how work is assigned, or how performance is appraised or rewarded. Prohibited from bargaining about "meat and potatoes issues," unions often become involved in seemingly petty issues such as how parking places will be assigned or how office moves will be conducted. In addition, federal employees are prohibited from using the two most powerful tools of their private sector counterparts—the strike and work stoppages—and union security provisions are almost nonexistent.

Three neutral entities are involved in the federal labor-management relations process. Functions of the bipartisan Federal Labor Relations Authority (FLRA) include certifying bargaining units, deciding appeals where agencies have determined an issue is nonnegotiable, overseeing elections of labor organizations as exclusive representatives, and resolving complaints of unfair labor practices. The Federal Mediation and Conciliation Service (FMCS) works with management and labor to resolve impasses in negotiations. If agreement cannot be reached, the Federal Services Impasses Panel (FSIP) can take whatever action is necessary to resolve the impasse. These impasse resolution mechanisms, which are also found in many state and local jurisdictions, have been put in place as an alternative to the use of the strike to resolve disputes between labor and management.

Despite its more limited scope, The labor-management relations process in the public sector was based on the private sector model and the assumption that management and employees' interests are divergent and often adversarial. Indeed, many battles have been fought before the FLRA and in the courts whereby labor organizations have sought to widen the narrow scope of bargaining permitted under the FLRS and management has fought to retain its authority. But unions have largely failed in their efforts to broaden their jurisdiction under the law, while agencies have grown weary of litigation. Thus, in the public as well as private sector, unions and employers have begun to experiment with an alternative model—labor-management cooperation.

In the federal sector, this has frequently meant that management has given unions the right to participate in decisions legally reserved for management in exchange for unions "accepting" a new program and giving up the right to litigate. In 1988, OPM published policy guidance encouraging agencies to engage in labor-management cooperation initiatives.[49] The National Treasury Employees Union and the Internal Revenue Service have successfully developed such cooperative ventures dealing with incentive pay and quality improvement.

Despite these success stories, labor-management cooperation is not the solution to every dispute. For example, an issue that has fueled considerable litigation in the federal arena as been privatization. The FLRS clearly gives management the right to make decisions with respect to contracting. However, because their members' jobs are often at stake, unions have fought all the way to the Supreme Court to gain entry into the decision-making process. Unfortunately, neither labor nor management believes that it can find a way to cooperate on an issue where their interests are so divergent. Union officials believe cooperation can only take place within the context of collective bargaining, where they at least have some leverage. Similar obstacles to successful labor-management cooperation initiatives exist at the state and local level, especially where there is a lack of trust between unions and managers, an unwillingness to sacrifice some authority, and where elections disrupt continuity through regular turnover among top decision makers.[50] Union skepticism toward cooperation or participation in management decisions where they have no statutory authority was perhaps best expressed by an official of the American Federation of Government Employees. A February 10, 1991 article in the *Federal Times* quoted him as saying: "I don't believe in participative management. Ever see two cats playing with a mouse? The mouse is participating. Participation is not the goal. The goal is collaboration."

Hopes for increased labor-management cooperation were further blighted when a General Accounting Office survey of federal union and management officials revealed that, while three-quarters of managers reported positive experiences with cooperative initiatives, less than one-half of union officials rated them positively. In a 1991 survey, union officials were asked to rate the importance of seven tactics for the 1990s, and the development of cooperative relations with management received the lowest rating of the seven.[51]

Nevertheless, despite this daunting backdrop of pessimism about labor-management cooperation, the Clinton administration undertook a new initiative in 1993 with the issuance of Executive Order 12871, which called for labor-management partnerships. The order established a National Partnership Council comprised of representatives from the Public Employee Department of the AFL-CIO, the three largest unions representing federal employees, and seven representatives from federal agencies. It further directed agency heads to create labor-management councils within their own agencies and to begin negotiating with employees over certain subjects that agencies had previously been permitted (but not required) to bargain over under the statute. The council's report, issued in January 1994, endorsed many of the National Performance Review's recommendations, including decentralization of hiring, the replacement of the current classification system with broadbanding, the establishment of a more flexible and decentralized performance management system, and increased investment in employee training and development. In addition, the council recommended the reexamination of rights as they currently exist in the Statute, with the possibility of expanding management rights and/or mandatory subjects of bargaining.[52]

It should be noted that collective bargaining is not the only arena open to unions to influence policies affecting employees. Unions are also actively involved in electoral politics and lobbying for changes in laws affecting federal employees. In the survey of union officials mentioned earlier, litigation and court challenges, electoral politics and campaigning, and public relations efforts were rated as even more important tactics for the 1990s than more aggressive collective bargaining.[53] Where collective bargaining by state employees is not permitted, it is common for those employees to form associations that press employees' interests before state legislators instead.[54]

In the state and local arena, there has been more variation in the scope and range of labor activity. Today nearly every state has some type of statute or administrative edict that regulates labor relations at the state and local levels of government.[55] Some states have models that emphasize consultation of labor by management who ultimately retains authority over personnel matters, while others bear more resemblance to the private sector model where nearly all personnel matters are subject to negotiation. Like the federal government, most states and localities prohibit strikes by public employees, although some allow them for certain categories of employees (see Table 10-6).

The scope of bargaining also differs from state to state. In most states (as in the federal sector) managers and unions are prohibited from bargaining over the criteria and process for hiring new employees, as allowing union involvement in this arena is seen as a threat to the merit system. Agencies' missions are also not open to discussion as, in a democracy, these are set through the legislative process. Most states allow bargaining on working conditions, grievance procedures, and union security. Some states also permit bargaining over compensation, layoffs, transfers, and promotions, while others do not.[56] During the 1980s, the issue of whether the contracting of public services should be a mandatory subject of bargaining became a hot topic in several states. While some commentators have suggested that the impact of privatization on employees' working conditions means that in most cases at least

Table 10-6

State and Local Government Employees with the Right to Strike

State	Employees Covered
Alaska	All public employees except police and firefighters
California	All but police and firefighters, *providing* a court of California PERB does not rule that striking is illegal
Hawaii	All public employees
Idaho	Firefighters and teachers
Illinois	All public employees except police, firefighters, and paramedics
Minnesota	All public employees except police and firefighters
Montana	All public employees
Ohio	All public employees except police and firefighters
Oregon	All public employees except police, firefighters, and correctional officers
Pennsylvania	All public employees except police, firefighters, prison guards, guards at mental hospitals, and court employees
Rhode Island	All public employees
Vermont	All public employees except correctional officers, court employees, and state employees
Wisconsin	All public employees except police, firefighters, and state workers

Note: Employee rights represent those effective as of 1990.

Source: Ban and Riccucci, 1993 (Jossey-Bass). Adapted from Kearney, 1992. Updated by *Labor Relations Reporter,* "State Labor Laws" Washington, DC: Bureau of National Affairs, 1989–1990.

some aspect of the process *is* a mandatory subject, at least two states determined it was *not* mandatory.[57]

Labor-management relations adds another wrinkle to the complex management of personnel in the public sector. Most public sector entities recognize the right of employees to organize to represent their own interests. But the power of unions must be balanced against the interests of the public that these entities are responsible for serving. In the federal government, neither federal managers nor labor officials are completely satisfied with the balance struck by the FLRS. As resources become more restricted, as the legal environment becomes more complex, and as technological and demographic transformations mount, both parties are looking for ways to ensure their constituents interests are not lost.

Emerging Challenges to the Civil Service System

The preceding discussion has examined the traditional personnel functions and some of the difficulties that are faced when functional areas encompass conflicting objectives. By now it should be apparent that public sector personnel systems have evolved over the last century to take on more functions, and the functions themselves have become more complex. The job of the personnel officer has become more than administering the procedures required to bring employees on board and keep them producing. Among other changes, the workforce has become more educated, skilled, mobile, and demanding. Technology has changed the nature of many jobs while facilitating communication and information processing. In recognition of an evolving organizational environment, many personnel offices have redefined their role as human-resource management. In other words, people are no longer thought of as replaceable pieces of the organizational machinery but as a valuable resource that an organization must make special efforts to manage and develop effectively. This responsibility falls not just to the personnel officer but to every manager who depends on an effective workforce to accomplish his or her part of the organization's mission.

A growing number of organizations are recognizing the need to allow their employees to better utilize their skills and creativity through employee empowerment, the creation of more flexible and discretionary work environments, and by breaking down traditional hierarchical structures. Much of the private sector has probably been ahead of the public sector in adapting to the new environment, but the public sector is rapidly catching up. The following discussion will highlight some of the new demands facing public sector personnel systems as a result of changes in the technological and demographic landscape and the very nature of how work is defined.

Transforming Demographics and Social Values

Two reports commissioned in the late 1980s by the Department of Labor and OPM, *Workforce 2000* and *Civil Service 2000*, respectively, warned of serious challenges awaiting employers in this country. Both reports, prepared by William Johnston of the Hudson Institute,[58] spoke of dramatic changes in the composition of the workforce, labor shortages, and mismatches between job skill requirements and employee skill levels. The reports rapidly became household words in private and public sector personnel offices as individuals scrambled to examine how their own organization's programs could contend with these formidable events on the horizon.

Since that time, many of the predictions made by the two reports have been questioned, and some of them refuted. For example, rather than a predicted labor and skills shortage, an economic recession in the early 1990s led to de-creased turnover in federal jobs and long lines of overqualified applicants wait-ing at job recruitment fairs. Moreover, the reports foresaw in the coming decade a dramatic change in the gender and ethnic makeup of the labor force; a prediction severely criticized by analysis with the Economic Policy Institute and the General Accounting Office, who argued that the growing participa-tion of women and minorities would merely be the continuation of an existing trend.[59] Nevertheless, after the critiques of the Hudson Institute studies, agreement remained that the gradual change in the demographic makeup of the workforce over the past few decades would continue, and personnel sys-tems must respond.

The most dramatic change in the last thirty years has been a tremendous increase in women's participation in the workforce. Census data show that the percentage of women in the labor force grew from 38 percent in 1960 to 58 percent in 1990.[60] Minority workforce participation has also grown, and is expected to continue to grow. Finally, as the "baby boom" moves through the pipeline, the workforce has become older. In its analysis of federal work-force demographics, GAO reported that the median age for the federal workforce rose from thirty-four years old in 1980 to thirty-seven in 1990 and is expected to reach forty-one by the year 2005.[61]

Growing participation by women has several implications for personnel systems. First, most of today's benefits programs, including that in the fed-eral government, were really designed with the assumption that men were in the workforce with their wives at home taking care of the children. Now that both parents are often working, there is considerable demand for child care, elder care, part-time and flexible schedules, family leave policies, and flexible work sites to allow parents' to accommodate the needs of their children. Most employers recognize that these benefits are important for employee re-cruitment and retention as well as productivity and morale. For public sector employers, the logic of increased benefits and the need for equitable distrib-ution of them can run headlong into budget constraints.

Second, the pay gap between women and men is a thorn that many women insist should remain in their employers' sides until it is resolved. Al-though employers have been required to pay men and women equally for the same work since the passage of the Equal Pay Act of 1963, the median weekly earnings for men in 1993 were 30 percent greater than for women.[62] The issue now is whether women are paid equally for *comparable* jobs.

The debate about the "comparable worth" of jobs, which reached its height during the 1980s, is complex and difficult to summarize. There are at least three schools of thought as to why women are paid less. One is that pay inequity is rooted in biased job evaluation that undervalues jobs traditionally held by women. Another is that pay for jobs is determined by market forces, and as long as women are willing to take lower-paid jobs, there is no incentive for employers to raise salary levels. The third attributes the problem to one of occupational segregation where women are steered into particular jobs that have historically paid less than those that have drawn men. Regardless of the argument one accepts, it is clear that increased participation of women in the workplace has not necessarily brought them commensurate opportunities. Personnel systems at the local, state, and federal levels will continue to be propelled to resolve the issue of disparate pay into the next century.

A third issue is that of sexual harassment. While sexual harassment, or unwanted sexual attention, is not new in the workplace, employers are growing increasingly aware of the need to eliminate it. In surveys conducted by the Merit Systems Protection Board in 1980, 1987, and 1994, more than 40 percent of women in the federal government reported that they had been harassed.[63] Awareness of the problem and pressure to rout sexual harassment have increased since the publication of MSPB's findings, as well as the famous Hill-Thomas hearings in 1991 where then Supreme Court justice nominee Clarence Thomas was accused by his former employee Anita Hill of sexual harassment. As more women enter the workforce, more demands are placed on personnel managers to ensure that employees are made aware of what actions constitute harassment and that it is illegal under several statutes. They also must ensure that avenues of redress are open and functioning for those who are victims of harassment. That opportunity for redress increased when the U.S. Supreme Court upheld the EEOC assertion that sexual harassment was sex discrimination that violates Title VII of the Civil Rights Act of 1964.[64]

The increase of women and members of minority groups in the workforce has compelled a growing concern with the issue of diversity. Even where discrimination has not been overt, women and minorities have felt shut out of organizations whose ways of doing business have been defined by the white male majority. A 1992 study by MSPB found, for example, that employees in professional and administrative positions who devote more than forty hours per week to their jobs are assumed to be more committed to their careers and therefore deserve visible work assignments, developmental opportunities, and promotions.[65] While evidence suggests women perform their jobs as well as men, child-rearing responsibilities sometimes make it more difficult for them to work long hours. Moreover, even if women are able to work overtime, it is assumed they cannot and so they are often passed over for promotions. A subtle yet discernible reason for this is the time availability criteria that usually does not bear any actual relationship to job performance or commitment. Women and minorities also often face stereotypes such as "women are not as career-oriented as men" or "minorities are not as qualified as nonminorities." These stereotypes can be more acute for the organization's first African American manager or the first female engineer.

In many public and private sector organizations, minorities and women are severely underrepresented in management positions in relation to their proportion of the workforce as a whole. For example, while women comprise nearly half of the federal workforce, only about 12 percent of federal senior executives are women.[66] In the 1980s, the term "glass ceiling" was coined to describe the subtle, almost invisible set of barriers that block the advancement of women and minorities into management.

Numerous studies have acknowledged that public sector agencies do not reflect the population they are intended to serve, especially at the upper levels. The Winter Commission noted in its report, "Women and minorities still continue to staff the front lines and not the front office."[67] Similarly, the National Performance Review criticized the federal government's record in integrating members of underrepresented groups into middle and upper management.[68]

Many public sector entities have separate Equal Employment Opportunity (EEO) offices that are specifically charged with designing programs to redress imbalances in the employment of protected groups. Nevertheless, personnel systems are also looking for ways to correct the imbalance through:

1. ensuring a lack of bias in how employees are selected for jobs or for training;

2. expanding recruitment mechanisms to ensure that women and minorities are included in applicant pools;

3. developing mentoring programs; and

4. training managers in the value of working with those who look "different" than the "typical" employee of the past.

With the passage of the CSRA, the federal government made the commitment to achieve a civil service that reflected the nation's diversity. While diversity has clearly grown overall in the workforce, the commitment to full representation at all grade levels has not been met. Changing traditional views and work habits is a difficult process, and the issue of valuing diversity in the workplace represents one of the greatest challenges of the decade.

The Technological Challenge

Advances in technology and the steep rise in labor costs have combined to make a technological revolution inevitable in the public as well as private sector during the last two decades. But with this technological revolution comes major impacts on office operations, the composition and roles of staff, and job satisfaction. Since the advent of the revolution, debates have raged as to

whether technology increases supervision or gives employees more autonomy, heightens the role of midmanagement or renders it irrelevant, enhances
or diminishes job satisfaction, and increases productivity or reduces it. The
very existence of the debate underlies the reality that the effect of technology
is not inherent in the technology itself, but in the hands of those who manage it. The role of human-resource management in this process is critical.

Technology challenges each of the traditional personnel functions. In an
automated organization, the technology may be doing the work, and employees are acting as interveners to correct the defects of the technology.
Outcomes are far less predictable, and employees must be given the flexibility to cross classification lines. A static position-classification system that relies on rigid definitions of jobs then becomes an anachronism. Tasks often
become much more complex and varied, and a single method of data collection for job analysis may be inadequate in providing information needed for
position classification.

A selection process based on finding people with a specific set of knowledge or skills becomes outdated as quickly as the knowledge and skills are
outpaced by technology. By the same token, training programs that just
teach employees what they need to know to do the job become outmoded.
Our personnel system is designed to match individual people to individual
jobs. But technology often calls for a wider range of skills and more flexibility than a single individual is capable of.

Technology is one of the driving forces that has, and will continue to have,
a major impact on organizations. Organizational structure and operations,
staff roles and composition, and the nature of supervision all undergo transition as an organization automates. The need and opportunity for flexibility
place serious demands on human-resource management systems that sought
to ensure merit by defining a single, uniform approach to personnel management. No longer must the personnel manager be concerned only with the
person-organization fit, but also with the person-technology-organization
fit. The respite found in a regulated system is pressured to give in to a proac-
tive and developmental system.

Changing Human-Resource
Management Strategies

The technological revolution and the changing composition of the workforce are just two of the factors that are demanding changes in the way work
is done. Much of our traditional personnel system grew out of the scientific
management movement, which conveniently dovetailed with the need for an

objective, neutral, merit-based system. Work was simple and prescribed, and it was assumed that a carefully performed job analysis could unearth its inherent content and qualifications. A simple examination procedure, based on the content of the job, could determine who was the best qualified individual to perform the job. Training would be skill oriented, designed to teach the employee how to complete his or her tasks more efficiently. A vertical promotion process would allow supervisors to be recruited from those who have performed and therefore know the job, and would be an incentive to employees to do well. Productivity and performance standards could be defined in terms of measurable output. Those who exceeded performance standards could be rewarded; those who fell short would be subject to disciplinary action. Employees would be expected to work at a specific location during specific hours, and supervision was direct.

This picture is obviously oversimplified. Managing people in organizations has never been that straightforward. The civil service has had more than just a single objective of getting work done, and these multiple objectives have added complexity to the process. But the fundamental roots of most public sector personnel systems do lie in that conventional approach.

Calls for personnel officials to rethink their approaches to managing the person-organization fit are coming from a number of fronts. These demands include a redefinition of merit. No one has decided yet what a new definition would be, but there is a strong desire to rid government of what is seen as overregulation of personnel in the name of neutral and objective personnel management. In addition, the realities of technological change, a more demanding workforce, and demographic change are commanding more flexibility and discretion.

Table 10-7 looks at how personnel functions might be redefined in a transformed personnel system. Position classification would be flexible, rather than rigid, to allow for changing technology and job requirements. A more useful selection process would be construct-oriented, geared toward finding individuals with an *aptitude* for learning and managing skills, rather than having a specific set of skills that technology may render extinct. Training that emphasizes cognitive skills and teaches employees to teach themselves the new skills as they become necessary becomes the wiser approach. For a variety of reasons, it becomes useful to define work responsibilities in terms of teams. Teamwork allows for the pooling of a broader range of skills and talent to accomplish a particular objective. It may better meet the demands of parents who need to be available to deal with family emergencies by ensuring that others are available to complete an assignment. Teamwork, in turn, calls for compensation, performance appraisals, and rewards to also be team-based.

Technology makes possible, and family-accommodating employment makes necessary, flexible locations and work schedules. Technology can

Table 10-7

Traditional and Transformed Personnel

Management	Traditional	Transformed
Job analysis	One-dimensional	Multidimensional
Position classification	Rigid	Flexible
Selection	Content-oriented	Construct-oriented
Training & development	Specialized, skill-oriented	Diverse pedagogical
Work arrangement	Individual	Team
Compensation	Individually based	Team-based
Performance appraisal	Individually based	Team-based
Work schedule	Fixed	Flexible
Work location	Centralized	Dispersed
Supervision	Direct	Indirect
Productivity	Output-oriented	Quality-oriented

provide the means for employees to work independently, and for supervision to be less direct. Flexible schedules and locations accommodate the needs of people who, for a variety of reasons, cannot work an 8:00 to 5:00 job.

Recently the public sector has joined a movement imported from Japan and initiated in the private sector. This movement, commonly known as total quality management (TQM) was introduced in Chapter 9. It emphasizes the provision of high-quality goods and services and the importance of service to the customer or client. While some jurisdictions use different names, the management philosophy is the same. For example, Indianapolis has developed a program they call "Total Quality Service" whereby teams work to develop and implement improvements to work processes that employees face on a daily basis. The state of New York is in the process of implementing what it calls "Quality through Participation."

Total quality management and its siblings are management approaches that are oriented toward teamwork and redefining the role of managers in order to continually improve products or services. While some critics believe TQM is just another fad that will go the way of other management initiatives, its tenacity may be rooted in the principles thus far discussed—a desire to find new ways to do work and to be more responsive to taxpayers or customers. Yet TQM also challenges the traditional personnel system in many of the ways already discussed. For example, many TQM proponents argue that any focus on individual job performance, such as with a traditional performance appraisal, runs counter to the focus on product quality and teamwork. But in most public sector jurisdictions, individual performance appraisals are fundamental to the employment contract. Written appraisals have become a primary means for documenting that any actions taken by the employer, whether to reward, advance, discipline, or remove the employee, are based on merit rather than whim. How can the fundamentally different philosophies underlying traditional personnel management and TQM be resolved?

Conclusion

Will there be another major, sweeping reform of the federal personnel system on the order of the Pendleton Act of 1883 or the Civil Service Reform Act of 1978? It is a difficult question to answer. While the pressure on the current system mounts, solutions that would resolve the conflicting goals of the system are not in the offing. Compromises would still have to be reached between management flexibility, employee rights, and the claims of veterans, unions and other interests groups.

Balances would still have to be struck between merit, neutrality, productivity, and a socially representative workforce. As a recent article in *Governing Magazine* reported, even the official termination of the state of Florida's civil service system on June 30, 1992, resulted in no changes to the way the personnel system was managed. One reason, according to the article, is that implementing the recommendations of the Reform Commission that came up with the plan would cost the several hundred million dollars.[69] Personnel management has been called the cornerstone of public administration. It is going to bear that weight for many years to come.

This chapter has used the U.S. federal civil service as an exemplar of problems in many levels of public service and across many countries. However, as should be clear from this chapter's examination of the Winter Commission review of state and local public service, and the National Performance Review's evaluation of the federal sector, there are many issues that different jurisdictions face in common when it comes to managing their workforces. While jurisdictions vary tremendously in their history, demographic makeup, political cultures, and other factors that can affect the way the government does business, they have also faced many of the same challenges in terms of budgetary constraints, "customer" (i.e., taxpayer) expectations, and legal requirements. State and local governments continually look to the federal government as the federal government looks to states and localities for ideas about approaches to common problems.

Similarly, there is much to learn from the way human resources are managed in other nations, although, again, discussion of personnel systems abroad was beyond the scope of this chapter. Nevertheless, researchers studying ways to improve personnel practices frequently look to other nations for examples. One example is an MSPB report on staffing practices in the Public

Service of Canada that included several recommendations aimed at applying to the federal civil service successful practices used for recruiting and selecting employees in Canada.[70]

In short, while this chapter may have understated some of the important differences between local, state, and federal human-resource management systems and those at work in other countries, it is hoped the reader has at least developed the understanding that while personnel systems the world over operate under similar constraints and face many of the same dilemmas, there is no one way to manage a personnel system. The greatest challenge is to acknowledge the key goals of the system, recognize the conflicts among them, and find a way to navigate a course toward those goals that provides the greatest benefit to the employee, the organization, and the public.

Notes

[1] See B. Guy Peters and Donald J. Savoie, eds., *Governance in a Changing Environment* (Ottawa: Canadian Center for Management Development, 1995).

[2] Jay M. Shafritz, Norma M. Riccucci, David H. Rosenbloom, and Albert C. Hyde, *Personnel Management in Government* (New York: Marcel Dekker, 1992).

[3] Al Gore, *Reinventing Human-Resource Management: Accompanying Report of the National Performance Review* (Washington, DC: Office of the Vice President, 1993), 2–3.

[4] Frank J. Thompson, ed., *Revitalizing State and Local Public Service* (San Francisco: Jossey-Bass, 1993).

[5] U.S. Civil Service Commission, *Biography of an Ideal* (Washington, DC: U.S. Civil Service Commission, 1973).

[6] *Personnel Administrator v. Feeney,* 442 U.S. 256 (1979).

[7] Shafritz, et al., *op. cit.*

[8] Patricia W. Ingraham, "The Reform Game," in P. W. Ingraham and D. H. Rosenbloom, eds., *The Promise and Paradox of Civil Service Reform* (Pittsburgh, PA: University of Pittsburgh Press).

[9] Government of Canada, *Public Service 2000* (Ottawa: Ministry of Supply and Services Canada, 1990).

[10] Ronald D. Sylvia, *Critical Issues in Public Personnel Policy* (Pacific Grove, CA: Brooks/Cole 1989).

[11] Patricia W. Ingraham and David Rosenbloom, "The State of Merit in the Federal Government." Occasional Paper prepared for the National Commission on the Public Service (unpublished), 1990.

[12] Thompson, *op. cit.*

[13] Gore, *Reinventing Human-Resource Management, op. cit.*

[14]See e.g., William B. Johnston, et al., *Civil Service 2000* (Washington, DC: U.S. Office of Personnel Management, 1988); and National Commission on the Public Service [Volcker Commission], *Leadership for America: Rebuilding the Public Service* (Washington, DC: Government Printing Office, 1989).

[15]Howard H. Risher and Brigitte W. Schay, "Grade Banding: The Model for Future Salary Programs?" *Public Personnel Management* 23 no. 2 (1994): 187–200.

[16]Carolyn Ban and Norma Riccucci, "Personnel Systems and Labor Relations: Steps toward a Quiet Revitalization," in Thompson, *op. cit.*

[17]Gore, *Reinventing Human-Resource Management, op. cit.*

[18]J. Donald Kingsley, *Representative Bureaucracy* (Yellow Springs, OH: Antioch University Press, 1944).

[19]National Commission on the State and Local Public Service [Winter Commission], *Hard Truths/Tough Choices: An Agenda for State and Local Reform* (Albany, NY: The Nelson A. Rockefeller Institute of Government, 1993), 31.

[20]*Luevano v. Campbell,* 93 F.R.D. 68 (D.D.C. 1981).

[21]132 L.Ed.2d 158 (1995).

[22]Thompson, *op. cit.*

[23]Gore, *Reinventing Human-Resource Management, op. cit.*

[24]David G. Carnevale, "Human Capital and High Performance Organizations," in Steven W. Hays and Richard C. Kearney, eds., *Public Personnel Administration: Problems and Prospects,* 3rd ed. (Englewood Cliffs, NJ: Prentice Hall, 1995); Donald F. Kettl, "Managing on the Frontiers of Knowledge: The Learning Organization," in Patricia W. Ingraham and Barbara S. Romzek, eds., *New Paradigms for Government* (San Francisco: Jossey-Bass, 1994).

[25]Gore, *Reinventing Human-Resource Management, op. cit.*

[26]Winter Commission, *op. cit.,* 41.

[27]Gore, *Reinventing Human-Resource Management, op. cit.,* 36.

[28]Thompson, *op. cit.*

[29]Ingraham and Rosenbloom, *The Promise and Paradox of Civil Service Reform, op. cit.*

[30]Gore, *Reinventing Human-Resource Management, op. cit.;* Thompson, *op. cit.*

[31]Al Gore, *Creating a Government that Works Better and Costs Less: Report of the National Performance Review* (Washington, DC: Office of the Vice President, 1993).

[32]George W. Downs and Patrick D. Larkey, *The Search for Government Efficiency: From Hubris to Helplessness* (New York: Random House, 1986).

[33]Gore, *Reinventing Human-Resource Management, op. cit.*

[34]Thompson, *op. cit.*

[35]David H. Rosenbloom, "What Every Personnel Manager Should Know about the Constitution," in Hays and Kearney, *op. cit.*

[36]408 U.S. 564 (1972).

[37]424 U.S. 319 (1976).

[38]Phillip J. Cooper, "Reinvention and Employee Rights: The Role of the Courts," in Patricia W. Ingraham and Barbara S. Romzek, eds., *New Paradigms for Government* (San Francisco: Jossey-Bass, 1994).

[39]470 U.S. 532 (1985).

[40]Shafritz, et al., *op. cit.*

[41]401 U.S. 424 (1971).

[42]490 U.S. 642 (1989).

[43]480 U.S. 616 (1987).

[44]Irving O. Dawson, 1993. "Trends and Developments in Public Sector Unions," in S. W. Hays and R. C. Kearney, eds., *Public Personnel Administration: Problems and Prospects,* 2nd ed. (Englewood Cliffs, NJ: Prentice Hall, 1993).

[45]U.S. Office of Personnel Management, *Union Recognition in the Federal Government as of December 31, 1992* (Washington, DC: Government Printing Office, 1992).

[46]Richard C. Kearney, "Federal Labor Relations 2000: Introduction to the Symposium," *International Journal of Public Administration* 16 no. 6 (1993): 781–791.

[47]Sylvia, *op. cit.*

[48]Richard C. Kearney, "Unions in Government," in Steven W. Hays and Richard C. Kearney, eds., *Public Personnel Administration: Problems and Prospects,* 3rd ed. (Englewood Cliffs, NJ: Prentice Hall, 1995).

[49]U.S. Office of Personnel Management, Office of Employee and Labor Relations, "Labor Management Cooperation: Policy Guidance" (FPM Letter 711-163), Washington, DC, 1988.

[50]Kearney, "Unions in Government," *op. cit.*

[51]Katherine C. Naff, "Toward the Year 2000: Issues and Strategies for Federal Labor-Management Relations," *International Journal of Public Administration* 16 no. 6 (1993): 813–840.

[52]National Partnership Council, *A Report to the President on Implementing Recommendations of the National Performance Review* (Washington, DC: Government Printing Office, 1994).

[53]Naff, "Toward the Year 2000," *op. cit.*

[54]Sylvia, *op. cit.*

[55]Ban and Riccucci, *op. cit.*

[56]Dennis L. Dressang, *Public Personnel Management and Public Policy* (New York: Longman, 1991).

[57]Katherine C. Naff, "Labor-Management Relations and Privatization: A Federal Perspective," *Public Administration Review* 51 (January/February 1991): 23–30.

[58]William B. Johnston, *Workforce 2000: Work and Workers for the 21st Century* (Indianapolis: Hudson Institute, 1987); Johnston, et al., *Civil Service 2000* (Washington, DC: U.S. Office of Personnel Management, 1988).

[59]Lawrence Mischel and Ruy A. Teixeira, *The Myth of the Coming Labor Shortage: Jobs, Skills, and Incomes of America's Work force 2000* (Washington, DC: Economic Policy Institute, 1991); U.S. General Accounting Office, *The Changing Workforce: Demographic Issues Facing the Federal Government* (Washington, DC: General Accounting Office, 1992).

[60]U.S. Bureau of the Census, *Statistical Abstract of the United States: 1994,* 114th ed. (Washington, DC: U.S. Bureau of the Census, 1994).

[61]U.S. General Accounting Office, *The Changing Workforce, op. cit.*

[62]U.S. Bureau of the Census, *op. cit.,* 429.

[63]U.S. Merit Systems Protection Board, *Sexual Harassment in the Federal Work Place: Trends, Progress, and Continuing Challenges* (Washington, DC: Government Printing Office, 1995).

[64]*Meritor Savings Bank v. Vinson,* 477 U.S. 57 (1986).

[65]U.S. Merit Systems Protection Board, *A Question of Equity: Women and the Glass Ceiling in the Federal Government* (Washington, DC: Government Printing Office, 1992).

[66]*Ibid.*

[67]Winter Commission, *op. cit.,* 31.

[68]Gore, *Reinventing Human-Resource Management, op. cit.*

[69]Jonathan Walters, "How *Not* to Reform Civil Service," *Governing* (November 1992): 30–34.

[70]U.S. Merit Systems Protection Board, *To Meet the Needs of Nations: Staffing the U.S. Civil Service and the Public Service of Canada* (Washington, DC: Government Printing Office, 1992).

Chapter 11

Public Sector Budgeting: Purse Strings, Politics, and Management

Budgeting has always been one of the most important decision-making processes for governments. Indeed, the budget has become one of government's most important reference documents. Budgets simultaneously record policy decision outcomes, list and rank priorities, articulate government program objectives, delineate and explain government's service and assistance efforts, and estimate public sector performance, impact, and overall effectiveness. In Aaron Wildavsky's famous definition, "A budget, therefore, may be characterized as a series of goals with price tags attached."[1] A public budget has four basic dimensions, all of which are interrelated. First, it is a political instrument that allocates scarce public resources of budgeting far beyond determining who gets what.

> If politics is regarded as conflict over whose preferences are to prevail in the determination of policy, then the budget records the outcomes of this struggle. Let us then conceive of budgets as attempts to allocate financial resources through political processes to serve differing human purposes.[2]

Public administration often speaks of two sides in the continuing debate over public expenditures. The first set of political arguments arise over what is often termed public finance and includes, among many other things, arguments about much money should be raised, who should pay, how much, and in what ways.[3] Answers to these issues involve decisions about the level and types of taxes, fees, and user charges to be employed (see Chapter 5). Decisions not to tax, as in policies that allow tax credits for various uses of income (called tax expenditures by advocates and tax loopholes by critics), or not to charge fees (called assistance by proponents and subsidies by opponents) are critical policy judgments. Of course, the answers to those debates depend on other political arguments about the assumptions on which revenue and expenditure policy should be based. An error of 1 percent in the estimation of revenues in a large state can mean a shortfall of more than $200 million. In a small state, or even a small nation, that may be running very close to the edge economically, several incorrect estimates in a row can mean a major financial crisis.

Spending decisions are equally political whether they involve building and launching space stations, paving roads, or paying for entitlement programs such as Medicare, Food Stamps, or school aid payments. Budgeting decisions can also involve credit and insurance issues where one level of government guarantees loans or credits. Credit decisions can involve a wide range of activities such as bank loans to college students, deposit insurance for investors in financial institutions, or loan credits for foreign nations. These promises to pay if the need arises are known as the government's contingent liability. For years, it was argued that such promises were not really the same as an expenditure because the legislators who voted for such policies usually did so on the argument that the beneficiaries are good risks and the government would never need to pay off, that is until the savings and loan disaster of the 1980s when countless institutions defaulted. Then there was the U.S. commitment to Mexico to help bail out a NAFTA partner whose economy nearly collapsed following political manipulations of the interest rates and the money supply during a hotly contested presidential election.

Second, governments at all levels and in many places around the world face increasingly difficult fiscal environments that now include intense media scrutiny about how government raises revenues, how it spends money, and to whom it loans or gives money in the pursuit of the public interest.[4] This type of scrutiny relates to another way of viewing budgeting. A budget is a managerial instrument. A budget should specify the ways and means of providing public programs and services. It establishes the costs and the criteria by which activities are evaluated for their efficiency and effectiveness. It is the budgetary process that ensures that all of the programs and activities of a jurisdiction are reviewed or evaluated during each fiscal year (or cycle). This managerial perspective entails a wide range of public administration activities, including fiscal and expenditure forecasting and planning, productivity and cost analysis, strategic planning and program design, and various forms of policy review and evaluation.

Third, it is clear that a budget is also an economic instrument that can direct a nation's and even state and local economic growth and development. At both the national level and the state and regional levels, government budgets are primary mechanisms for evaluating redistribution of income, stimulating economic growth and development, promoting full employment, combating inflation, and maintaining stability (see Chapter 5).

Once the economic dimension of budgeting was considered primarily the domain of the national government, but this has also changed. Subnational governments, states, counties, cities, and metropolitan authorities are just as likely to be active competitors in the economic marketplace as they bid on and attempt to attract sports franchises, theme parks, industrial plants, or even shopping malls to local within their boundaries. As Chapter 5 indicated, they do this by offering delayed or lower taxes and construction and development loans, or by constructing supporting infrastructure such as roads, parking lots, mass-transit lines or utilities.

Fourth, a budget is an accountability instrument (often discussed as financial management) that holds public officials legally liable for the expenditures and revenues appropriated to support programs that have been entrusted to them. As the politics, economics, and management issues inherent in public sector resource allocation have become more complex and controversial, there has been a major effort made to develop better financial information. Financial management is much more than simple auditing. It means having uniform cost data and standardized categories to report a jurisdiction's fiscal situation and the results of its programs.

Part of the purpose, of course, is to make budgeting compatible with accounting and auditing systems. But, as public managers have learned to their dismay, the lack of consistent and acceptable financial information breeds a special chaos of its own. In the mid-1970s, when the city of New York teetered on the brink of bankruptcy, the entire fiscal crisis was compounded by the existence of three different sets of books with conflicting numbers. In the two decades since, there has been great progress in bringing governments to accept generally accepted accounting principles (GAAP) and adopt and conform to consistent accounting standards. Much of the driving force behind the financial management aspect is the substantial amount of funding that is passed through one government to another: from federal to state, from state to local governments, and between state and local governments and nonprofit organizations that contract to provide public services. To account for intergovernmental transfers properly means having common financial management procedures and accounting techniques.

The Current State of Public Sector Budgets

Over the past two decades, it has become increasingly apparent that the interconnections among these dimensions are what is vital. For example, the very premise of the accounting dimension means that budgets are to hold governments accountable in the aggregate. After all, the basic concept of a budget implies that there is a ceiling or a spending limitation, which literally requires governments to live within their means. The nation's persistent budget deficit, however, has now come to be viewed as one of the top political and economic problems, How is it that the very instrument designed to ensure balanced spending and funding decisions is viewed as the major factor that is destroying that balance?

The failure to respond to that question has certainly not been the result of lack of effort. Since the late 1970s, Congress and six presidents have waged veritable budget warfare over controlling spending and changing taxes. Similar efforts have been undertaken by other countries around the world, with developing countries struggling to cut expenditures even when the demand for social services has been increasing dramatically. In 1990, the Congress and the Bush administration concluded a now-infamous budget summit. They put together a deficit reduction package for $500 billion in cuts. Still, the deficit persists. The Clinton administration and leaders of the Republican controlled Congress did, however, collaborate to implement a balanced budget deal in August 1997.

The reality is that budgeting links control to political and economic choice, or as Michael White and the late Aaron Wildavsky made clear in their study, *The Deficit and the Public Interest:*

> Budgeting involves meeting obligations, keeping promises. It involves choices about values, about which purposes are of highest priority. It involves questions of power: How are we governed, and by whom? Most of all, tax and spending decisions involve real people with real pain and real benefits. What happens to any of us—the fate of farmers, the poor, or General Dynamics—may have meaning to others. In the rhetoric of deficit reduction, these other matters are either disparaged as "special interests" or worse, ignored. Persistent deficits are blamed on a lack of courage or good will. Wrong. Deficits persist because all choices are banned. Choices are hard because important values are helped or hurt by alternatives.5

However, from its beginnings, budget theory has recognized its central importance in shaping such choices. This was to a great extent what budget reform in government was all about. Indeed, at the turn of the twentieth century, the development of the executive budget, as opposed to a legislative budget, for the American system of government was absolutely crucial to the development of public administration in the United States.

Not surprisingly, the executive budget did not develop first in the federal government. It came primarily from the Progressive reform tradition associated with the state and local experience. The classical treatment of this development was written by one of public administration's leading early scholars, William Willoughby. In his 1918 book, *The Movement for Budgetary Reform in the States,* Willoughby identified three main threads of budget reform:

1. providing for and advancing popular control (i.e. the public),
2. developing and enhancing legislative and executive cooperation,
3. improving administrative and managerial efficiency.[6]

These threads must be intertwined if budgeting is to be effective.

The Budget-Reform Saga

Of course, the development of the executive budget itself was considered the first step of budget reform. It is important to remember that public budgets, as we know them today, are a relatively new phenomenon. Prior to the twentieth century, budgets were little more than piecemeal complications of appropriations reports adopted by a legislature. The Budget and Accounting Act that began the establishment of today's federal budgeting mechanism was not enacted until 1921. Earlier budgeting efforts at the state and local levels go back to experiments and developments in New York City and other localities in the early 1900s. Prior to that, there was little perceived need for sophisticated budgeting mechanisms because government expenditures were relatively insignificant.

The Transformation of Legislative Budgeting (1789–1921)

Early federal budgeting, if it can even be dignified with that label, was primarily an exercise in getting rid of surplus funds accumulated from tariffs or in finding ways to fund major land purchases. In retrospect, the nation's first great public administrator, Alexander Hamilton, may have succeeded too well in establishing the new republic on a solid financial footing. However, there were instances throughout the nineteenth century, such as the financial panic of 1837 and Abraham Lincoln's efforts during the 1860s to finance the Civil War, that generated concern that there might be a need for a budgeting system. Later, political and social forces, such as the progressive reform movement, the scientific management movement, and the emergence of more diverse and specialized government programs, provided the impetus for advocates of a budgeting system.

Pioneering work done in some states and municipalities provided the federal government with further examples of the direction to go in budgeting. Indeed, the federal nature of the U.S. system of government was an essential factor in budgetary reform. Such reforms often emerged from "experiments" in state and local laboratories, whether they were in New York City in the 1900s, with the development of performance-based budgets, or in Georgia in the 1970s, with the advent of zero-based budgeting.

The thrust for reform came to a head in the report of the Taft Commission of 1912, which argued strenuously for a national budgeting system to serve the executive branch. Even in its infancy, a recurring theme of governmental budgeting was already apparent. It was the conflict between the legislative and executive branch as to who would control the budgeting process. Not surprisingly, Congress quickly rejected the Taft Commission recommendations.

After World War I, President Wilson rekindled the idea of an executive budget mechanism, but Congress proposed its own legislation. President Wilson vetoed it on grounds that it lacked control by the executive. The Congress and president then feuded over the enabling legislation that created what was perhaps the first round in what would be a long tradition of rancor and noncooperation over budget issues between the legislative and executive.[7]

Congress waited until Wilson had left office before enacting in 1921 what became the Budget and Accounting Act. It established a Bureau of the Budget (lodged in the Treasury Department), a formal budgeting mechanism to be controlled by the executive branch, and a General Accounting Office that was to be accountable to Congress.

The Development of Executive Budgeting (1921–1955)

It was another eighteen years, however, before the Bureau of the Budget became a direct staff branch of the chief executive's office.[8] During this period, budget processes focused primarily on accountability and control. The initial technology of budgeting was the line-item budget, a systematic accounting-oriented method of recording public expenditures against various classification categories, such as salaries, travel, supplies, equipment, and so on.

Against this backdrop, in 1940, V. O. Key, Jr., wrote a searching inquiry about the state of the art of budgeting entitled, "The Lack of a Budgetary Theory."[9] Greatly concerned about the overemphasis on mechanics, Key posed what is still widely regarded as the central question of budgeting: "On what basis shall it be decided to allocate X dollars to activity A instead of activity B?" He then went on to elaborate on what he felt were the major areas of inquiry that should be researched to answer that question and develop a budgetary theory.

In the 1940s and 1950s, following the recommendations first issued by the Brownlow Commission and later codified by the Hoover Commission, performance budgeting emerged as the dominant budgeting system. Performance budgeting was, above all, a management-oriented approach, heavily focused on efficiency through an examination of the relationship between costs and outputs. Its appearance during these two decades was well-timed to match dramatic increases in both the size and scope of governmental undertakings. As the New Deal gave way to World War II mobilization, the era of what Paul Appleby termed *Big Democracy*[10] had truly arrived. There was confidence among public administrators that the new techniques and processes behind large-scale public budgets were adequate to the large-scale, more efficiency-oriented structures of administrative operations. Vision on budgeting in the 1940s was blurred by the unprecedented scale of operations of the war and the preceding economic battled waged against the Great Depression.

Improved efficiency, however, was not an adequate response to Key's question of choice. Larger budgets, fueled by economic growth, made choices more important and increased concern about how budgets should facilitate the idea of direct consideration of alternatives. The 1960s brought even more definitive responses. Wildavsky argued that Key's question, as posed, was unanswerable. His 1961 article entitled "Political Implications of Budgetary Reform"[11] paralleled the argument made by Charles E. Lindblom in his famous essay, "The Science of Muddling Through."[12] Budgeting, Wildavsky argued, was really a mode of incremental conflict resolution aimed principally at ordering political preferences. The question of which criteria should determine what goes into the budget is synonymous with the question of what government ought to do in the first place. If an answer were possible, it would mean nothing less than a total resolution of conflict over government's role in society.

Systems Budgeting in the 1960s (1955–1975)

Of course, the 1960s marked a new era of increased governmental activity. Policy and programs were recast in bolder, more innovative terms, with social intervention as a major premise. A new budgeting system, emphasizing multi-year planning, policy analysis, and program objectives focused on effectiveness emerged. It was called the Planning Programming Budget System (PPBS).

Developed first in the Department of Defense, PPBS attempted to take the rational actor of policy making (critiqued in Chapter 6) seriously. The effort was to identify all possible options for a given policy problem and analyze the cost effectiveness of each. If this challenge could be met it would presumably result in better policy decisions that were also far more effective and efficient than the old incremental approach. It was a prescription, and it was the very antithesis of the Lindblom/Wildavsky explanation about how important policy choices were really made.

The PPB system was widely heralded as a major breakthrough for public administration and was nicknamed by critics as the "pristine path to budget salvation." The PPBS approach dominated public budgeting like no other system before it.

The case for depicting budgeting systems as an evolutionary process of management development was effectively outlined by Allen Schick in a 1966 article entitled "The Road to PPS: The Stages of Budget Reform."[13] The budget literature has particularly adopted his typology of budgetary reform that illustrated shifts in emphasis from accounting-strict expenditure control (the line-item budget) to management/work efficiency (the performance budget) to planning/program effectiveness (PPBS).

Budgeting in an Era of Resource Scarcity (1975–?)

By the 1970s, though, PPBS had failed. It was discontinued during the Nixon administration. Budget reform in the 1970s was beset by two more compelling developments: (1) a new period of legislative/executive competition over who would control budgets; and (2) a new "era of resource scarcity" in which economic growth was no longer a constant. Unquestioning popular support for increased budgets was no longer available. And as dramatic growth was replaced in the early 1970s by a dramatic downturn in the economy, it was clear that increased taxes would be needed to pay the difference between rising costs and stagnating revenues. It was then that a new lesson was learned about the fact that social service costs rise dramatically because of widespread economic need at the same time that tax revenues from existing sources are in decline.

The other two threads of budget reform were now fully as important as the once-dominant managerial thread. Reflecting on the new political/economic environment, Charles B. Levine described how organizations must learn to adapt and alter budget strategies. His discussion of "cutback management"[14] recognized that a half century of "positive budgeting" was over and that a new era of " negative budgeting" was at hand. The vulnerability of public budgets to expenditure and revenue limitation initiatives (like California's Proposition 13, limiting property tax increases) was inescapable.

Partly because of these new economic realities, budget reforms in the 1970s were marked by intense rivalry between the legislature and the executive. These disputes came to a head as a result of two events. First, the Nixon administration asserted wide-ranging executive powers over not only the budget, but the entire economy. The president imposed a wage/price freeze by executive order.[15] With respect to the budget itself, the president asserted broad authority to impound funds that had already been appropriated by Congress.[16] Second, Congress began to rediscover its power as it drove Richard Nixon from office in 1974.[17] Congress pressed its claims by enacting new legislation entitled the Congressional Budget and Impoundment Act of 1974. The battle leading up to this statute was so intense that Schick labelled it the "seven-year budget war."

Relations between state legislators and governors have also been complex. While state legislators gave governors more budgetary authority in some states in an effort to keep control of administrative agencies,[18] they were not prepared to give away too much. Indeed, a 1980s survey of state officials found:

> Because of the formal authority possessed by the state legislature, that institution has more influence over state administration than any other external political actor. In particular, the power of the purse and general lawmaking

authority are two prerogatives which make the legislature the most influential external actor in state administration.[19]

While state agencies could rely on significant amounts of direct federal financial support, they had more insulation from state legislatures.[20] When that federal funding dropped off dramatically during the early 1980s, the state legislatures regained some of the leverage they had lost in the 1960s and 1970s.

There was one more major development within budget reform in the 1970s, the arrival of zero-based budgeting (ZBB) with the Carter administration. Launched with great fanfare in 1977, ZBB promised to counter the traditional incrementalist bias of budgets (the assumption that next year's budget would start from last year's base plus some incremental increase). The idea was to use an elaborate system of decision packages, alternatives that laid out what would happen at the same funding next year, and others that indicated what would be gained or lost if an agency's budget were increased or decreased by stipulated increments. Supposedly, each program would be required in effect to justify its existence every year and there would be no more budgeting by inertia.

It was an illusion. In the first place, it was impossible to reconsider every single budget decision every year. The amount of staff time consumed in attempting a serious analysis threatened to dwarf any savings that might realistically be expected to result. Indeed, it turned out that Jimmy Carter's use of ZBB as the governor of Georgia did not result in an end to incremental assumptions. Thomas Lauth found that administrators tended to build their decision packages around incremental calculations from the previous year.[21]

Finally, critics called ZBB decremental budgeting in disguise, since its primary purpose seemed to be to eliminate any program that could not defend itself against attack. Ironically, the ZBB system that was designed to make ordered cuts in the event of fiscal stress was ignored when those circumstances actually presented themselves. The ZBB process was eliminated by the Reagan administration in 1981.

In 1980, budget reform stood at a crossroads. Clearly, the coming decade would be one of increasing complexity and difficulty. The outgoing, but widely respected, Comptroller General Elmer B. Staats encouraged a continuing effort at budget reform, but the political and economic situation was changing so rapidly that it was unclear whether the new rules of the game would permit systematic reform efforts.

The 1980s may be remembered as the decade when budgeting was turned upside down. At the federal level, this was the era of President Ronald Reagan, who termed the whole budget process "Mickey Mouse"; of a budget director named David Stockman who was nicknamed "The Terminator"; and of major changes to the congressional budget process. Congress incorporated automatic budget-deficit reduction provisions in the Gramm-Rudman-Hollings legislation (which, incidentally, was tagged "Grammbo," a hybrid of Senator Gramm and the film character Rambo). The media took to calling executive budgets D.O.A. (dead on arrival) the moment they came to the Congress.

The year 1985 was one of several intense budget-crisis years. Reagan's first term was marked by the passage of major tax legislation. The rates of personal income tax were cut dramatically, some 23 percent over three years. Congress and the administration remained deadlocked over where to make cuts in the domestic spending while there was a simultaneous and unprecedented buildup in defense expenditures. As Chapter 5 indicated, tax indexing may have eliminated "bracket creep," but it also exacerbated the revenue shortfall.[22] The resulting dramatic deficit increase supported a demand for deficit reduction that would allow an attack on previously untouchable domestic spending programs.

The Balanced Budget and Emergency Deficit Control Act, known as Gramm-Rudman-Hollings, sailed through Congress within ninety days without even the benefit of hearings. What the statute did was to create a series of deficit reduction targets that would be met each year to balance the budget in five fiscal years. If the Congress and the president could not agree on a combination of spending cuts or revenue increases to meet the target, then automatic reductions (sequestrations) would be triggered from domestic, defense, and foreign affairs appropriations.

Because the person who would make the decision whether it was necessary to sequester previously appropriated funds was the comptroller general, who reported to the Congress, the Supreme Court overturned the statute.[23] Congress modified the statute to have the Office of Management and Budget make the determination, but the political reality was that the targets would not be treated seriously. For one thing, such dramatic expenditures as the savings and loan bailout and Operation Desert Shield (and later Desert Storm) were taken "off budget" (not counted as part of the budget for deficit-estimating purposes under the act).

In the end, a deficit deal was struck known as the Budget Enforcement Act of 1990, which called for a $500 billion five-year plan of spending cuts and tax increases to reduce the deficit. The new law limited categories of discretionary spending and restricted the ability to transfer funds from one budget category to another. The federal budgeting process would be forced to follow a concept of PAYGO—or *pay as you go*—in which newly approved or augmented programs would have to come with funding sources or find cuts in existing programs adequate to fund the new initiative.

The situation was different politically for many other nations that use a parliamentary form of government. After all, there are no separation of powers problems to tolerate. On the other hand, the same kinds of fiscal difficulties and international economic competition confronted those countries. In addition, many parliamentary governments faced tax revolts quite similar to what happened in the United States. The difference is that their tax burdens tended to be much higher than those common in the United States. So it was no surprise when the Margaret Thatcher government was able to employ many of the same kinds of strategies and tactics later used by the prime minister's American colleague, Ronald Reagan, to attack previously untouchable social programs.

Two other financial management developments came along with the 1990 statute. Stung by huge financial losses incurred by the federal government over the cleaning up of the savings and loan fiasco, the Credit Reform Act of 1990 provided new regulations and protections for loans and loan guarantees. Furthermore, the 1990 act was matched with the creation of the Chief Financial Officers Act, which designated financial management responsibilities in an established position, the chief financial officer, to oversee reporting, accounting, and budgeting in their respective agencies.

Ironically, by the time President Clinton took office in January 1993, the 1990 budget deal had been completely undone. This time the fault lay with the poor performance of the economy. The political dimension of budgeting had been overtaken by the economic. Despite putting together a $500 billion reduction package in the 1990 deal, the .05 percent rate of growth produced the highest rate of increase in the deficit as a percentage of GDP (gross domestic product) in over a quarter of a century, 4.6 percent.

To understand how deficits are affected by economic conditions, one need only look at a set of estimates provided by the Congressional Budget Office. In 1993, they projected these levels of change in the deficit for each of the following:

Economic Change Factors	FY 1994 Deficit Increase
1 percent lower annual growth rate	$25 billion
1 percent higher annual unemployment rate	$50 billion
1 percent higher annual inflation rate	$2 billion
1 percent higher annual interest rates	$16 billion

It is little wonder that President Clinton felt compelled to deal with the economic aspects of the budget and why his first budget submission included both major revenue and spending proposals.

Power and Politics in Budgeting

The federal experience in legislative and executive budgetary interaction is complex and fascinating, but it makes generalizations difficult. It must be remembered that the power of the legislative appropriations process is strongly affected by the legal rules and procedures that have been established.

Legislative/executive budgeting relationships are illustrated by two widely divergent models. In the strong-executive/weak-legislative model, the chief executive is allowed to have the more formidable budgeting powers, foremost among them the line-item veto. The line-item veto sets executive budget recommendations as a ceiling. The legislature can reduce a program's budget, but if the legislature attempts to increase the spending recommendations for a program, the executive may veto anything over the initial recommendation. This veto power can extend to each individual line item in a budget measure.

At the other end of the scale is the strong-legislature/weak-executive model. Here the line-item veto is forbidden in the federal case or limited with provisions available for an override of the veto. This model is characterized as one where legislatures can virtually rewrite the entire budget to their own liking, submit it as one package incorporating all of a government's expenses, and present it to the chief executive on a take-it-or-leave-it basis.

The Line-Item Veto

Clearly, the line-item veto stands at the heart of the argument over how to control the budget process. This veto over specific appropriations is generally considered to be an innovation pioneered by the Confederacy during the Civil War. Despite numerous attempts to incorporate it into the federal budget process, it was only recently adopted and made available to President Clinton. Before Clinton could exercise the new authority, the legislation was struck down by a federal court. However, the Supreme Court rejected the challenge for lack of standing at the end of its term in 1997, leaving open the likelihood of a new round of legal battles when the president first tries the item veto. In contrast, forty-nine out of the fifty states have some form of line-item veto for years.

Whether line-item vetoes make the difference that their advocates claim for them is another matter. The general conclusion is that line-item vetoes are not effective mechanisms in terms of fiscal restraint. While there is no evidence to support the conclusion that expenditures would decrease if the president had an item veto, there would likely be a change in interbranch relationships. The experience in the states is that the item veto restructures the negotiation process between the chief executive and the legislature. It is a leverage device to get a better deal rather than a budget-cutting tool.

Earmarking of Funds

Weak executive models often present an extensive use of what is called earmarked expenditures, the result of which is a relatively large amount of uncontrollable spending. There is earmarking where revenues from specific sources or in set amounts are legislatively dedicated solely to particular programs. The most common example is the commitment of gasoline tax revenues for road repairs. There is considerable debate over the practice. The positive side is the political attractiveness of convincing the public that a tax to be collected from them will be used for a specific purpose or that a user charge will be funneled back into the program from which it came. The standard example of that phenomenon is the return of fishing or hunting license fees to wildlife management programs.

On the negative side, earmarking dramatically limits flexibility and adaptability, since new legislation is needed to alter spending patterns to meeting rapidly changing conditions. The Dade County, Florida, restaurant tax commitment to providing funds for the homeless is an example of some of the problems that can arise. For example, the restaurant tax will produce less revenue in bad economic times when the needs and numbers of the homeless are highest. Proponents can argue that the single ear-marked tax is not the only funding source for a program, but it is politically difficult to give more money to a program that already has its own designated funding source. School districts that have received funds from state lottery programs have had difficulty of this sort because legislators tend to think they have resolved a funding need once they have guaranteed access to a particular revenue stream. Administratively, earmarked funds make it virtually impossible to transfer funds to accounts where the money may be most needed.

The Uncontrollable Spending Problem

Another aspect of budget politics in action concerns the issue of discretionary spending versus what is often referred to as uncontrolled spending. The latter are programs where the annual appropriations cannot be changed easily. Social service entitlement programs are the most commonly cited examples, but they are by no means the only ones. If a person qualifies for benefits, then they must be provided at the level specified in the law. Hence, a significant portion of the budget is demand-driven. The level of expenditures for each year cannot be set in advance, since it is not clear how many eligible clients will demand services. That is one reason why Medicaid expenditures are creating nightmare scenarios in many states. The client demand for services is matched by dramatically escalating service costs. There can be tension within a legislature in this kind of case because the appropriations committees that are responsible for the budget may take a very different position from the authorization committees that write the substantive legislation, which establish the funding obligations for particular programs and define eligibility for services.

The Welfare Reform Act of 1996 was a major assault on the idea of entitlements. It was popular to different constituencies for different reasons. The president and members of Congress liked the idea because it was an opening wedge in the battle to eliminate entitlement programs. No longer would the federal government be compelled by law to provide funds more or less automatically to any applicant who appeared to meet program qualifications. State-level political leaders expressed support because it appeared to give them more discretion over social programs rather than serving merely as pass-through agents for entitlement programs. The public supported it largely because welfare spending is a target everyone seems to love to attack even though it represents a very modest proportion of the budget and cannot possibly play a significant role in balancing the federal budget. However, there are very serious questions about the impact of that kind of legislation on the states and localities. For example, the bill cut off certain kinds of benefits for legal aliens, but communities like Los Angeles have large numbers of elderly resident aliens who have worked all of their lives and paid taxes. Some of them rely on social programs, but with the cutoff of federal dollars, the state and county must decide whether to absorb a very large expense to maintain the programs at the local level or deal with a significant number of impoverished senior citizens who have throughout their lives contributed to the community and the economy of the area. It is also not at all clear what will happen to federal expenditure patterns in the years ahead, once entitlements are trimmed or eliminated. Some state officials now fear what could become a kind of silent unfunded mandate, a shifting of political as well as economic burden from Washington to the states and localities.   # 13

One of the unexplored dimensions of this move to attack entitlements has to do with its impact on the balance of legislative and executive power. As programs are cut or transferred, the executive branch loses resources, staff, and, to one degree or another, policy influence. A very important aspect of executive power is the ability to manage grants and federally funded programs that affect states and localities. Another way of putting that is to say that they affect the congressional constituencies. The executive's flexibility in these areas is leverage that can and is used to obtain congressional cooperation. The loss of those dollars means a loss of leverage.

On another dimension of the legislative/executive relationship, chief executives do not like earmarked funds for the obvious reason that such programs dramatically limit the executive's flexibility. That is why the existence of large amounts of earmarked funds is an indicator of a legislatively dominated budget process. The frustration level over this kind of program is exacerbated by the fact that the executive branch, particularly at the state level, feels that its judgment should prevail since the legislature lacks the expert knowledge possessed by the executive branch agencies that actually administer the programs. The degree to which legislatures will accept the idea that budget preparation and execution are executive functions and budget adoption is legislative varies from jurisdiction to jurisdiction. This is obviously one area in which parliamentary governments have a distinct advantage.

The fact that there are different committees in both houses of a bicameral legislature that carry out three different functions—authorization, appropriation, and oversight—suggests that there are many internal battles as well as interbranch conflicts. That is all the more true because appropriations committees often attempt to address substantive program provisions on the argument that the committee's task is to ensure that appropriated funds are being properly and efficiently utilized. Obviously, a bad expenditure is neither proper nor efficient. The result is that administrators can get cross-pressured between committees in the same house of the legislature or between committees in both houses.

The Balanced Budget Battle

There remains a final aspect that speaks to the power politics in budgeting, the question of a balanced budget amendment. By legal requirements, state and local governments must ensure that expenditures proposed in a budget do not exceed revenues. Now it should be noted that balancing a budget is a much more flexible process than it might seem. Jurisdictions can and often do roll over or delay payments from one fiscal year to the next, over- and underestimate revenues and expenditures, or even borrow funds using short-term bonds called revenue anticipation notes to balance their budgets. Still, over a period of two or three fiscal years, states and local governments must bring their financial situations into some sort of balance. Normally, that puts pressure on legislatures and executives to cooperate in budgeting, but pressure does not always result in action. Hence, the state of New York has been perpetually late with its budget, borrowing huge amounts of funds on the open market to pay necessary expenses until the new budget is adopted. The appropriations bills should be passed in time for the April 1 fiscal year, but, in 1996 for example, the state went into the end of June with no budget in sight.

The Call for a Balanced Budget Amendment. There has been a recurring demand that a balanced budget amendment be adopted for the federal government. The 1996 debate, led by Senator Paul Simon of Illinois, a Democrat, proposed requiring that any budget that is not balanced would need a 60-percent vote for approval. Even this version of a balanced budget amendment recognizes the economic realities that might require the national government to engage in deficit spending to stimulate the economy in a recession, combat economic downturns, or provide funds in emergency situations like the savings and loan crisis or natural disasters. The states and localities, in theory at least, can balance because they can expect that, if disaster strikes, the federal government will be available to provide help.

Ultimately, critics say that there is no reason to accept all of the obvious problems that would come with a balanced budget amendment. After all, the Congress could simply refuse to pass anything other than a balanced budget. However, while everyone is in favor of balanced budgets in the abstract, few people are willing to sacrifice their pet programs to achieve the reality. Although the balanced budget amendment proposal was defeated in 1997, there is every reason to believe that it will reemerge at some point in the future.

The Tale of Train Wrecks and Budget Cycles. Short of a balanced budget amendment, however, 1995 saw balanced budget politics twice bring the federal government to near paralysis. The clash came to be known as the budgetary train wreck, as an ideologically committed group in Congress—fresh from a major election victory in 1994 and under the leadership of Speaker Newt Gingrich (a Republican from Georgia)—thought that they saw an opportunity to muscle whom they perceived to be a weak president into a budget deal by threatening not to approve legislation needed to keep the government operating.

The story is reflective of some of the continuing tensions at play in the effort to deal with budget deficits. The president introduces a budget in late winter. The congressional committees examine the economic assumptions underlying the executive's proposal and move toward passage of a first budget resolution that sets targets for the individual appropriations committees to use as they work toward enactment of the thirteen separate appropriations bills that make up what we call the federal budget. Of course, it comes as no surprise that committees face pressures to exceed their target for popular programs and projects, which means that a set of negotiations ensues in late summer leading to a second budget resolution that is needed to resolve the overall package before final work can be completed on the individual appropriations bills. That work should be done before the beginning of the new fiscal year, which occurs on October 1 for the federal government.

It has often been the case in recent memory that the details cannot be resolved in time and the new bills are not ready before the deadline. The

Congress has normally adopted a continuing resolution that allows the government to continue to operate at the same level of expenditures until the appropriations bills are passed, at which time a budget reconciliation process resolves the ambiguities that arise because of this method of financing. In 1995, however, Republicans declared their intention to use the threat of shutting down the government by refusing to adopt a continuing resolution to force the White House to accept congressional cuts. Then, in order to turn up the heat, the congressional negotiators warned that they would also refuse to extend the statutory ceiling on the national debt; this would prevent the government from borrowing to meet its obligations, effectively putting the federal government into default.

The government actually was brought to a standstill on two separate occasions. Of course, not everyone left since essential personnel such as military forces, security agencies, and the like were kept on duty. Even then, there were arguments about just who was essential. Ironically, the tactics backfired on the congressional forces because some of the people who first felt the impact of the shutdown were businesses who needed loans, licenses, permits, information, and other services or regulatory decisions. Then middle-class vacationers felt the shutdown as national parks and other attractions closed their gates. In short, some of the budget warriors fired without realizing that they would hit their own constituents.

And then, as the war of words was escalating, the congressional forces pressed the attack by accusing the secretary of the treasury of using illegal techniques to maintain borrowing and payments for federal programs. However, as it became increasingly clear from Wall Street and Main Street that a federal default would have catastrophic results and that there would be huge costs involved in making up for all of the work lost because of the shutdowns, Congress blinked.

The White House faced both a threat and an opportunity. President Clinton was able to use developing sentiment against the new class of Republican members of Congress and their leader to rally support against the proposals and to make the Republican leadership look reckless and impetuous. On the other hand, he had little choice. He was under attack for a failure of political will and had to demonstrate political courage or face the prospect of an uphill battle for reelection.

It came as no surprise to anyone that when the 1996 budget negotiations began, well after the campaign season had begun for both presidential and congressional candidates, all sides declared their intention to avoid a government shutdown at all costs! Clearly, the congressional brinkmanship resulted not only in a loss of prestige but also in a weakening of its future ability to use the debt limit and budget deadline to gain power in interbranch budgetary power games. That consequence was demonstrated when the Republicans made another attempt at coercing executive approval for budgetary dead-locks in 1997. It backfired again. This time they tried to hold hostage a bill providing relief to flood-ravaged Midwestern communities hostage only to reap a barrage of predictably unfavorable publicity.

Budgeting Systems and Public Management

Any discussion of the management dimension of budgeting properly begins with the budget systems developed to improve efficiency and effectiveness. In this sense, it is important to remember that the line-item budget was itself intended as an improvement in fiscal management. Line-item budgets codi-fied spending rules, allowed comparisons by expenditure category across organizations, and, most importantly, injected the accounting dimension permanently into public expenditures. Behind every object of expenditure category there was a body of rules that were enforced by the line-item budget.

Consider some of the contemporary management dimensions behind three primary budgetary systems. They include performance budgeting, PPBS, and ZBB. We will then turn to some of the most recent efforts to find budgeting strategies that will enhance management effectiveness.

Performance Budgeting and Productivity Management   # 14

Perhaps the major criticism of line-item budgeting, with its extensive empha-sis on classification by objects of expenditure, was the consequent lack of in-formation about the total programs and functions of government. Although the first line-item executive budgets marked a significant advancement in budgetary technology, many public managers were becoming increasingly dissatisfied with the deficiencies of this process by the end of World War II. They were demanding more information about management, processes, planning, and the efficiency of programs than line-item budgets were able to provide.

Budget systems that were concerned with work data performance and ef-ficiency indicators were first developed just before World War I by the New York Bureau of Municipal Research. The first federal efforts at performance budgeting were in the Department of Agriculture and the Tennessee Valley Authority during the 1930s, and then, under the auspices of the Hoover Commission of 1949, the designation "performance budgeting" was offi-cially sanctioned as the preferred budgeting method. The Hoover Commis-sion stated its recommendations bluntly: "A program of performance bud-geting should be substituted for the present budget, thus presenting in a document of much briefer compass the Government's expenditure require-ments in terms of services, activities, and work projects rather than in terms of the things bought."[24]

Jesse Burkhead, in one of the first budgeting textbooks, maintained that there could be no precise definition of performance budgeting because per-formance budgeting systems tend to be so varied in their operations. But, generally, performance budgeting presents purposes and objectives for which are funds are being allocated, examines costs of programs and activities es-tablished to meet these objectives, and identifies and analyzes quantitative data measuring work performed.

One problem that has arisen over time is that the terms performance bud-geting and program budgeting have tended to be used interchangeably, but they are not synonymous. In performance budgeting, programs are generally linked to the various higher levels of an organization and serve as labels that encompass and structure the subordinate performance units. These units, the central element of performance budgeting, are geared to an organization's operational levels, and information about them is concrete and meaningful to managers at all levels. Program budgeting, on the other hand, might or might not incorporate performance measurements and yet still be useful for delineat-ing broad functional categories of expenditure for review at the higher levels. Overall, performance budgeting tends to be retrospective, focusing on previ-ous performance and accomplishments, while program budgeting tends to be forward looking, involving policy planning and forecasts.

Although the predominant orientation of performance budgeting was for the purpose of better management and enhanced efficiency, most of its early advocates expressed hope that its associated processes would further executive/legislative budgeting relationships. Indeed, the generally recog-nized success of performance budgeting was instrumental in obtaining Con-gressional approval of the Budgeting and Accounting Procedures Act of 1950, which allowed the president greater discretion over the format and content of executive budget submissions. Certainly, systematic performance-measurement data are more useful to appropriations committees than are traditional line-item submissions, and they better serve the purpose of leg-islative oversight.

Over the last decade, a considerable body of literature has emerged on productivity analysis and measurement. Ironically, the contentions of this new productivity field are very reminiscent of earlier claims for performance budgeting. Performance budgeting sought to establish management's last right and responsibility to ascertain how much work was being accom-plished, at what cost, and for what results as measured against specified per-formance standards. In the 1990s the questions are still the same, only it seems that they are being asked by different people.

PPBS and the Systems Approach

The 1960s witnessed the departure of performance budgeting and the reemergence of a new development in budgeting technology. Some contended that performance budgeting simply faded away, in part because its requirements for immense amounts of data from lower levels of management generated a less than enthusiastic response. Further, as government programs continued to expand, budget officials, already faced with a considerable burden of calculation in making resource-allocation decisions, were less and less interested in a micro-oriented budgeting system and more inclined to some form of macro-oriented system that would facilitate budgeting in aggregate terms. Others contended that the demise of performance budgeting was a slight exaggeration, although conceding its replacement in some jurisdictions. Nevertheless, performance budgeting, with its concern for databases, paved the way for the next major innovation in governmental budgeting.

In the 1960s PPBS took the budgetary world by storm. It promised much. Its advocates began by insisting that it could interrelate and coordinate the three major processes constituting its title. Planning would be related to programs that would be keyed to budgeting. To further emphasize the planning dimension, PPBS pushed the horizon out to half a decade, requiring five-year forecasts for program plans and cost estimates. The PPBS placed a whole new emphasis on program objectives, outputs, and alternatives and stressed the new watchword of evaluation, the *effectiveness criterion*. Finally, PPBS required the use of new analytical techniques from strategic planning, systems analysis, and cost/benefit analysis to make decision making more systematic and rational.

The PPB system succeeded at the Department of Defense both in terms of producing better quality decisions and by building more control for the secretary of defense. President Johnson made PPBS mandatory for all federal agencies in 1965. He saw it as a steering mechanism for his Great Society programs. By 1970, PPBS was expanding in some jurisdictions while contracting in others. Opposition came from various quarters, especially from bedeviled agency administrators and staff who experienced one difficulty after another in complying with PPBS's submission requirements. While President Nixon formally canceled the PPBS experiment in 1971, what really happened was that jurisdictions all over the nation modified it to fit their needs.

Zero-Base Budgeting: An Appealing but Problematic Idea

The zero-base concept is first and foremost a rejection of the incremental model of budgeting. It demands a rejustification of the entire budget submission every cycle, whereas incremental budgeting essentially respects the

#18

outcomes of previous budgetary decisions and focuses on the margin of change from year to year. While legislatures have great practical difficulties in assessing so many decisions at one time, the executive branch could choose to make it the focus of attention.

Zero-base budgeting (ZBB) was also keyed to another old idea, the direct consideration of alternatives within the context of administrative control. First articulated by Verne B. Lewis in 1952,[25] the idea of budget alternatives is based on the preparation of incremental budget submissions that permit evaluation of various funding amounts in terms of levels or quantities of service. The managerial dimension of alternative budgeting provides a dual advantage. Budget submissions can be prepared in a manner that will facilitate comparison and demonstrate a range of choices for service and funding levels. At the same time, the final choice will provide a realistic contract, that is, specific, realistic expectations for the program manager.

The ZBB approach also focuses on the concept of priorities, which is more than an elaboration of the consideration of alternatives. It reflected a concern that the things that governments do should be the most important of all of the things that they could do. In examining public programs, administration first stressed accountability, then efficiency, then effectiveness and impact, and now relevance.

The difficulties arose not in theory but in practice. When the administration itself did not employ the techniques it advocated when the financial chips were down, it was clear that no one would take the process seriously any longer. It is one of those management strategies that seems to have all of the rational calculating elements in place, but has so many difficulties in operation that its value is limited.

Cutback Management and Resource Scarcity

If there has been a characteristic that marked budgetary dynamics in the 1980s and 1990s it is a change in the old understanding of success. It has generally been considered that a manager is successful if she was able to get more money, people, and power. However, that changed during the 1980s, as people who could cut and downsize became more valuable. In part, the ability to identify how many dollars had been cut from an organization's budget and how many people had been eliminated from its payroll was a simple case of meeting a need to cut back. On the other hand, it was also a skill that garnered political praise. It was one thing more as well. It became a way to leverage change that would not be possible under ordinary fiscal conditions because those with vested interests in projects and programs would be able to block change and protect those resources.

Charles Levine's work on cutback management recognized all of these elements.[26] Levine laid out the management rules for cutback management.

Briefly, public sector managers would respond to revenue shortfalls based on the degree of political uncertainty (i.e., the probability of the cuts being restored) and the magnitude of the budget shortfall. The responses could range from simply stretching the budget to get through the fiscal year, to "rationing demands" by limiting services or charging fees, to "selective withdrawal" by redrawing geographic divisions of the organization or terminating specific programs, to "retrenchment" by permanently altering the structure, programs, and staffing of the organization.

Various techniques in cutback management could be employed to address fiscal stress. In Levine's overview of cutback methods, he presented these techniques in the form of a series of questions for managers to ask.

1. What activities are required by law?
2. What activities can be terminated?
3. What additional revenues can be raised? (user charges and fees)
4. What activities can be assigned to other service providers?
5. What can be done more efficiently? (productivity)
6. Where can low-cost or no-cost labor be used? (volunteers, etc.)
7. Where can capital investments be substituted for labor?
8. Where can information-gathering methods be installed?
9. Where can demand be reduced and services rationed?
10. What policies can help strengthen the economic base (promote private-sector investment)?
11. What arrangements can be made to identify and strengthen the leadership of the cutback management process?

As this list indicates, cutback management was not intended to be a budget system, but rather a process to fuse political and economic realities with management strategies that would establish a solid operating base under weakened organizations.

Contemporary Directions in Budget Development

It is generally agreed that many of the old assumptions about budgeting do not work well any longer.[27] In fact, the National Performance Review read what it hoped was an obituary for old budget techniques in 1993. The NPR argued for what it termed mission-driven, results-oriented budgeting.[28] The NPR report identified three principles that should guide the future budget process.

#21

1. Strengthen accountability for results, with political leadership defining political priorities first, then reaching agreements with managers on what they are expected to accomplish and how their accomplishments will be measured.

2. Once decisions have been reached, empower managers to achieve expected results by providing the necessary resources, unburdened by excessively detailed restrictions.

3. Streamline and improve the budget-development process to give managers more time to manage their programs; provide managers with more timely information on policy priorities and funding levels in order to more effectively use resources; provide links between budgetary resources, missions, goals, and results.[29]

Much of the discussion calls for a variation on performance budgeting, but there are three specific ideas that are different. First, the report calls for an end to what is termed the end of the fiscal year splurge. This argument notes that agencies race at the end of the fiscal year to find ways to spend whatever remaining funds they might have before they lose them. The fear is not merely that the unencumbered funds would disappear, but also that the legislature would conclude that the agency obviously did not need all of the funds that were appropriated and that a budget cut is in order. There is debate about whether there really is a great deal of unnecessary spending or whether managers simply defer planned purchases until they are certain that they will not have need of additional available funds for the rest of the fiscal year. In any case, the NPR recommends that agencies should be permitted to "roll over 50 percent of their unobligated year-end balances in annual operating costs to the next year."[30]

Second, the NPR urges that managers should be given greater flexibility to reprogram funds within their existing budgets. The idea is to avoid a situation where a manager is forced to spend more than he needs in one category but lacks the funds necessary to accomplish the mission in another category. The effort to improve on this problem has been underway in a number of states for some years now.

#23

The most radical innovation called for by the NPR is the suggestion to move to something that is called target-based budgeting. Under this approach, an agency would be given a target. If its budget came in over that, it would be cut back to the target level. If it was under, the agency could keep the difference between their actual budget and the targeted amount. The object is to give agencies the incentive to be as efficient as possible so that they can invest the extra resources in an entrepreneurial fashion to get the most mission performance for a given dollar.

24

There are two difficulties with some of the recommendations that have been advanced that essentially call for providing administrative agencies with greater budget flexibility and discretion. The first is the obvious fact that the budgetary politics of legislatures in recent years have demonstrated less, not more, confidence in executive branch management of the resources. The NPR calls, among other things, for a two-year budget cycle. While that may make perfectly good sense from a management point of view, it is highly unlikely that the legislature is going to be willing to give up that much leverage over the executive branch. Similarly, there are still too many legislators, at all levels of government and in many countries around the world, who continue to build their campaigns around issues of fraud, abuse, and waste. They want more controls over executive branch agencies, not less.

The other problem is that the NPR recommendations call for more flexibility, but they also introduce a performance-based system that has significantly increased reporting requirements and accountability rules. One cannot help but be struck by reading the NPR, the executive orders involved, and the legislation supported by the administration that has insisted on decentralization and empowerment, that there is still a very strong desire for top-down control. In sum, there are a variety of new ideas. It is likely to take considerable time and effort to get them enacted, implement them, and overcome the usual cynicism that accompanies new budget techniques.

Conclusion

While students of public administration have traditionally shown greater interest in the political, economic, and managerial aspects of budgeting, the accounting and audit dimension has also reemerged. The literature of public budgeting gives the impression that the politics of budgeting ends with the legislature's approval of the final budget document. Of course, nothing could be further from the truth. There is great managerial discretion in the actual execution of the assigned budget. Chief executives can advance or delay payments, enlarge or depress revenue and expenditure estimates, allocate funds liberally or conservatively, and in many other ways manipulate surpluses, deficits, and corresponding budgetary behavior. All of these factors mean that we may only know what the real budget for the year was by looking at the end of the audit of accounts rather than by paying attention to either the budget as submitted to the legislature or the appropriation that emerged from it.

Of course, the advent of more powerful desktop computer systems have greatly affected the ability to maintain accountability in more dynamic ways than in earlier times. Indeed, estimates are that the financial management and budgetary functions are the most heavily automated functions in all of government. The drive to automate reporting; the use of spreadsheet software and graphics to improve analysis and consider alternatives; the development of information systems for integrating tax and revenue, user charges, expenditures, cash management, and even investments is nothing less than extraordinary.

In sum, the budgetary reform's management thread has changed dramatically. Absent any one dominant budgeting system to lead, public sector organizations have resorted to developing their own eclectic budget systems. The emergence of a loose body of strategies and tactics under the general rubric of cutback management has captured much of the management attention in public budgeting. More recently, the pressures have been to attempt to deregulate and decentralize budgeting with the hope that it will be possible to encourage entrepreneurial financial management. Whether the political forces in the legislature or the chief executive's office are ready to grant that much flexibility and whether the techniques and resources required for successful entrepreneurial efforts will be ready when managers need them remains to be seen.

Notes

[1]Aaron Wildavsky, *The Politics of the Budgetary Process,* 2nd ed. (Boston: Little, Brown, 1974), 1–2.

[2]Aaron Wildavsky, *Budgeting: A Comparative Theory of Budgetary Processes* (Boston: Little, Brown, 1975), 5.

[3]Fremont J. Lyden and Marc Lindenburg, *Public Budgeting in Theory and Practice* (New York: Longman, 1983), 207.

[4]Charles L. Schultze, *The Private Use of the Public Interest* (Washington, DC: Brookings Institute, 1977).

[5]Michael White and Aaron Wildansky, *The Deficit and the Public Interest* (Berkeley, CA: University of California, 1989), xviii–xix.

[6]William F. Willoughby, *The Movement for Budget Reform in the States* (New York: D. Appleton and Company, for the Institute of Government Research, 1918).

[7]See Howard E. Shuman, *Politics and the Budget: The Struggle between the President and the Congress,* 2nd ed. (Englewood Cliffs, NJ: Prentice-Hall, 1988).

[8]Larry Berman, *The Office of Management and Budget and the Presidency* (Princeton, NJ: Princeton University, 1979), Ch. 1.

[9]*American Political Science Review* 34 (1940): 1137–1140.

[10]Paul Appleby, *Big Democracy* (New York: Alfred A. Knopf, 1945).

[11]Aaron Wildavsky, "Political Implications of Budgetary Reform," *Public Administration Review* 21 (Autumn 1961): 183–190.

[12] Charles E. Lindblom, "The Science of Muddling Through," *Public Administration Review* 19 (Spring 1959): 79–88.

[13] Allen Schick, "The Road to PPB: The Stages of Budget Reform," *Public Administration Review* 26 (Dec./Jan. 1966): 243–258.

[14] Charles B. Levine, "Organizational Decline and Cutback Management," *Public Administration Review* 38 (July/August 1978): 316–325.

[15] E.O. 11615 and Proclamation 4074 (1971). See generally Stanley H. Friedelbaum, "The 1971 Wage-Price Freeze: Unchallenged Presidential Power," *Supreme Court Review* 1974 (1974): 33–80.

[16] Shuman, *op. cit.,* Ch. 7.

[17] James L. Sundquist, *The Decline and Resurgence of Congress* (Washington, DC: Brookings Institute, 1981).

[18] Glenn Abney and Thomas P. Lauth, *The Politics of State and City Administration* (Albany, NY: State University of New York Press, 1986), 40.

[19] *Ibid.,* 63.

[20] *Ibid.,* 67.

[21] Thomas P. Lauth, "Zero-Base Budgeting in Georgia State Government: Myth and Reality," *Public Administration Review* 38 (Sept./Oct. 1978): 420–430.

[22] See Paul E. Peterson, *The Price of Federalism* (Washington, DC: Brookings Institute, 1995), 77–78.

[23] *Bowsher v. Synar*, 478 U.S. 714 (1986).

[24] *The Hoover Commission Report on the Organization of the Executive Branch* (New York: McGraw-Hill, 1949).

[25] Verne B. Lewis, "Toward a Theory of Budgeting," *Public Administration Review* 12 (Winter 1952): 42–52.

[26] Charles B. Levine, *Managing Fiscal Stress* (Chatham, NJ: Chatham House, 1980).

[27] Irene S. Rubin, "Strategies for the New Budgeting," in James L. Perry, *The Handbook of Public Administration,* 2nd ed. (San Francisco: Jossey-Bass, 1996). See also Allen Schick, *The Federal Budget* (Washington, DC: Brookings Institution, 1995), Ch 1.

[28] Al Gore, *Mission-Driven, Results-Oriented Budgeting: Accompanying Report of the National Performance Review* (Washington, DC: National Performance Review, 1993); see also Gore, *Improving Financial Management: Accompanying Report of the National Performance Review* (Washington, DC: National Performance Review, 1993).

[29] Gore, *Mission-Driven, Results-Oriented Budgeting, op. cit.,* 4–5.

[30] *Ibid.,* 45.

Chapter 12

International Affairs and Public Administration

The last decade of the twentieth century has been marked by the end of the Cold War, the unification of Germany, the dissolution of the Soviet Union, the emergence of new states, the transformation of South Africa after the end of apartheid, a major new presence of Asia and the Pacific Rim countries in trade and finance, and dramatic changes in the social, political, and economic realities of developing countries. Some observers believe that these events signal the beginning of a new era in international relations, one that will be characterized by enhanced cooperation among nation-states and an increasing role for international organizations in the keeping and enforcement of peace. Others contend, however, that the so-called "new world order" will more likely resemble a "new world disorder." That more pessimistic scenario suggests that conflict will become more, rather than less, likely and that efforts to build international political and economic institutions will be unsuccessful. Certainly the sad plight of Somalia, the adventurism of Iraq, the volatile condition of North Korea, the political and economic brinksmanship of China, the carnage of Rwanda, Burundi, and Zaire, the economic and political turmoil of Mexico, the outspoken criticism of the U.N. role in Bosnia, and the unwillingness of some developed countries—notably the United States—to live up to international commitments support the pessimistic assessment.

Regardless of which view of the future international system proves to be accurate, students of public administration need to be aware of emerging trends in international affairs. The purpose of this chapter is to offer an overview of international economic and security affairs that highlights those issues that will affect the making and administration of public policy in the twenty-first century. It is not enough merely to compare what is taking place in various countries or regions of the globe. It is essential to examine the way that nation-states, regional bodies, and international institutions deal with one another. These external actions shape domestic policymaking and influence the environment of public administration at all levels. In order to understand those relationships it is essential to consider how international relations are structured, what the processes of international debate are, and what trends are shaping the future of international politics and business.

Cooperation amidst Anarchy

International relations among nation-states are generally described as "cooperation amidst anarchy." The international system differs from the nation-state in that there is no higher political authority to enforce norms and standards of international behavior. Nation-states exist in a situation of anarchy, in which they are left to their own devices to provide for their security. The large armies and navies of the great powers historically have been the result, as are efforts by middle and lesser powers, to build similar military establishments.

If this is true, then why are relations among nation-states described as cooperation amidst anarchy? What incentives exist for states to cooperate with each other? Why do nations choose to cooperate with one another to achieve their objectives? Cooperative behavior between nation-states has both costs and benefits. With respect to costs, cooperation generally decreases flexibility in policy making. The pursuit of collective security arrangements, for example, links one's behavior in a crisis or other threatening situation to a collective response by other states who share a perception of threat to their security interests. Hence there was anxiety from European states about joining with the United States in Bosnia. Similarly, national decisions to participate in regional economic institutions such as the European Union (formerly the European Community), NAFTA, and the World Trade Organization are taken at the cost of reduced independence and flexibility in international economic policy. With respect to benefits, cooperation will often enable nations to achieve goals collectively that are not feasible unilaterally. Although collective security arrangements may decrease flexibility, they often offer cost-effective ways of dealing with external threats. This is precisely the argument used by President Clinton in support of NATO expansion. And while regional economic institutions may constrain national economies, they may enhance the competitiveness of those economies over the long term.

The growth of complex interdependence since the 1970s has enhanced the value of international cooperation. As nations have lost control over their environments they have become more aware of their sensitivity and vulnerability to the actions of others. And while nations often take unilateral steps in an effort to decrease their vulnerability to the actions of others, they may also engage in cooperative behavior to enhance the predictability of international relations. The trend toward increasing cooperation is particularly evident in international economic affairs, as nations have created international institutions such as the European Community and the North American Free Trade Area to enhance their international economic positions.

The increasing permeability of national borders that has accompanied the growth of complex interdependence has broken down the traditional boundaries between domestic policy and foreign policy. The faster that means of transportation and communication become, the less important those boundaries will be. This trend is most evident in the realm of economic policy, where the new conditions of dependence and interdependence have serious consequences for the economic prosperity of states and local communities. The adoption of protectionist policies by Japan and members of the European Community in the 1980s has had a direct effect on the competitiveness of American products abroad. And decisions by American firms to relocate manufacturing plants to the developing world, where the cost of doing business is dramatically reduced, have also had direct—and negative—effects on the economic circumstances of many local communities that stand to lose those businesses and the jobs they provide to the local economy. The movement of capital on the world markets also influences the amount of funds that are available to purchase local government bonds and the cost of those funds in terms of interest rates.

The tendency to view domestic policy and foreign policy as a seamless web extends to the political and security area, where its effects are heightened by the broader view of national security that emerged with the end of the Cold War. National security is no longer defined separately from international security. The security of one nation now seems to be tied to the existence of stability in the international system.

Moreover, security issues are no longer defined strictly in politico-military terms. The economic crisis in Russia has raised very real concerns that their nuclear weapons materials and expertise may be finding their way into the global weapons marketplace. During the last decade, issues such as the environment, education, and public health have been added to the national and international security agendas. These issues, in particular, are difficult to isolate as questions of either domestic *or* foreign policy. Rapid spread of the AIDS virus, for example, is an issue that demands the attention of both domestic *and* foreign policy makers in the United States and around the globe.

What are the implications of these international trends for the field of public administration? Stated succinctly, differences between public administration and management in the national and international arenas are narrowing due to the growth of complex interdependence and the increasing permeability of national borders. It is clear that serious challenges lie ahead for policy makers and administrators at the local, state, national, and international levels. These challenges will demand a broader understanding of the international system and clear knowledge of the linkages between political and economic phenomena across local, state, and national boundaries. When, for example, a thaw in international relations encourages the closure of a military base like Plattsburgh Air Force Base in upstate New York, that decision affects the economy of a significant region of that state. The inability of political leaders to control their political and economic environments will increase pressure on governmental institutions. More demands are likely to be placed on those public administrators who work for agencies that provide services directly to the public, not only to be able to react to the consequences of forces in the international arena, but also to understand and even to anticipate them.

What kinds of skills will be needed to operate effectively in this new environment? Greater reliance on persuasion as a tool of policy making will create a demand for political leaders, administrators, and managers with strong communications, organizational, and negotiating skills. Moreover, these challenges will demand public servants with the ability to view problems across traditional governmental lines and with the commitment to solve problems collectively with their counterparts in other states, regions, and countries.

This section addresses these issues in greater detail. First, the chapter provides an overview of the international economic system. The purpose is to review the growth of mutual dependence, the concept of international regimes, and the implications of these phenomena for the making and administration of public policy. This discussion focuses on international monetary and trade issues, regional integration, and international development to illustrate the impact of complex interdependence on international economic relations. Finally, this part of the chapter assesses the relevance of linkage politics, power sharing, and the concept of "soft power" for international relations in the twenty-first century.

The second part of this chapter focuses on the international security system. We will review the contribution of security "regimes," both during the Cold War and after.

The chapter also discusses the role of the United Nations in international peacekeeping and the growing debate about peace-enforcing missions. Finally, the chapter examines the emergence of mechanisms to address nontraditional security issues associated with the environment and the problem of assuring security in a post–Cold War world.

The specific issues addressed in this discussion suggest the revolution that is occurring in international affairs. If it had been written at the height of the Cold War, it is unlikely that a section on the environment would have been included. Moreover, current debates about international security are likely to focus on issues of international trade policy as well as on issues of war and peace. And there clearly are strong linkages between economic development and the environment—as evidenced by the emerging movement in support of sustainable development. In short, distinctions between the international economic and international security systems are rapidly disappearing.

The International Economic System: Money and Trade, Regional Integration, and Development

Perhaps the most impressive development in the twentieth century has been the growth of a truly global society characterized by interdependence among nations. It has become increasingly difficult for any nation, including the United States, to control the political environment. The rapid growth of new actors, such as multinational corporations, that operate across national boundaries, has led to the emergence of transnational special-interest groups (usually referred to as NGOs for nongovernmental organizations)[1] that share the international stage with nation-states and supranational organizations.[2]

National power in this new environment depends not only on military capabilities, but also on the control of resources and markets, trade balances, exchange rates and capital flows, and technology. Power relationships among nations in a situation of interdependence vary with the issue area. While military power remains dominant in debates about national survival, the exercise of military power has become more costly. Moreover, economic power assumes center stage in discussions of quality of life. Thus, the World Bank and the International Monetary Fund (IMF) have become enormously important in dictating constraints in domestic policy in developing nations around the world. The shock therapy applied to the Russian economy and the effects of structural adjustment on social service delivery in many Latin American countries are two obvious examples.

The formulation and implementation of national economic policy is influenced by a range of external factors, including the rapid growth of multinational corporations and the emergence of regional economic communities. The rise of the Organization of Petroleum Exporting Countries (OPEC) in the 1970s drove up petroleum prices with significant impact on economies around the world. Conversely, the national economic policies of particularly influential states, such as the United States, Germany, and Japan, often have serious effects abroad.

The economic circumstances of states and even local communities are directly affected by these new conditions of dependence and interdependence.

For example, the decisions by German and Japanese automobile manufacturers to build manufacturing plants in the United States have direct and immediate effects on local economies through the creation of jobs. In 1992, Japanese companies in the United States employed more than 350,000 Americans.[3] Decisions by some American firms to move their manufacturing operations to countries such as Mexico, where the costs of doing business are lower, also have direct and immediate, but negative, effects on local economies.

Another result of this new environment has been greater reliance on international regimes. That term refers to the agreed procedures, rules, or institutions that have been designed to help manage international economic relations. As policy makers have become increasingly aware of the linkages between domestic and international affairs, they have pursued the negotiation and implementation of international arrangements to deal with the negative effects of interdependence. Regional arrangements, such as agreements to create a single unified market in Europe and the Canada/United States Free Trade Agreement, are examples of this trend.[4]

Complex Interdependence and Regimes: The Growth of Mutual Dependence

Since the end of World War II, there has been a dramatic increase in economic interaction among the developed economies. In part this increased interaction has been the result of reliance on the American dollar as a common medium of exchange. The growth of international trade during this period, as a consequence of the removal of trade barriers and economic growth and investment, has been accompanied by the internationalization of production. All of these trends have been the products of decisions made by the developed market economies.[5]

This increased economic interaction among the developed economies has led to a situation of interdependence. Each of the major actors has become sensitive to, or mutually dependent on, other actors in the system.[6] Clearly, the monetary, trade, and investment policies adopted by one country can have dramatic and often negative effects on the monetary, trade, and investment policies of other actors in the international system.[7]

Some nations were better able than others to adapt to these circumstances during the early postwar period. Countries such as the United States, Japan, and Germany, due to the strength and relative independence of their economies, have historically been less vulnerable to major shifts in the international economic system. That is, the governments of these nations had more success, particularly in the 1950s and the 1960s, in controlling the negative effects of interdependence through the adoption of public policies that shielded their domestic economies. While they were sensitive to these trends, they were less vulnerable to them precisely because domestic political actors intervened.

This situation had changed dramatically by the 1980s. The diffusion of power in the international system and the emergence of new actors, such as multinational corporations, further decreased the autonomy of the developed market economies.[8] From the perspective of the national decision maker, the problem of managing the domestic economy has become inextricably linked to the problem of managing the international economy. The adoption of policies designed to deal with domestic concerns such as inflation and unemployment are constrained by the international environment. For example, the creation of jobs at home and the protection of domestic industries may undercut a nation's long-term economic competitiveness.[9] As a result, it has become more difficult for national policy makers to control their own economies.[10]

At the same time that the economies of the developed world were becoming increasingly interdependent, important changes were occurring in North-South relations—that is, in the interaction between developed and developing markets. Joan Spero has argued that these relationships were more accurately characterized as dependence rather than interdependence, because the developing economies were both sensitive to and vulnerable to the actions of the developed economies.[11] This dependence extended to trade, investment, money, and aid, and was reinforced by political and security arrangements. The impact of this situation on the developing world was to perpetuate underdevelopment.

During the 1970s and the 1980s, major changes were occurring in the relations between the developed and the developing worlds. Nations in the developing world began to adopt strategies that were designed to move them beyond dependence. These strategies shared the assumption that the interests of developing nations would be better served by collective, rather than independent action. The result was a proposal for a New International Economic Order (NIEO) to replace the international economic order created after World War II. Specific proposals flowing from the NIEO, including a greater commitment by the developed world to foreign assistance and renegotiation of debt in the developing world.

Major changes occurred as well in East-West relations, namely between the planned economies of Eastern Europe and the Soviet Union and the developed market economies of the West. For most of the Cold War, the nature of the relationship between the economies of East and West was characterized by independence. There was little interaction between them, and this situation was reinforced by political and security arrangements arising from the military confrontation in Europe. East-West relations began to change, albeit only slowly, during the 1970s, plateaued in the 1980s, and were transformed in the early 1990s with the end of the Cold War, the unification of Germany, and the dissolution of the Soviet Union. While it is too early to assess the specific long-term economic effects of these changes, it seems clear that mutual dependence is likely to increase rather than decrease.

The Role of Regimes in a Situation of Complex Interdependence

The growth of mutual dependence since the end of World War II has led some scholars to challenge traditional assumptions about international politics. The realist perspective on international affairs assumes that nation-states are the dominant actors in the international system, that military force is the primary instrument of policy, and that the "high politics" of military security issues dominate the "low politics" of social and economic concerns.[12]

Robert Keohane and Joseph Nye have offered an alternative perspective on international affairs, which they label "complex interdependence." A situation of complex interdependence is characterized by multiple actors in the international system, of which nation-states comprise only one. Military force is not effective as an instrument of policy, and a clear hierarchy of issues does not exist in international affairs.[13] The United States can no longer effect change in China or Russia by military threats, nor can it force action in developing economies when it is no longer able to offer large amounts of foreign aid.

There are clear advantages to cooperation among nations in a situation of complex interdependence. Cooperation should enable nations to manage international economic and political relations in ways that decrease the costs, or the negative effects, of interdependence. This is because cooperation enables nations to establish mutual expectations about their behavior and facilitates the development of working arrangements that will allow them to adapt their policies to changing circumstances.[14]

While international cooperation is beneficial in an interdependent global economy, however, it is especially difficult to achieve in international politics because of the anarchic nature of the international system.[15] Unlike domestic politics, international politics unfolds in the absence of a final arbiter. There is no higher political authority to which nation-states can turn as a guarantor of their security. As a consequence, nation-states must exercise self-reliance in international affairs. This is not to say that international organizations such as the United Nations and alliances such as NATO have not played an important role in international affairs. But because these organizations and alliances are unable to impose their views on sovereign nation-states, they are unable to enforce cooperation. The result is a situation in which nation-states will cooperate only when they deem such behavior to be in their national interest.

The problem for international relations in a situation of complex interdependence is how to create incentives for international and interregional cooperation. In general, this means convincing policy makers that cooperative arrangements will offer long-term benefits to their nations and establishing mechanisms to facilitate that cooperation. The creation of procedures, rules, or institutions for particular activities is one way in which nation-states attempt to regulate international economic and political relations. These governing arrangements are known as *regimes.*[16]

International regimes have emerged since World War II as "intermediate factors"[17] between the structure of the international system (defined as the distribution of power and resources among the major actors) and the political and economic interaction that occurs between nation-states. Regimes may be as informal as understood rules of international behavior (as existed, for example, between the United States and the Soviet Union during the Cold War) or as formal as international agreements, treaties, and organizations.

Regimes have emerged since World War II to regulate international behavior concerning environmental protection, international monetary policy, international trade, and aid to the developing world. For example, the foundations for postwar international monetary and trade regimes were laid at Bretton Woods in July 1944. At Bretton Woods the international community created a system of fixed exchange rates and created two public international organizations, the International Monetary Fund (IMF) and the International Bank for Reconstruction and Development (IBRD). A commitment to nondiscriminatory trade practices was codified by the General Agreement on Tariffs and Trade (GATT) in 1947. The Bretton Woods "System," as it became known, operated until 1971 under the leadership of the United States.

Regimes enable nation-states to cope with uncertainty in a situation of complex interdependence. By establishing formal and informal rules of behavior in international affairs, regimes enhance the predictability of nation-state behavior in a variety of issue areas. Regimes decrease the potential costs of cooperation among nation-states by establishing clear standards and expectations concerning international behavior. They provide important vehicles for the exchange of information, and they facilitate burden-sharing among nation-states.

Implications for Public Policy and Administration

While the growth of complex interdependence has captured the attention of international relations scholars and foreign policy makers alike, it has generally been ignored by the field of public management. Public administration involves the translation of decisions by legislatures or political executives into action. Putting policy into effect also involves creating and managing government structures to achieve this objective.[18]

The growth of complex interdependence has contributed to a situation in which national governments are losing control over their political, economic, and social systems. Consider the impact of demographic trends on economic development and political stability. The massive migration of Germans from East to West following German unification has placed serious demands on the Federal Republic's social safety net and contributed to protests by the right and left in Germany during 1992. The United States faces a major challenge from the south and from the Far East, as between 200,000 and 2 million (estimates vary) illegal aliens enter the country each year.[19] That migration is fueled by the harsh impacts of dramatic economic change in Mexico and the chaotic scramble of 800,000,000 Chinese workers to find an economic future for their families and themselves. Both the United States and the Federal Republic of Germany must deal with the domestic economic and social effects of these trends, including the impact on unemployment rolls and the increased burden placed on the health, education and welfare systems. In the United States at least, the costs of addressing these issues have essentially been left to state and local governments. These trends need to be taken into account in the making and administration of public policy.

Regimes and International Economic Relations: International Monetary and Trade Issues

The international monetary system provides the essential framework for international economic interaction. The absence of a common currency makes it difficult for nations to engage in trade and other forms of interaction. To facilitate international economic interaction nations must create a mechanism to determine the value of currencies in relation to one another. Agreement on currency rates of exchange is a necessary first step in ensuring the effective operation of the international economic system. The international exchange rate for a particular currency may be set by market forces or by international agreement. Often these arrangements assume characteristics of regimes.

Bretton Woods and After

The Bretton Woods system was designed to help regulate the international economic system in the post–World War II world. Bretton Woods introduced a system of fixed exchange rates and established the International Monetary Fund (IMF) and the International Bank for Reconstruction and Development (IBRD) as public institutions charged with implementation of this system. Inherent in the Bretton Woods regime was the assumption that an open system would benefit all. The system worked because the United States enforced the rules and because there was no challenger to American dominance of the system. Under the terms of Bretton Woods, the International Monetary Fund provides reserves and formulates administrative rules relating to currency exchange. The IBRD, or the World Bank, made loans and underwrote private investments to aid in rebuilding Europe after World War II. The postwar period was one of American dominance of the international monetary system.

By the 1960s, however, the system had begun to change. The increasing U.S. balance of payments deficit and the decline in U.S. gold holdings led to the decline of the dollar-based international monetary system. The emergence of multinational corporations as major actors on the international stage was one factor contributing to the increasing interdependence of the developed economies. Growing interdependence led to cooperation among finance ministers and the central banks in dealing with their common problems, if only in an ad hoc way. The emergence of Europe and Japan as fully recovered economies led them to challenge the privileged position of the dollar and American dominance of the international economic system.

By the early 1970s, the U.S. balance-of-payments situation had reached crisis proportions. The United States had historically attempted to offset its balance-of-payments deficits with trade surpluses. By the early 1970s, however, Europe and Japan's share of international trade had increased, and the United States suffered its first trade deficit of the twentieth century.[20] In response to these trends, the United States announced that America would no longer exchange dollars for gold. This decision marked the end of the Bretton Woods system and replaced that regime's fixed exchange-rate system with free-floating exchange rates. In large part, these actions were products of growing American dependence on other international actors and the realization that the United States could no longer exercise unilateral leadership of the international monetary system.

By the early 1980s, rising interest rates, a deepening recession, and the decline in inflation had led to a dramatic rise in the value of the dollar. The strong dollar made it increasingly difficult for American manufacturers to compete on the international scene because it meant increased costs to international purchasers of U.S. goods. As a consequence, the American trade deficit grew at the same time that the United States increased its reliance on borrowing from foreigners as a way to finance growing budget deficits. The dollar had dropped by the mid-1980s, but foreigners continued to finance the budget deficit. At the same time, the international monetary system was confronted with a severe debt crisis as many countries in the developing world that could no longer afford to pay their interest costs, let alone the principal, were forced to reschedule payments of their debts. This situation led to tremendous uncertainty in the international monetary system.[21]

GATT and NAFTA

The emergence of complex interdependence as an international fact of life has led the United States and other developed economies to pursue predictability and stability through international cooperation and the creation of regimes. Within the European Community, for example, the European Monetary System has served to fix the national currencies against each other while allowing them to move up and down together against the dollar, the yen, and other non–European Community currencies.[22] However, by the early 1990s, movement toward future economic and monetary union in Europe was complicated by the unification of Germany and fears that the Federal Republic would soon dominate European economic relations.[23]

Since the end of World War II there have also been consistent efforts to promote cooperation in international trade through the General Agreement on Tariffs and Trade (GATT). The international trade regime embodied in GATT was drawn up in 1947 during a Geneva conference to negotiate tariff reductions. This regime was based on the assumption that a system of open and free trading would benefit everyone. The three main principles underlying GATT are nondiscrimination, transparency, and reciprocity. Nondiscrimination implies that all trading partners will be treated equally by extending most favored nation status to each other. (Most favored nation status had been a system under which nations selected some trading partners for special favorable trading rules.) Transparency suggests that if barriers exist, they should be tariffs rather than quotas (meaning fees on imports rather than prohibitions or fixed limits on quantities of goods). And reciprocity implies that if one nation lowers its tariffs against another's goods, the other nation should do the same. One major limitation of the GATT regime, however, is that GATT has no authority to apply sanctions against members who fail to comply.

Between 1947 and 1967 the United States initiated six trade negotiations that proved successful in lowering tariff barriers. The dramatic growth in world trade that occurred during this period, fostered by the rules of behavior inherent in the GATT system, was accompanied by falling tariffs. But while the United States pursued a policy of open trade during the 1950s and the 1960s, the Europeans and Japan engaged in protectionism. The seeds of future conflict were sowed with the creation of the European Economic

Community in 1957. In one of its first actions, the EEC removed all internal tariffs between the member nations and imposed an external tariff which was lowered substantially during the Kennedy round of GATT. More problematic for the long term, however, was the adoption of a common agricultural policy by the EEC that was based on protectionism rather than free trade.[24] *Protectionism* is a term of criticism used to denote policies designed to protect local businesses at the expense of free and open markets. By the 1980s this policy threatened the exports of U.S. agricultural producers, who were unable to penetrate the European market.[25]

The Tokyo round of trade negotiations that began in 1973 coincided with the emergence of protectionist sentiment in the United States. By the mid-1970s, the United States was no longer willing to support an open economic system at the expense of its national interests. During this period many nations began introducing nontariff barriers such as quotas and voluntary export restraints (VERs) in response to increased international competition. Within the United States, specific industries such as steel, textiles, and shipbuilding exercised strong political pressure to gain government protection.[26] Similar actions by Japan and members of the European Community have severely weakened GATT. By the late 1970s it was clear that domestic interest groups, both in the United States and in other developed nations, were important players in the politics of economic protection.

The end of U.S. dominance in international trade, declining support for liberal trade practices, and the GATT system will characterize international economic relations into the twenty-first century. In response to these trends, the United States has joined with other nations to create new regimes to deal with the negative consequences of complex interdependence. Two of the most recent examples are the Canada/United States Free Trade Agreement and the North American Free Trade Agreement (NAFTA). The Canada/United States negotiations, concluded in 1988, enabled both sides to demonstrate bilateral progress in areas such as energy products, services, and investment measures that were not under consideration in GATT.[27] The NAFTA agreement, signed in 1992, lifted barriers between Canada, Mexico, and the United States.

The problems of managing the international monetary and trade systems will be more difficult in the future than they have been since World War II. The decline of American dominance of the international economic system and the growth of protectionist pressures around the globe have put serious pressure on the trading system that emerged after World War II. While monetary policy is still handled primarily by political and economic elites, trade policy has become the purview of domestic interests such as the European farmers or American automobile manufacturers.[28] The result is increased uncertainty and unpredictability in international economic relations.

International regimes have played important roles in managing the international monetary and trade systems since World War II. Despite growing protectionist sentiment and emerging unilateralism (attempts to go it alone) in international affairs, nations will continue to rely on regimes to help reduce uncertainty and unpredictability in international economic relations. Tensions remain, however, between the ideal of free and open trade and monetary relations and the reality of the regionalization of world trade and monetary systems. It is in the long-term interests of the United States that these regional arrangements develop within the context of the GATT system.[29]

Regional Integration

Another approach to dealing with complex interdependence involves cooperative efforts among nations that go beyond the creation of rules, procedures, and institutions designed to deal with specific issues such as monetary or trade relations. Political integration entails building political communities and associated institutions that transcend national boundaries and represent more permanent solutions to dealing with the uncertainty and unpredictability of international affairs. Because political integration demands that nation-states voluntarily compromise their sovereignty, more is required than simply the desire to cooperate.

Political integration is facilitated by a number of structural factors, such as similar historical experiences and culture, compatible political and economic systems, geographical proximity, and shared perceptions of external threats. But structural factors are not sufficient. Economic and political incentives are required. Nation-states must appreciate the benefits of cooperative behavior, such as access to markets and cheaper imports. Participation in international monetary and trade regimes as well as other forms of multilateral cooperation such as military alliances can lay the foundations for political integration. Attitudes must change as well. The socialization of domestic publics accustomed to identifying with the nation-state rather than with a supranational organization as the prime guarantor of their political, economic, and military security is a major obstacle to political integration.

The emergence of complex interdependence is a major factor in explaining regional integration, particularly in Europe. The European Community represents the most ambitious effort to date. The creation of the European Economic Community (EEC), or Common Market, in 1958 grew out of cooperative efforts by the participating nations to rebuild the European economies after World War II. The fundamental assumption underlying the creation of the EEC was that international economic cooperation was essential in the postwar world. Initial efforts to remove customs duties and the creation of a common external tariff were accompanied by the establishment of freedom of movement for capital and workers. The EEC also introduced common policies with respect to taxation, transportation, and agriculture.[30]

Despite the early focus on economic issues, the ultimate objective of the European Community was political. The preamble to the Treaty of Rome, which was signed in March 1957 and which created the European Economic Community, states that its purpose was to lay the foundation for a closer union among the peoples of Europe.[31] This objective proved much more difficult to achieve in practice, however. By the late 1950s, European economic recovery had removed much of the pressure for economic cooperation. Moreover, there existed no clear plan for moving from economic to political integration. And British reluctance to accede to the European Community until 1973 further slowed the pace of political union.

During the 1970s, political commitment to unification also declined in response to the global economic crisis created in 1973 and 1974 by sharp increases in oil prices, inflation, balance-of-payments problems, and recession. The European Community was divided on how to deal with these new challenges, which affected some members more seriously than others. Some attempted to secure their own supplies through the negotiation of bilateral arrangements with oil producers. Others implemented rationing, and still others accepted shortages.[32] By the late 1970s, the growth of protectionism in Europe signaled an even bleaker future for political integration. The worsening recession and increasing unemployment reinforced neomercantilist tendencies within the European Community.

Beginning in the early 1980s, however, the situation began to change. The increasing dependence on trade, and on trade among members of the European Community, in particular, that occurred during the 1970s and the early 1980s focused the attention of political and economic leaders on the value of the EEC as an export market.[33] The desire to create greater economies of scale in domestic production, as a way of dealing with the problem of "stagflation"—the coincidence of economic stagnation and inflation—increased pressure to expand exports.[34] The creation of the European Monetary System (EMS) in 1979 facilitated this process by stabilizing exchange rates and prices.[35]

These trends provided the foundation for the third stage of economic and monetary union embodied in the Single European Act, which went into effect on July 1, 1987. The objective of the Single European Act was the creation of an "area without internal frontiers," namely, commitment to achieve a single internal market by the end of 1992. Critical to the implementation of this act were agreements reached in 1991 between members of the EEC at Maastricht in the Netherlands. The Maastricht Treaty represents a commitment on the part of member nations to move toward an economic and monetary union by January 1, 1999, through creation of a European central bank and a single currency.

Many thought that the end of the Cold War, symbolized by the fall of the Berlin Wall and the unification of Germany, would speed the process of regional integration.[36] But within two years, serious doubts had emerged about the ability of European governments to follow through on the ambitious commitments made at Maastricht. Concern expressed by Britain about "excessive German hegemony" and German opposition to the proposal for a single currency and a central bank undermined expectations for early progress.[37]

The experience of the European Community illustrates both the promise and the problems associated with regional integration. In terms of the promise, the community has facilitated cooperation among its members on a wide array of trade and monetary issues. In terms of problems, however, the EEC has faced serious obstacles in its efforts to achieve economic and monetary union. Moreover, prospects for political union are uncertain, even after Maastricht. Agreement on a common currency would clearly facilitate political union. But serious problems remain, among them the fact that as of early 1993 neither Denmark nor Britain had ratified the Maastricht Treaty. Thus, while the growth of complex interdependence has increased the benefits of international cooperation, concerns remain in national capitals about whether the costs of surrendering sovereignty are worth the benefits associated with political integration.

The issue of regional integration shares a common theme with the monetary and trade issues discussed above. Community politics and national politics are linked, just as are the politics of domestic and international monetary and trade issues. Much of the opposition to British ratification of the Maastricht Treaty, for example, stems from domestic concerns about the impact of economic and monetary union on the competitive positions of certain British industries. Thus, domestic considerations have dominated discussions of regional integration in the past and are likely to do so in the future.

International Development

International relations since the end of World War II have been characterized by a development gap between rich and poor nations. Debate surrounding creation of the International Bank for Reconstruction and Development (IBRD) in 1944, now the largest source of multilateral aid, highlighted the emerging split between the developed and developing worlds. The developed world, particularly the Europeans and the Soviet Union, argued that the major focus of the IBRD should be on the "reconstruction" of the

The discovery of mad cow disease in Britain not only forced British farmers to sell off their herds at giveaway prices, but it also created a strong fear and reaction from the rest of the European Community. The resulting boycott of British livestock illustrates that there is much to be settled before a "single Europe" will become a reality.
(Photo courtesy of Jonathan Player/NYT Permissions.)

European and Soviet economies.[38] For their part, representatives of the developing world pressed for an emphasis on the "development" of the economies of all member nations, not just Europe.[39] In the late 1940s, however, the focus was clearly on European recovery. The IBRD adopted conservative loan terms, and restrictions on borrowers made it extremely difficult for nations in the developing world to obtain loans.

By the mid-1950s there had been a major shift in Western views of the developing world. In response to the emergence of the Soviet threat, the United States and other Western allies focused increasingly on the use of foreign aid. Foreign aid was not necessarily related to economic growth and development, but was designed to win the political support of the developing world in the Cold War against international communism. The impact of aid to the developing world was very different, however, than aid to post–World War II Europe. Rather than fostering development, the nature of American and allied assistance simply perpetuated underdevelopment. By the mid-1960s, domestic political support for foreign assistance programs had declined precipitously.

At about the same time, the developing world began to raise serious concerns about structural barriers to economic development. The formation of the United Nations Conference on Trade and Development (UNCTAD) in 1964, as an arm of the United Nations General Assembly, provided a forum for the developing world to express its concerns about such issues as aid, protectionism, technology transfer, food, and the environment. The UNCTAD, which meets every three years, has had little impact on the international trading system, however, because it has no enforcement powers.[40]

The growth of interdependence in the 1970s led to another shift in perspective as policy makers in the developed world recognized the importance of developing economies as markets for rapidly expanding exports.[41] The dramatic rise in the price of oil in 1973 and 1974 increased the foreign assistance needs of non–oil-producing states in the developing world. And the emerging debt crisis reinforced the view that economic development and the long-term economic interests of the developed world were inextricably linked. These broader views of the importance of the developing world led to increased reliance on trade and foreign direct investment, in addition to foreign aid, as tools of economic development.

By the 1980s, debt relief had become the major issue in relations between the developed and the developing worlds. Argentina, Brazil, and Mexico, the largest debtor states in Latin America, and many smaller countries as well, rescheduled their debts and agreed to strict austerity measures under the guidance of the International Monetary Fund (IMF). By the middle of the decade, however, the consensus was that these measures were economically ineffective and politically destabilizing. In 1985, the IMF decided to deal with the debt crisis by emphasizing economic growth. This signaled a major role for multilateral aid in general, and the IBRD in particular, in addressing the problem of Third World debt.[42] It also implied the commitment of new funds from private banks, regional banks, the World Bank, and national governments.[43]

Alternative voices have emerged in the 1990s, however, making the case for new approaches to development that move beyond the goal of improving economic living standards. These voices, generally coming from the developing world, have criticized the free-market model of development in favor of new approaches that emphasize grassroots participation, equity, and the concept of sustainable development. The end of the Cold War has broadened the development debate from ideological arguments over the benefits of capitalism and communism to a more pragmatic focus on the roles of government and market forces.[44]

There are clear linkages between trends in international monetary and trade relations and international development. For example, implementation of the North American Free Trade Agreement (NAFTA) will help promote economic growth in Mexico and reduce incentives for Mexicans to seek a better life in the United States.[45] In short, the emergence of complex interdependence has highlighted the need to focus on the critical relationships between money, trade, and development.

The Management of International Economic Relations: Linkage Politics

The most far-reaching change in international relations since the end of World War II has been the emergence of complex interdependence. Since the end of World War II there has been an explosion in the movement of information, people, money, natural resources and technology across national boundaries. The revolution in transportation and communications has led Americans, as well as the citizens of other nations, to conceptualize domestic and foreign policy as a seamless web. It has also led to the clear linkage of domestic and international politics.

These linkages are particularly dramatic in the area of economic policy. Decisions made within the United States about whether to raise taxes to help control the growth of the federal deficit affect not only the American taxpayer but also potential foreign investors, trading partners, and the value of the dollar. The types of jobs available to Americans in the future will depend in large part on decisions concerning the regulation of imports and exports. Domestic interests such as the American automobile industry and automotive workers exert strong protectionist pressures on our political leaders to counter unfair trade practices by Japan and the Federal Republic of Germany.

Decisions made within other national capitals and supranational organizations such as the European Union have a direct effect on the competitiveness of American products abroad and on the quality of life at home. Changes in OPEC prices and production policies had a direct impact on Americans in the 1970s. Protectionist policies adopted by members of the European Union and Japan in the 1970s and the 1980s are clear examples of the impact of international decisions on domestic economic conditions. These trends illustrate the need for greater coordination of domestic and international economic policies.

Complex Interdependence and "Power Sharing"

Another way of looking at the consequences of complex interdependence for international economic relations is the notion of power sharing. Power sharing is a familiar concept in domestic policy. The separation of powers among the president, Congress, and the judiciary is often described as a condition of separate institutions sharing power. The formulation of U.S. trade policy illustrates this phenomenon. Both the executive and legislative branches of government play central roles, and conflict between the two has led to serious problems in the coordination of trade, monetary, and industrial policy. These problems are likely to become more severe in the 1990s, as the Congress exerts pressure on the executive branch to use trade as a means of improving the international competitiveness of American business.[46]

But the concept of separate institutions sharing power also describes the relationship between domestic and international institutions in a situation of complex interdependence. Once decisions about national economic policy were made at home, but now decisions by other nations and supranational organizations impose serious constraints on the formulation of national economic policy. The behavior of multinational corporations also can affect the achievement of domestic economic objectives. This reinforces the point that nation-states have lost control of their economies.

The implementation of policy is as equally affected by these trends as is the formulation of policy. The emergence of transnational interests has led to the penetration of government bureaucracies by extra-national pressure groups seeking to make policy more responsive to their interests. The dramatic growth in the number of registered foreign lobbyists in Washington, D.C., during the 1970s and the 1980s is only one indicator of this trend.

"Soft Power" and International Economic Relations

The growth of complex interdependence is associated with a decline in the utility of military force as an effective instrument of policy. The end of the Cold War and the dissolution of the Soviet Union have not removed all military threats to the security of the United States, but they have elevated non-military threats to the central attention of policy makers. In the future, American power will be measured not in terms of military might but in the ability to control the political and economic environments and convince other actors to do what it wants.[47]

These tasks place a premium on access to information, responsive political and economic institutions, and political leaders with strong communications, organizational, and negotiating skills. Joseph Nye characterizes this revolution as the emergence of "soft power" in international relations.[48] The increased visibility of international regimes as tools for minimizing the negative consequences of complex interdependence provides an obvious forum for the use of these skills. Nations that become experts in the exercise of soft power will be more successful in manipulating international regimes to their own ends.

Soft power skills are also essential in domestic policy making and implementation. The artificial dichotomy between politics and administration has long been recognized and rejected by students of public administration.[49] The penetration of government bureaucracies by transnational interest groups will enhance the need for individuals in the public service who are flexible, issue-oriented, and who clearly understand the complexities and dilemmas posed by the growth of complex interdependence.

International Security and Change: Collective Security, Peacekeeping, and the Environment

The end of the Cold War has removed the single, dominant challenge to the security of the United States since 1945. While Russia remains an important concern for America because it controls nuclear weapons that could pose a threat to our interests or the interests of our allies, the dissolution of the Soviet Union has lessened the immediacy of that threat and has opened new opportunities for international cooperation. The dissolution of the Warsaw Pact, the fall of the Berlin Wall, and the unification of Germany have combined with the emergence of the European Community to encourage new thinking about prospects for European security after the Cold War. Moreover, the United Nations has staked out a prominent position as a major actor on the international stage.

In terms of structure, the international system is in flux. The bipolar structure that dominated international relations after World War II has disintegrated. The dissolution of the Soviet Union created, if only for a brief time, a unipolar world where the United States was the only superpower. Most observers of the international scene believe that the unipolar moment has already passed, and that the international system is moving toward multipolarity. International relations in the early twenty-first century will be characterized by interactions among several major powers—the United States, Russia, Germany (or Europe), Japan, and China. With the dramatic increases in population, growing significance of supplies of raw materials and labor, and critical environmental resources, developing countries will be important as well, though it is as yet unclear how the developed country dominance of international relations will change as a result.

While there has been much debate about the consequences of the end of the Cold War for international stability, a consensus is emerging that international relations in the post–Cold War world will be characterized by conflict within and between nations. The multipolarity of the post–Cold War world has introduced a great deal of instability. During the Cold War the United States and the Soviet

With the end of the bipolar superpower struggle between the United States and the former Soviet Union, and the mediating influence that both powers exercised on conflicts not directed toward that main struggle, smaller conflicts both within and among countries have come to the surface. Afghanistan, once the victim of overt invasion, now brings destruction upon itself—through such acts as the burning of whole villages that leave grieving women and children homeless—as internal factions battle for control.
(Photo courtesy of Alan Chin/NYT Permissions.)

Union relied on alliances to help maintain discipline in international relations. The existence of nuclear weapons fostered cautious behavior by the superpowers, for fear of the terrible consequences of nuclear war. The superpowers developed agreed rules of behavior that structured their relationship. And the high politics issues of military security dominated the agenda of international relations. All of these factors contributed to stability during the Cold War.

The end of the Cold War has created a very different international environment. The permanent alliances of the Cold War have been replaced by a system of flexible coalitions whose makeup may vary from issue to issue. The proliferation of nuclear weapons to non–status quo powers who may be less cautious in their behavior raises serious concerns about the future of international security. The absence of agreed-upon rules of behavior in the New World Order contributes further to the unpredictability of international affairs. Finally, the emergence of nontraditional "low-politics" issues such as economics and the environment to assume an equal place on the international affairs agenda with traditional "high-politics" concerns suggests that the problem of ensuring international security after the Cold War will be more complex. Some analysts have suggested, in fact, that we will soon miss the Cold War.[50]

How we think about international security after the Cold War is the subject of much debate, in large part due to the emergence of a situation of complex interdependence. It has become increasingly difficult for nation-states to control their environments. National power is no longer measured in terms of military capabilities, but in terms of whether states can influence the behavior of other actors through the use of an array of instruments of policy—political, economic, and military. As the exercise of military power has become more costly, nation-states have chosen other, less expensive, instruments to achieve their objectives.

Moreover, the traditional view of security as military and defense policy is changing. Economic issues are assuming an equal place alongside military issues in debates about national security. There is increased concern about the impact of population growth and migration on the integrity of national borders and the quality of life within those nations that have experienced a major influx of refugees. Access to water has also become a question of national survival, particularly in the Middle East. Some analysts have even gone so far as to characterize environmental concerns such as global warming as questions of national and international security.

These changes in how we think about national security and the role of military force have led to an increased focus on peaceful methods of conflict resolution. The declining role of hard power and the emergence of soft power[51] have already been addressed earlier in this chapter. The successful exercise of soft power demands access to information, responsive political and economic institutions, and political leaders with strong communications, organizational, and negotiating skills. The increased costs of the exercise of military power have led policy makers to reassess the utility of other instruments of diplomacy, including international negotiation, as means of achieving their political, economic, and military objectives. Clearly, soft power will have an increasingly important role to play in dealing with future challenges to international security.

International regimes have made a significant contribution to international security in the past, and are likely to become even more important in the future. During the Cold War, both the United States and the Soviet Union relied on a system of alliances in defense of their security interests. Moreover, the superpowers reached agreement on informal rules of behavior as well as on their respective spheres of influence. The United States and the Soviet Union pursued arms control negotiations within a broad framework that by 1993 had led to an agreement to reduce their nuclear arsenals to less than a third of their size at the height of the Cold War. Also, from the 1950s until the beginning of the 1990s, the United Nations Security Council played an important role in peacekeeping efforts around the world.

One of the consequences of the trends noted above is that international regimes will be increasingly central in maintaining international security after the Cold War. The tendency of nation-states to engage in coalition behavior, whether based on informal arrangements that vary from issue to issue, or in terms of more formal alliances and institutions, will contribute to international stability. The European Community is emerging as a security vehicle as well as an economic arrangement. The United Nations is playing a much greater role, as evidenced by its actions during the Persian Gulf War and in the former Yugoslavia in the early 1990s. Although it is too early to suggest that a "new international order" has emerged to replace the "old Cold-War order," (and, in fact, some would characterize the current situation as the "new international disorder"), it may not be too soon to suggest that multilateral cooperation is becoming an increasingly important vehicle in the pursuit of international security.

It is too soon to predict that international regimes will replace the nation-state as the prime guarantor of security. Despite the growth of complex interdependence, the international system remains anarchic—an environment in which no nation will be willing to surrender its sovereignty entirely to an international regime. On the other hand, we can expect international regimes to play an increasingly active role in the maintenance of international security.

It is important to consider an overview of the changing international security system and to indicate why students of public administration will need to be aware of these dynamics as they pursue careers in the public sector. This discussion is organized around four topics. First, there is a consideration of the role of security regimes, both Cold War regimes such as alliances and emerging regimes that are dealing with the security issues of the twenty-first century. Second, a discussion of the role of the United Nations in international peacekeeping operations is important. Third, there is an assessment of the emergence of regimes designed to address nontraditional security issues associated with the environment. Finally, there is an examination of the problem of assuring security in the post–Cold War world and the emergence of "new interventionist"[52] tendencies in the United States.

Regimes and International Security: "Traditional" Security Regimes

Nation-states have relied on international regimes throughout history to help provide for their security. Since the end of World War II, alliances and collective-security regimes have been the primary vehicles that nation-states have used to defend their interests against external military threats.

Alliances are formal coalitions of nation-states that are designed to enhance the security of their members. They are often viewed by policy makers as a substitute for increasing their own military capabilities. The concept of burden-sharing underlies most alliances, because nation-states assume that members of an alliance will share the political, economic, and military costs associated with the common defense. Nations generally form alliances to counter a perceived external threat to their security interests with which they are unable to deal unilaterally. Alliances form in response to threats, not simply power. In other words, nations will oppose any perceived threat to international stability, whether or not the threat is represented by the most powerful actor. (A good example of this phenomenon was the coalition arrayed against Saddam Hussein in 1990 and 1991.) In many respects, then, alliances perform a balancing function in international relations. Nation-states are more secure because they know that any potential aggressor will face the combined opposition of others.[53]

During the Cold War, the U.S. experiences with the North Atlantic Treaty Organization (NATO) illustrate the contributions that alliances make to international security. For the United States, NATO provided crucial political and military links to Western Europe. For the European members of NATO and Canada, NATO enhanced deterrence by linking the defense of Europe to the defense of the United States. Because an attack on one was deemed an attack on all, within the language of the North Atlantic Treaty, the alliance served to enhance the security of both the United States and Europe while providing the foundations for future political, economic, and military relationships among the participating nation-states.

A critical question for NATO after the end of the Cold War and dissolution of the the Soviet threat involves the future purpose of the alliance. While a potential threat remains in Russia, most analysts believe that in the near term Russian leaders will concern themselves with the domestic economy and will not be interested in foreign ventures. Of broader interest, particularly given events in the former Yugoslavia during 1992 and 1993, is whether there is a role for NATO in dealing with the consequences of ethnic strife and economic dislocation in other European countries. And, as the debate surrounding the participation of the Europeans in the Gulf War suggests, there may be increasing discussion of a so-called "out-of-area" role for NATO in the future.

It is clear, however, that alliances will play a very different role in the post–Cold War world than they played during the last forty years. Dramatic changes in the structure of international relations will have significant effects on the way alliances operate in the post–Cold War world. The emergence of a multipolar international system will encourage flexible alliance relations instead of the more permanent alliance system that reinforced bipolarity during the Cold War.[54] Flexibility is key if alliances are to play the critical role of balancing potential threats to international security. Nation-states must be free to move from one alliance relationship to another in order to defend against the rise of overwhelming powers that threaten the stability of the international system.

Moreover, complex interdependence means that alliances created to deal with one potential threat may not be appropriate for dealing with other threats. This is because power in a situation of complex interdependence is relative to the issue under consideration. While, hypothetically, the United States and Japan might join together to counter a future economic threat to their interests by the European Community, it would probably make little sense for the United States and Japan to join together to counter a future military threat to their interests by Russia. Put differently, alliances that make sense with respect to economic threats may bring little in the way of value added (particularly for the United States, in this example) against military threats.

A second approach to the use of regimes to enhance international security relies on collective security arrangements, such as the one represented by the United Nations. The assumptions underlying collective security are very different from those underlying a reliance on alliances. Whereas alliance systems assume that the behavior of nations is motivated by self-interest, collective-security arrangements are based on the assumption that nation-states share responsibility for each other's security. While alliance systems are based on the concept of balancing, collective-security arrangements focus on action by all in response to threats of violence by any nation-state. In short, collective-security arrangements deter aggression (or serve to punish aggression if it occurs) by virtue of the fact that the entire international community is arrayed against any potential aggressor.

The first attempt at the construction of a collective-security arrangement during the twentieth century was the League of Nations. Designed in response to the terrible loss of life that occurred during World War I, the league had the ambitious objective of ensuring that World War I would, in fact, be "the war to end all wars." The failure of the league was due to a number of factors, including the refusal of the United States to participate and the inability of the members to reach agreement on the circumstances that would prompt a collective response to aggression. The nature of the international system—characterized by a situation of anarchy in which nation-states were unwilling to compromise their sovereignty—helps to explain the failure of the league.

The United Nations Charter, which was signed in July 1945, attempted to address some of the shortcomings of the League by including a provision enabling any of the five permanent members of the Security Council (the

Figure 12-1
United Nations Organization

To avoid the impotence of the League of Nations, the creators of the United Nations placed responsibility for collective security in the hands of the Security Council, which included five permanent members, any of which could veto proposed actions. The chart below lists some of the military forces that report directly to the council. Reorganization continues at this writing.

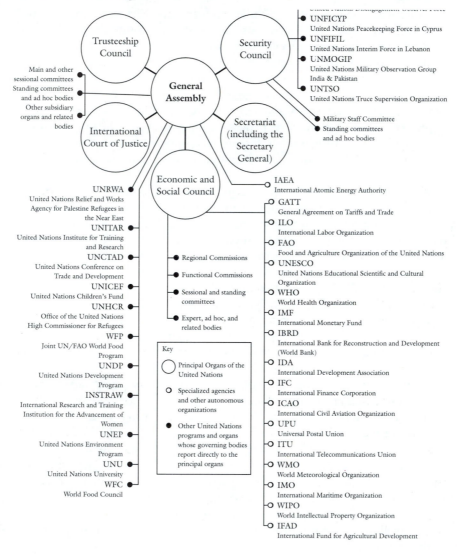

Source: Jon Martin Trolldalen, *International Environmental Conflict Resolution* (Washington, DC: World Foundation for Environment and Development, 1992).

United States, the Soviet Union, Great Britain, France, and China) to veto any proposed action (see Figure 12-1). Moreover, the charter severely restricted the power of the United Nations General Assembly to engage in collective action by limiting its power to studying conflict situations and making recommendations and to providing support for peacekeeping operations.[55]

It was difficult in practice to sanction the use of United Nations forces in the late 1940s because of the potential for a Soviet veto. Agreement to use United Nations forces in response to the North Korean invasion of South Korea in 1950 was made possible only because of the Soviet Union's boycott of the Security Council (in protest of the U.N. refusal to seat the Communist government of the People's Republic of China). The adoption of the Uniting for Peace Resolution, which authorized the continued use of these forces after the Soviet Union returned to its seat on the Security Council, established a very important precedent, namely that the United Nations General Assembly could assume responsibility for security issues in the event of deadlock in the Security Council.[56] Despite this action, there have been relatively few examples of the United Nations' exercise of collective security through the use of military force since the end of World War II. A recent example involves the response of the international community to the Iraqi invasion of Kuwait in August 1990.

The experience of the coalition arrayed against Iraq during the Gulf crisis and war of 1990 and 1991 illustrates the problems and prospects for U.N. involvement in collective-security operations and the kind of flexible alliances that will characterize post–cold War international relations. For the first time in the history of the Security Council, the five permanent members were united in their condemnation of Iraq's action, which violated the United Nations Charter's prohibition of the use of military force to resolve international conflicts.[57] The quick passage of United Nations Resolution 661 after the Iraqi invasion of Kuwait provided an initial framework for the economic embargo. A crucial turning point in building the international coalition occurred on August 25, 1991, with the passage of U.N. Resolution 665, which included a mandate for the use of military force to enforce the embargo.[58] And, finally, for the first time since the Korean War, the United Nations authorized (U.N. Resolution 678, passed on November 29, 1991) the use of military force to remove Iraqi troops from Kuwait.[59]

United Nations Peacekeeping

Over the past thirty-five years, the United Nations has played a rather limited role in collective-security operations designed to cope with threats to international security. During this same period, however, the United Nations *has* focused on the use of peacekeeping techniques that were not envisioned by the United Nations Charter. Peacekeeping activities are different from both the peaceful settlement of disputes and collective-security approaches to dealing with conflict. The purposes of peacekeeping efforts vary, but may include preventing fighting between two or more parties, imposing a buffer between opposing military forces, maintaining order, and enforcing a cease-fire. Peacekeeping forces are impartial and strictly neutral; they use weapons only in self-defense; and they must have the consent of the parties and/or an invitation from one or more of the parties before intervening. Peacekeeping forces have been involved in disputes between nation-states and in domestic conflicts that have threatened to erupt into civil war.[60]

Whereas collective-security operations tend to draw forces from the "great powers," peacekeeping attempts to keep the great powers out of conflict situations. Medium or small powers who are clearly neutral are more likely to contribute to peacekeeping forces. During the past thirty-five years, Austria, Canada, India, Denmark, Finland, Sweden, Norway, and Ireland have been major participants in U.N.-sponsored peacekeeping activities.[61] With some exceptions, the major powers tend to contribute logistical support, transportation, and financial support, rather than military forces.[62]

Peacekeeping operations must be approved by the United Nations Security Council. The United Nations General Assembly assumes responsibility for the creation of the force, its direction, and the challenges of assessing the costs of operations.[63] The financing of peacekeeping operations has been a major concern, with some nations arguing that the major powers should be responsible for footing the bill.[64] There has been increasing opposition, particularly within the United States, to the idea that the major powers should bear primary responsibility for supporting peacekeeping operations. To put the debate about financing in perspective, however, it is interesting to note that all United Nations peacekeeping operations around the world could have been supported for one year with the funds expended during just two days of Operation Desert Storm.[65]

The history of United Nations peacekeeping operations since the early 1950s is mixed. There have been nearly twenty examples of United Nations peacekeeping operations, the most recent being the creation of a United Nations Protection Force (UNPROFOR) to deal with the crisis in the former Yugoslavia. Nearly fourteen thousand military personnel have been committed to UNPROFOR. As of mid-1992, Argentina, Belgium, France, Nepal, the Netherlands, Russia, and the United Kingdom had made military or civilian contributions to this effort. This force was charged with maintaining peace and order, and its responsibilities included verifying the cease-fire, overseeing and disarming combatants, and supervising the activities of local police and authorities.[66]

By early 1993 the situation in the former Yugoslavia had deteriorated. There appeared to be no overriding goal or plan behind United Nations intervention, and the U.N. did not have the resources necessary to deal with growing atrocities in Bosnia.[67] The U.N.-sponsored peace process, chaired by Lord Owen and former U.S. Secretary of State Cyrus Vance, had stalled, as the parties used these talks to gain tactical advantage rather than to seek a permanent solution to the conflict. International outrage about the use of rape and torture as instruments of policy increased pressure for American intervention. In an effort to bring the three warring factions to the negotiating table, the United States decided in February to begin parachuting relief supplies into Bosnia. Prospects for quick resolution of the crisis in Bosnia appeared dim, however, and many Americans called for direct military intervention.

One of the major issues for international relations in the post–Cold War world concerns the contribution of United Nations peacekeeping operations to international security. What functions does peacekeeping serve that are not served by collective-security operations? What are the limits of peacekeeping? How do differences between peacekeeping and peacemaking affect the creation of international regimes designed to enhance security?

Despite the growth of complex interdependence and the trend toward increased cooperation among nation-states in international affairs, there are limits to the use of collective-security regimes. While nation-states may be more willing to cooperate with others in the pursuit of common objectives, they are reluctant to surrender their sovereignty to larger institutions. Successful collective-security operations, such as the Gulf War of 1991, require the formation of a consensus about common objectives and interests that is often difficult and always time consuming. For this reason, and because at times it may be impossible to reach a consensus on the necessity for action, collective-security regimes cannot—and will not, for the foreseeable future—substitute for unilateral action.

There are also limits to the role of peacekeeping regimes in enhancing security after the Cold War. Peacekeeping operations do not use or employ military force as such. Their purpose, rather, is to engage in other activities that will decrease the likelihood that military force will be needed. Moreover, the fact that peacekeeping operations require the agreement of the parties to a conflict before U.N. forces can become involved seriously constrains their impact on ongoing disputes. And, finally, peacekeeping operations cannot solve, or resolve, conflicts. They can contribute to the resolution of conflicts by providing breathing space—both literally and figuratively—to enable other instruments of diplomacy and conflict resolution to be brought to bear on the problem. While peacekeeping regimes, and United Nations–sponsored peacekeeping forces in particular, will continue to play an important role in enhancing security after the Cold War, there are limits to the contribution they can make to international security.

Uncertainty about the differences between peacemaking and peacekeeping complicates the use of both strategies to ensure security after the Cold War. Peacekeeping implies the absence of an enemy, and the success of peacekeeping is directly tied to maintaining strict neutrality. Peacemaking (or peace-enforcement), on the other hand, implies the explicit identification of an aggressor and the use of military force to defeat the aggressor militarily.[68] The United Nations involvement in Bosnia in 1993 illustrates the former; the United Nations involvement in the Persian Gulf in 1990 and 1991 the latter.

Another issue concerning the role of the United Nations in the post–Cold War world is the demand for U.N. involvement in civil wars for humanitarian purposes. The United Nations response to the plight of Iraqi Kurds following Operation Desert Storm illustrates the involvement of the U.N. in humanitarian exercises.[69] The experience of the United Nations in Somalia during 1992 and 1993 illustrates the problems of humanitarian intervention in conflict situations. In many respects, the UN response can be characterized as too little, too late. Although the military task in Somalia was less dangerous than in Iraq or Bosnia, the United Nations debate about the creation of an international force to ensure the delivery of food aid delayed a response until more than 100,000 Somalis had starved.[70]

In short, while the end of the Cold War has decreased fears of the veto and, as a consequence, has facilitated decisions by the United Nations to become involved in collective-security and peacemaking operations, serious concerns remain about the ability of the United Nations to effectively cope with emerging conflict situations, particularly those involving humanitarian relief and intervention in civil wars. A primary issue stems from the increasingly blurred lines between domestic jurisdiction and international responsibility.[71] The creation of international regimes designed to enhance security is an important objective of international policy in the post–Cold War world. It is an objective that will be at least as difficult, if not more difficult, to achieve than it was during the Cold War. The growth of complex interdependence, which is a major cause of the increasingly blurred lines between domestic politics and international relations, clearly cuts both ways.

Security and the Environment

An important consequence of the rise of complex interdependence and the end of the Cold War has been a new focus on nontraditional aspects of international security. For the past forty-five years, most discussions of security have focused on the military dimension of international security. Other aspects of security, including the economy, education, health, and the environment, have received less than their fair share of attention. Beginning in the late 1970s, however, greater attention was paid to the economic dimensions of international security. Several of these dimensions—the international monetary system, the international trade system, and international development—were addressed earlier. During the past decade, the focus on nontraditional aspects of international security has increased dramatically. Scholars and policy makers alike are discussing such issues as the federal deficit,[72] U.S. economic competitiveness,[73] low literacy rates,[74] acquired immune deficiency syndrome (AIDS),[75] migration of populations[76] and global warming[77] as threats to national and international security.

This shift to nontraditional issues is a product of several trends in international affairs. In the first place, the growth of complex interdependence is associated with a dramatic increase in the flow of information, people, and ideas across national boundaries. The emergence of a global economic system, particularly in the areas of monetary and trade affairs, has broken down traditional barriers between domestic and foreign economic policy. Population migration has increased as a result of several factors. The end of the Cold War has encouraged migration from the former Eastern Europe and Soviet Union as individuals seek new political, economic, and social opportunities[78] and as they flee from the crisis in the former Yugoslavia. Migration has also increased from North Africa to southern Europe as large numbers of Muslims also seek a better life.[79] And access to potable water has become critical to national survival—and, thus, national security—in the Middle East and the Persian Gulf.[80]

Environmental problems have received particular attention. These problems cross national boundaries, as illustrated by the conflict over water management in the Middle East and North Africa—where nations share surface water or groundwater with neighboring states.[81] Moreover, the effects of climate change cannot be isolated. One of the effects of greenhouse warming will be sea-level rise. It has been estimated that the rising sea level could cost the United States $100 billion by 2100 for the building of dikes at shorelines and other activities to deal with the effects of a three-foot rise in sea level.[82] In the developing world, global warming will produce serious economic and social dislocations. Bangladesh and the Maldives will face serious threats to their territorial integrity. In Bangladesh, for example, it has been estimated that about 16 percent of the total land area will be lost and 10 percent of the population will have to be relocated in response to rising sea levels.[83]

It is clear that multilateral efforts will be necessary to deal with emerging environmental problems. Bilateral arrangements, while useful in dealing with specific, relatively limited issues such as the conflict between the United States and Canada concerning acid rain, will not be sufficient. Multilateral arrangements involving nation-states from both the developed and the developing world will be required, as well as active involvement by the United Nations and other international governmental organizations.[84] International regimes will have a critical role to play in addressing environmental problems and their security implications.

There have been several attempts to create international regimes dealing with nontraditional security issues. One example is the Third United Nations Law of the Sea Conference, which met from 1973 to 1982. The purpose of this conference was to resolve concerns of the developed and developing worlds dealing with the use of the seas for economic purposes while preserving them as the so-called common heritage of mankind. The institutional objective was to create regimes for areas beyond the control or jurisdiction of any state.[85] The issue was complicated by the fact that the value of the seas' resources is directly linked to whether a nation has access to the technology necessary to exploit them. The developed and developing worlds split on this point. Moreover, landlocked nations expressed concern that they would not have access to the oceans' resources.

The treaty that was adopted in 1982 established a regime for the production and regulation of deep-seabed minerals.[86] The Reagan administration rejected the treaty, however, arguing that its provisions were designed to promote a new world order aimed at redistribution of the world's wealth.[87] By 1989, the treaty had received only forty-two of the sixty votes required for ratification.[88] The experience of the Law of the Sea process demonstrates the problems involved in creating international regimes to deal with nontraditional security issues.

The most recent attempt to deal with environmental issues through the creation of international regimes is illustrated by the United Nations Conference on Environment and Development held in Rio de Janeiro in June 1992. The purpose of the Rio Earth Summit, as it has been called, was to achieve consensus on the priorities for environment *and* development. The underlying assumption of those present was that problems of the environment and development could no longer be treated separately.[89] The Rio Earth Summit produced several nonbinding documents: (1) the Rio Declaration on Environment and Development; (2) a statement on the management of forests; and (3) Agenda 21, a guide to sustainable development for use by governments.[90] The Rio Earth Summit also created a new Commission on Sustainable Development under the supervision of the U.N. Economic and Social Council (ECOSOC) to examine the implementation of Agenda 21 at national, regional, and international levels.[91]

The contrast between the inability to overcome obstacles that impeded progress in the Law of the Sea case and the ability of nations to move beyond similar obstacles at the Rio Earth Summit is clear. In part the differences between the two situations are due to changes that have occurred in international relations during the last decade. Increasing attention has been paid to nontraditional security issues, and particularly issues of the environment, by the mass media. Television has played a significant role in highlighting the challenge posed by global warming. The increasing prominence of the concept of the "global village"[92] reinforces the notion that complex interdependence is a fact of life. These trends may have contributed to the achievements at Rio in June 1992. It is important to recognize, however, that much remains to be done to ensure that the *nonbinding* commitments made at Rio are implemented. Despite the construction of an international regime to deal with questions of sustainable development, actions by nations and international organizations will be required to make the goals of the Rio Earth Summit a reality. And, as of the five year assessment of Agenda 21 in June 1997, the U.N. General Assembly found only limited progress and many challenges ahead.

Conclusion

The end of the Cold War has created an opportunity to move beyond traditional approaches to national and international security. The expected deep cuts in U.S. military capabilities that will occur during the last decade of the twentieth century are directly linked to the decline of the Soviet threat and the absence of any new major military challenge to American security interests in the foreseeable future. Moreover, and perhaps more significantly for the long term, the clear recognition that the United States exists in an international system characterized by complex interdependence will have dramatic effects on how we think about international security.

The first implication of these trends is that American policy makers—at local, state, and federal levels—need to pay more attention to nontraditional security issues. The relationship between security and economics, or put differently, between American economic policy and American national security policy is clear not only to policy makers but also to average Americans.[93] The belief that national security is also linked to the quality of the environment, to the American educational system, and to the accessibility of health care is not as widely popular, but is growing in part because of increased media attention devoted to these issues.

The linkage between domestic policy and foreign policy, particularly in the area of economics, has become an accepted premise in policy-making circles. Moreover, policy makers are also beginning to recognize the increasingly blurred lines between the domestic and international arenas for other issue areas, such as the environment, public health, and human resources.

These trends suggest that policy makers at all levels will feel increased public pressure to deal with questions of national and international security, broadly defined.

Complex interdependence is associated with the decline in the utility of military force as an instrument of policy. The ability to control one's political and economic environments and to convince other nations to follow one's lead will be the measures of American power in the future.[94] The emergence of "soft power" in international relations suggests that different tools will be of value to policy makers as they deal with these new challenges. Communication, negotiation, and conflict resolution skills will be in great demand at all levels of government.

It is not clear, however, that the end of the Cold War means that military force has lost all of its utility to deal with future threats to national or international security.[95] Collective security, as we note below, will continue to be an important instrument of policy. At the same time, an increased focus on nontraditional issues of national security may enhance the role of communication, negotiation and conflict resolution. The growing attention to environmental issues as security concerns, illustrated by the Rio Earth Summit, provides a good example. The process of international environmental negotiation has been much smoother in the 1980s than it was during the 1970s, when confrontation characterized the discussions about creation of a New International Economic Order.[96] The use of tradeoffs to satisfy the interests of North and South seems to have worked in these cases. This does not mean, however, that the same approach will necessarily work in efforts to resolve the crisis in the former Yugoslavia.

While the end of the Cold War has enabled policy makers to pay more attention to nontraditional issues of national and international security, this does not mean that traditional issues will be ignored. The humanitarian relief effort in Somalia in 1992 and 1993 and the war in Bosnia in 1993 are only two examples of the kinds of issues that will face the United States in the future.

The election of President Bill Clinton in November 1992 brought a new perspective on international affairs to the White House. The Clinton administration has adopted an interventionist view of the American role in the world. This view has surprised some analysts, who assumed that the domestic-policy focus that characterized the campaign would characterize the administration as well. This has not turned out to be the case. The Clinton administration's perspective has been described as being a combination of liberal internationalism and an awareness that civil war is a critical issue of international security. The approach places emphasis on the international community's moral obligation to intervene in domestic conflicts around the world.[97]

The instruments of this "new intervention" are varied. The United Nations tends to be the preferred actor, whether in a peacekeeping, peacemaking, or peace-enforcing role. This suggests that international regimes, more broadly defined, will have an increasingly important role to play in enhancing national and international security after the Cold War. It also suggests that the responsibilities of these regimes will be varied and highly demanding. The experiences of the United Nations in Somalia in 1992 and 1993 and in Bosnia in 1993 demonstrate the difficulties that will confront multilateral efforts to deal with new challenges to national and international security.

The United Nations' intervention on behalf of the Kurds in northern Iraq at the end of the Gulf War set an important precedent—namely, the use of military force for humanitarian purposes. The existence of that precedent facilitated United Nations action in Somalia. Despite the problems faced by the United Nations in Somalia, the principle of international intervention for humanitarian purposes is now well-established. The United Nations efforts to deal with the crisis in Bosnia in 1993 confirmed the precedent of intervention by the international community in domestic conflicts.[98]

In at least one respect, these trends have confirmed the logical result of complex interdependence. The new interventionism implies that the interests of individuals are more important than the interests of nation-states. United Nations efforts in Iraq, Somalia, and Bosnia override the principle of state sovereignty for the good of human beings. Widespread international support for these activities may indicate the beginnings of a political response to the effects of complex interdependence and the belief in a global village that demands responsibility *from* all of its citizens *for* all of its citizens. This may strengthen the role of international regimes in enhancing national and international security in the twenty-first century.

Notes

[1]See e.g., Thomas Princen and Matthias Finger, *Environmental NGOs in World Politics* (London: Routledge, 1994).

[2]Joseph S. Nye, Jr., *Bound to Lead: The Changing Nature of American Power* (New York: Basis Books, 1990), 176.

[3]Stephen W. Bosworth, "The United States and Asia," *Foreign Affairs* 71 no. 1 (1991/92), 124.

[4]Carnegie Endowment National Commission, *Changing Our Ways* (Washington, DC: Carnegie Endowment for International Peace, 1992), 23.

[5]Joan Edelman Spero, *The Politics of International Economic Relations,* 2nd ed. (New York: St. Martin's, 1981), 13.

[6]Robert O. Keohane and Joseph S. Nye, *Power and Interdependence,* 2nd ed. (New York: Harper Collins, 1989), 8.

[7]Spero, *op. cit.,* 13.

[8]Nye, *op. cit.,* 182–188.

[9]Paul Kennedy, *The Rise and Fall of the Great Powers* (New York: Vintage Books, 1987).

[10]Carnegie Endowment National Commission, *op. cit.,* 14.

[11]Spero, *op. cit.,* 15–16.

[12]Hans J. Morgenthau, *Politics Among Nations* (New York: Alfred A. Knopf, 1948).

[13]Keohane and Nye, *op. cit.,* 24–25.

[14]Robert O. Keohane, *After Hegemony* (Princeton: Princeton University Press, 1984), 46.

[15]Robert J. Lieber, *No Common Power: Understanding International Relations,* 2nd ed. (New York: Harper Collins, 1991), 5.

[16]Keohane and Nye, *op. cit.,* 19.

[17]*Ibid.,* 21.

[18]B. Guy Peters, *The Politics of Bureaucracy,* 3rd ed. (New York: Longman, 1989), 2.

[19]Charles W. Kegley, Jr. and Eugene R. Wittkopf, *World Politics: Trend and Transformation,* 4th ed. (New York: St. Martin's, 1993), 314.

[20]*Ibid.,* 224.

[21]Jeffrey A. Frieden and David A. Lake, eds., *International Political Economy: Perspectives on Global Wealth and Power,* 2nd ed. (New York: St. Martin's, 1991), 232–233.

[22]Dick Leonard, *Pocket Guide to the European Community* (London: Basil Blackwell and The Economist Publications, 1988), 84–86.

[23]Walter Goldstein, "EC: Euro-Stalling," *Foreign Policy* 85 (Winter 1991/92): 129–147.

[24]Leonard, *op. cit.,* 9.

[25]David H. Blake and Robert S. Walters, *The Politics of Global Economic Relations,* 3rd ed. (Englewood Cliffs, NJ: Prentice-Hall, 1987), 18–19.

[26]Spero, *op. cit.,* 93.

[27]J. H. Warren, "Multilateralism and Regionalism: A North American Perspective from a Canadian Viewpoint," in *The Trilateral Commission Working Group Papers, 1991–92* (New York: The Trilateral Commission [North America], 1992), 54.

[28]Glenn P. Hastedt and Kay M. Knickrehm, *Dimensions of World Politics* (New York: Harper Collins, 1991), 331.

[29]Carnegie Endowment National Commission, *op. cit.,* 23.

[30]Anne Daltrop, *Politics and the European Community,* 2nd ed. (London: Longman, 1986), 14.

[31] *Ibid.*, 15.

[32] *Ibid.*, 160.

[33] David R. Cameron, "The 1992 Initiative: Causes and Consequences," in Alberta M. Sbragia, ed., *Euro-Politics: Institutions and Policymaking in the "New" European Community* (Washington, DC: Brookings Institution, 1992), 38.

[34] *Ibid.*, 45.

[35] *Ibid.*, 46.

[36] C. Fred Bergsten, "The World Economy," *Foreign Affairs* 69 (Summer 1990): 107.

[37] Walter Goldstein, "Europe after Maastricht," *Foreign Affairs* 72 (Winter 1992/93): 120–121.

[38] Spero, *op. cit.*, 150.

[39] *Ibid.*, 148.

[40] Robert A. Isaak, *International Political Economy* (Englewood Cliffs, NJ: Prentice-Hall, 1991), 91–92.

[41] Spero, *op. cit.*, 173.

[42] Blake and Walters, *op. cit.*, 149.

[43] A. LeRoy Bennett, *International Organizations: Principles and Issues,* 5th ed. (Englewood Cliffs, NJ: Prentice-Hall, 1991), 275.

[44] Robin Broad, *et. al.*, "Development: The Market Is Not Enough," *Foreign Policy* 81 (Winter 1990/91): 145–160.

[45] M. Delal Baer, "North American Free Trade," *Foreign Affairs* 70 (Fall 1991): 133.

[46] Bruce Stokes, "Organizing to Trade," *Foreign Policy* 89 (Winter 1992/93): 38.

[47] Nye, *op. cit.*, 175.

[48] *Ibid.*, 188.

[49] Peters, *op. cit.*, 4.

[50] John J. Mearsheimer, "Back to the Future: Instability in Europe after the Cold War," *International Security* 15 (Summer 1990): 5–56.

[51] Nye, *op. cit.*, 188.

[52] Stephen John Stedman, "The New Interventionists," *Foreign Affairs* 72 no. 1 (1992/93): 1–16.

[53] Stephen M. Walt, *The Origins of Alliances* (Ithaca, NY: Cornell University Press, 1987).

[54] Kenneth N. Waltz, *Theory of International Politics* (Reading, MA: Addison-Wesley, 1979).

[55] Kegley and Wittkopf, *op. cit.*, 514.

[56] Margaret P. Karns and Karen A. Mingst, "Multilateral Institutions and International Security," in Michael T. Klare and Daniel C. Thomas, eds., *World Security* (New York: St. Martin's, 1991), 270.

[57] *Ibid.*, 291.

[58] Roland Dannreuther, "The Gulf Conflict: A Political and Strategic Analysis" *Adelphi Papers* #264 (Winter 1991/92): 28–30.

[59] *Ibid.*, 41.

[60] Bennett, *op. cit.*, 140.

[61] Central Intelligence Agency, *United Nations Peacekeeping Operations, 1992* (Washington, DC: Central Intelligence Agency, 1992).

[62] Bennett, *op. cit.*, 141.

[63] *Ibid.*, 143.

[64] *Ibid.*

[65] Sir Brian Urquhart, "The UN: From Peace-Keeping to a Collective System?" *Adelphi Papers* #265 (Winter 1991/92): 28.

[66] Central Intelligence Agency, *op. cit.*

[67] Edward C. Luck, "Making Peace," *Foreign Policy* 89 (Winter 1992/93): 148.

[68] Stedman, *op. cit.*, 11.

[69] Thomas G. Weiss and Kurt M. Campbell, "Military Humanitarianism," *Survival* 33 (Sept./Oct. 1991): 451.

[70] Luck, *op. cit.*, 148.

[71] Weiss and Campbell, *op. cit.*, 462.

[72] Jeffrey E. Garten, "The 100-Day Economic Agenda," *Foreign Affairs* 72 (Winter 1992/93): 16–31.

[73] Theodore H. Moran, *American Economic Policy and National Security* (New York: Council on Foreign Relations Press, 1993), 13–26.

[74] Peter G. Peterson with James K. Sebenius, "The Primacy of the Domestic Agenda," in Graham Allison and Gregory F. Treverton, eds., *Rethinking America's Security: Beyond Cold War to New World Order* (New York: W. W. Norton, 1992).

[75] Barry B. Hughes, *Continuity and Change in World Politics* (Englewood Cliffs, NJ: Prentice-Hall, 1991), 443–444.

[76] Myron Weiner, "Security, Stability, and International Migration," *International Security* 17 (Winter 1992/93): 91–126.

[77] David A. Wirth, "Catastrophic Climate Change," in Michael T. Klare and Daniel C. Thomas, eds., *World Security* (New York: St. Martin's, 1991).

[78] Edward Mortimer, "European Security after the Cold War," *Adelphi Papers* #271 (Summer 1992): 15–16.

[79] *Ibid.*, 16–17.

[80] Joyce R. Starr, "Water Wars," *Foreign Policy* 82 (Spring 1991): 17–36.

[81] Natasha Beschorner, "Water and Instability in the Middle East," *Adelphi Papers* #273 (Winter 1992/93): 3.

[82] Wirth, *op. cit.*, 390.

[83]Shaukat Hassan, "Environmental Issues and Security in South Asia." *Adelphi Papers* #262 (Autumn 1991): 22–23.

[84]Jessica Tuchman Mathews, "The Environment and International Security," in Michael T. Klare and Daniel C. Thomas, eds., *World Security* (New York: St. Martin's, 1991), 377.

[85]Karns and Mingst, *op. cit.,* 278.

[86]Leigh S. Ratiner, "The Law of the Sea: Crossroads for U.S. Policy," *Foreign Affairs* 60 (Summer 1982): 1006–1021.

[87]James L. Malone, "Who Needs the Sea Treaty?" *Foreign Policy* 54 (Spring 1984): 45.

[88]Peter A. and Robert F. Gorman, *International Relations* (Pacific Grove, CA: Brooks/Cole, 1991), 297.

[89]Richard N. Gardner, *Negotiating Survival* (New York: Council on Foreign Relations Press, 1992), 4.

[90]*Ibid.,* 1.

[91]Carnegie Endowment National Commission, *op. cit.,* 39.

[92]Brian Groth, "Negotiating in the Global Village: Four Lamps to Illuminate the Table," *Negotiation Journal* 8 (July 1992): 241–257.

[93]Alan Murray, "The Global Economy Bungled," *Foreign Affairs* 72 no. 1 (1992/93): 158–166.

[94]Nye, *op. cit.,* 188.

[95]James G. Blight and Andrew W. Lynch, "Negotiation and the New World Disorder," *Negotiation Journal* 8 (October 1992): 357.

[96]I. William Zartman, "International Environmental Negotiation: Challenges for Analysis and Practice," *Negotiation Journal* 8 (April 1992): 121.

[97]Stedman, *op. cit.,* 1–2.

[98]*Ibid.,* 6–7.

Chapter 13

Comparative Public Administration: Different Problems, Common Trends

It is ironic that so many public administration students spend their time looking inward and backward at the field when the history of our profession shows that the first major scholars of the field and many of its most distinguished practitioners spent their earlier years learning from the experiences of other nations. As far back as the Roman empire, public administration was a borrower profession that took lessons from anywhere it could find them. Roman administrators learned from the Egyptians and the Greeks. Public administrators in Europe not only took over the heritage left to them by the Romans but also learned from each other through acts such as watching the efforts of Russia to develop an efficient tax-collection system and analyzing the organization of the Roman Catholic Church as it extended its reach and influence around the globe.

Early in the history of the United States, lessons were learned from other colonies and from the Native Americans of the areas in which colonists were striving to build their own communities. The effort at Constitution building was rooted in a study of what had and had not worked in other countries from the contemporary period back into antiquity. Indeed, the *Federalist Papers* and debates of the framers are filled with considerations of the experiences of others.[1]

When Woodrow Wilson, who is considered to be the intellectual founder of our field, moved into public administration he became a student of German (though he had his fair share of trouble with the language) so that he could study the practices of what was then the leading Western government in the development of public administration techniques. He argued vigorously for a comparative approach to the study of public administration, though he recognized that lessons learned would have to be filtered through the cultural lens of the person seeking to learn those lessons and borrow techniques.[2] One need not accept Prussian government and lifestyles to learn from their public management experience. Wilson considered the work of

Frank Goodnow, a professor at Columbia University who was trained in Berlin, to be the best texts available for the education of American public administrators. One of Goodnow's two major texts was *Comparative Administrative Law*.[3] Goodnow's best-known student was another German-trained lawyer, Ernst Freund, who went on to do comparative administrative law studies among state and local governments within the United States while a professor at the University of Chicago.[4] Soon the isolation of the early twentieth century set in and the value of the comparative study of the field vanished. Moreover, the United States came to be convinced of its superiority and behaved as if we had little to learn from others. One should hasten to add, in the spirit of comparative study, that other great powers were making the same mistake. As colonial powers compelled their colonies to adopt their own systems, historically evolved systems of governance were displaced by the British, French, or Spanish regimens, to name a few.

There appeared a possibility that the post–World War II period would bring a renewed willingness to take a wider view around the world, but the reaction against the war, pressing domestic demands, and the rapidly intensifying "red scare" of the 1950s and 1960s commanded attention to matters domestic. Attention was also drawn to more esoteric academic debates as battles raged among those who wanted to make public administration a more scientific social science and to move the field toward theory and away from a direct concern with the task of governing.[5]

It appeared that the study of comparative public administration was back to stay during the 1960s as former colonial powers in Africa and elsewhere gave up control and turned to helping with development administration. In the United States, the Comparative Administration Group (CAG) developed, with well-known scholars writing on a range of topics,[6] though with more attention to how the developed nations could help the developing than to lessons that all countries might learn from each other. Dwight Waldo, writing in 1968, found the rise of comparative and development administration study—most notably the work of the CAG led by Fred Riggs[7]—to be one of the three most important developments in academic public administration in the postwar period.[8]

Once again, however, domestic tensions took center stage, the war on poverty intensified internal efforts at change, and Vietnam caused many in the United States to seek a return to isolation notwithstanding the continuation of the Cold War. The 1970s and 1980s were as turbulent economically as the 1960s had been socially. The energy crisis, double-digit inflation, 'stagflation,' global competition for investment, currency fluctuations, and technological revolution meant hard times, and in hard times many societies turn inward. Even cosmopolitan Europe saw the rise of political parties seeking to eliminate foreign influences.

Comparative and development administration, as advocated by Professor Dwight Waldo of the Maxwell School at Syracuse University, focused on helping developing countries to establish and improve their administrative abilities.
(Photo courtesy of the American Society for Public Administration.)

In short, particularly in the United States but elsewhere as well, most observers who have thought much about the state of academic study of comparative public administration have expressed considerable disappointment at the progress that has been made to date.[9]

The forces of isolation are still very much alive around the world, but the global dynamics of the 1990s command the attention of public administrators to developments around the world. There are a number of major developments that are shaping the administrative environment, including:

- the creation of critically important regional pacts such as the European Union and NAFTA;
- the development of global governing structures like the World Trade Organization;
- the obvious immediate impact of a twenty-four-hour-a-day global marketplace;
- the clear impacts to the global community from tensions and violence from Rwanda to the former Yugoslavia to the Newly Independent States of the former Soviet Union and Eastern Europe;

- increasing demands for participation by formerly excluded groups around the world, as demonstrated in part by the claims of indigenous peoples at the Rio Earth Summit in 1992 and the debates over policy at the UN Conference on Women in Beijing in 1995.

For all these reasons, it is critically important to renew our commitment to a comparative perspective on public administration. The last chapter explained that there is a complex international bureaucracy that plays an important role in global governance. This chapter emphasizes ways in which public administration professionals can best learn practices and gain awareness of new opportunities from around the world. Specifically, we will consider how to think comparatively, to identify elements of global convergence and cultural distinctiveness, to recognize forces that have shaped the structure of governments, to view the interactions between nations and their subunits and international institutions, and to consider trends in contemporary comparative administration.

Thinking Comparatively

At the local level, comparison is a standard method of action. It is when comparisons are made between units of government and communities that are considered foreign or distant that comparison suddenly drops off and seemingly becomes threatening.

One community will watch as one or a few of its neighbors deal with a problem and then use the lessons from that experience to meet future challenges. That process has become institutionalized as cities have selected peer communities to be benchmarks against which to compare their own actions on a wide range of issues—from levels of taxation, to public employee salaries, to types of responses to federal mandates. This comparative process has even gone commercial, as companies selling codification services will, for a fee, provide a community with copies of a number of ordinances on the same topic from a variety of cities with similar characteristics.

We should be doing precisely the same thing with other neighboring countries and other regions of the world. Public administrators should regard the wide range of countries, cultures, and governmental institutions as a palette, the elements of which can be shaded slightly in one setting, contrasted sharply in another to highlight important features of a problem, or even applied directly to a new challenge if the circumstances and context warrant it. Of course, we cannot compare what we do not understand. It is amazing that even today such close neighbors as Mexicans, Americans, and Canadians do not understand each other very well.

The first challenge then is to ensure that the second of what Professor Dwight Waldo has called the two critical questions must always be taken seriously. The first question to be asked with respect to any assertion is "So What?" In other words, Why does anyone care? What difference does it make (whatever "it" may be)? The second is, "As compared to what?" The question of considering comparison is not something to be done after everything else has been addressed, but must become a central part of the reasoning process in public administration.

The second important factor is that comparison is both a guide to analysis and action and also a means to enhance understanding, communication, and cooperation. At the most obvious level this effort will repay those seeking to attract international firms to their states and communities. But at a much more fundamental level, the effort to take comparison seriously, coupled with the current ability to communicate instantly and inexpensively with most parts of the international community, creates the foundation for a wider and more constructive international conversation about how to improve professional performance and how to work better together.

Global Convergence versus Cultural Distinctiveness: The Dynamic Tension

Whether we like it or not, there are forces in the global community that are causing some degree of convergence among approaches to public administration. At the same time, and perhaps in part because of the pressures to move toward what is common, there are increasingly strong tensions to establish and maintain cultural distinctiveness. Neither of those sets of forces appears likely to decline in the years to come. That is true among nations and across groups within regions and nations as well.

There are a number of forces of convergence, including many of the important influences in the contemporary context of public administration described in the introductory chapter to this volume. Of particular interest in terms of convergence are population growth and shift, the information technology revolution, the birth of a rapid-response global marketplace, the growing importance of environmental limits, and rising expectations in communities around the world.

No longer can societies be simply defined as urbanized and developed or underdeveloped and rural. It is also no longer possible to speak of developing nations as small and developed nations as large. Many developing nations are among the most rapidly growing in the world and most have experienced substantial shifts of population from rural areas to the urban centers, particularly in Latin America and Asia (see Figure 13-1).

Figure 13-1
Urban and Rural Population Projections, 1950–2025

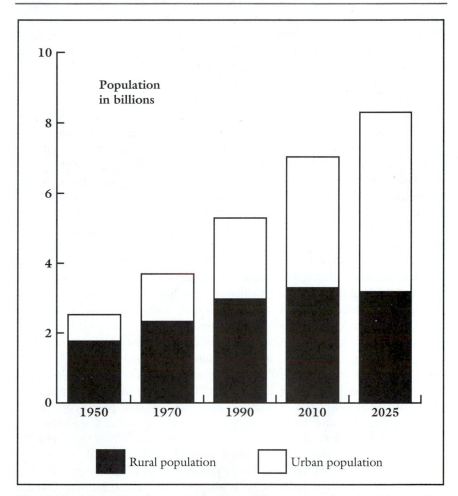

The world's cities are growing at a rate of one million people each week, with most of that growth represented in people relocating from the countryside as they seek a better life. This continuing population shift from rural to urban areas—most pronounced in Latin America and Asia—means that more than two-thirds of the world's population will be living in a city by 2025.

Source: United Nations Habitat II.

Of course, in some cases the move to the cities follows environmental problems in the rural areas where desertification, salinization, water-logging, erosion, or the like have forced farmers from the land. Ironically, of course, the move to the cities for a better life has often meant less clean air, less available clean water, and diets that are not as healthy as were sometimes available in the rural areas. These migrants within their own lands have felt the effects of environmental limits in the country and in the cities.

At the same time, demands for economic growth and increased productivity have been one result of the establishment of a truly global market that operates around the clock every day. The ability to move investments almost instantly from one industry to another and from one economy to another has meant increased competition, not just with neighboring communities or adjacent countries, but also with many countries in several regions of the globe simultaneously. That has meant pressure for increased productivity, which frequently in modern markets has not necessarily meant more product but the same level of production with fewer or less costly employees. That has, in turn, meant that individual countries are faced with more complex needs for health care, retirement financing, and even the prospect of finding a sizeable portion of their populations without any benefits beyond moderate salaries, and an expectation that government will respond to their obvious needs. At the same time, global competition has made it harder for countries like the Scandinavian societies, which have traditionally valued social-support programs, to keep pace. In the current global market, firms can avoid paying the taxes that are needed to support such social programs by moving operations to a developing country that does not require those business costs.[10]

The key to the rise of the global marketplace, however, is the revolution in information technology of the 1980s and 1990s. For all intents and purposes the personal computer is a creature of the 1980s. It had prototypes in the preceding decade—and indeed the space race had produced miniaturized computers even before that—but it was not until the 1980s that personal computers became small enough, simple enough, and affordable enough to make them standard office tools for professionals. That capability, plus the growth in networking technology leading to the Internet, has literally changed the world. In developed countries, some grade school children can sit in the comfort of their homes and roam the world in search of information of every kind at little cost beyond the initial purchase of the computer. Even the smallest developing countries have created home pages on the World-Wide Web. That computer technology, along with the burgeoning growth in international cable and satellite television, has changed politics as well as markets around the world.

One result of these changes has been a set of rising expectations around the world for a different kind of life: social, economic, and political. The fact that what people see on television is often a completely mythical reality has not changed their desire to achieve the lifestyle they see. It is truly astounding for any American travelling abroad to realize just how many people think that most Americans actually lead the kind of lives portrayed on prime-time dramas and soap operas.

The issue is not simply one of lifestyle concerns in the popular sense, but a general sense that the kinds of freedoms, quality of life, and rights that one sees portrayed in another country should be available to everyone in the world. Associated with that expectation is a growing demand that governments should be accountable for their treatment of their citizens. Indeed, people in many countries who used to regard themselves as subjects in a kingdom now think of themselves as citizens in a democratic community and expect that they have rights to protect them against abuses of power. Indeed, they expect that the courts will protect those rights. That is a considerable leap in those nations where courts have not traditionally behaved as a co-equal branch of government that allows citizens to win battles in court that they might not be able to win in Parliament. Increasingly, constitutional courts around the world have been asserting greater authority in such cases.[11] More than that, other bodies, like the European Court, are being used to obtain relief internationally against what have traditionally been regarded as local decisions, like zoning rulings and determinations about the issuance of liquor licenses. At the same time, countries such as the United States that have focused much of the accountability discussion on legal mechanisms have moved more toward political means of accountability. Into this mix has come a global move to impose market mechanisms of accountability, ranging from simplistic measures of costs of services to much more complex devices like customer-satisfaction surveys and market-choice strategies involving vouchers for public services.

All of these factors have moved us toward convergence. The positive side of this is that administrators the world over have more in common than ever before. They are seeing common problems and challenges even if they work in very different environments. However, at the same time that we are addressing these forces tending to make our societies look more alike, there are concomitant forces moving in the other direction, reactions against what is sometimes viewed as a homogenization of distinctive political, social, and cultural communities. Certainly the effort to come to grips with cultural distinctiveness is a critically important example.

Cultural Distinctiveness: A Reaction against Commonality

It may in part be because of these forces of convergence, but there has been an unmistakable tendency to assert and address differences at a time when there seem to be more and more similarities. Ethnicity has in some cases intensified as groups have felt threatened by globalization. The more we are faced with a loss of our distinctiveness, the more we seek mechanisms that will restore our self-image and reinforce our sense of uniqueness. The more embattled our foundations seem to be from contending factions or ethnic groups, the more we feel called upon to defend, sometimes in the most horrible ways, our own heritage. The need to belong becomes increasingly intense as a sense of anomie increases.

One of the forms that this claim to uniqueness has taken is the increasingly common assertion of the preeminence of cultures. This has been true not only in individual nations, but also in regions. Witness, for instance, the growing importance for many Asians that they be seen as having an unique Asian identity and status. Despite their participation as global businesspersons and in every other walk of life, that need to feel a unique identity has become increasingly important. And there have been similar responses in Latin American and Europe. It is little short of amazing to anyone with a nodding acquaintance of history that we could be in the twentieth century and speaking of citizenship in Europe as an identity that would be acceptable to a wide range of Europeans.

Culture, as the term is used here, incorporates ethnicity as well as ways of life that are passed down from generation to generation. That ethnic component also is often associated with a particular religious affiliation. Religious strife has increased in part as a reaction to the increasingly active search for converts in lands dominated by other traditions. As people search for their roots, they may reawaken long-dormant religious tensions. Taken together, these forces have emerged as powerful and sometimes dangerous influences in places like the Middle East and the former Yugoslavia.

Ironically, there is also the fact that failures in development have brought a reaction that is culture-centered. As fiscal stress or corruption have weakened efforts at development, reversion to older, more traditional patterns of social organization have been natural places to turn. In a philosophical or even psychological sense, these responses may be an effort to get grounded in a time of turbulence. On the other hand, they may be nothing more than an effort to return to old ways that seemed to work on a day-to-day basis.

At a subnational level, there are also important efforts at cultural identity. Indeed, there have been movements within republics of the former Soviet Union to break away from what were already considered relatively small states. Even in a country like the United States that has traditionally ignored or even rejected cultural identity (given the common tendency to speak of the melting pot), it is interesting what a wide diversity of cultures there are among the states. Indeed, Daniel Elazar has indicated that those distinctions are among the most important in terms of understanding American federalism.[12]

At an even lower level of generalization, there has been a growing effort to recognize differences in organizational culture as an important determinant in management strategies and tactics. Schein has argued very effectively that the failure to recognize the distinctive culture of different organizations is a recipe for disaster for any manager either operating within that organization or dealing with the organization as a negotiating partner or competitor[13] (see Chapter 9).

The Power Problem: Parliaments, Presidencies, and other Institutions

To be sure, there are other factors that affect the unity or division of power, among which are the structure and processes according to which governments are organized. Ideally, of course, those institutions and processes should reflect the political culture of the country for which they were designed. However, there are a variety of devices through which governments are formed—including colonial transplantation, institutional borrowing, and institutional synthesis—which do not always relate the form to foundation culture.

Governments formed from former colonies, not surprisingly, were usually not entirely new creations. Rather, these new regimes built their new governance structures on the foundations of colonial institutions, though perhaps within a very different social, political, and economic reality. Benjamin Franklin was reputed to have said that revolutionary governments often come into the world "half improvised, half compromised." Neither is it unusual for the governments that emerge following revolutions or voluntary withdrawal of colonial rule to move through several stages of change and adaptation, sometimes in a more or less evolutionary manner and at other times in more conflict-laden and difficult processes.

In a number of cases, those sometimes fragile new governments fall at the hands of a military coup d'état. Military regimes may retain the colonial forms for ease of administration rather than as any kind of effort to reflect a political culture or even a clearly articulated ideology. When a nation like Brazil experiences a lengthy colonial domination followed by an additional lengthy period of military rule, the adjustment to civilian constitutional government can be a difficult process. After all, where do the framers of the new government look for the kinds of shared values that make up political culture in a society in which citizens have never had the opportunity freely to debate and define a common ground?

Similarly, there have been difficulties where a people are suddenly faced with a dramatic change of regime, as in the case of the republics of the former

Soviet Union. When such drastic change is accompanied by other major forces, such as internationally imposed economic "shock therapy," there may be what seems to be an institution and process vacuum. In that situation, there may be a dramatic need for new governmental forms but insufficient stability and resources to support the difficult task of institution building.

Until relatively recently there had not been much attention paid to the special problems of structuring and administering island states and small nations. The Earth Summit accords called for development of information sharing on this issue, and an international conference on the subject was held in Barbados in 1994. The pressure on many Pacific island nations and on newly emerging small nations in Europe, Africa, and Asia, along with the problems of development in the Caribbean and Latin American small states, have convinced the international community of the necessity to pay attention to the special needs of these nations. One of the dimensions of this discussion has been a growing recognition of the importance of nongovernmental organizations (NGOs) in the development and administration of programs in nations that lack the institutional infrastructure or resources to undertake the work themselves. The benefits of these relationships between official power and unofficial players in the political and administrative world are obvious, but it is becoming clear that there are dangers as well. Leaders in some smaller states have felt somewhat overwhelmed by the desire of NGOs—which are after all interest groups with their own policy and ideological preferences—to exercise a power role, particularly in smaller or less developed states.

At the end of the day, despite many forces of convergence in the contemporary world, there remain a plethora of institutional arrangements among governments. There are a few generalizations that can be made. First, most public administrators work for ministries of their national government or local governments. The federalism arrangements in the United States in which more than 85 percent of all public servants are state and local employees is an exception rather than the rule. Even though there has been a worldwide movement for decentralization in the past two decades, most national governments retain ultimate authority in the capital. Second, notwithstanding the overall national power and traditional divisions between domestic and foreign ministries, it is increasingly common for administrators in many agencies to work directly with their counterparts in other countries and regions around the world. Third, direct interaction is increasing as the number of international agreements on everything from air-traffic control to environmental regulation grows, with many calling for articulation of national, and in some cases even subnational, administrative systems. Fourth, even where administrators are not dealing with one another in projects or programs, they are often communicating through international organizations or through the

Internet. The more technology penetrates previously isolated countries, the more likely it is that cross-boundary communication will grow.

Dealing with the Global Community from a Comparative Perspective

Although all of these facts of global community administrative life are true, there are still many complexities that make life in a comparative and international world interesting to say the least. For one thing, the rules of the road are different. As we increasingly cross over, around, and through boundaries, we must still deal not only with the international structures described in the previous chapter, but also with increasing global expectations and the continuing importance of regional realities.

International Institutions

Just as life in American public administration has become more complex by virtue of the many people and resources that must be brought together to get policies implemented and to operate them on a day-to-day basis, so too cross-national and -international exchanges involve many players. That is particularly the case when developing or transitional nations are involved. The United Nations, the World Bank, and the International Monetary Fund are of particular importance for many public administration activities.

The United Nations has recently celebrated its fiftieth anniversary. It is appropriate at this time that the U.N. has enacted a resolution on the importance of public administration in social and economic development. Indeed, the resumed session of the General Assembly in the spring of 1996 had that subject as its primary agenda. A group of experts on public administration from around the world was convened at the U.N. in the summer of 1995 to make recommendations to the General Assembly on ways to enhance public administration globally.

In addition to this broad effort at administrative development, the United Nations has sponsored conferences and training activities around the world in such areas as sustainable development administration, privatization, decentralization, and administration of social programs. In addition, there have been more specialized programs offered by policy-specific organizations such as World Health Organization (WHO), the Food and Agriculture Organization (FAO), and the United Nations Environment Program (UNEP). Some of the major global conferences, such as the 1992 Earth Summit in Rio de Janeiro and the 1995 Social Summit in Copenhagen, produced ambitious accords. Agenda 21 and the Copenhagen Declaration set forth a range of policy commitments by national and international institutions.

Many administrative activities in developing countries are connected with projects sponsored by the United Nations Development Program (UNDP). This organization facilitates development projects and maintains country offices in many nations around the world. Those projects include programs aimed at capacity building in various program areas, though traditionally the primary focus has tended to be on policy design rather than administration. As a major funding organization, UNDP plays an important role in a wide range of activities, from institution building to providing support for program design.

The World Bank, described in Chapter 12, is also an important funding agency for international projects. The bank has until recently tended to finance larger projects, such as infrastructure developments like roads, dams, and the like. However, responding to relatively harsh criticism, it has moved to place more emphasis on environmental, educational, and small-scale enterprise activities. The bank continues to take criticism on grounds that it has not been sufficiently open in terms of providing information to people affected by their loans or in offering them an opportunity to participate fully in important decisions. Although the bank has added personnel in these sensitive areas, it is as yet unclear what direction this important institution will take in the future.

The International Monetary Fund was also described in the previous chapter. For present purposes, its importance lies in the fact that, in providing support (which often takes the form of what is called a "structural adjustment" of a nation's debt), the IMF has imposed a range of conditions that accompany the assistance. The argument runs that such changes as deregulation and privatization are essential to ensure that a nation's economy will be healthy enough to be a good financial risk. However, many critics have read this as a way to bludgeon poor nations into adopting what may be at least as much an ideological program as one intended to ensure effective development. Among other things, the unwillingness of IMF to consider the domestic social consequences of these changes has brought considerable reaction. The international concern about these pressures has been intense. More than one hundred nations committed themselves to a firm position on the subject.

> We commit ourselves to ensuring that when structural adjustment programmes are agreed to they include social development goals, in particular eradicating poverty, promoting full and productive employment, and enhancing social integration.[14]

Nevertheless, the demands of international lenders have led to significant institutional and process changes in the target governments.

One of the difficulties that emerges from international pressures for internal change is that it may produce a mismatch between the political and social culture of the country and what is demanded from external institutions. Among other things, these demands may force nations to make economic development in a strict market sense a priority over other values, such as maintenance of traditional cultures, environmental protection, or cooperative social arrangements in favor of a policy structure that is cash-based, competition-oriented, export-focused, and monetarily-driven. If that happens, there is the very real danger that public administrators will be operating programs and systems that are at odds with the basic cultural infrastructure of the country they are attempting to govern. This problem has been particularly acute in Latin America, but also in portions of Africa.

Global Expectations

At the end of the day there is every reason to believe that administrators who have seen themselves as strictly local functionaries will increasingly come into contact with their counterparts in other nations and the international institutions that play important roles in global governance. One reason for that is the rising set of global expectations. Because there is an awareness of the interconnectedness of policy consequences, various nations are demanding an opportunity to have international consideration of goals and the means of their attainment.

There are several contemporary examples that will likely affect administrators at all levels of government. The Copenhagen Declaration of 1995, also known as the Declaration of the Social Summit, is a comprehensive document that addresses a wide range of policies and the methods of their administration in the social sector. In addition to its general terms, the Declaration calls for a number of actions to be taken by governments and for there to be follow-up discussions on implementation. The United Nations Commission on Social Development was created to oversee that effort. The Cairo conference on global population issues of the preceding year had laid the groundwork for recommendations adopted at the Copenhagen meeting but did not go as far. The United Nations World Conference on Women, held in Beijing in September 1995, was one forum in which the results of the Cairo and Copenhagen meetings were considered further. A less well-known but important follow-up to the Copenhagen meeting was the Conference on Administration of Social Policy in Stockholm in October 1995, at which efforts were made to take a more detailed look at how to structure and operate social policies more effectively and in terms of the needs of the future. The Habitat II conference in Istanbul, formally known as the U.N. Conference on Human Settlements, held during June 1996, produced a global plan of action that is particularly interesting to local government administrators since it focuses on the development of sustainable communities.

Another set of global expectations emerged from the 1992 Earth Summit in Rio de Janeiro. That meeting produced a number of treaties on the environment but also gave birth to Agenda 21, which is a global plan for sustainable development that is much more comprehensive than anything that had come before. Institutionally, it produced the U.N. Commission on Sustainable Development with counterpart commissions in each nation. It also produced agreements on a mechanism for funding sustainable development projects around the world, known as the Global Environmental Facility. Between the broad Agenda 21 process and the more specific treaties on various areas of the environment, the United States and many other nations had to develop administrative infrastructure and modify existing information practices to meet the global agreements. To get some sense of the scope of these activities, one need only consult U.S. government and environmental listings on the World-Wide Web of the Internet.

While the examples of this growing set of international expectations are increasing rapidly, there is one more example of which public administrators at all levels of government, even local communities in the heartland of the United States, must be aware. It is the General Agreement on Tariffs and Trade, known by its acronym, GATT. The World Trade Organization, created by GATT, is designed to address a wide range of trade issues, including disputes over regulations within nations and their subdivisions that are considered to pose barriers to trade. Thus, there have already been a number of nations considering whether to bring action against the United States or individual states where it is perceived that excessively strong regulations prevent the importation or distribution of goods manufactured abroad. There is also concern with local purchase policies and the degree to which they form barriers to trade. Under the procedures of the World Trade Organization, states and local governments are dependent on the national government to defend them before the WTO or to grant permission for the subnational units (states or local governments) to defend themselves. While it is as yet uncertain exactly how the WTO will figure in domestic administration, there is no doubt that GATT and similar international agreements are expected to play an increasing role.

Regional Realities

At the regional level, the North American Free Trade Agreement (NAFTA) is already an important reality. Presently consisting of Canada, Mexico, and the

United States, there are efforts under way in Central and South America to expand NAFTA to cover all of the Americas. This is only one of a number of important regional efforts around the world to develop strength among the nations of a region that none of them possesses individually. Certainly that effort has been a critical fact of life in Europe, where, for example, European Union decisions have in many important areas displaced national policies in important areas of regulation. Member states have been brought to answer for violation of EU standards. Great Britain was one of the first to experience the enforcement effort, as it was called, to respond to charges of beach pollution in excess of EU environmental rules. In Asia, efforts have been under way to bring the so-called Asian tigers together with less politically or economically powerful states to meet the challenge of Europe and NAFTA. The ASEAN nations, as their alliance is called, are increasingly expressing their views with one voice. Latin America appeared headed for its own regional alliance until several nations began the movement toward an expansion of NAFTA to cover all of the western hemisphere, an effort that is under way at the time of this writing.

The first to feel the effects of NAFTA were the local governments near major border crossing points, such as the one in Laredo, Texas. The implementation of such agreements does not just mean the dismantling of tariff barriers; it also implies the development of a governance infrastructure to support a variety of expanded interactions, of which trade is certainly an important element. However, it is unclear whether the states entering into regional agreements are ready to build an administrative structure adequate to fully implement and operate the regional agreements.

On the other hand, there are small-scale regional efforts that are having immediate administrative impact. For example, a number of Caribbean islands have cooperated to keep well-trained environmental administrators who are tempted by attractive private-sector offers to leave public service by hiring those highly skilled people as regional experts working for several countries. It is a way to keep human resources regionally that none of the small island states could have individually. This kind of cooperative effort will be more important in future years.

Common Trends in Comparative Public Administration

There is a range of common trends in administration across nations today, quite apart from these large regional or international activities. They include deregulation, delayering, decentralization, reengineering, privatization, accountability enhancements, and technological development.

Deregulation

There is no question that there has been an international trend toward deregulation and increased use of market mechanisms to achieve public sector goals. Moreover, one of the most common themes in political change of the past decade has been the effort to get rid of what are termed *command-and-control regulation systems*.[15] Indeed, as the size of government shrinks, there will necessarily be greater reliance on market-based policy tools.[16]

There are five essential elements to this drive. First, regulations should not be imposed unless they are truly necessary. Second, they are not truly necessary if there is some less intrusive mechanism for obtaining the same results. Third, there are market-oriented tools that rely on incentives, information, and market choice that avoid the need for regulation. Fourth, if regulations do appear to be needed, it is essential to ensure that the potential impacts of those programs are carefully analyzed before they are imposed. Finally, if they are imposed, they should be as flexible as possible and oriented toward a risk-assessment approach to determine how much action is truly needed given enforcement costs.

At the same time that there has been international demand for deregulation, there have been equally loud calls for more and better health care, working conditions, and protection of the environment. Indeed, it has become very clear that regulation is needed to protect markets from abuses by traders. In one case, a young securities trader brought down one of the world's oldest and most established banks. In another, a single trader working for a major Japanese bank caused instability in the world copper market through manipulations of accounts in the copper mining field. Regulation is, and will continue to be, a critically important task of government. Some forms of behavior simply will not be tolerated by society, and no effort at providing incentives would ever likely be adequate to stop that behavior without a threat of sanctions. Moreover, many of the recently adopted international agreements call for more regulation, rather than less. That is true of regional governing structures like the EU as well as for specific international agreements like environmental treaties or human rights accords. Finally, the ability to employ market-based tools depends on market supports and the availability of resources to support incentives. However, the international financial support has not been available to build some of these structures.[17] Indeed, some of the difficulties with structural adjustment policies and other requirements imposed by the international community (including some by those who are the most vigorous advocates of deregulation) have exacerbated economic difficulties and have made it very difficult to use alternatives to regulation.[18]

For all these reasons, the future will involve the use of traditional and alternative techniques of regulation based on market principles like the use of incentives, fees, permits, and the like. Even these techniques, which do not purport to have a command-and-control character to them, present problems not unlike those administrators have dealt with in other contexts. A permitting system means that administrators must have standards against which to evaluate applications, enforcement techniques to ensure that the terms of the permits are honored, and devices by which to suspend or revoke permits if those standards are violated.

There is another factor to be considered apart from the questions of the relationships between older regulatory techniques and newer alternatives. Market-based policy tools do not run themselves. Special-use fees, specialized taxes, and subsidies all require creation of an infrastructure and regular operating techniques. Devices that call for pricing that incorporates all costs, including things like pollution or social impacts, must be paid to someone who must in turn take action to clean up pollution or provide the social services. Labelling requirements that inform consumers, who presumably take the place of a regulator by making market choices, must still be monitored to ensure the accuracy and availability of all necessary information in forms that consumers can understand. Programs that are based on the performance of impact analyses or risk assessments for proposed industrial activity must also provide means and resources for government organizations to evaluate both the integrity and the substance of the assessments submitted.

Decentralization

Decentralization has been just as popular as deregulation, but the term can mean different things to different people. In its fullest form, decentralization involves an attempt to increase participatory democracy by sending not only the responsibility for program implementation, but also authority for decision making to the local community, or at least to the closest level possible to those most directly affected by the policy. Thus, there has long been a desire to decentralize social-service programs—from education to health care to housing—down to the local-government level. Such efforts had been undertaken in many developing countries even before decentralization became popular in developed countries like the United States. Compared to countries in Latin America, Africa, and parts of Europe, the United States is a latecomer to the process. That is all the more ironic in light of the fact that the United States has a federal structure while most of the other countries that have already implemented various types of decentralization employ unitary governments.

On the other hand, it is important to look closely at what is meant by *decentralization*. If all that is involved is the operation of local offices, schools, or clinics, without delegation to those units of significant decision-making authority, it is not true decentralization. Moreover, where responsibilities are transferred to the state (called by different names in different countries) or local level without resources, the delegation amounts to little more than what we have discussed earlier as unfunded mandates. Unfortunately, it has been a common model in Latin America and in Africa to retain most significant policy-making authority at the national level and to transfer service delivery responsibility to local governments. Scandinavian countries have a long tradition of important local government involvement, but in some instances they also use a model in which local governments become contractors paid to provide certain types of services. Local governments in Finland, for instance, provide services to refugees under contracts with the national government.[19]

One of the most interesting tests of whether decentralization is serious involves handing subnational units significant budgetary discretion. There has been a trend in many countries to provide more spending authority to individual agencies or units of government and then to increase accountability demands in terms of performance standards and actual enhanced accounting requirements.[20] As Naomi Caiden has pointed out, however, these experiments are relatively new, and it remains to be seen how they will fare over time, particularly in periods of financial scarcity.[21]

As the intergovernmental relations chapters indicated, the experience in the United States with decentralized expenditure discretion has been mixed. Interestingly enough, revenue sharing, which represents the most discretionary money available to states and localities, was eliminated by a conservative Republican administration, although it had been originally developed on precisely the grounds that it was a way of really moving decision authority to local communities. Block grants gave the next widest range of latitude, but they were constrained as well, with substantial budget cuts coming with modest increases in local discretion. The most recent efforts to move toward block grants is an experiment that may very well be in trouble before they are even implemented. That is true because state and local administrators already anticipate that the amounts of federal dollars will be decreased over the next few years and may even be eliminated if the federal government succeeds in removing legal entitlement of qualified recipients to have those dollars. For that reason, many local administrators fear that the current talk of decentralization really means a devolution of responsibility but not a true decentralization of government.

Reengineering

When these discussions about the restructuring of authority and responsibility take place within organizations rather than between levels of government, they are generally referred to as reengineering. Reengineering emerged as a preferred concept after it became clear that "downsizing" (simply reducing the size of an organization) and "right sizing" (downsizing, but only to the level at which the organization could function effectively) were too narrow. Reengineering argues for a complete reconfiguration of organizations and a continuous effort to fine-tune in order to achieve a high-performance organization.

Based on the idea that what should matter are results, reengineering suggests that organizations must be remade in the manner that renders the agency best able to meet its mission, whatever that might be. An organization that continually learns from its experiences and can meet the changes in its environment must be adaptable not merely in minor incremental ways, but must also be capable of transforming itself when necessary. That is no small task, for reasons pointed out in the earlier chapters on organization theory and behavior (see chapters 8 and 9).

One of the most popular trends associated with reengineering is "delayering," which refers to the effort to make organizations flatter by eliminating layers of middle management. The object, in addition to achieving savings associated with those cuts, is to move the top management closer to the level of line managers and their service delivery personnel. In theory, that should reduce communications difficulties and render the organization more responsive as well as more efficient.

However, delayering is one of the least well understood of the public management trends of the 1990s. The idea was that what middle managers primarily do is to work on issues of control which, it is said, could be accomplished by more effective use of computer systems. However, it turns out in practice that when those managers leave there are other functions that get lost in the transformation.[22] Middle managers mitigate conflict, plan, coordinate, and ensure accountability beyond simple control. It is clear that there are also issues of morale associated with their departure. It is not easy to recruit and retain high-quality line managers and service professions into an organization in which they have no real hope of significant career progression because the middle rungs on the career ladder have been eliminated.

To meet the cut in middle management, top managers use teaming in which line managers are brought together as problem-solving groups. Another alternative is the use of internal consulting arrangements in which individual line managers with special expertise are identified to help out in other parts of the organization when there is a need. The plus side of that arrangement is that, in theory at least, line managers would be empowered as they came to play more important decision-making roles in the organization. In practice, however, it also means fewer people accepting more responsibility to do more work without little or no additional compensation. It also means that the energy that top managers devote to working directly with their line supervisors cannot be used to deal with other organizations in their agency's environment at a time when that environment is more turbulent than ever. All of these forces have a tendency to lead to burnout.

The difficulties with organizations that are finely tuned for high performance is not unlike what we see in high-performance racing cars or racehorses. They can be honed to a razor's edge for high performance in a very special kind of task. However, they require a great deal of care if they are to remain at that level since high performance leads to burnout and breakdown if they are pushed too hard or too long. The most important problem is that they are also not designed for change. A formula-one racing machine is designed for a very special kind of task and nothing else. It cannot be easily adapted for a different kind of race. If one prefers an organic metaphor instead of a mechanical picture, a thoroughbred racehorse trained for normal races cannot be expected to be a pacer or a trotter or to beat quarter horses in their race.

The point is that there are dangers in reengineering that we are only beginning to recognize. A finely tuned organization may break down more easily than one with some flexibility built into it. Moreover, adaptability requires some amount of slack resources within an organization. Which value matters most, efficiency or adaptability? Do we want maximum performance from the public service in the short term, or do we want to ensure the maintenance of a highly qualified and well-motivated body of public managers over the longer term? These are all difficult choices.

There is another difficulty in attempts to create and operate high-performance organizations. It is one thing to fine-tune delicate, high-performance machines in a sophisticated government with the resources to allow for specialization. It is quite another to do so in developing countries where the conditions just do not exist to build and operate a grand-prix racing machine. A good, strong plow horse may be needed far more than a thoroughbred.

The Empowering Effects of High Technology

Much of the reengineering effort assumes that complex information management technologies will make these dramatic transformations possible. We expect not only that computers will speed communications and put decision support techniques at every manager's fingertips, but they will also provide a thread linking the pieces of complex loosely coupled organizations together. Beyond that internal use of technology, though, is the effort to link organizations and even create virtual organizations in cyberspace, that place "out there" on the Internet where everyone in the world can instantly communicate. In fact, the question is not merely how organizations will be able to make use of the torrent of information that can be acquired on the Net, but also how those organizations will be changed by that process.[23]

While there is a much wider use of computers and on-line communications in developed countries than anyone would have anticipated only a few short years ago, we are not all "wired" as the expression goes. Although most offices in developed countries have a computer, many people use them only for word processing or, if they are particularly adventuresome, for electronic mail. Even then, a great deal of organizational time and resources are dedicated to the purchase and maintenance of computer hardware and software. Hard-pressed employees often have little or no time to attend training sessions on how to use particular pieces of software, let alone to design more effective management strategies that take advantage of the capabilities of the equipment. Even very sophisticated organizations still have considerable difficulty developing and maintaining effective and user-friendly systems.

These problems exist in well-resourced sophisticated organizations in the developed countries. The situation is considerably worse in developing countries. The history of public administration is rich with examples of what happens when efforts are made to transfer technology to developing countries when they are not well-adapted to the situation. Reengineering assumes more than the presence of a few personal computers in a number of offices within a ministry. It requires complex systems of compatible hardware and software as well as customized communications systems that simply do not exist in many developing countries. Beyond the technology itself, there are important implications for the behavior patterns within organizations that flow from the introduction of high technology into the workplace. It takes a great deal of effort to render that technology, and the work ways that come with it, an integral part of the organization's day-to-day operation. And if one equips, trains, and alters an agency's culture to meet high-technology standards, there remains the question of communicating and coordinating with other parts of the government that may not have achieved that level of progress. Even in developed countries at the turn of the century there are still many offices that do not have easily accessible e-mail systems or ready access to the World-Wide Web of the Internet.

There is no doubt that high technology is and must be an important part of management in the modern world, but it is dangerous simply to assume too much about how that technology can be brought into organizations. It is important as to study how that technology will be used by organizations, but we must also consider how it will transform them.

Privatization

One of the most widely discussed trends in contemporary public management is privatization. Actually, the term is often applied to contract delivery of services, but there is often no true privatization because the basic authority and responsibility for delivery of services is retained by the public sector. Certainly, contracted government is at the heart of the reinventing government movement.[24]

Interestingly, privatization has been in use in developing countries for many years and not just in developed countries. Even so, public administration still has much to learn about how to operate a government by contract,

Very few places on the globe today are entirely unaffected by modern technology. In Bangladesh, one of the world's poorest nations, the old technology represented by a hand-pushed freight cart is juxtaposed with the modern technology embodied in a sophisticated camera shop.
(Photo courtesy of Phillip Cooper.)

particularly in contracting for services. This is an area in which the United States can learn from the experience of the Scandinavian countries. A great deal of attention has been paid in many governments to bid processes to prevent corruption in the awarding of contracts. However, the more complex challenges concern the actual administration of contracts.

That means, among other things, that it is important to recruit and train public managers with strong negotiations skills. They must also be educated in contract administration skills, which in many countries are different in the public sector than they are in private business. For ministries that are not able to recruit new people, this necessity will require major retraining efforts.

Contracts have been popular for several reasons, including the fact that it is possible to keep the size of the public ministries small. It is also presumed that there will be increased flexibility that comes from administering by agreement rather than by public bureaucracies governed by complex systems of rules. On the other hand, contracts are sets of rules that are accepted by the contracting parties. They are just as binding, and may be just as constraining as administrative regulations. In some cases, firms that provide services to developing countries require that disputes be settled in courts in the firm's home country under the contract law of that jurisdiction. From the firm's point of view, the problem is that they simply are not prepared to submit themselves to the tender mercies of courts that may not be considered wholly neutral. From the contracting ministry's perspective there is a new kind of problem. They have gone from operating under regulations that they administer to the situation under contracts in which they are merely one party. If there is a difficulty, the agency is not the authoritative decision maker but merely one participant in a dispute to be decided by a court over which they have no control and that is not easily accountable to their political institutions. There is also every likelihood that the firms involved can hire more legal talent than small countries can retain in foreign tribunals.

On the other hand, contracts offer an opportunity to foster employment in the private sector, particularly in basic service organizations that can hire people with limited education and skills and bring them into the formal economy as taxpaying participating citizens. This approach also means that where there are market competitors, ministries can take advantage of the efficiencies that can be obtained with market forces. Contracts also provide a mechanism for working more effectively with international nongovernmental organizations that can bring experience and expertise to complex problems on a temporary basis rather than by setting up more or less permanent agencies.

There is every reason to believe that privatization will continue to be an important force in public management around the globe. It is, however, not a panacea but a tool. Like all tools, it can be potentially dangerous if not used properly. Specifically, mechanisms of accountability must be constructed and maintained if contract government is to be a servant of the public interest rather than a danger to it.

Accountability

For many developed countries, the effort to ensure that unelected public officials remain accountable has been a central concern of public administration for more than a century. There have been two important sets of issues with respect to accountability in recent years.

First, the mechanisms of accountability have been changing. Until relatively recently, countries with a parliamentary tradition, particularly those using the so-called Westminster model found in Great Britain and countries in its sphere of influence, have employed a system that is known as ministerial responsibility. In that approach, ministers are individually responsible for the performance of their ministries and collectively responsible, under the leadership of the prime minister, for the actions of their government.[25] Career public servants are to be dealt with within the ministry. Ministers are responsible to answer on the floor of Parliament for problems within their agencies and, in theory at least, to resign if the maladministration is serious enough. In practice they do not resign but are expected to explain what has been done to correct the problem and ensure that it does not happen again. The idea is not so much to respond to an individual claim by an injured citizen who asserts a kind of legal right but to have political accountability. The form is different in other parliamentary countries, but the tendency to emphasize political accountability through ministers has been common.

On the other hand, the United States and a few other countries have emphasized legal accountability in which citizens demand recompense for injuries, monetary or otherwise, that they have suffered as result of maladministration. Few Americans accept the idea that legislative oversight is an adequate mechanism for ensuring an accountable administration. Thus, American administrative law features a complex system of administrative appeals, judicial review, and even the possibility of suing individual officials or communities for damages.

There has been a tendency in recent years for those two poles to converge. There have been numerous examples of subjects in parliamentary regimes thinking of themselves as citizens rather than subjects and asserting what they regard as their individual legal rights in court against public officials and their ministries.[26] In the United States, by contrast, there has been a criticism of traditional legal approaches to accountability and a move to consider overall political accountability more important than in the past.[27]

Into the midst of this convergence, however, has come the growing importance of market accountability as a third force.[28] Market accountability emphasizes performance measures of accountability in which service to customers is the metaphor used to guide assessment. Market accountability emphasizes an economic efficiency premise that may take several forms. There is a cost dimension in which the assumption is that anything that costs less is better. That is a statement about economy rather than what is normally considered efficiency,[29] but the distinctions are often lost in the political arena. The second dimension of market accountability is a cost/benefit approach in which a government action meets the test of market accountability if, and only if, it has a positive cost/benefit calculation. The cost/benefit approach may vary from a simple admonition to show that the real impacts of government action have been carefully considered in advance of implementation to a far more complex set of calculations. Third, there are performance standards, often anchored in a kind of input/output efficiency model, with the emphasis on outputs and outcomes. The focus, indeed, is most often on measurable outcomes. The measurement of results is valued over control by rules or by hierarchical authority. Finally, there is an approach emphasizing client satisfaction. It assumes that if customers receive adequate levels of quality service at a good price, then accountability is achieved. This approach views citizens or subjects as consumers or customers. One variation on this model is the market-choice perspective typified by voucher programs. Again, the assumptions of the marketplace concerning knowledge and competition are applied. If given choices, consumers will select the better services. Those organizations that win the customers, whether they are public or private institutions, will prosper by virtue of their performance.

There are a number of difficulties with these approaches, including the premises that assume that public policies should function as fee-for-service operations. Social development policies, for example, are not created by governments as fee-for-service programs. Indeed, most of those considered customers are poor and cannot pay enough taxes to begin to defray the costs of the services. It is one thing to design programs to treat clients of social services well but quite another to assume that that is how one should structure accountability. In many developing countries, for example, market-based systems only ensure that existing two-tier structures of social services are reinforced. Finally, there is the fact that market-based approaches failed to distinguish between clients and constituents. Policies affect many citizens who are not the primary clients targeted for service. Ministries have an obligation to address accountability concerns both for the clients and for that wider constituency.

Second, developing countries have largely been ignored in international discussions of accountability. There has been a tendency to ignore accountability issues in developing countries, apparently on the theory that where countries have had a long history of colonial, military, or authoritarian rule there is little reason to talk of administrative accountability as that concept has been traditionally understood. In some developing countries, courts have not traditionally been places where those aggrieved by government actions could obtain redress, and political systems have not been concerned with mass support that must be maintained with attention to accountability.

However, there is growing evidence that citizens of developing countries are demanding accountability. The recent history of South Africa, Haiti, Mexico, Brazil, Venezuela, and some of the Newly Independent States of Eastern Europe shows an effort to force accountability, even at the highest levels of government. To the degree that those demands are meeting with sympathetic listeners who are also treaty partners of the country involved, there are also international expectations of accountability, though much remains to be done before it will be clear just what form that accountability will take.

Conclusion

There has never been a time when public administration could not benefit from a comparative perspective. Unfortunately, there has been a tendency of many systems of public management to look inward, consumed by day-to-day problems. In the current environment, with global connections not in the future but right at hand, there is no choice for any wise administrator but to occasionally look up from the pile on the desk and learn from counterparts in other jurisdictions and other parts of the world.

There are forces that are indeed moving different systems of public administration closer to one another. At the same time, comparability does not mean a lack of difference, and there are forces tending to emphasize uniqueness even as the world seems to be shrinking. Precisely because of these competing tendencies, it is important to consider what can be shared but remain alert to the different ways in which ideas, institutions, and processes look and act in different political and cultural settings.

Amidst all of the differences, it is relatively easy to identify a set of trends in public administration. A comparative perspective on these approaches to meeting the future needs of the field will reveal far more than assessments that look only to our own backyard.

Notes

[1]Alexander Hamilton, James Madison, and John Jay, *The Federalist* (New York: Mentor, 1961).

[2]Woodrow Wilson, "The Study of Administration," *Political Science Quarterly* 2 (1887): 209–213.

[3]Frank Goodnow, *Comparative Administrative Law* (New York: Putnam, 1893).

[4]Ernst Freund, *Administrative Powers over Persons and Property* (Chicago: University of Chicago Press, 1928).

[5]See e.g., Robert A. Dahl, "The Science of Public Administration: Three Problems," *Public Administration Review* 7 (Winter 1947): 1–11; and Herbert A. Simon, "A Comment on 'The Science of Public Administration,'" *Public Administration Review* 7 (Summer 1947): 200–203.

[6]See Ferrel Heady, *Public Administration: A Comparative Perspective* (Englewood Cliffs, NJ: Prentice-Hall, 1966).

[7]"Trends in the Comparative Study of Public Administration," *International Review of Administrative Sciences* 38 no. 1 (1962): 9–15; *Administration in Developing Countries* (Boston: Houghton-Mifflin, 1964); see also Dwight Waldo, ed., "Comparative and Development Administration: Retrospect and Prospect," *Public Administration Review* 36 (Nov./Dec. 1976): 615–654.

[8]Dwight Waldo, "Public Administration," *Journal of Politics* 30, no. 2 (May 1968): 469–473.

[9]See e.g., Montgomery Van Wart and N. Joseph Cayer, "Comparative Public Administration: Defunct, Dispersed, or Redefined?" *Public Administration Review* 50 (Mar./Apr. 1990): 238–248; and B. Guy Peters, *The Politics of Bureaucracy,* 4th ed. (White Plains, NY: Longman, 1995), 12.

[10]See e.g., Tim Knudsen, ed., *Welfare Administration in Denmark* (Copenhagen: Danish Ministry of Finance, 1991).

[11]C. Neal Tate and Torbjorn Vallinder, eds., *The Global Expansion of Judicial Power* (New York: New York University Press, 1995.)

[12]Daniel Elazar, *American Federalism: A View from the States* (New York: Crowell, 1966).

[13]Edgar Schein, *Organizational Culture and Leadership,* 2nd ed. (San Francisco: Jossey-Bass, 1992).

[14]World Summit for Social Development, *The Copenhagen Declaration and Programme of Action* (New York: United Nations, 1995), Commitment 8, 27.

[15]David Osborne and Ted Gaebler, *Reinventing Government* (New York: Penguin, 1992); Report of the National Performance Review, *From Red Tape to Results: Creating a Government That Works Better and Costs Less* (Washington, DC: Government Printing Office, 1993).

[16]Lester M. Salamon, ed., *Beyond Privatization: The Tools of Government Action.* (Washington, DC: Urban Institute, 1989).

[17]See e.g., Roger D. Stone, *The Nature of Development* (New York: Alfred A. Knopf, 1992).

[18]Barbara Jancar-Webster, ed., *Environmental Action in Eastern Europe: Responses to Crisis* (Armonk, NY: M.E. Sharpe, 1993).

402 CHAPTER 13 | Comparative Public Administration

[19]Interview with Mr. Jouni Helenius, Ministry of Social Welfare, Helsinki, Finland, July 7, 1994.

[20]See Naomi Caiden, "The Management of Public Budgeting," in Randall Baker, ed., *Comparative Public Management* (Westport, CT: Praeger, 1994).

[21]*Ibid.*, 147.

[22]Patricia W. Ingraham and Dale Jones, "The Pain of Organizational Change: Managing Reinvention," unpublished paper presented at the Third National Public Management Research Conference, Lawrence, Kansas, October 1995.

[23]Chris C. Demchak, "'Webbing' American and European Public Agencies," unpublished paper presented at the Third National Public Management Research Conference, Lawrence, Kansas, October 1995.

[24]See Osborne and Gaebler, *op. cit.*

[25]S. L. Sutherland, "The Al-Mashat Affair," *Canadian Public Administration* 34 (Winter 1992): 573–603.

[26]See Tate and Vallinder, *op. cit.*

[27]Report of the National Performance Review, *op. cit.*

[28]This argument is present in more detail in "Accountability and Administrative Reform," in B. Guy Peters and Donald J. Savoie, eds., *Governance in a Changing Environment* (Ottawa: Canadian Centre for Management Development, 1995).

[29]Henry Mintzberg, "A Note on that Dirty Word 'Efficiency'," *Interfaces* 5 (October): 101–105.

Bibliography

The following works are recommended as leading references on each of the topics addressed in the text. They are organized by chapter.

Chapter 1   Public Administration for the Twenty-First Century: Beyond Reform

Bailey, Stephen K. "Ethics and the Public Service," in Roscoe Martin, ed. *Public Administration and Democracy* (Syracuse, NY: Syracuse University, 1965).

Cooper, Terry L. and N. Dale Wright, eds. *Exemplary Public Administrators* (San Francisco: Jossey-Bass, 1992).

Daly, Herman E. *Beyond Growth: The Economics of Sustainable Development* (Boston: Beacon Press, 1996).

Doig, James W. and Erwin C. Hargrove. *Leadership and Innovation* (Baltimore: Johns Hopkins University Press, 1990).

Downs, George W. and Patrick D. Larkey. *The Search for Government Efficiency* (New York: Random House, 1986).

Gerth, H.H. and C. Wright Mills, eds. *From Max Weber: Essays in Sociology* (New York: Oxford, 1946).

Gladden, E.N. *History of Public Administration* (London: Frank Cass, 1972).

Goodsell, Charles. *The Case for Bureaucracy, 3rd ed.* (Chatham, NJ: Chatham House, 1994).

Gore, Al. *From Red Tape to Results: Creating A Government That Works Better & Costs Less*. Report of the National Performance Review (Washington, DC: Government Printing Office, 1993).

Gulick, Luther and Lyndal Urwick. *Papers on the Science of Administration* (Fairfield, NJ: Augustus M. Kelley Publishers, 1977 [originally published by the Institute of Public Administration, New York, 1937]).

Hamilton, Alexander, James Madison, and John Jay. *The Federalist Papers* (New York: Mentor, 1961).

Hauchler, Ingomar and Paul M. Kennedy. *Global Trends* (New York: Continuum Publishing, 1993).

Ingraham, Patricia W. and Barbara S. Romzek, eds. *New Paradigms for Government* (San Francisco: Jossey-Bass, 1994).

Jacoby, Henry. *The Bureaucratization of the World* (Berkeley, CA: University of California Press, 1973).

Kennedy, Paul. *Preparing for the Twenty-First Century* (New York: Random House, 1993).

Link, Arthur S., ed. *The Papers of Woodrow Wilson* (Princeton, NJ: Princeton University Press, 1968–69).

Nalbandian, John. *Professionalism in Local Government: Transformations in the Roles, Responsibilities, and Values of City Managers* (San Francisco: Jossey-Bass, 1991).

Osborne, David and Ted Gaebler. *Reinventing Government* (New York: Penguin, 1993).

Reagan, Michael. *The New Federalism* (New York: Oxford University Press, 1972).

Rohr, John. *To Run A Constitution* (Lawrence, KS: Kansas University Press, 1986).

Rusk, David. *Cities Without Suburbs* (Washington, DC: Woodrow Wilson Center Press, 1993).

Schumpeter, Joseph. *Capitalism, Socialism, and Democracy,* 3rd ed. (New York: Harper & Row, 1950).

Stone, Roger D. *The Nature of Development* (New York: Alfred A. Knopf, 1992).

Tate, C. Neal and Torbjorn Vallinder, eds. *The Global Expansion of Judicial Power* (New York: New York University Press, 1995).

Waldo, Dwight. *The Enterprise of Public Administration* (Novato, CA: Chandler & Sharp, 1980).

White, Leonard D. *Introduction to the Study of Public Administration,* 4th ed. (New York: Macmillan, 1955).

Wilson, James Q. *The Moral Sense* (New York: Free Press, 1993).

Wilson, Woodrow. "The Study of Administration," *Political Science Quarterly* 2 (June 1887): 209–213.

Wood, Robert. *Suburbia* (Boston: Houghton Mifflin, 1958).

World Resources Institute. *World Resources,* 1992–93 (New York: Oxford, 1992).

Chapter 2   Legal Basis and Framework of Public Administration

Easton, David. *The Political System* (New York: Knopf, 1971).

Finer, S.E., ed. *Five Constitutions* (New York: Penguin, 1979).

Fisher, Louis. *Constitutional Conflicts Between Congress and the President,* 4th ed. (Lawrence, KS: Kansas University Press, 1997).

———— . *Constitutional Dialogues* (Princeton, NJ: Princeton University Press, 1988).

Gerth, H.H. and C. Wright Mills, eds. *From Max Weber: Essays in Sociology* (New York: Oxford University Press, 1946).

Hamilton, Alexander, James Madison, and John Jay. *The Federalist* (New York: Mentor, 1961).

McIlwain, Charles Howard. *Constitutionalism: Ancient & Modern* (Ithaca, NY: Cornell University Press, 1947).

Rohr, John. *To Run A Constitution* (Lawrence, KS: Kansas University Press, 1986).

Wilson, Woodrow. "The Study of Administration," *Political Science Quarterly* 2 (1887): 209–213.

Chapter 3   Law Against Ethics: Legal Accountability and Ethical Responsibility

Chapman, Brian. *The Profession of Government* (London: Unwin University Books, 1971).

Cooper, Phillip J. *Hard Judicial Choices* (New York: Oxford University Press, 1988).

_____ . "The Supreme Court on Governmental Liability: The Nature and Origins of Sovereign and Official Immunity," *Administration & Society* 16 (November 1984): 259–288.

Cooper, Terry. *The Responsible Administrator* (Port Washington, NY: Kennikat, 1982).

Finer, Herman. "Better Government Personnel: America's Next Frontier," *Political Science Quarterly* 51 (December 1936): 569–599.

_____ . "Administrative Responsibility in Democratic Government," *Public Administration Review* 1 (Summer 1941): 335–350.

Fleishman, Joel L., Lance Liebman, Marck H. Moore, eds. *Public Duties: The Moral Obligations of Government Officials* (Cambridge, MA: Harvard University Press, 1981).

Friedrich, Carl. "Public Policy and the Nature of Administrative Responsibility," in C.J. Friedrich and E.S. Mason, eds. *Public Policy* (Cambridge, MA: Harvard University Press, 1940).

Hamilton, Alexander, James Madison, and John Jay. *The Federalist Papers* (New York: Mentor, 1961).

Harriger, Katy J. *Independent Justice: The Federal Special Prosecutor in American Politics* (Lawrence, KS: Kansas University Press, 1992).

Hirschman, Albert O. *Exit, Voice, and Loyalty* (Cambridge, MA: Harvard University Press, 1970).

Mosher, Frederick C. *Democracy and the Public Service,* 2nd ed. (New York: Oxford University Press, 1982).

Richardson, William and Lloyd Nigro. "Administrative Ethics and Founding Thought: Constitutional Correctives, Honor, and Education," *Public Administration Review 47* (September/October 1987): 367–376.

Rohr, John. "Ethical Issues in French Public Administration: A Comparative Study," *Public Administration Review 51* (July/August 1991): 283–297.

_____ . *Ethics for Bureaucrats,* 2nd ed. (New York: Marcel Dekker, 1989).

Rosenbloom, David. "Public Administrators, Official Immunity, and the Supreme Court: Developments During the 1970's," *Public Administration Review* 40 (March/April 1980): 166–173.

Suleiman, Ezra N. *Politics, Power, and Bureaucracy in France* (Princeton, NJ: Princeton University Press, 1974).

Wood, Robert. *Remedial Law* (Amherst, MA: University of Massachusetts Press, 1991).

Chapter 4   The Intergovernmental Policy Structure and Action

Advisory Commission on Intergovernmental Relations. *Multi-State Regionalism* (Washington, DC: Government Printing Office, 1972).

_____ . *Regulations, Regulatory Federalism: Process, Impact, and Reform* (Washington, DC: Government Printing Office, 1984).

Conlan, Timothy, J. and David R. Beam, "Federal Mandates: The Record of Reform and Future Prospects," *Intergovernmental Perspective,* 18 (Fall 1992): 7–11.

Council of State Governments. *The Book of The States,* 1992–93 ed. (Lexington, KY:

The Council of State Governments, 1992).

Elazar, Daniel J. *American Federalism: A View from the States,* 2nd ed. (New York: Thomas Y. Crowell, 1972).

Grodzins, Morton. *The American System: A New View of Governments in the United States* (Chicago: Rand McNally, 1966).

Henry, Nicholas. *Governing at the Grassroots: State and Local Politics* (Englewood Cliffs, NJ: Prentice-Hall, 1980).

National Research Council. *Toward an Understanding of Metropolitan America* (San Francisco: Canfield, 1975).

Rusk, David. *Cities Without Suburbs* (Washington, DC: Woodrow Wilson Center Press, 1993).

Schuman, David and Dick W. Olufs III. *Public Administration in the United States,* 2nd ed. (Lexington, MA: D.C. Heath and Company).

Saidel, Judith R. "Resource Interdependence: The Relationship Between State Agencies and Nonprofit Organizations," *Public Administration Review 51* (November/December 1991): 543–553.

Wright, Deil S. *Understanding Intergovernmental Relations,* 3rd ed. (Pacific Grove, CA: Brooks/Cole Publishing, 1988).

Chapter 5   Fiscal Federalism and Its Constitutional Foundations

Buchanan, James M. and Gordon Tullock. *The Calculus of Consent* (Ann Arbor, MI: University of Michigan Press, 1962).

Musgrave, Richard A. and Peggy B. Musgrave. *Public Finance Theory and Practice,* 2nd ed. (New York: McGraw Hill, 1976).

Osborne, David and Ted Gaebler. *Reinventing Government* (New York: Penguin, 1993).

Ostrum, Vincent. *The Intellectual Crisis in American Public Administration,* 2nd ed. (Tuscaloosa, AL: University of Alabama Press, 1989).

Peterson, Paul E. *The Price of Federalism* (Washington, DC: Brookings, 1995).

Reagan, Michael. *The New Federalism* (New York: Oxford University Press, 1972).

Rivlin, Alice M. *Reviving the American Dream: The Economy, the States, and the Federal Government* (Washington, DC: Brookings Institution, 1992).

Rusk, David. *Cities Without Suburbs* (Washington, DC: Woodrow Wilson Center Press, 1993).

Schwartz, Bernard. *Super Chief* (New York: New York University Press, 1980).

U.S. General Accounting Office. *Block Grants: Characteristics, Experience, and Lessons Learned* (Washington, DC: Government Printing Office, 1995).

Waldo, Dwight. *The Administrative State* (New York: Ronald Press, 1948).

Wright, Deil. *Understanding Intergovernmental Relations,* 3rd ed. (Pacific Grove, CA: Brooks/Cole Publishers, 1988).

Wright, Deil and Harvey L. White. *Federalism and Intergovernmental Relations* (Washington, DC: American Society for Public Administration, 1984).

Chapter 6   Public Policy in Administration

Adams, Guy B., ed. *Policymaking, Communication, and Social Learning* (New

Brunswick, NJ: Transaction Books, 1987).

Allison, Graham. *Essence of Decision* (Boston: Little, Brown, 1971).

Anderson, Charles W. *Statecraft* (New York: John Wiley and Sons, 1977).

Bullard, Robert D. *Dumping on Dixie* (Boulder, CO: Westview Press, 1990).

Bardach, Eugene. *The Implementation Game* (Cambridge, MA: MIT Press, 1977).

Bullock, Charles S., III, et al. *Public Policy in the Eighties* (Monterey, CA: Brooks/Cole Publishing, 1983).

Castles, Frances, ed. *The Comparative History of Public Policy* (Cambridge, MA: Polity Press, 1989).

Dahl, Robert. *Who Governs* (New Haven, CT: Yale University Press, 1961).

deLeon, Peter. *Advice and Consent* (New York: Russell Sage Foundation, 1988).

Domhof, Eric. *The Higher Circles* (New York: Random House, 1970).

Dror, Yehezkel. *Design for the Policy Sciences* (New York: American Elsevier, 1971).

————— . *Public Policymaking Reexamined* (San Francisco, Chandler, 1968).

Dubnick, Melvin J. and Barbara A. Bardes. *Thinking about Public Policy* (New York: John Wiley and Sons, 1983).

Formaini, Robert. *The Myth of Scientific Public Policy* (New Brunswick, NJ: Transaction Publishers, 1990).

Goldwin, Robert A., ed. *Bureaucrats, Policy Analysts, Statesmen: Who Leads?* (Washington, DC: American Enterprise Institute, 1980).

Halligan, John. "Policy Advice and the Public Service," in B. Guy Peters and Donald Savoie, *Governance in a Changing Environment* (Montreal: McGill/Queens University Press, 1995).

Hegeman, J.H. *Justifying Policy* (Amsterdam: Free University Press, 1989).

Hill, Michael and Glen Bramley. *Analyzing Social Policy* (Oxford: Basil Blackwell, 1986).

Hofferbert, Richard I. *The Reach and Grasp of Policy Analysis* (Tuscaloosa, AL: The University of Alabama Press, 1990).

Kingdon, John W. *Agendas, Alternatives, and Public Policies* (New York: Harper Collins, 1984).

Lerner, Daniel and Harold D. Lasswell, eds. *The Policy Sciences* (Palo Alto, CA: Stanford University Press, 1951).

Lindblom, Charles. "The Science of Muddling Through," *Public Administration Review* 19 (Spring 1959): 79–88.

Lowi, Theodore J. "Public Policy, Politics, and Political Theory," *World Politics* 17 (July 1964): 677–715.

Meltsner, Arnold J. *Policy Analysts in the Bureaucracy* (Berkeley, CA: University of California Press, 1976).

Mills, C. Wright. *The Power Elite* (New York: Oxford University Press, 1956).

Mosher, Frederick C. "The Changing Responsibilities and Tactics of the Federal Government," *Public Administration Review* 40 (November/December 1980): 541–548.

Organization for Economic Cooperation and Development. *Economic Instruments for Environmental Protection* (Paris: OECD, 1989).

Ostrum, Vincent. *The Intellectual Crisis in American Public Administration*, 2nd ed.

(Tuscaloosa, AL: University of Alabama Press, 1989).

Pressman, Jeffrey L. and Aaron Wildavsky. *Implementation* (Berkeley, CA: University of California Press, 1973).

Rourke, Francis E. *Bureaucracy, Politics, and Public Policy* (Boston: Little, Brown, 1968).

Salamon, Lester M., ed. *Beyond Privatization: The Tools of Government Action* (Washington, DC: Urban Institute, 1989).

Salisbury, Robert H. "An Exchange Theory of Interest Groups," *Midwest Journal of Political Science* 13 (February 1969): 1–32.

Schattschneider, E.E. *The Semi-Sovereign People* (New York: Holt, Rinehart, and Winston, 1960).

Schubert, Glendon. "The Public Interest: Theorem, Theosophy, or Theory" in Carl Friedrich, ed. *Nomos: The Public Interest* (New York: Atherton Press, 1962).

Shotland, R. Lance and Melvin M. Mark, eds. *Social Science and Social Policy* (Beverly Hills, CA: Sage, 1985).

Simon, Herbert. *Administrative Behavior,* 3rd ed. (New York: Free Press, 1976).

Trolldalen, Jon Martin. *International Environmental Conflict Resolution: The Role of the United Nations* (Oslo: World Foundation for Environment and Development, 1992).

Wald, Emmanuel. "Toward a Paradigm of Future Public Administration," *Public Administration Review* 33 (July/August 1973): 466–472.

Wilson, James Q. *The Politics of Regulation* (New York: Basic Books, 1980).

Chapter 7   Policy Implementation, Evaluation, and Termination

Ball, Howard, Thomas Lauth, and Dale Krane. *Compromised Compliance* (Westport, CT: Greenwood Press, 1982).

Bardach, Eugene. *The Implementation Game* (Cambridge, MIT Press, 1974).

————— . "Policy Termination as a Policy Process," *Policy Sciences* 7 (1976): 123–131.

Becker, Theodore L. and Malcolm M. Feeley. *The Impact of Supreme Court Decisions,* 2nd ed. (New York: Oxford University Press, 1973).

Behn, Robert. "The Three Big Questions of Public Management," *Public Administration Review* 55 (July/August 1995): 319–324.

Bullard, Robert D., ed. *Confronting Environmental Racism* (Boston: South End Press, 1993).

Bullock, Charles S., III and Charles M. Lamb. *Implementation of Civil Rights Policy* (Monterey, CA: Brooks/Cole Publishers, 1984).

Canon, Bradley C. "Courts and Policy: Compliance, Implementation, and Impact," in John B. Gates and Charles A. Johnson, *The American Courts: A Critical Assessment* (Washington, DC: Congressional Quarterly, 1991).

Cohen, Michael D., James G. March, and Johan P. Olsen. "A Garbage Can Model of Organizational Choice," *Administrative Science Quarterly* 17 (March 1972): 1–25.

deLeon, Peter. "Public Policy Termination: An End and a Beginning," *Policy Analysis* 4 (Summer 1978): 369–392.

Johnson, Charles and Bradley C. Canon. *Judicial Policies: Implementation and Im-*

pact (Washington, DC: Congressional Quarterly, 1984).

Jones, Charles O. *Introduction to the Study of Public Policy* (Monterey, CA: Brooks/Cole, 1984).

Levine, Charles H. "Organizational Decline and Cutback Management," *Public Administration Review* (July/August 1978): 316–325.

Lipsky, Michael. *Street-Level Bureaucracies* (New York: Russell Sage, 1980).

Mazmanian, Daniel A. and Paul A. Sabatier. *Effective Policy Implementation* (Lexington, MA: D.C. Heath, 1981).

Nakamura, Robert T. and Frank Smallwood. *The Politics of Policy Implementation* (New York: St. Martin's Press, 1980).

Peters, B. Guy and Donald Savoie, eds. *Governance in a Changing Environment* (Montreal: McGill/Queens University Press, 1995).

Pressman, Jeffrey L. and Aaron B. Wildavsky. *Implementation* (Berkeley, CA: University of California Press, 1973).

Rogers, Harrell R. and Charles S. Bullock, III. *Coercion to Compliance* (Lexington, MA: D.C. Heath, 1976).

Rossi, Peter H. and Howard E. Freeman. *Evaluation: A Systemic Approach,* 4th ed. (Newbury Park, CA: Sage Publications, 1989).

Stone, Deborah A. *Policy Paradox and Political Reason* (Glenview, IL: Scott Foresman, 1988).

U.S. General Accounting Office. *Block Grants: Characteristics, Experience, and Lessons Learned* (Washington, DC, Government Printing Office, 1995).

Van Meter, Donald and Carl Van Horn. "The Policy Implementation Process: A Conceptual Framework," *Administration & Society* 6 (Feb 1975): 445–488.

Wasby, Stephen L. *The Impact of the United States Supreme Court: Some Perspectives* (Homewood, IL: Dorsey Press, 1970).

Chapter 8   Managing Public Organizations

Beckhard, Richard. *Organization Development: Strategies and Models* (Reading, MA: Addison-Wesley, 1969).

Bennis, Warren G. *Organization Development: Its Nature, Origins, and Prospects* (Reading, MA: Addison-Wesley, 1969).

Bolman, Lee G. and Terrence E. Deal. *Reframing Organizations: Artistry, Choice, and Leadership* (San Francisco: Jossey-Bass, 1991).

Cox, Taylor, H. Jr. *Cultural Diversity in Organizations: Theory, Research & Practice* (San Francisco: Berrett-Koehler, 1993).

Deming, W. Edwards. *Out of the Crisis: Quality, Productivity and Competitive Position* (Cambridge, UK: Cambridge University Press, 1988).

Fayol, Henri. *General and Industrial Management,* trans. by C. Storrs, 1949 (London: Pitman Publishing, Ltd., 1916).

Gerth, H. and C. Wright Mills, eds. *Max Weber: Essays in Sociology* (Oxford, UK: Oxford University Press, 1946).

Gilbreth, Frank B. *Motion Study: A Method for Increasing the Efficiency of the Workman* (New York: D. Van Nostrand, 1911).

————— . *Primer of Scientific Management* (New York: D. Van Nostrand 1912).

Gulick, Luther and Lyndall Urwick, eds. *Papers on the Science of Administration* (New York: Institute of Public Administration, 1937).

Held, Walter G. *Decision Making in the Federal Government: The Wallace S. Sayre Model* (Washington, DC: Brookings Institution, 1979).

Ingraham, Patricia. "Building Bridges or Burning Them? The President, the Appointees, and the Bureaucracy," *Public Administration Review* 47 (1987): 425–435.

Jaques, Elliott. "In Praise of Hierarchy," *Harvard Business Review,* (January-February 1990): 127–133.

Juran, Joseph J. *On Planning for Quality* (New York: Collier Macmillan, 1988).

Kaufman, Herbert. *The Forest Ranger* (Baltimore, MD: Johns Hopkins Press, 1960).

Lawler, Edward E., III, Susan Albers Mohrman, and Ferald E. Ledford, Jr. *Employee Involvement and Total Quality Management* (San Francisco: Jossey-Bass, 1992).

Lipsky, Michael. *Street-Level Bureaucracy* (New York: Russell Sage Foundation, 1980).

McConkey, Dale D. *MBO for Nonprofit Organizations* (New York: AMACOM, 1975).

McWhinney, Will. *Paths of Change: Strategic Choices for Organizations and Society* (Newbury Park, CA: Sage, 1992).

Mosher, Frederick C. *Democracy and the Public Service,* 2nd ed. (New York: Oxford University Press, 1982).

Odiorne, George, S. *Management by Objectives* (New York: Pitman, 1965).

Ott, J. Steven, Albert C. Hyde, and Jay M. Shafritz, eds. *Public Management: The Essential Readings* (Chicago: Nelson-Hall, 1991).

Ouchi, William G. *Theory Z: How American Business Can Meet the Japanese Challenge* (Reading, MA: Addison-Wesley, 1981).

Pascale, Richard T. and Anthony G. Athos. *The Art of Japanese Management: Applications for American Executives* (New York: Simon & Schuster, 1981).

Peters, Thomas J. and Robert H. Waterman, Jr. *In Search of Excellence* (New York: Harper & Row, 1982).

Rourke, Francis E. *Bureaucracy, Politics, and Public Policy,* 3rd ed. (Boston: Little, Brown, 1984).

Schein, Edgar H. "Reassessing the 'Divine Rights' of Managers." *Sloan Management Review,* 30 (Winter 1989): 63–68.

Shafritz, Jay M. and J. Steven Ott. "Classical Organization Theory" in, J. Shafritz and S. Ott, eds. *Classics of Organization Theory,* 4th ed. (Belmont, CA: Wadsworth, 1996).

Taylor, Frederick Winslow. *The Principles of Scientific Management* (New York: Norton, 1911).

Thompson, James D. *Organizations in Action* (New York: McGraw-Hill, 1967).

U.S. General Accounting Office. *Block Grants: Characteristics, Experience, and Lessons Learned* (Washington, DC: General Accounting Office, 1995).

Walton, Mary. *The Deming Management Method* (New York: Dodd Mead, 1986).

Weber, Max. "Bureaucracy," in H. Gerth and C. Wright Mills, eds. *From Max Weber: Essays in Sociology* (New York: Oxford, 1946).

Welles, James F. *Understanding Stupidity: An Analysis of the Premaladaptive Beliefs and Behavior of Institutions and Organizations* (Orient, NY: Mount Pleasant Press, 1986).

Yates, Douglas, Jr. *The Politics of Management* (San Francisco: Jossey-Bass, 1985).

Zuboff, Shoshana. *In the Age of the Smart Machine: The Future of Work and Power* (New York: Basic Books, 1988).

Chapter 9   Organization Development, Participation, and Culture

Argyris, Chris. *Intervention Theory and Methods* (Reading, MA: Addison-Wesley, 1970).

————— . "Some Limits of Rational Man Organization Theory," *Public Administration Review* 33 (March/April 1973): 263–267.

Barnard, Chester. *The Functions of the Executive* (Cambridge, MA: Harvard University Press, 1938).

Barzelay, Michael. *Breaking Through Bureaucracy* (Berkeley, CA: University of California Press, 1992).

Beckhard, Richard. *Organization Development: Strategies and Models* (Reading, MA: Addison-Wesley, 1969).

Blank, Renee and Sandra Slipp. *Voices of Diversity* (New York: AMACOM, 1994).

Bolman, Lee G. and Terrence E. Deal. *Reframing Organizations: Artistry, Choice, and Leadership* (San Francisco: Jossey-Bass, 1991).

Cox, Taylor H., Jr. *Cultural Diversity in Organizations: Theory, Research & Practice* (San Francisco: Berrett-Koehler, 1993).

Cox, Taylor H. Jr., and Stacy Blake. "Managing Cultural Diversity: Implications for Organizational Competitiveness." *The Executive*, 5 (August 1991): 45–56.

Deming, W. Edwards. *Out of the Crisis: Quality, Productivity and Competitive Position* (Cambridge, UK: Cambridge University Press, 1988).

Federal Quality Institute. *Introduction to Total Quality Management in the Federal Government* (Washington, DC: U.S. Office of Personnel Management, 1991).

Follett, Mary Parker. "The Giving of Orders," in H. C. Metcalf, ed. *Scientific Foundations of Business Administration* (Baltimore, MD: Williams & Wilkins, 1926).

French, Wendell L. and Cecil H. Bell, Jr. *Organization Development: Behavioral Science for Organization Improvement,* 5th ed. (Englewood Cliffs, NJ: Prentice-Hall, 1994).

Habermas, Jurgen. *Toward a Rational Society,* trans. by Jeremy J. Shapiro (Boston: Beacon Press, 1970).

Helgesen, Sally. *The Female Advantage: Women's Ways of Leadership* (New York: Doubleday Currency, 1990).

Hummel, Ralph P. *The Bureaucratic Experience,* 4th ed. (New York: St. Martin's Press, 1994).

Ingraham, Patricia. "Quality Management in Public Organizations," in Guy Peters and Donald Sovoie. *Governance in a Changing Environment* (Ottawa: Canadian Centre for Management Development, 1995).

Juran, Joseph J. *On Planning for Quality* (New York: Collier Macmillan, 1988).

Maslow, Abraham. "A Theory of Human Motivation," *Psychological Review* 50 (July 1943: 370–396.

Mayo, G. Elton. *The Human Problems of an Industrial Civilization* (Boston, MA: Division of Research, Harvard Business School, 1933).

McGregor, Douglas M. *The Human Side of Enterprise* (New York: McGraw Hill, 1960).

Morrison, Ann M. *The New Leaders: Guidelines on Diversity in America* (San Francisco: Jossey-Bass, 1992).

Munsterberg, Hugo. *Psychology and Industrial Efficiency* (Boston: Houghton Mifflin, 1913).

Osborne, David and Ted Gaebler. *Reinventing Government* (Reading, MA: Addison-Wesley, 1992).

Ott, Ellis R. and Edward G. Schilling. *Process Quality Control,* 2nd ed. (New York: McGraw-Hill, 1990).

Ott, J. Steven. *Classic Readings in Organizational Behavior,* 2nd ed. (Belmont, CA: Wadsworth, 1996).

———— . *The Organizational Culture Perspective* (Belmont, CA: Wadsworth, 1989).

Ouchi, William G. *Theory Z: How American Business Can Meet the Japanese Challenge* (Reading, MA: Addison-Wesley, 1981).

Pascale, Richard T. and Anthony G. Athos. *The Art of Japanese Management: Applications for American Executives* (New York: Simon & Schuster, 1981).

Roethlisberger, Fritz J. and William J. Dixon. *Management and the Worker* (Cambridge, MA: Harvard University Press, 1939).

Rogers, Judy L. "New Paradigm Leadership: Integrating the Female Ethos." *Journal of the National Association of Women Deans, Administrators, & Counselors* 51 (No. 9 1988): 1–8.

Rosener, Judy B. "Ways Women Lead." *Harvard Business Review* (Nov./Dec. 1990): 119–125.

Schein, Edgar H. *Organizational Culture and Leadership,* 2nd ed. (San Francisco: Jossey-Bass, 1992).

———— . *Organizational Psychology,* 3rd ed. (Englewood Cliffs, NJ: Prentice-Hall, 1980).

Schein, Virginia. "Would Women Lead Differently?" in William Rosenbach and R. Taylor, eds. *Contemporary Issues in Leadership* (Boulder, CO: Westview Press, 1989).

Shafritz, Jay M. and J. Steven Ott. "Classical Organization Theory," in J. Shafritz and J. Ott, eds. *Classics of Organization Theory,* 4th ed. (Belmont, CA: Wadsworth, 1996).

Silverman, David. *The Theory of Organizations* (New York: Basic Books, 1971).

Skinner, B.F. *Science and Behavior* (New York: Macmillan, 1953).

Stiver, Camilla. *Gender Images in Public Administration: Legitimacy and the Administrative State* (Newbury Park, CA: Sage Publications, 1993).

Thayer, Frederick K. *An End to Hierarchy and Competition,* 2nd ed. (New York: Franklin Watts, 1981).

U.S. Government Accounting Office. *Organizational Culture: Techniques Companies Use to Perpetuate or Change Beliefs and Values* (Washington, DC: Government Printing Office, 1992).

Walton, Mary. *The Deming Management Method* (New York: Dodd, Mead, 1986).

Weick, Karl E. *The Social Psychology of Organizing,* 2nd ed. (Reading, MA: Addison-Wesley, 1979).

White, Orion F. and Cynthia J. McSwain. "Transformational Theory and Organizational Analysis," in Gareth Morgan, ed. *Beyond Method: Strategies for Social Research* (Beverly Hills, CA: Sage, 1983).

Chapter 10   Personnel Policy and Human Resource Management

Ban, Carolyn and Norma Riccucci. "Personnel Systems and Labor Relations: Steps Toward a Quiet Revitalization," in Frank J. Thompson, ed. *Revitalizing State and Local Public Service* (San Francisco: Jossey-Bass, 1993).

Carnevale, David G. "Human Capital and High Performance Organizations," in Steven W. Hays and Richard C. Kearney, eds. *Public Personnel Administration: Problems and Prospects,* 3rd ed. (Englewood Cliffs, NJ: Prentice-Hall, 1995).

Cooper, Phillip J. "Reinvention and Employee Rights: The Role of the Courts," in Patricia W. Ingraham and Barbara S. Romzek, eds. *New Paradigms for Government* (San Francisco: Jossey-Bass, 1994).

Dawson, Irving O. "Trends and Developments in Public Sector Unions," in Steven W. Hays and Richard C. Kearney, eds. *Public Personnel Administration: Problems and Prospects,* 2nd ed. (Englewood Cliffs, NJ: Prentice-Hall, 1993).

Downs, George W. and Patrick D. Larkey. *The Search for Government Efficiency: From Hubris to Helplessness* (New York: Random House, 1986).

Dressang, Dennis L. *Public Personnel Management and Public Policy* (New York: Longman, 1991).

Gore, Al. *Creating a Government that Works Better and Costs Less.* Report of the National Performance Review (Washington, DC: Office of the Vice President, 1993).

————— . *Reinventing Human Resource Management:* Accompanying Report of the National Performance Review (Washington, DC: Office of the Vice President, 1993).

Government of Canada. *Public Service 2000* (Ottawa: Ministry of Supply and Services Canada, 1990).

Ingraham, Patricia W. "The Reform Game," in Patricia W. Ingraham and David Rosenbloom, eds. *The Promise and Paradox of Civil Service Reform* (Pittsburgh, PA: University of Pittsburgh Press).

Johnston, William B., et al. *Civil Service 2000* (Washington, DC: U.S. Office of Personnel Management, 1988).

Johnston, William B. *Work force 2000: Work and Workers for the 21st Century* (Indianapolis: Hudson Institute, 1987).

Kearney, Richard C. "Federal Labor Relations 2000: Introduction to the Symposium," *International Journal of Public Administration* 16 no. 6 (1993): 781–791.

————— . "Unions in Government," in Steven W. Hays and Richard C. Kearney, eds. *Public Personnel Administration: Problems and Prospects,* 3rd ed. (Englewood Cliffs, NJ: Prentice-Hall, 1995).

Kettl, Donald F. "Managing on the Frontiers of Knowledge: The Learning Organization," in P. Ingraham and B. Romzek, eds. *New Paradigms for Government* (San Francisco: Jossey-Bass, 1994).

Kingsley, J. Donald. *Representative Bureaucracy* (Yellow Springs, OH: Antioch University Press, 1944).

Mischel, Lawrence and Ruy A. Teixeira. *The Myth of the Coming Labor Shortage: Jobs, Skills, and Incomes of America's Work force 2000* (Washington, DC: Economic Policy Institute, 1991).

Naff, Katherine C. "Labor-Management Relations and Privatization: A Federal Perspective," *Public Administration Review* 51 (January/February 1991): 23–30.

————. "Toward the Year 2000: Issues and Strategies for Federal Labor-Management Relations," *International Journal of Public Administration* 16 no. 6 (1993): 813–840.

National Commission on the Public Service (Volcker Commission). *Leadership for America: Rebuilding the Public Service* (Washington, DC: Government Printing Office, 1989).

National Commission on the State and Local Public Service [Winter Commission]. *Hard Truths/Tough Choices: An Agenda for State and Local Reform* (Albany, NY: The Nelson A. Rockefeller Institute of Government, 1993).

National Partnership Council. *A Report to the President on Implementing Recommendations of the National Performance Review* (Washington, DC: Government Printing Office, 1994).

Peters, B. Guy and Donald J. Savoie, eds. *Governance in a Changing Environment* (Ottawa: McGill/Queens University Press, 1995).

Risher, Howard H. and Brigitte W. Schay. "Grade Banding: The Model for Future Salary Programs?" *Public Personnel Management* 23 no. 2 (1994): 187–200.

Shafritz, Jay M., Norma M. Riccucci, David H. Rosenbloom, and Albert C. Hyde. *Personnel Management in Government* (New York: Marcel Dekker, 1992).

Sylvia, Ronald D. *Critical Issues in Public Personnel Policy* (Pacific Grove, CA: Brooks/Cole Publishers, 1989).

Thompson, Frank J., ed. *Revitalizing State and Local Public Service* (San Francisco: Jossey-Bass, 1993).

U.S. Bureau of the Census. *Statistical Abstract of the United States: 1994,* 114th ed. (Washington, DC: U.S. Bureau of the Census, 1994).

U.S. Civil Service Commission. *Biography of an Ideal* (Washington, DC: U.S. Civil Service Commission, 1973).

U.S. General Accounting Office. *The Changing Work Force: Demographic Issues Facing the Federal Government* (Washington, DC: General Accounting Office, 1992).

U.S. Merit Systems Protection Board. *A Question of Equity: Women and the Glass Ceiling in the Federal Government* (Washington, DC: Government Printing Office, 1992).

————. *Sexual Harassment in the Federal Work Place: Trends, Progress, and Continuing Challenges* (Washington, DC: Government Printing Office, 1995).

————. *To Meet the Needs of Nations: Staffing the U.S. Civil Service and the Public Service of Canada* (Washington, DC: Government Printing Office, 1992).

U.S. Office of Personnel Management. *Union Recognition in the Federal Government as of December 31, 1992* (Washington, DC: Government Printing Office, 1992).

————. Office of Employee and Labor Relations. *Labor Management Cooperation: Policy Guidance* (Washington, DC: Government Printing Office, 1988).

Chapter 11   Public Sector Budgeting: Purse Strings, Politics, and Management

Abney, Glenn and Thomas P. Lauth. *The Politics of State and City Administration* (Albany, NY: State University of New York Press, 1986).

Appleby, Paul. *Big Democracy* (New York: Alfred A. Knopf, 1945).

Berman, Larry. *The Office of Management and Budget and the Presidency* (Princeton, NJ: Princeton University, 1979).

Friedelbaum, Stanley H. "The 1971 Wage-Price Freeze: Unchallenged Presidential Power," *Supreme Court Review* (1974): 33–80.

Gore, Al. *Improving Financial Management:* Accompanying Report of the National Performance Review (Washington, DC: National Performance Review, 1993).

————— . *Mission-Driven, Results-Oriented Budgeting:* Accompanying Report of the National Performance Review (Washington, DC: National Performance Review, 1993).

Hoover Commission, *The Hoover Commission Report on the Organization of the Executive Branch* (New York: McGraw-Hill, 1949).

Key, V.O. "The Lack of a Budgetary Theory." *American Political Science Review* 34 (1940): 1137–1140.

Lauth, Thomas P. "Zero-Base Budgeting in Georgia State Government: Myth and Reality," *Public Administration Review* 38 (September/October 1978): 420–430.

Levine, Charles B. *Managing Fiscal Stress* (Chatham, NJ: Chatham House, 1980).

————— . "Organizational Decline and Cutback Management," *Public Administration Review* 38 (July/August 1978): 316–325.

Lewis, Verne B. "Toward a Theory of Budgeting," *Public Administration Review* 12 (Winter 1952): 42–52.

Lindblom, Charles E. "The Science of Muddling Through," *Public Administration Review* 19 (Spring 1959): 79–88.

Lyden, Fremont J. and Marc Lindenburg. *Public Budgeting in Theory and Practice* (New York: Longman, 1983).

Peterson, Paul E. *The Price of Federalism* (Washington, DC: Brookings, 1995).

Rubin, Irene S. "Strategies for the New Budgeting," in James L., Perry, ed. *The Handbook of Public Administration*, 2nd ed. (San Francisco: Jossey-Bass, 1996).

Schick, Allen. *The Federal Budget* (Washington, DC: Brookings Institution, 1995).

————— . "The Road to PPB: The Stages of Budget Reform," *Public Administration Review* 26 (December/January 1966): 243–258.

Schultze, Charles L. *The Private Use of the Public Interest* (Washington, DC: Brookings, 1977).

Shuman, Howard E. *Politics and the Budget: The Struggle Between the President and the Congress,* 2nd ed. (Englewood Cliffs, NJ: Prentice-Hall, 1988).

Sundquist, James L. *The Decline and Resurgence of Congress* (Washington, DC: Brookings Institution, 1981).

White, Michael and Aaron Wildavsky. *The Deficit and the Public Interest* (Berkeley, CA: University of California Press, 1989).

Wildavsky, Aaron. *Budgeting: A Comparative Theory of Budgetary Processes* (Boston: Little, Brown, 1975).

————— . "Political Implications of Budgetary Reform," *Public Administration Re-*

view 21 (Autumn 1961): 183–190.

————— . *The Politics of the Budgetary Process,* 2nd ed. (Boston: Little, Brown, 1974).

Willoughby, William F. *The Movement for Budget Reform in the State* (New York: D. Appleton and Company, 1918).

Chapter 12   International Affairs and Public Administration

Baer, M. Delal. "North American Free Trade," *Foreign Affairs* 70 (Fall 1991): 132–149.

Bennett, A. LeRoy. *International Organizations: Principles and Issues,* 5th ed. (Englewood Cliffs, NJ: Prentice-Hall, 1991).

Bergsten, C. Fred. "The World Economy," *Foreign Affairs* 69 (Summer 1990): 96–112.

Blake, David H. and Robert S. Walters. *The Politics of Global Economic Relations,* 3rd ed. (Englewood Cliffs, NJ: Prentice-Hall, 1987).

Bosworth, Stephen W. "The United States and Asia," *Foreign Affairs* 71 no. 1 (1991/92): 124–135.

Broad, Robin, et al. "Development: The Market is Not Enough," *Foreign Policy* 81 (Winter 1990/91): 145–160.

Cameron, David R. "The 1992 Initiative: Causes and Consequences," in A. Sbragia, ed. *Euro-Politics: Institutions and Policymaking in the "New" European Community* (Washington, DC: Brookings Institution, 1992).

Carnegie Endowment National Commission. *Changing Our Ways* (Washington, DC: Carnegie Endowment for International Peace, 1992).

Central Intelligence Agency. *United Nations Peacekeeping Operations* (Washington DC: Central Intelligence Agency, 1992).

Daltrop, Anne. *Politics and the European Community,* 2nd ed. (London: Longman, 1986).

Frieden, Jeffrey A. and David A. Lake, eds. *International Political Economy: Perspectives on Global Wealth and Power,* 2nd ed. (New York: St. Martin's Press, 1991).

Gardner, Richard N. *Negotiating Survival* (New York: Council on Foreign Relations Press, 1992).

Garten, Jeffrey E. "The 100-Day Economic Agenda," *Foreign Affairs* 72 (Winter 1992/93): 16–31.

Goldstein, Walter. "Europe after Maastricht," *Foreign Affairs* 72 (Winter 1992/93): 120–121.

————— . "EC: Euro-Stalling," *Foreign Policy* 85 (Winter 1991/92): 129–147.

Gorman, Peter A. and Robert F. *International Relations* (Pacific Grove, CA: Brooks/Cole Publishers, 1991).

Groth, Brian. "Negotiating in the Global Village: Four Lamps to Illuminate the Table," *Negotiation Journal* 8 (July 1992): 241–257.

Hastedt, Glenn P. and Kay M. Knickrehm. *Dimensions of World Politics* (New York: Harper Collins Publishers, 1991).

Hughes, Barry B. *Continuity and Change in World Politics* (Englewood Cliffs, NJ: Prentice-Hall, 1991).

Isaak, Robert A. *International Political Economy* (Englewood Cliffs, NJ: Prentice-Hall, 1991).

Karns, Margaret P. and Karen A. Mingst. "Multilateral Institutions and International Security," in Michael T. Klare and Daniel C. Thomas, eds. *World Security* (New York: St. Martin's Press, 1991).

Kegley, Charles W., Jr., and Eugene R. Wittkopf. *World Politics: Trend and Transformation,* 4th ed. (New York: St. Martin's Press, 1993).

Kennedy, Paul. *The Rise and Fall of the Great Powers* (New York: Vintage Books, 1987).

Keohane, Robert O. *After Hegemony* (Princeton, NJ: Princeton University Press, 1984).

Keohane, Robert O. and Joseph S. Nye. *Power and Interdependence,* 2nd ed. (New York: Harper Collins Publishers, 1989).

Leonard, Dick. *Pocket Guide to the European Community* (London: Basil Blackwell and The Economist Publications, 1988).

Lieber, Robert J. *No Common Power: Understanding International Relations,* 2nd ed. (New York: Harper Collins Publishers, 1991).

Luck, Edward C. "Making Peace," *Foreign Policy* 89 (Winter 1992/93): 137–155.

Mathews, Jessica Tuchman. "The Environment and International Security," in Michael T. Klare and Daniel C. Thomas, eds., *World Security* (New York: St. Martin's Press, 1991).

Mearsheimer, John J. "Back to the Future: Instability in Europe After the Cold War," *International Security* 15 (Summer 1990): 5–56.

Moran, Theodore H. *American Economic Policy and National Security* (New York: Council on Foreign Relations Press, 1993).

Morgenthau, Hans J. *Politics Among Nations* (New York: Alfred A. Knopf, 1948).

Nye, Joseph S. Jr. *Bound to Lead: The Changing Nature of American Power* (New York: Basis Books, 1990).

Peters, B. Guy. *The Politics of Bureaucracy,* 3rd ed. (New York: Longman, 1989).

Peterson, Peter G. with James K. Sebenius. "The Primacy of the Domestic Agenda," in Graham Allison and Gregory F. Treverton, eds. *Rethinking America's Security: Beyond Cold War to New World Order* (New York: W. W. Norton & Co., 1992).

Princen, Thomas and Matthias Finger. *Environmental NGOs in World Politics* (London: Routledge Press, 1994).

Ratiner, Leigh S. Ratiner. "The Law of the Sea: Crossroads for U.S. Policy," *Foreign Affairs* 60 (Summer 1982): 1006–1021.

Spero, Joan Edelman. *The Politics of International Economic Relations,* 3rd ed. (New York: St. Martin's Press, 1981).

Starr, Joyce R. "Water Wars," *Foreign Policy* 82 (Spring 1991): 17–36.

Steadman, Stephen John. "The New Interventionists," *Foreign Affairs* 72 no. 1 (1992/93): 1–16.

Stokes, Bruce. "Organizing to Trade," *Foreign Policy* 89 (Winter 1992/93): 36–52.

Walt, Stephen M. *The Origins of Alliances* (Ithaca, New York: Cornell University Press, 1987).

Waltz, Kenneth N. *Theory of International Politics* (Reading, MA: Addison-Wesley Publishing Co., 1979).

Warren, J.H. "Multilateralism and Regionalism: A North American Perspective from a Canadian Viewpoint," in *The Trilateral Commission Working Group Papers, 1991–92* (New York: The Trilateral Commission [North America], 1992).

Weiner, Myron. "Security, Stability, and International Migration," *International Security* 17 (Winter 1992/93): 91–126.

Weiss, Thomas G. and Kurt M. Campbell. "Military Humanitarianism," *Survival* 33 (Sept./Oct. 1991): 451–465.

Zartman, I. William. "International Environmental Negotiation: Challenges for Analysis and Practice," *Negotiation Journal* 8 (April 1992): 113–123.

Chapter 13 Comparative Public Administration: Different Problems, Common Trends

Caiden, Naomi. "The Management of Public Budgeting," in Randall Baker, ed. *Comparative Public Management* (Westport, CT: Praeger, 1994).

Cooper, Phillip J. "Accountability and Administrative Reform," in B. Guy Peters and D. Savoie, eds. *Governance in a Changing Environment* (Ottawa: McGill/Queens University Press, 1995).

Dahl, Robert A. "The Science of Public Administration: Three Problems," *Public Administration Review* 7 (Winter 1947): 1–11.

Elazar, Daniel. *American Federalism: A View From the States* (New York: Crowell, 1966).

Freund, Ernst. *Administrative Powers Over Persons and Property* (Chicago: University of Chicago, 1928).

Goodnow, Frank. *Comparative Administrative Law* (New York: Putnam, 1893).

Gore, Al. *From Red Tape to Results: Creating A Government That Works Better & Costs Less.* Report of the National Performance Review. (Washington, DC: Government Printing Office, 1993).

Hamilton, Alexander, James Madison, and John Jay. *The Federalist Papers* (New York: Mentor, 1961).

Heady, Ferrel. *Public Administration: A Comparative Perspective* (Englewood Cliffs, NJ: Prentice-Hall, 1966).

Knudsen, Tim, ed. *Welfare Administration in Denmark* (Copenhagen: Danish Ministry of Finance, 1991).

Jancar-Webster, Barbara, ed. *Environmental Action in Eastern Europe: Responses to Crisis* (Armonk, New York: M.E. Sharpe, 1993).

Mintzberg, Henry. "A Note on that Dirty Word 'Efficiency'," *Interfaces* 5 (October): 101–105.

Osborne, David and Ted Gaebler. *Reinventing Government* (New York: Penguin, 1992).

Peters, B. Guy. *The Politics of Bureaucracy,* 4th ed. (White Plains, NY: Longman, 1995).

Riggs, Fred. *Administration in Developing Countries* (Boston: Houghton-Mifflin, 1964).

————. "Trends in the Comparative Study of Public Administration," *International Review of Administrative Sciences* 38 no. 1 (1962): 9–15.

Salamon, Lester M., ed. *Beyond Privatization: The Tools of Government Action* (Washington, DC: Urban Institute, 1989).

Schein, Edgar. *Organizational Culture and Leadership,* 2nd ed. (San Francisco: Jossey-Bass, 1992).

Simon, Herbert A. "A Comment on 'The Science of Public Administration'," *Public Administration Review* 7 (Summer 1947): 200–203.

Stone, Roger D. *The Nature of Development* (New York: Alfred A. Knopf, 1992).

Sutherland, S.L. "The Al-Mashat Affair," *Canadian Public Administration* 34 (Winter 1992): 573–603.

Tate, C. Neal and Torbjorn Vallinder, eds. *The Global Expansion of Judicial Power* (New York: New York University Press, 1995).

Van Wart, Montgomery and N. Joseph Cayer. "Comparative Public Administration: Defunct, Dispersed, or Redefined?" *Public Administration Review* 50 (March/April 1990): 238–248.

Waldo, Dwight, ed., "Comparative and Development Administration: Retrospect and Prospect," *Public Administration Review* 36 (November/December 1976): 615–654.

Waldo, Dwight. "Public Administration," *Journal of Politics* 30 (May 1968): 469–473.

Wilson, Woodrow. "The Study of Administration," *Political Science Quarterly* 2 (1887): 209–213.

World Summit for Social Development. *The Copenhagen Declaration and Programme of Action* (New York: United Nations, 1995).

Cases Cited

Index